# WRITING THE PERFECT RESUME

## KARL WEBER AND ROB KAPLAN

### Learn the techniques that get you hired

**www.petersons.com**

**PETERSON'S**

THOMSON LEARNING

Australia • Canada • Mexico • Singapore • Spain • United Kingdom • United States

**PETERSON'S**

**THOMSON LEARNING**

**About Peterson's**

Founded in 1966, Peterson's, a division of Thomson Learning, is the nation's largest and most respected provider of lifelong learning online resources, software, reference guides, and books. The Education Supersite$^{SM}$ at petersons.com—the Web's most heavily traveled education resource—has searchable databases and interactive tools for contacting U.S.-accredited institutions and programs. CollegeQuest$^{SM}$ (CollegeQuest.com) offers a complete solution for every step of the college decision-making process. GradAdvantage$^{TM}$ (GradAdvantage.org), developed with Educational Testing Service, is the only electronic admissions service capable of sending official graduate test score reports with a candidate's online application. Peterson's serves more than 55 million education consumers annually.

Thomson Learning is among the world's leading providers of lifelong learning, serving the needs of individuals, learning institutions, and corporations with products and services for both traditional classrooms and for online learning. For more information about the products and services offered by Thomson Learning, please visit www.thomsonlearning.com. Headquartered in Stamford, Connecticut, with offices worldwide, Thomson Learning is part of The Thomson Corporation (www.thomson.com), a leading e-information and solutions company in the business, professional, and education marketplaces. The Corporation's common shares are listed on the Toronto and London stock exchanges.

**Dedication**

*For Jakob, who will boast one of the outstanding resumes of the Class of 2020 (KW); and*
*For Tina, for all her love, encouragement, and support (RAK)*

For more information, contact Peterson's, 2000 Lenox Drive, Lawrenceville, NJ 08648; 800-338-3282; or find us on the World Wide Web at: www.petersons.com/about

ISBN 0-7689-0595-8

Printed in Canada

10  9  8  7  6  5  4  3  2  1     02  01  00

# Acknowledgements

We're grateful to numerous colleagues, advisers, and friends who've helped us explore and comprehend today's exciting and complex career universe. In particular, we'd like to thank:

John Bakos, president of Bakos Career Management Professionals, who generously provided expert insights into resume development based on his years as one of the most respected career counselors in the United States;

Susan Gordon, president of Lynne Palmer Executive Recruitment, and Robert Defendorf of Scholastic, Inc., whose stories, suggestions, and ideas about job-search strategies were invaluable;

Laura Harrison McBride, whose artful research and writing were crucial in the creation of the chapters on the electronic resume;

Janee Woods Weber and Laura Weber, who provided extensive research help that added immeasurably to the completeness and timeliness of the book;

Nancy Brandwein, who contributed a fascinating collection of cover letters based on her own unusual career story; and

Karen Weber, whose administrative support was invaluable.

Finally, a word of thanks to our editor, Dave Henthorn, whose picture should appear in all future dictionaries to illustrate the meaning of the word *patient*.

Karl Weber and Robert A. Kaplan
Chappaqua and Cortlandt Manor, New York

# About the Authors

Karl Weber is a well-known editor, author, and publishing consultant specializing in books dealing with business, personal finance, and current affairs. An expert on strategies for scoring high on standardized tests, he is the author of *The Insider's Guides to the SAT, ACT, GMAT, and GRE*. He was the editor of two of the best investment books of all time, as selected in 1997 by *Worth* magazine, and also worked with former President Jimmy Carter on two best-selling books about his religious faith. He lives with Mary-Jo Weber, his wife of 25 years, in Chappaqua, New York.

Rob Kaplan, himself a veteran of numerous successful job searches, has held senior-level editorial positions with several major New York-based publishers and now heads his own literary services firm. He is also the co-editor (with Harold Rabinowitz) of *A Passion for Books* (Times Books, 1999), an anthology on books and book collecting, and *Science Says* (W. H. Freeman, 2000), a collection of quotations on science and scientists. He lives with his family in Cortlandt Manor, New York.

# Contents

Introduction ................................................... xiii

## Part I Who Are You and Where Are You Going?... 1

**Chapter 1 Realities of Today's Career Marketplace** ........ 2
Job Hunting in a Booming Economy............ 3
The Numbers Game ........................ 7
Technological and Social Change ............. 8
Time and Money Pressures.................. 12
Getting Your Piece of the Action .............. 13
Just the Facts ............................ 16

**Chapter 2 You and Your Goals** .................... 17
Identify Your Personal Interests............... 18
Recall Your Dreams....................... 19
Determine Your Work Values ................ 20
Determine Your Life Values ................. 22
Pulling It All Together ..................... 24
A Diamond Is Forever—But a Job Rarely Is ...... 28
Just the Facts ............................ 30

**Chapter 3 Evaluating What You Have to Offer** ............ 31
Your Education and Training ................. 32
Your Previous Employment .................. 32
Your Personal Achievements................. 34
Your Volunteer/Community Service............. 36
Your Hobbies and Activities ................. 38
Focusing Your Career Choice................. 38
Just the Facts ............................ 43

## Part II Resume Basics.................... 45

**Chapter 4 Classic Resume Formats** ...................... 46
The Chronological Format .................. 46
The Functional Format..................... 53
The Combination Format .................. 59
How to Choose the Right Format for You ........ 67
Customizing Formats to Highlight
        Your Strengths................. 68
Just the Facts ................................ 82

**Chapter 5 Words That Shout "Hire Me!"** . . . . . . . . . . . . . . . . . **83**
Advertising Yourself. . . . . . . . . . . . . . . . . . . . . . . . 83
Secrets of the Word Spinners. . . . . . . . . . . . . . . . . 88
Being Concise . . . . . . . . . . . . . . . . . . . . . . . . . . 89
Just the Facts . . . . . . . . . . . . . . . . . . . . . . . . . . . 104

**Chapter 6 Details That Matter: Your Resume from Top**
**to Bottom** . . . . . . . . . . . . . . . . . . . . . . . . . . **105**
Name and Contact Information . . . . . . . . . . . . . . . 105
The Headline: Objective or Summary . . . . . . . . . . . 110
Work Experience . . . . . . . . . . . . . . . . . . . . . . . . . 115
Educational Background . . . . . . . . . . . . . . . . . . . . 119
Other Information: What to Include,
What to Omit . . . . . . . . . . . . . . . . . . . . . . . 122
Other Elements to Include or Omit . . . . . . . . . . . . 125
Endorsements . . . . . . . . . . . . . . . . . . . . . . . . . . . 127
Just the Facts . . . . . . . . . . . . . . . . . . . . . . . . . . . 128

**Chapter 7 Effective Resume Design** . . . . . . . . . . . . . . . . . . . . **129**
Design That Communicates . . . . . . . . . . . . . . . . . 129
Type Styles and Sizes . . . . . . . . . . . . . . . . . . . . . 131
Other Elements of Resume Design . . . . . . . . . . . . . 138
Printing Your Resume . . . . . . . . . . . . . . . . . . . . . 148
Just the Facts . . . . . . . . . . . . . . . . . . . . . . . . . . . 149

**Part III Resumes for the Online Job Search** . . . . . . . . **151**

**Chapter 8 How the Online Job Search Works** . . . . . . . . . . . . **152**
Job Hunting Comes to the Internet . . . . . . . . . . . . . 152
Starting Your Online Job Search . . . . . . . . . . . . . . 155
Researching Employers Online—A Case Study . . . 157
Working the Net in Search of Job
Opportunities . . . . . . . . . . . . . . . . . . . . . . . 160
Mining Interest-Specific Web Sites . . . . . . . . . . . . . 163
Passive Searching—Pros and Cons . . . . . . . . . . . . 163
Using Your "Expert" Status to Get Recognized . . . 164
Case Study: Terri's Online Job Search . . . . . . . . . . 165
Using the Web to Supplement Other Job-Search
Strategies . . . . . . . . . . . . . . . . . . . . . . . . . . 166
Just the Facts . . . . . . . . . . . . . . . . . . . . . . . . . . . 166

**Chapter 9  The Web-Based Resume** . . . . . . . . . . . . . . . . . . . . .   **168**
    Three Kinds of Web-Based Resumes . . . . . . . . . . .   168
    How the Scannable Resume Works . . . . . . . . . . . .   169
    Basic Steps to a Scannable Resume . . . . . . . . . . .   170
    Choosing and Using the Right Keywords . . . . . . . .   173
    From the Scannable Resume to the Plain-Text
        Resume . . . . . . . . . . . . . . . . . . . . . . . . . . . . .   177
    How Many Resumes? . . . . . . . . . . . . . . . . . . . . . .   177
    Just the Facts . . . . . . . . . . . . . . . . . . . . . . . . . . .   178

**Part IV  Resumes for Special Circumstances** . . . . . . . .   **179**

    **Chapter 10  The Recent Graduate** . . . . . . . . . . . . . . . .   **180**
    Defining Your Career Objective . . . . . . . . . . . . . . .   181
    Discovering Your Relevant Experience . . . . . . . . . .   183
    Striking the Right Balance . . . . . . . . . . . . . . . . . . .   189
    Just the Facts . . . . . . . . . . . . . . . . . . . . . . . . . . .   200

    **Chapter 11  The Seasoned Veteran** . . . . . . . . . . . . . . . .   **201**
    Prospects for Today's Older Job Seeker . . . . . . . . .   201
    Job-Search Strategies for the Fifty Plus . . . . . . . . . .   203
    The Gentle Art of Camouflage . . . . . . . . . . . . . . . .   207
    Interviewing Tips for the Seasoned Veteran . . . . . .   218
    Just the Facts . . . . . . . . . . . . . . . . . . . . . . . . . . .   221

    **Chapter 12  The Career Changer** . . . . . . . . . . . . . . . . .   **222**
    Why People Are Changing Careers . . . . . . . . . . . .   223
    Finding a New Career . . . . . . . . . . . . . . . . . . . . . .   225
    Determining What You Have to Offer . . . . . . . . . . .   226
    Redefining Your Experience . . . . . . . . . . . . . . . . . .   227
    Deciding on a New Career . . . . . . . . . . . . . . . . . .   229
    Getting It Down on Paper . . . . . . . . . . . . . . . . . . .   230
    Just the Facts . . . . . . . . . . . . . . . . . . . . . . . . . . .   247

    **Chapter 13  Resumes for the "Problem" History** . . . . . . . . . . . .   **249**
    Missing Years of Work . . . . . . . . . . . . . . . . . . . . . .   250
    Too Many Jobs . . . . . . . . . . . . . . . . . . . . . . . . . . .   252
    Too Few Jobs . . . . . . . . . . . . . . . . . . . . . . . . . . . .   263
    Lack of Formal Education . . . . . . . . . . . . . . . . . . .   266
    Learning Experiences: Layoffs, Firings, Scandals . .   269
    Just the Facts . . . . . . . . . . . . . . . . . . . . . . . . . . .   280

## Part V   Cover Letters That Open Doors . . . . . . . . . . .   281

**Chapter 14**   **The Cover Letter: A Great First Impression** . . . . . . .   282
Why a Cover Letter? . . . . . . . . . . . . . . . . . . . . . . .   283
Cover Letter Basics . . . . . . . . . . . . . . . . . . . . . . .   286
Fine-Tuning Your Letter . . . . . . . . . . . . . . . . . . . .   294
The Finishing Touches . . . . . . . . . . . . . . . . . . . . .   298
Just the Facts . . . . . . . . . . . . . . . . . . . . . . . . . .   302

**Chapter 15**   **Networking Letters** . . . . . . . . . . . . . . . . . . . . . . .   303
Getting Your Network Started . . . . . . . . . . . . . . . .   303
Making Contact . . . . . . . . . . . . . . . . . . . . . . . . .   306
Drafting Your Networking Letter . . . . . . . . . . . . . .   309
Following Up Your Networking Letter . . . . . . . . . . .   315
Planning the Networking Meeting . . . . . . . . . . . . . .   315
Following Up After a Networking Meeting . . . . . . .   318
Just the Facts . . . . . . . . . . . . . . . . . . . . . . . . . .   318

**Chapter 16**   **Job-Tailored Letters** . . . . . . . . . . . . . . . . . . . . . . .   320
Making Contact with Potential Employers . . . . . . . .   321
Making the Job-Tailored Cover Letter Work
     for You . . . . . . . . . . . . . . . . . . . . . . . . . . . .   322
Drafting Your Job-Tailored Letter . . . . . . . . . . . . . .   323
Fine-Tuning Your Job-Tailored Letter . . . . . . . . . . .   329
Following Up Your Job-Tailored Letter . . . . . . . . . .   333
One Job Hunter's Tale: Six Letters for Six Jobs . . .   334
Just the Facts . . . . . . . . . . . . . . . . . . . . . . . . . .   341

**Chapter 17**   **Follow-Up Letters** . . . . . . . . . . . . . . . . . . . . . . . .   342
Networking Interview Follow-Up Letters . . . . . . . . .   342
Job Interview Follow-Up Letters . . . . . . . . . . . . . .   345
Job Acceptance Follow-Up Letters . . . . . . . . . . . . .   349
Job Turndown Follow-Up Letters . . . . . . . . . . . . . .   349
Job Rejection Follow-Up Letters . . . . . . . . . . . . . .   352
Follow-Up Letters to Networking Contacts . . . . . . .   352
Just the Facts . . . . . . . . . . . . . . . . . . . . . . . . . .   355

**Part VI   The Next Steps. . . . . . . . . . . . . . . . . . . . . . . . .   357**

    Chapter 18   **From the Interview to the Offer** . . . . . . . . . . . . . . .   358

                Preparing for the Interview. . . . . . . . . . . . . . . . . . .   359

                How to Shine in an Interview. . . . . . . . . . . . . . . . . .   363

                After the Interview. . . . . . . . . . . . . . . . . . . . . . . . .   366

                What to Do When the Call or Letter Comes . . . . .   368

                Negotiating the Deal. . . . . . . . . . . . . . . . . . . . . . . .   369

                Juggling Offers . . . . . . . . . . . . . . . . . . . . . . . . . . . .   372

                You've Got the Job—Now What? . . . . . . . . . . . . .   375

                Just the Facts . . . . . . . . . . . . . . . . . . . . . . . . . . . . .   376

**Part VII   Appendices. . . . . . . . . . . . . . . . . . . . . . . . . . . .   379**

    Appendix A   **More Sample Resumes** . . . . . . . . . . . . . . . . . . . . .   380

    Appendix B   **Web Sites for the Job Hunter** . . . . . . . . . . . . . . . .   441

    Appendix C   **Trade Journals, Industry Guidebooks, and
                      Directories.** . . . . . . . . . . . . . . . . . . . . . . . . . . . . .   445

# Learn about grad and business school options
## with the **QuickStart Counselor–**

real-time, online education advice you can trust.

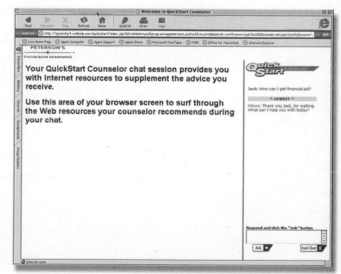

# Introduction

No one enjoys writing a resume. It's easy to see why. As soon as you sit down to begin crafting your mind shifts into the job-search mode—and for most people, that's an uncomfortable place to be. We associate looking for a job with all sorts of unpleasantness: with being interviewed (in terms of sheer stress an experience second only to making a speech), with competing against strangers, with *being judged*.

No wonder resume-writing, the first stage in the job-search process, provokes anxiety and dread in most people. As soon as you put pen to paper, or fingers to keyboard, you begin thinking, "What will *they* think about *me*?"

## YOU NEED A HELPFUL GUIDE

The truth is, writing a resume (and the cover letter to go with it) will probably never rank with skiing, sunbathing, or gourmet dining on most lists of pleasurable activities. But it needn't be the extreme stressor it is for many job seekers. In *The Insider's Guide to Writing the Perfect Resume,* we'll provide you with a clear, comprehensive, step-by-step process for crafting a brilliant resume and an alluring cover letter that will maximize your chances in the job-search sweepstakes. We may not make the task fun, but we'll make it a lot easier than you've found it in the past.

Furthermore, by debunking some of the common myths about resumes (including some you'll find repeated in competing books), we hope to demystify the resume-writing process and make it work *for* you, not against you.

We'll explain why your resume is *not* some sort of sworn affadavit presenting "the whole truth and nothing but the truth" about your career. Instead, it's an "advertisement for you," which should be artfully tailored to emphasize your strengths and camouflage your weaknesses. We'll teach you exactly how to do so.

We'll show why the "one-page myth" of resume length is wrong, and we'll teach you how to determine the optimum length for *your* resume—including some little-known tips for making your resume more concise and noticeably more powerful.

We'll help you sort out which resume styles and word choices work (and don't work) with the new online job-search methodologies. As you'll see, some of the "rules" that you may have heard of for Web-based resumes are *not* accurate. Our chapters on this topic will set you straight.

We'll reveal the kinds of common words, phrases, and sentences that turn off many potential recruiters, and we'll provide alternative expressions that unmistakeably shout, "Hire me!"

We'll discuss the sorts of personal details that can make your resume stand out attractively from the crowd as well as the ones you should *never* include.

And we'll show you how to tailor a cover letter for every stage of the job-search process, from networking meetings to blind job applications to follow-ups after interviews.

In short, we'll provide you with dozens of strategies, facts, tips, and ideas that can free you from the outmoded, paralyzing attitudes too many job seekers bring to the resume-writing task. After reading this book, you should no longer think of the resume as a weapon to be used against you by an eagle-eyed recruiter seeking reasons to reject you. Instead, it'll be a tool to be wielded by you as a door-opener and an attention-grabber.

A word about the sample resumes you'll find throughout this book. Each one is based closely on the real-life resume of a successful job-search candidate. However, the names, addresses, phone numbers, company listings, and other identifying details have been altered for reasons of privacy. If the real name of any individual appears on a resume in this book, it's purely coincidental and unintentional.

We've selected our sample resumes to illustrate various resume strategies, styles, and designs, and we hope you'll find them enlightening and inspiring. Every career and every job seeker is unique. Your own resume will undoubtedly draw elements from more than one of the sample resumes you'll find in these pages—as well as a special twist or two of your own. That's as it should be. Don't approach the sample resumes as rigid forms to be followed precisely but rather as sources of great ideas to be adopted and molded to fit your own personality and style.

# Part I

# Who Are You and Where Are You Going?

# Chapter 1

# Realities of Today's Career Marketplace

## Get the Scoop On . . .

- The good news *and* the bad news for job hunters
- Rapid changes caused by economic and social forces
- Skills and strategies to achieve success

Unless you're a professional writer, you'll probably devote more time and energy to crafting your resume than to any other document you'll ever create—including your best-ever college term paper, your most crucial business report, and even that special poem to the one and only love of your life. And that's appropriate. Because, for most people, their resume is the single most important piece of writing they'll ever do. A great resume can make the difference between landing the job of your dreams and not even getting your foot in the door—it matters just that much.

As a piece of writing, the resume is an eminently *practical* device—a job-hunting tool intended for prying open a world of career opportunities. And like any tool, it must be properly designed to do the job effectively. Each element of the resume—from its length, format, and style to the precise wording of each detail and even the color of the paper on which it's printed—must be chosen with practical effectiveness in mind.

Other considerations may come into play. To a lesser extent, the resume may be a vehicle for personal self-expression . . . a source of aesthetic pleasure . . . a factual record of your work experience, education, and other data. But above all, the resume is a *tool for persuasion*. As we'll explain in greater detail in later chapters—and as we'll reiterate frequently throughout the book—the resume is a kind of advertisement. It's an 8½ × 11-inch billboard designed to catch the eye of a potential customer (that is, an employer) and begin the process of selling her on your most important product: you.

Every piece of advice we offer in this book will be designed with that purpose in mind: To make your resume the most powerful possible tool for capturing the interest of a potential employer and then for persuading her that *you* are the right person for the job.

The resume, then, is a selling tool. And as any good salesperson will tell you, it's impossible to do a truly effective job of selling without knowing the territory—that is, without knowing a little about your customer, about her needs, and about the competitive marketplace in which you're doing business.

When it comes to selling your skills to an employer, of course, the marketplace we're referring to is the job market; and understanding the nature of today's job market and the peculiar pressures it's creating on both sellers and buyers of human talent will go a long way toward preparing you for being your own best possible salesperson. That's the purpose of the rest of this chapter.

## JOB HUNTING IN A BOOMING ECONOMY

### First, the Good News

*Question: Are you a salesperson? Don't answer based on what your business card or your resume says. No matter what your title, the answer is, Yes. Whenever you are looking for your next job—and, nowadays, for many people, that means at all times—you are a salesperson for yourself. That's the frame of mind in which to approach the job search: to be a salesperson for what you have to offer an employer and to do the best possible job of selling yourself.*

As you've undoubtedly heard, the economy of the United States (and of much of the rest of the developed world) is enjoying an almost unprecedented boom as we enter the twenty-first century.

The good news takes several forms. The rate of economic growth, as measured in business productivity statistics, is high—a healthy 2 percent annually, according to current U.S. data. The value of businesses, as reflected in the prices of stocks trading on the world's exchanges and in electronic marketplaces, has never been higher and continues to climb at a record pace. Partly as a result of all the newfound paper wealth enjoyed by investors, many people's sense of personal prosperity is high, which generates confidence among consumers and a willingness to spend money—further stimulating economic growth.

Furthermore, interest rates, which affect the ease with which businesses can get access to the capital they need to finance expansion and growth, were consistently low during the '90s. And price inflation, which can stymie economic expansion, also remained remarkably low throughout the last decade—just 1.6 percent in 1998, for example. (The fact that both interest rates and inflation have remained low during a period of strong economic expansion has many economists scratching their heads; this benign combination is exceedingly rare, and most of the experts are at a loss to account for it.)

However, the key statistics for you as a job hunter have to do with unemployment—the percentage of people who are involuntarily out of work. For several years, the officially measured rate of unemployment in the United States has been at a historic low. As of July 1999, that rate was 4.3 percent of the workforce—lower than at any other time in the past thirty years.

(To put this in perspective, consider this. During the '70s and '80s, economists debated what the "full employment" rate might be—that is, the rate of unemployment below which no modern industrial economy could reasonably be expected to fall. Most believed that the full employment rate was somewhere between 5 and 6 percent. Thus, today's rate of less than 4.5 percent would have been considered *practically impossible* by most economists less than a generation ago.)

Naturally, the employment market varies from industry to industry, with a few ultra-hot fields leading the way (and some fields lagging). The information technology sector (IT), including companies in the computer, software, Internet, and electronics businesses, is generally considered today's economic leader. IT companies added more than 1 million new jobs to the U.S. economy between 1993 and 1999, and as of this writing the unemployment rate among IT professionals was below 2 percent.

Furthermore, there appears to be no end in sight to the phenomenal growth of information technology. A 1999 Commerce Department report estimated that another 1.3 million IT workers will be needed over the next decade.

Information technology isn't the only booming field. Employment in health care, engineering, sales and marketing, travel and tourism, financial services, retailing, accounting and other business services, and many other areas is also growing rapidly. And although each of these job markets is insulated from the others to some extent (nurses generally aren't competing for jobs with CPAs), great demand in one area tends to increase the positive pressure on every field over time, as workers migrate from one industry to another.

Thus, we're encountering all kinds of evidence, both anecdotal and statistical, about today's positive job marketplace. Some straws in the wind:

- At conferences attended by company human resource managers, a hot topic is how to attract and keep good employees in an era when some jobs actually go begging. Consultant Gary Cluff urges companies to "start by making your current employees happy campers." Yes, companies are listening—because they must.

- Eager to retain good workers, some companies are offering unprecedented employee benefits, such as child care. Staples, Inc., the office-supply superstore chain, has just opened an 8,000-square-foot child-care center for employees at its corporate headquarters in Framingham, Massachusetts. Other companies are following suit.

- Great running backs and third basemen aren't the only workers receiving "signing bonuses." Many employers in health care, IT, and other highly competitive fields are offering such bonuses to attract new workers, ranging from $1,000 to $10,000 or more.

- Many companies are paying their current employees fancy bonuses for referring their friends to jobs. MasterCard International, for example, routinely pays $1,000 to $3,000 for successful referrals, depending on the level of the job. Carolyn Koenig, an HR specialist with the company, says, "I've had some people make $20,000 in a year off of referrals."

- Groups once considered "hard to employ" due to prejudice or a perceived lack of skills are now finding it easier to land good jobs. The unemployment rate among young African-American men—while still larger than among their white counterparts—has fallen dramatically during the '90s. And even adults (of all races) who lack high school diplomas are finding jobs; their unemployment rate is just 6 percent, the lowest level since that statistic was first recorded.

- Technology companies, unable to fill jobs for engineers, programmers, scientists, and other highly skilled workers, are lobbying the federal government to loosen immigration restrictions so that more foreign workers can enter the United States

Demographics—that is, the study of changing population patterns—help to explain today's tight labor markets. As the members of the vast Baby Boom generation age (in the late 1990s, the advance guard of the Baby Boomers began entering their 50s), a smaller cohort of Generation Xers moves up to take their place. Thus, there's relatively less competition for jobs usually held by people in their 20s and 30s than existed twenty years ago, when the flood of Boomers hit the streets. And as the Boomers begin to retire, the sellers' market for labor will follow them up the business ladder, creating new higher-level openings over the next two decades.

So, in many ways, today is the best of times for job seekers.

Or is it?

## On the Other Hand . . .

Yet at the same time, some equally valid facts and statistics (as well as the common experiences of millions of Americans) suggest a very different economic picture.

One set of statistics that paints a less glowing picture of the economy has to do with personal income. According to most measurements, salaries and family incomes were stagnant during most of the 1990s, rather than increasing (as is usual during an economic expansion). In fact, once inflation is taken into account, most economists believe that the average family income is actually *lower* today than it was in the 1970s. (As we write, recent figures appear to suggest that the period of wage stagnation may be ending, with small gains starting in the third quarter of 1998.)

*"In April [1999], the computer industry—hardly anyone's candidate as a troubled sector—announced the most job cuts that month, more than 10,000. Electronics, another high-technology star, was second, with 8,900. According to the Challenger survey [by Challenger, Gray & Christmas, a leading outplacement firm], between 1993 and 1998 the computer industry announced almost 273,000 job cuts, about the same as retail trade and second only to the aerospace-military industry."*
*—The New York Times*

Furthermore, to the extent that some families have improved their incomes, this is mainly due to the fact that more women with children are working than in the past, and that more workers are taking on second jobs than ever before. Millions of families are finding that it takes two incomes (or even two and a half, counting extra part-time work) to sustain the middle-class lifestyle that one good job could support a generation ago.

There's disagreement, too, about the value of the millions of new jobs being created by the booming economy. Dueling economists with differing statistics have reached varying conclusions, but it seems clear that many of the new jobs, especially those in the rapidly growing service sector, are low-paying, often low-growth positions.

Take health care as an example. Under pressure from employers, insurers, and the federal government to reduce the costs of healthcare, hospitals and other providers are looking for ways to trim salary expenses. Consequently, many are gradually replacing relatively high-paid workers with others who are less skilled and lower paid. Thus, as registered nurses retire, many are being replaced, not by other registered nurses, but by aides and technicians of various kinds, who can perform similar (not identical) work for less money.

Even today's low rate of inflation is a mixed blessing. It's sustained, in large part, by the wage stagnation we've already mentioned. Of course, business managers love the fact that wages—the largest single cost of doing business for most companies—have barely grown in recent years, making it easier for businesses to control their costs. But many working people, receiving salary increases of 1 to 3 percent annually rather than the 5 to 10 percent that was common only a decade ago, are finding it harder to pursue their dreams of the good life.

Perhaps the most striking paradox of today's economy is that, even as unemployment rates continue to fall, companies are announcing record numbers of layoffs. During 1999, layoff announcements (mostly from large companies) were running 40 percent higher than in 1998—which was itself a record-breaking year.

Nearly every week seems to bring another bad-news announcement. In July 1999 alone, we read about almost 20,000 jobs being eliminated at Eastman Kodak, 15,000 laid off at Procter & Gamble, and 6,000 more at Levi Strauss. The economies of entire towns and regions have been devastated by such cuts.

The record-setting layoff numbers are being registered even in industries that are the drivers behind today's economic boom, such as computers and electronics. Recent layoffs in the computer business have been truly enormous—and hard to understand during a time of supposed "boom."

What's going on here?

## THE NUMBERS GAME

One fact emerges clearly: Today's job market features remarkably high rates of turnover. According to the U.S. Bureau of Labor Statistics, over 13 million workers now "change their employment status" in a typical month. (This means entering or leaving the work force, finding a new job after a period of unemployment, or joining the ranks of job seekers by quitting or being laid off or fired.) Note that most of these people are changing jobs voluntarily; with big-company layoffs running at about 60,000 per month, it's clear that they account for just a small fraction of all the turnover.

Furthermore, the Labor Department estimates that about 50 million workers—about 40 percent of the U.S. workforce—changes jobs in any given year. Of course, this doesn't necessarily mean 50 million *different* workers; if Joe Jones works for four companies in a single year, that counts as three job changes. Nonetheless, the picture is one of an extraordinarily mobile workforce.

Yet there are still many people who work for the same company for many years. Henry Farber, a Princeton University economist, estimates that, of all workers 35 years old or older, 35 to 40 percent have been working for the same company for at least ten years—stability by almost any measure.

What overall picture do these statistics suggest? There are at least three subgroups of American workers, loosely defined but identifiably different:

- A large bloc of working people who are happy with, or at least accepting of, their current jobs, and ready to remain there for a decade or longer

- Another large bloc of people who change jobs frequently, either voluntarily or otherwise

- An intermediate group who change jobs occasionally—perhaps once every two or three years

*Your* perception of the job market (and of the overall strength of the economy) probably depends in large part on which of these groups you and the people you know belong to. For some people, the economic boom has produced satisfying, lucrative, long-term jobs; for others, it has provided the welcome opportunity to job-hop at will; and still others have not benefited from it at all.

However, it's plain that the U.S. job market is a highly volatile place, with millions of jobs to be filled and millions of people jostling to fill them at any given time. When you enter this market in search of your next job, you're throwing yourself into a grueling competition on a mass scale.

# TECHNOLOGICAL AND SOCIAL CHANGE

Why is all this happening now? There are many reasons. Here are a few of the most important.

### The Industry Churn

As everyone knows, the 1990s were a period of phenomenal change as technologies, developed during the preceding decades (the computer, digital electronics, the Internet, and various biological and medical breakthroughs), revolutionized entire industries. As a result, millions of jobs are now being created in businesses that didn't exist ten years ago, while millions of other positions, now becoming obsolete, are gradually vanishing. We call this *industry churn*.

Technology, of course, is not the only driver of this phenomenon. Demographics is another. As the huge cohort of the Baby Boomers ages, industries that cater to older people —predominately health care, but also tourism, entertainment, education, and other "adult lifestyle" industries—are booming. Most experts expect this growth to continue for at least the next two decades.

Consider the data in the following table. Of the ten fastest-growing jobs for the coming decade (as projected by the U.S. Bureau of Labor Statistics), four are in the information technology sector, six in the health-care industry. That's technology and demographics at work.

## Ten Jobs with the Fastest Projected Rate of Employment Increase, 1996–2006

1. Database manager (118%)
2. Computer engineer (109%)
3. Systems analyst (103%)
4. Personal/home aide (85%)
5. Physical-therapy assistant (79%)
6. Home health aide (76%)
7. Medical assistant (74%)
8. Desktop publisher (74%)
9. Physical therapist (71%)
10. Occupational therapist (69%)

### The Functional Churn

*Putting a New Age spin on career trends in the* Utne Reader, *journalist Brad Edmondson summarizes tomorrow's "hot jobs" as "Healing . . . Peacemaking . . . Storytelling." Relying on U.S. government data, he forecasts rapid job growth by the year 2006 for physical therapists ("healers"), dispute mediators ("peacemakers"), and writers, artists, editors, musicians, and entertainers ("storytellers").*

Not only is there tremendous migration of labor from one industry to another; there are also massive shifts occurring between job categories. We refer to this as the *functional churn*.

For many reasons, businesses in the United States (and elsewhere) are under huge financial pressures today. The sustained bull market in stocks means that investors in companies are demanding ever-higher rates of return on their money. This, in turn, means that corporate managers are required to produce ever-increasing profit margins, which can only be done by reducing costs and improving productivity—doing more with less.

Similar pressures exist, for related reasons, in the nonprofit world. Some sectors, such as health care, are being driven to reduce costs by demands for savings from the companies that foot the bills (insurance companies and the employers who pay them). Other nonprofit sectors are being affected by government downsizing and the reduction in funds available for research, grants, and other purposes; these include institutions in the arts, sciences, education, and social services.

So both for-profit and not-for-profit organizations are under continuing pressure to reduce or eliminate thousands of staff positions that are viewed as nonproductive. Layers of bureaucracy are being shed, and departments such as human resources, purchasing, corporate communications, and public relations are being slashed.

Generally speaking, in most companies, the only departments that are growing are those that can *prove* they bring revenue into the organization. If all you can do is *spend* the company's money—however wisely—watch your back! Your job may be on next month's chopping block.

## The Geographic Churn

Yet another cause of labor turnover is the continuing, massive shift of population from the American Northeast and Midwest to the Sunbelt—that wide swatch of the southern United States stretching from the Carolinas through Georgia and Florida west to Texas, Arizona, and California. Not only are millions of Americans moving south and west, but so are thousands of businesses, taking jobs with them. We call this the *geographic churn*.

The Census Bureau figures in the following table suggest that this trend, which has been under way for three decades now, is still in full swing.

Naturally, there are still millions of good jobs to be had in the North and Midwest, and some industries remain largely centered in specific "Rust Belt" cities—automaking in Detroit; finance, fashion, and publishing in New York; optics in Rochester; futures and options trading in Chicago, and so on. But as more and more firms migrate from cities like Philadelphia, Buffalo, and Milwaukee to new homes in and around cities like Atlanta, San Diego, and Phoenix, hundreds of thousands of workers follow suit. Further job mobility is a natural consequence.

Technology plays a major role in this geographic churn. The Sunbelt would never have boomed without the invention and postwar spread of air conditioning. The development of affordable air travel played a role, too; today, when millions fly between cities and states every year, moving halfway across the country in search of a new job doesn't seem quite as daunting a prospect as it did in our parents' day.

### Fifteen U.S. Metro Areas with the Greatest Projected Employment Growth, 1998–2025

1. Atlanta, Georgia
2. Phoenix, Arizona
3. Houston, Texas
4. Dallas, Texas
5. Washington, D.C.
6. Los Angeles, California
7. San Diego, California
8. Seattle, Washington
9. Orange County, California
10. Tampa, Florida
11. Orlando, Florida
12. Denver, Colorado
13. Minneapolis, Minnesota
14. Boston, Massachusetts
15. Chicago, Illinois

And in the final years of the twentieth century, the information technology revolution accelerated the geographic churn by making it easier than ever for a business to operate almost anywhere. Thanks to the Internet and other cheap, convenient forms of instantaneous communication, companies can tap the talents of employees, suppliers, and consultants located elsewhere.

Some U.S.-based software companies, for example, now employ teams of programmers in Singapore, India, South America, and other distant lands who hand off their work electronically to teams in Boston, Austin, or San Jose, creating, in effect, global, round-the-clock software factories. Similarly, with the spread of electronic securities trading, U.S. financial firms located anywhere in Florida, New Mexico, or Maine can buy and sell stocks on exchanges in New York, London, Tokyo, or Frankfurt at any hour of the day or night.

It's an exaggeration to say that technology has made geography irrelevant. In many fields, there are still clear advantages to being located where the greatest collection of talent and energy is found. But technology is making geography less and less of a limiting factor for businesses—and the careers of individuals need to adapt accordingly.

For some, technology is opening up marvelous opportunities, making it possible, for example, to "telecommute" to work with colleagues hundreds of miles away without ever leaving your home. For others, it is posing challenges. For instance, as the IT industry becomes ever more geographically dispersed, an ambitious manager in the field may have to choose among job openings in Boston, Seattle, Austin, San Jose, and New York. For a parent with two kids in school (for example), such a decision can be agonizing.

### The Rise of Free Agency
Finally, job mobility has been accelerated by the weakening of some of the traditional links that once connected employees to companies. As a result, more and more working people are thinking of themselves as "free agents" rather than as long-term members of any corporate family.

- As global competition has intensified, large corporations that once prided themselves on virtual "lifetime employment contracts" now don't hesitate to lay off workers when necessary. In the 1980s, it sent shock waves through corporate America when IBM first broke its decades-old policy against layoffs; but in subsequent years, nearly ever other major U.S. firm has followed suit.

- More and more companies are making temporary, contract ("piecework"), seasonal, and part-time employees a major part of their workforce. The proliferation of so-called contingent work has produced a mass of working people with no strong sense of loyalty or commitment to any single company.

- Downsized companies are outsourcing many services they once handled in-house, often rehiring some of their former employees as independent contractors. As a result, there are more self-employed Americans than ever before—about 2.5 million, according to one recent estimate. Their chief loyalty, of course, is to themselves (and their families) rather than to any company client.

- The traditional corporate pension plan, which encouraged a long-term career with a single employer, has been largely replaced by portable retirement plans like the 401(k). The new plans don't penalize job hopping, which is yet another reason for why employee loyalty has eroded.

Each of these trends helps to feed a free-agent mindset on the part of many working people. It says: I'm fundamentally on my own, with no guarantees that Mammoth Industries or The Little Corporation will watch out for or protect my long-term interests—even if I happen to be working for them at the moment. Therefore, I've got to look out for myself—and when a better opportunity comes along, I've got to grab it.

As trends like these continue and accelerate, it's likely we'll see job turnover continue to grow, at least for the foreseeable future.

## TIME AND MONEY PRESSURES

For all the reasons we've explained so far, today's workplace is a hotbed of change, including an exceptionally high rate of employee turnover. It all adds up to a job market featuring millions of people seeking work at any given time, millions more ready to consider a change in jobs for the right opportunity, and millions of open job positions seeking the right person to fill them.

One result is that, in many fields, job hunting is an increasingly frantic, high-paced process—something like jostling for position among 20,000 runners in the Boston Marathon. Examples of some of the effects:

- Literally millions of resumes are now flooding cyberspace, available through thousands of job-search Internet sites maintained by employers, headhunters, and e-commerce companies.

- More and more companies (and job seekers) are using job fairs to streamline the job-search process. The fairs bring together hundreds of employers and thousands of job seekers to conduct scores of interviews within a few hours.

- On-campus recruiting by companies has reached new highs at hundreds of colleges. At Daytona Beach during 1999 spring break, 2,000 students (many in bathing suits and flip-flops) were interviewed by recruiters eager to get a jump on their corporate competitors.

- Grads of top business schools are being pursued by "handholders"—personal recruiters from banking, consulting, and industrial firms assigned to become the new grads'"best friends" in hope of short-circuiting the job-search process.

In today's superheated job market, companies in search of excellent employees are feeling intensely pressured to move quickly, lest they lose out on the opportunity to hire a top-notch candidate. Cisco Systems, the maker of computer-networking equipment, boasts of its "just-in-time" recruitment systems, by which they woo potential employees *constantly*, even in the absence of any actual job openings; and Allergan, Inc., a biotech company, has ordered its recruiters to contact job candidates within 48 hours—or risk losing them.

In some cases, the time pressure is causing everyone—job seekers and employers alike—to skip or streamline steps in the hiring process that were once considered sacrosanct. Personality tests? Reference checking? More and more often, these steps are simply dropped from the process. The pressure is to hire someone—fast—and hope that he or she won't leave too quickly, forcing the employer to start the race all over again.

# GETTING YOUR PIECE OF THE ACTION

What does all this mean for today's job hunters? We think the most important lessons are clear.

### You Need to Make the Job Search a Full-Time Occupation

Career counselors have long urged their clients to regard job hunting as a job in itself. The advice is more relevant today than ever before. With the job market in such a state of flux, and with so many sources of job information available—from newspapers and magazines to headhunters, employment agencies, and thousands of locations on the Internet—most working people need to block out significant time in order to just keep abreast of the trends and the opportunities they're creating.

Naturally, if you have a job, you don't want to leave it just to have more time to search for your next one. But when you're ready to embark on your next job search, don't assume it'll be as simple as making a few phone calls, mailing a handful of resumes, and choosing among offers. Instead, expect to spend weekends and a few evenings a week networking with people who may have job information you can use, tracking down the facts about companies and jobs you may be interested in, and preparing and distributing resumes and cover letters. And plan to spend a significant amount of time in interviews—often two, three, or more interviews for a single job.

Above all, be prepared to respond promptly when an inquiry comes in from a headhunter or a prospective employer. With so many fish in the sea, a delay of a day or two may cost you a spot in line for the job of your dreams. Don't take that chance.

### There Are Fewer Obstacles for the Determined Job Hunter Than Ever Before

Today's lively, ever-changing job market provides several clear advantages for job hunters. One is that, with so many jobs to fill, many companies are casting their nets wider than in the past. Biases that might have excluded some job candidates a generation ago are being broken down. (Other positive social forces are at work as well, of course.)

So women, older and younger workers, people of color, nonnative Americans, and the differently abled—all of whom found themselves disadvantaged in past job hunts—are finding the doors at least partly open today.

### Today's Job Market Puts a Premium on Flexibility.

As you embark on a job search, your chances of finding the perfect job will be enhanced if you're prepared to move quickly and flexibly. As the business and work worlds change, you need to be prepared to change with them—or risk overlooking opportunities that might have been remarkably fulfilling and rewarding.

Flexibility means, for example, being open to considering jobs whose description might not, at first, sound ideal for you. In an era of downsizing and streamlining, more and more employees are being asked to fill roles that are broadly, perhaps vaguely, defined. Today, many jobs are what you make of them rather than rigid, narrowly defined functional slots. In such a situation, the self-directed, self-starting professional who can define his or her own role and make it work to benefit the company is highly prized.

Flexibility also means being open to jobs in industries or business sectors you might have assumed were inappropriate for you. It may mean making a lateral career shift in order to learn a new technology or a new business rather than insisting on a traditional promotion when changing companies. Or it may mean moving from a relatively high-prestige, high-perk job (in a dead-end business) to a less-impressive job (in a dynamic, growing field).

### The Only Skills That Are Universally Prized Are People Skills

As for people skills, we mean such things as: the ability to work with many kinds of people and get along with them productively; the ability to remain calm, optimistic, and focused in times of stress or crisis; the ability to communicate clearly and persuasively both to individuals and to groups of people; the ability to manage relationships "upward," "downward," and "sideways" in the corporate hierarchy; and the ability to positively influence others over whom you have no formal power or authority.

Clearly these are skills that have always been important. What makes them especially significant in today's rapidly changing world of work? When industries, technologies, organizations, and relationships are in flux, even in turmoil, the one constant is *human potential*.

Whatever business you're in, chances are good that the specific industry knowledge, technical expertise, and factual information you possess today will soon be dated—if it isn't already. It's important, of course, to continually update your skills as thoroughly as possible. But most employers today are looking for something different from, and deeper than, technical skills. They're looking for people with the potential to adapt, learn, and grow in any working environment—an ability that can *never* become dated no matter how drastically our universe changes.

Thus, you may find, as you work your way through the job-search process, that employers are focusing to a surprising degree on "cultural" and "social" issues—how well you might fit into the climate of their workplace and the contribution your personality would make to the existing team. *These are factors that you, too, should be focusing on.* As we move into the twenty-first century, it is increasingly these people skills that will help determine how productive, satisfied, and successful you'll be in your career.

### Don't Be Shy About Tooting Your Own Horn
Most people have been raised to be diffident about self-praise. And in many contexts, modesty is appropriate and becoming. But in today's job market, it's important to be willing to trumpet your own strengths, skills, and accomplishments. If you're too shy or modest to do so, your credentials are apt to be overlooked. It's a crowded marketplace out there; the low-key competitor is all too likely to end up lost in the crowd.

Throughout this book, as we delve deeply into the art of crafting your resume and the cover letters to accompany it, we'll explain in detail how and where to toot your own horn—and, more importantly, how to do so without appearing conceited or self-centered. But we urge you, beginning now, to become accustomed to a mindset different from the one you're probably used to. Stop thinking of putting yourself forward as "bragging" and think of it instead as "self-marketing." It's one of the crucial business skills of our time.

### No One Else Will Manage Your Career for You
At one time—so the myth goes—millions of Americans followed career tracks mapped out and maintained by others. There was a predictable

path awaiting the talented grad: lifelong work at one of America's great industrial firms featuring a slow, steady rise from some entry-level job to a managerial position and ultimately retirement with a comfortable pension. That's the way we tend to picture careers from, say, the 1950s. It all seems very middle-class, secure, and a little dull.

In truth, few careers were so cut-and-dried back then. Plenty of people changed companies or professions; a good number were fired or laid off at one time or another; and technological and economic trends laid waste to some industries and nurtured others. The whole litany of changes we see around us today were certainly not uncommon in the past.

But it's safe to say that unpredictable change is now the normal order of business. As a result, it's clear that no benign corporate or government entity stands ready to ensure you a tranquil, secure, lifelong career path.

Today more than ever, your career is something you'll create through all the decisions, large and small, you'll make in your working life. Chances are good that you'll change jobs many times; you'll probably even shift from one industry to another, perhaps several times, before your work is done. At one time or another, it's quite likely you'll work for yourself, hold down one or more part-time jobs, or follow the entrepreneurial route of founding your own business. These once off-the-beaten-track career choices are becoming less the exception and more the norm in twenty-first century America.

For some people, this prospect of an uncharted career path is exhilarating; for others, it's intimidating. Don't let the unpredictability—and freedom—of the new world of work scare you. If you learn to recognize and seize the opportunities that most excite you, the results can be wonderfully fulfilling.

## JUST THE FACTS

- Today's booming economy holds tremendous potential for job seekers . . . but the tumult of change also holds risks.

- Economic, technological, and social changes have made the job marketplace more dynamic and unpredictable than ever before.

- To be truly successful, today's job hunter must be flexible, people-oriented, and responsive to a wide range of opportunities.

- Above all, in a world where job turnover is more rapid than ever, be prepared to take charge of your career. The resume is one crucial tool for doing so.

# Chapter 2

# You and Your Goals

## Get the Scoop On . . .

- Identifying your personal interests
- Linking your interests to your career choices
- Making your childhood dreams come true
- Determining your work values
- Determining your life values
- Identifying your dream job
- Recognizing and adapting to changes in the future

W ork is an essential element of our lives. We work to fulfill our dreams, to develop our potential, and to obtain those material things we need to survive and flourish. Work also enables us to contribute to our families, our communities, and the world at large. It's no wonder that, for most people, finding and succeeding at work that is worthwhile and personally satisfying is one of life's most basic and important quests.

As we said in the previous chapter, a resume is essentially a tool for persuasion, a means of convincing a potential employer that you are the right person for an available job. But before you even start thinking about how to craft a convincing argument, you must first know exactly what you're arguing for. That is, you need to determine your goals, both personal and professional, before you begin planning the ways and means by which you can achieve those goals.

Perhaps you've just graduated from high school, college, or grad school and have yet to decide exactly what you'd like to do with your life. If so, you're in an enviable position. Your choices are virtually unlimited, and the journey on which you're about to embark can be an extraordinarily exciting one. We'll help you take the first steps of that journey.

On the other hand, you may have already decided on a career path and taken the first—if not many—steps along that path. The fact that you're reading this book, however, means that you are about to take another series of steps, possibly in a new direction, and have chosen to seek some help in doing so. You may know in which direction you'd like to go, but it's also possible that you haven't yet found your bearings and could use a little help.

*"For three years I was a managing director in a big brewery. I have no sort of quarrel with brewing. It is an admirable trade, and beer is an admirable drink. But I have never been so bored in my life as I was during those three years. I learned then the lesson that nothing is so depressing as to spend one's life doing something in which one is not interested."*
—Geoffrey Faber, British publisher, in a speech to booksellers, 1931

But regardless of whether you're just starting your working life, already firmly ensconced in a career, or seeking to make a career change, it's essential that you know own your goals before you put pen to paper or fingers to keyboard to start writing your resume.

In determining those goals, bear in mind that work is not only an end in itself but also a means to an end. That is, while what you do for a living is important in and of itself, it can also have an enormous impact on every other aspect of your life.

For that reason, in determining a career path you will have to take into account several factors, including your personal interests, your dreams, your work values, your life values, what's likely to happen in the future, and, of course, your career-related skills. In this chapter, we'll help you evaluate most of these factors in relation to your career. The subject of career-related skills, however, is of such importance that we'll devote all of the next chapter to it.

## IDENTIFY YOUR PERSONAL INTERESTS

In determining what you want to do for a living, the first thing to do is identify those areas in which you have a personal interest. The most successful people usually love what they do for a living, so much so that it often doesn't even seem like work to them ("They *pay* me to do this? I'd do it for nothing!"). Conversely, those who are not genuinely interested in their jobs tend to be both less successful and less satisfied with their lives in general.

In order to start defining your goals, the first thing you should do is sit down and make a list of those things you're interested in. Just put down

---

**My Personal Interests**

1. _____
2. _____
3. _____
4. _____
5. _____
6. _____
7. _____
8. _____
9. _____
10. _____

whatever comes into your mind. The list might include everything from "cross-country skiing" to "Italian opera" to "refinishing antique furniture" to "reading about African history."

Remember, at this point you're just thinking about what your personal interests are, *not* what you want to do for a living, so there's no reason to limit yourself in any way. Ignore the voices within that whisper, "That's not practical!" "How can you make a living doing *that?*" "What will your parents say?" "What does *that* have to do with your college degree?" There's plenty of time later to consider those sorts of concerns.

## RECALL YOUR DREAMS

The next step in the process of developing your career goals is to recall your dreams. Although it may have been a long time ago—or at least seem like it—the chances are that as a child or an adolescent you imagined yourself at various times in one occupation or another. Maybe you dreamed of being a nurse, a firefighter, a construction worker, a doctor, an actor, a sportswriter, a teacher, a scuba diver, a dancer. You may, even as an adult, still be dreaming such dreams—and perhaps living them.

Since you are about to embark on a job search, now is the time for you to resurrect or reconsider those dreams. It's possible that at some point you will determine that those dreams aren't achievable, but don't limit yourself prematurely. Just write down whatever you can remember about the kind of career or careers you have imagined for yourself. Start here and add additional pages if you need them.

| My Dreams |
|---|
| 1. _____ |
| 2. _____ |
| 3. _____ |
| 4. _____ |
| 5. _____ |
| 6. _____ |
| 7. _____ |
| 8. _____ |
| 9. _____ |
| 10. _____ |

# DETERMINE YOUR WORK VALUES

**FYI**

*If you feel that you've lost track of your childhood dreams, try closing your eyes and imagining yourself as a child again. Doing so is sure to trigger at least some memories—for good or ill—and may very well remind you of some of the roles in which you imagined yourself at the time.*

The third element in developing career goals is determining your *work values*—that is, deciding on the kinds of things you want and expect to get out of work.

The most obvious of those things you expect to get out of work is a salary. Unless your great Uncle Moshe left you several million dollars in his will—and few of us are in that situation—working is the only way you're going to earn a living. So making money is always going to be a consideration.

If, as it sometimes is the case, making money is the *only* thing you're really interested in, choosing a career path will be relatively easy: You can simply aim for professions that provide high incomes, such as medicine or law.

However, while we certainly don't mean to belittle the importance of an income, the chances are that you expect work to provide you not only with money but with other, nonmaterial benefits as well. So in trying to determine the path your career should take, you should ask yourself not only "What do I want to have?" but also "What do I want to *be?*"

There are any number of possible answers to this question, and ultimately only you can determine the right answers for yourself. But it's important to ask and answer the question, because if you don't know what kind of person you want to be, it's extremely unlikely that you'll ever become that person. To give you an idea of what we're talking about and to help you get started thinking about it, here are a few of the most common nonmaterial benefits people hope to get out of work.

### A Sense of Accomplishment

*"Well, it's no trick to make a lot of money. . . if all you want is to make a lot of money."*
—"Mr. Bernstein," character played by Everett Sloan in the classic film *Citizen Kane*

For many of us, it's important to reach the end of the day feeling that we've completed our work with some degree of finality and closure. Being able to tick off the number of patients cared for, contracts signed, trees planted, students taught, crimes solved, or any other list of concrete achievements is uniquely satisfying and necessary to make work enjoyable.

### Doing Something Worthwhile

Another benefit many of us seek in work is a sense that we are doing something worthwhile. Of course, everyone has his own definition of what's worthwhile. Being the best refrigerator repairman in the world, may be deeply rewarding and meaningful for one person, an utter bore to another. Even jobs that enjoy enormous prestige and income may not *feel* worthwhile to the people who have them, as shown by the fact that famous, outwardly successful people sometimes commit suicide or get hooked on drugs or alcohol. These actions suggest an inner sense of hopelessness or lack of meaning. Only you can decide what feels worthwhile to you.

### A Creative Outlet

The opportunity to exercise creativity may be an important factor for you as well. Most people define the word *create* the same way the dictionary does: "to produce or bring about by a course of action or behavior." By this definition, making anything, tangible or intangible, constitutes creativity. Others define it in a more limited way, such as "to produce through imaginative skill," as in creating a work of art. But we know a CPA who's proud of his "creative accounting"—his talent for working around the myriad complex tax rules and regulations that would otherwise hamper the business activities of his clients. Perhaps creativity is simply the ability to use your talents, whatever they are, to their fullest.

### Helping Others

The sense that their work benefits other people is an important factor for some people as well. Of course, in a sense, virtually every job involves helping others; if your work benefits no one, it's unlikely anyone will pay you for it. But you may well think of "helping others" in a more traditional sense, such as being a social worker, physician, counselor, or nurse or working for a charitable organization.

### Learning

For some of us, one of the most important elements of work is having the sense that we are always learning something new. We're not talking only about learning how to do a job; at some point in time, everyone will have learned that. What we are talking about is the opportunity to be continuously learning by virtue of doing the job. For example, newspaper reporters, in the process of doing their jobs, are continuously learning about what's going on in their communities, their countries, or in the world.

### Leading Others

Some people appear to be born followers, while others are born leaders. If you're in the latter group, you won't be satisfied unless you are in a position in which you'll have the opportunity to influence, guide, or shape the beliefs and actions of others. Business managers, of course, exercise leadership skills on the job. So, in different ways, do school teachers, head nurses, orchestra conductors, city planners, and members of the clergy.

### A Sense of Community

Many people find their most rewarding social connections at work. For these people, work offers a chance to be part of a team, helping and supporting one another, tackling shared challenges in pursuit of common goals. The camaraderie of the workplace is as important for such people as the biweekly paycheck.

### Independence and Freedom

While some people relish being part of a team at work, there are others for whom working on their own—even within an office or other working environment—is more desirable. We know, for example, a man who worked for the New York City Transit Authority providing directions over the telephone to people who wished to get from one point to another on the subway. For over thirty years he sat in his cubicle, rarely spoke to any of his coworkers, and was perfectly happy. If being in control of your work and how you do it is important to you, list that as one of your work values.

These are only a few of the more common answers people have to the question, "What do I want to get out of work?" You may have other answers as well. Make a list of all those things that you would like to get out of a job so you can take them into consideration in developing your career goals.

*"I am certainly not one of those who need to be prodded. In fact, if anything, I am a prod."*

—Winston Churchill, in a speech to Parliament, November 11, 1942

# DETERMINE YOUR LIFE VALUES

The fourth element in developing career goals is determining your *life values*—that is, deciding what you want and expect to get out of life in general. It's a career-planning step that many people neglect to take, primarily because they don't think about such broader issues in

---

### What I Hope To Get Out of Work

1. _____
2. _____
3. _____
4. _____
5. _____
6. _____
7. _____
8. _____
9. _____
10. _____

---

deciding on the kind of work they wish to do. But the fact is that these life values are no less important than the work values we've already discussed.

Like your work values, your life values should influence your career choices. If spending a significant amount of quality time with your children is one of the things you most deeply value right now, it would not be a good idea for you to take a job that requires you to work particularly long hours or to work in the evenings when the rest of your family is at home.

Again, you are ultimately the only person who can determine what you want to get out of life. It's a broad and potentially profound question, of course, one that many people spend a lifetime exploring. But if you don't make an effort to consider it *before* you start on your career path, you may very well find that you've chosen wrongly.

While the following list of life values is by no means exhaustive, it should give you an idea of the kind of things you should be thinking about.

### Free Time
There seem to be relatively few true 9-to-5 jobs anymore; no one we know leaves the office at five on the dot. But some jobs require longer hours than others. If you live by yourself, and expect to continue to do so, and have no passionate avocations to which you want to devote much time, this may not be an issue for you. But if you have a spouse and, especially, children, you may want to spend as much time with them as possible.

### Time at Home

*"The man who doesn't spend time with his family isn't a real man."*
—"Don Vito Corleone," title character in the movie *The Godfather*

For many of those who like the idea, there are increasing opportunities to work at home. Both new technologies and the changing attitudes of employers are making it increasingly possible to operate out of home offices, either full-time or one or two days a week.

### Commuting Time
Most people commute to work every day—some for as little as 15 minutes and some for as long as two hours or more. We know one corporate executive who lives in rural Bucks County, Pennsylvania, and commutes to her office in New York City, spending a total of nearly 30 hours on the road each week. Many commuters take advantage of the time they spend on a train or bus by reading, working, or getting in a little extra sleep. But if the idea of a lengthy commute doesn't appeal to you, you'll obviously want to seek employment closer to rather than farther from your home.

### Schedule Flexibility
Some jobs involve relatively fixed working shifts, while others can be done at almost any time. Some employers insist on full-time work with

no long holidays, while others accommodate part-time schedules, job sharing, periodic sabbaticals, and unpaid leave. The desired degree of freedom to manipulate and change your own calendar is a factor to consider in deciding what sorts of jobs will or will not suit you.

### The Length of the Umbilical Cord

*"It is the first of all problems for a man to find out what kind of work he is to do in this universe."*

—Author/ philosopher Thomas Carlyle, in an address at Edinburgh University

With certain kinds of work, as soon as you walk out the workplace door, the job is a million miles away and you feel psychologically free to focus on your personal life. With other jobs, just the opposite is true: The sense of responsibility and concern for what is happening at the workplace never fully disappears, even on weekends and holidays. Some jobs require workers to remain in touch at all times via cell phone or e-mail; some even require workers to be available late at night to manage crises or opportunities in remote parts of the globe. A few people relish this sort of constant connection to work; others hate it. Better figure out which group you belong to before committing to a career path.

Everyone has their own life values, and these particular values may or may not be important to you. The only way to ultimately determine which values *are* important to you is to sit down and think about them. Make a list using the worksheet below so you'll be able to remember them in making your career decisions.

## PULLING IT ALL TOGETHER

So far, we've been discussing ideal situations—what you would most like to do and how you would like to do it, if you had complete control of your options. Now it's time to begin factoring in the requirements of real life.

---

### What I Hope to Get Out of Life

1. _____
2. _____
3. _____
4. _____
5. _____
6. _____
7. _____
8. _____
9. _____
10. _____

---

There are still two more steps you have to take in the process of establishing your career goals. The first is to make a connection between the ideals you've already listed—your interests, dreams, work values, and life values—and a job in which you can pursue them. The second step, which we'll discuss in the next chapter, is to determine whether or not you have, or can acquire, the job skills you need to do the kind of work you'd like.

It's entirely possible—perhaps even likely—that you can already see some connections between your ideals and the world of work. Even if unconsciously, you've probably begun thinking about the kinds of job that would enable you to pursue your interests and your dreams while honoring your work and life values. You may, for example, have included "children" on your list of personal interests and have dreamt of becoming an elementary school teacher. You may have listed "writing" among your interests and dreamt of being a newspaper reporter. Perhaps "working outdoors" is an interest of yours, expressed in the dream of being a forest ranger or outdoor guide. Or perhaps "organizing information" is an activity in which you're interested, and you've dreamed of working as a librarian, a database manager, or the information officer of a corporation.

No matter how far you've gone in the quest for a job that will fit your personality, the chances are that, regardless of your interests, dreams, and values, there is a job—or jobs—that can enable you to pursue them. However, if you're having a little difficulty figuring out exactly what that job might be, it would be helpful to examine the following chart, "The Career Matchmaker." While this chart is by no means comprehensive, it should help you begin the process of deciding how to translate what you'd like to do and how you'd like to turn it into a career. The vast number of other possibilities are limited only by your imagination.

Obviously, just a few of your possible interests have been listed here, but hopefully this chart has given you some idea of how to translate your interests, dreams, and values into career possibilities. Now it's time for you to figure out exactly what kind of career would be the right one for you to pursue. This is where the lists you've already made will come in particularly handy.

On the following checklist, write down in the appropriate column all the possible careers that appeal to you. Don't worry at this point about whether or not they represent jobs that you can do; you'll be able to resolve those questions in the next chapter. All you're looking for now is whether or not they represent jobs that you might like to do.

Then, having listed all your possible careers, go back over your interests, dreams, work values, and life values lists and rate them based

| The Career Matchmaker | |
|---|---|
| **If you are interested in . . .** | **Consider exploring a career in . . .** |
| animals | veterinary medicine, zoo management, wildlife management |
| art | architecture, computer graphics, decorating, art gallery management, museum administration, interior design, jewelry design, photography |
| buildings | architecture, construction, city planning, engineering, electrical work, plumbing |
| business | accounting, finance, business administration, management, marketing, sales, insurance, banking |
| cars | auto maintenance and repair, engineering, driving |
| children | child care, elementary education, pediatrics, counseling |
| clothing | tailoring, fashion design, fashion buyer, fashion reporter or writer |
| communications | advertising; television; radio; public relations; book, magazine, or newspaper publishing; Web design |
| computers | computer programming, computer systems design, e-commerce, network management, software, database management |
| criminal justice | police work, law, corrections, security, investigation, intelligence |
| dispute resolution | law, paralegal services, diplomacy, arbitration, public administration, labor relations |
| food | cooking, catering, nutrition, restaurant management, hospitality |

on the extent to which those careers seem to fit your criteria for the perfect job. You can use a scale of one to five, one being the farthest from meeting your criteria and five being the closest.

Although it's likely that you'll know whether those jobs are appropriate to your personal interests and dreams, it's possible that you may not know whether they'd meet your expectations as far as work and life values are concerned. If so, it would be a good idea for you to do some research to find out more about those professions.

There are many books available that discuss jobs in a variety of fields. In addition, virtually every industry has one or more magazines or journals devoted to it. (Many are listed in Appendix C, "Trade Journals, Industry

| **The Career Matchmaker** | |
| --- | --- |
| **If you are interested in . . .** | **Consider exploring a career in . . .** |
| furniture | interior design, retail or wholesale furniture sales |
| health | nursing, medicine, medical administration, physical therapy, public health, medical records administrator, insurance |
| languages | diplomacy, human and social services, language instruction, translating, church or missionary work |
| machines | engineering, manufacturing, mechanics, lab technician, machine operator, repairer, or inspector |
| math/science | engineering, research and development, teaching, financial analysis, risk management, chemistry |
| music | entertainment, music production, artist representation, radio production, record industry |
| outdoors | travel agencies, tourism, forestry, environmental science, oceanography, park and recreation management, landscape architecture |
| physical activity/sports | athletics, athletic coaching, athletic training, dance instruction, physical therapy |
| psychology | psychology, counseling, social work |
| teaching/training | primary or secondary education, human resources, corporate training, librarianship |
| travel | travel agencies, tour guiding, travel writing, hospitality, airlines, cruise lines |

Guidebooks, and Directories." A single trip to the library will probably unearth a large amount of information about careers that may be of interest to you. Even better, though, would be a conversation with someone already working in a field in which you think you might be interested. You can probably arrange such an interview by networking, and we provide information on how to go about doing that in Chapter 15.

In doing this research—either in the library or through networking—it would be advisable for you to find out not only what your dream jobs are actually like but also as much as possible about the education and skills each require. In the next chapter, we'll help you evaluate your background in terms of what's required for any particular job, showing how to realistically evaluate your chances of getting such a position.

| Making the Connections | | | | | | |
| --- | --- | --- | --- | --- | --- | --- |
| Possible Career | Personal Interests | Dreams | Work Values | Life Values | Education Values | Skills |
| 1. _____ | _____ | _____ | _____ | _____ | _____ | _____ |
| 2. _____ | _____ | _____ | _____ | _____ | _____ | _____ |
| 3. _____ | _____ | _____ | _____ | _____ | _____ | _____ |
| 4. _____ | _____ | _____ | _____ | _____ | _____ | _____ |
| 5. _____ | _____ | _____ | _____ | _____ | _____ | _____ |
| 6. _____ | _____ | _____ | _____ | _____ | _____ | _____ |
| 7. _____ | _____ | _____ | _____ | _____ | _____ | _____ |
| 8. _____ | _____ | _____ | _____ | _____ | _____ | _____ |
| 9. _____ | _____ | _____ | _____ | _____ | _____ | _____ |
| 10. _____ | _____ | _____ | _____ | _____ | _____ | _____ |

In filling out this checklist, once you've determined the extent to which the potential jobs you've selected meet your criteria, insert your ratings in the appropriate columns. While there may be some careers that come close to meeting your criteria in only one or two of the four areas listed, it's likely that there will be some to which you can give high ratings in three or all four categories.

Finally, add up the ratings for each of the possible careers listed on the checklist. Even if you've given a low rating to a job in one or two categories, generally speaking those with the highest overall ratings are probably the jobs you should be looking into further.

## A DIAMOND MAY BE FOREVER—BUT A JOB RARELY IS

*Not only is "job hopping" no longer considered a problem, but potential employers have come to be somewhat wary of job candidates who have stayed in the same job for a long time.*

In making these efforts to determine your "perfect" job, remember that you're not making any irrevocable choices. It may be that when your parents or grandparents started working, they expected, and were expected, to keep those jobs until they retired. But that's simply not true anymore.

Your chances of having one job for the rest of your life are remote at best, due to the societal changes we discussed in the last chapter. A history of "job hopping," which used to be considered a potential problem for those seeking new positions, has now become so common that, except in extreme cases, no one thinks twice about it.

Not only is it likely that you will change jobs, it's almost equally likely that you will change careers. Once rare, this has now become a very common occurrence. While this is in part due to economic, social, and technological changes that have created thousands of new industries in recent decades, it is also partly due to a changing attitude toward work and the role it plays in our lives.

Even if your grandfather was miserable because he hated what he did for a living, it might never have occurred to him that he should look for another kind of job—one that he would be *happy* doing. That's all changed. While some people still think of work only as a way of feeding, housing, and clothing themselves and their families, most people expect to get more out of their jobs than just a paycheck. So people who are unhappy in their careers are likely to seek new ones.

Sometimes people who change careers stay in the same industry in which they started. For example, we know one man who started his working life as a book editor, then went on to run a book club, went back to editing, and eventually set himself up in business as a literary agent. While many of the skills required for these positions were similar, the jobs themselves were very different, as were the working conditions. On the other hand, sometimes people who are changing careers move into entirely different fields. We've heard stories, for example, of corporate executives who got tired of the rat race and quit their high-paying jobs to take over and operate country inns, small wineries, art galleries, and other modest, low-pressure businesses.

*"I must not rust."*
—Clara Barton, founder, American Red Cross

If you've been in the workforce for some time, you may have already had more than one career and may be thinking of changing careers again. But even if you're just starting your working life, don't assume you'll be stuck for the rest of your life with the job or career you choose right now. Not only does the world change, but our priorities change as well. Today's actuary may be tomorrow's florist, and the woman who starts her career as a department store buyer may wind up taking care of children in a day-care center. Fortunately, in today's world you have plenty of opportunity to make those kinds of changes.

In fact, not only will you be able to make those changes, it's likely that you will *have* to. Although change has always been one of the great constants in life (along with death and taxes), the world is changing faster today than ever in the past. So if you settle into one job and stay with it for the rest of your life, you may find yourself stagnating. In order to keep up with the rest of the world, you will have to continue growing, learning, and changing, in both your personal and professional lives. To enjoy the process, don't fight it—embrace it.

# JUST THE FACTS

- The first step in developing your career goals is identifying your personal interests.

- The second step is recalling your childhood dreams—remembering the kinds of jobs you imagined yourself holding when you were young—regardless of how farfetched they may seem to be now.

- The third step is determining your work values—the things that are important to you in considering your ideal job.

- The fourth step is determining your life values—those personal but work-related aspects of your life that can have an impact on, and be impacted by, the job or career you choose to pursue.

- The fifth step is evaluating all the information you've gathered about your interests, your dreams, and your values in order to make an intelligent selection of a job or career.

- No job or career is forever, and you can and must change to adapt to the changing world and your own changing priorities.

# Chapter 3

# Evaluating What You Have to Offer

## Get the Scoop On . . .

- Evaluating your education and training
- Evaluating and documenting your work history
- Evaluating and documenting your personal achievements
- Presenting your volunteer/community service work
- Activities you should—and should not—include
- Selecting your best job or career

In the last chapter we helped you identify both your career and career-related life goals—what you would ideally *like* to do for a living. In this chapter, through a series of worksheets, we'll help you evaluate your background and the skills you've already acquired to help you determine exactly what you have to offer a potential employer.

Filling out these worksheets will serve three purposes. First, they will enable you to start creating a database of information about you and your history that you'll find useful in your search for appropriate careers as well as appropriate jobs.

Second, they will more specifically enable you to determine whether or not you currently have the background and skills you need for the "dream" jobs you identified in the last chapter.

Third, because each of the various worksheets correspond to one of the sections of your resume, they will provide you with the raw information from which you can construct your resume. (Detailed suggestions for how to put it all together, including how to translate this raw information into appropriate language, begins in Part II, "resume Basics.")

This chapter is divided into six sections: education and training, previous employment, personal achievements, volunteer/community service, hobbies and activities, and making a choice about what career to pursue. Although the worksheets included in each section are largely self-explanatory, we'll provide you with all the additional information you'll need to fill them out.

# YOUR EDUCATION AND TRAINING

**FYI**

*Although only some of the information you provide in these worksheets may actually be used in your resume, you're likely to have need for all of it at some point during your job search, and by including it here it will always be readily available. So don't skip quickly through the worksheets! The time you spend now will be time saved later in the process.*

Although information about your education and training will not be the first item on your resume (it's usually placed near the end), we've started with it because it usually comes first chronologically.

The education and training worksheet that follows is divided into two sections. The first, "education," asks you to provide general information about your high school, college, postgrad, or professional training experience. Much of this information will eventually be included in your resume.

The second section, "Relevant Course Work," asks for information about those courses you took which were specifically applicable to your job search, including the knowledge and skills you gained from them and any significant projects, papers, or presentations you created in connection with them.

Make copies of the worksheet so you can use one for each institution you've attended (high school, college, postgraduate work, or professional training).

# YOUR PREVIOUS EMPLOYMENT

While potential employers take into account all the information provided in your resume when trying to decide whether or not to ask you in for an interview, in most cases your work history is the element to which they pay the most attention. (The recent grad applying for an entry-level position is an obvious exception.) So, unless and until a potential employer chooses to interview you, he or she will rely primarily on job-related information—where you've worked, the kinds of positions you've held, and the achievements you've had—in trying to determine what kind of employee you are likely to be.

For that reason, it's essential that you get all the relevant information down on paper. In order to help you do that, we've included the employment worksheet that follows.

Fill out a copy of this worksheet for each job you've held. While much of this information—employers, job titles, employment dates, responsibilities, achievements, and promotions or awards—will eventually be transferred directly to your resume, some of it will not. We have, for example, included two questions regarding what you liked and disliked about each job. As with the information you've already provided on your education, having this information will be helpful in determining how closely your past jobs matched your interests, dreams, and values and thus enable you to make better decisions about the future.

**Education and Training**

**Education**

Name of institution/program: _____

Location: _____

Major: _____

Minor: _____

Attendance/graduation dates: _____

Degree/diploma/certificate: _____

Overall GPA: _____     Major GPA: _____

Class rank: _____

Honors/distinctions/awards/fellowships: _____

_____

_____

Study abroad/summer study/work study: _____

_____


**Relevant Course Work**

Course name: _____

Knowledge/information gathered: _____

_____

_____

Skills learned or utilized: _____

_____

_____

Important projects/papers/presentations: _____

_____

_____

References/contacts: _____

_____

_____

You will also note that the worksheet includes a question concerning your personal achievements. We've raised this question to get you to start thinking about those achievements; they'll eventually be included in your resume as part of your employment history. However, we recognize that if you've never thought about this issue before, you may not be entirely clear on exactly what such an "achievement" might be.

For that reason, we've included a personal achievement worksheet in this chapter. So if you do have any questions about this, you might want to consider filling out those worksheets first, and then coming back to complete the previous employment forms.

## YOUR PERSONAL ACHIEVEMENTS

*"The greatest accomplishment is not in never falling, but in rising again after you fall."*

—Legendary Green Bay Packers football coach Vince Lombardi

As we've already mentioned, unless you're a recent grad, a potential employer is likely to pay more attention to the employment history on your resume than to anything else. And the achievements you attained in the course of performing those jobs is an extremely important aspect of that history.

The following personal achievement worksheet is intended to be used, if necessary, in conjunction with the previous employment worksheet. It'll help you determine whatever achievements you attained in each of your previous positions so you'll be able to identify them as clearly as possible in your resume. Of course, if you've been through this process before, you may not need any help in identifying those achievements.

On the other hand, if you haven't, you may be a little unclear about exactly what we mean by an "achievement." What does this word mean in terms of your work history? It could mean that you were named "Employee of the Month" by your company or that you exceeded your sales quota by a substantial percentage. It could also mean, for example, that you:

> Administered a $1.2 million budget, improving your agency's financial performance for three consecutive years.

> Were named "Manager of the Year" by the Northern California Association of Sales Managers.

> Signed up 30 new accounts at Housewares, Hardware, Gourmet Products, and Premium and Gift shows.

> Instituted TQM program that achieved 75% reduction in outgoing defect rate, cut delivery service installation time 30%, and grew productivity 25% through health and safety training.

**Previous Employment**

Employer: _____

Type of business: _____

Job title: _____

Employment dates: _____

Responsibilities: _____

_____

_____

_____

_____

Skills learned or utilized: _____

_____

_____

_____

Achievements: _____

_____

_____

Promotions or awards: _____

_____

_____

References/contacts: _____

_____

What I liked most about this job: _____

_____

_____

_____

What I liked least about this job: _____

_____

_____

Because potential employers are more inclined to interview job applicants who have demonstrated their ability to achieve, you'll want to include any such achievements on your resume. And don't understate your achievements. Modesty may be considered a desirable character trait, but it won't help you get an interview—or a job. Accordingly, we suggest you fill out a worksheet for *everything* that you think might represent an achievement. Once you've done them all, you can always go back and select those you think are most important, impressive, and/or relevant to your job search.

The worksheet essentially asks four questions:

1. What was the success or accomplishment? This can be listed as simple as "As sales manager, exceeded the department's quota for three years in a row."

2. What was the problem or situation? That is, in what area of your job did the events occur and why was some action required? For example, "Salespeople were not meeting their quotas, leading to substantial revenue losses for the company."

3. What specific action(s) did you take? This can be something you did yourself or, if you were a supervisor or manager, something you instructed your staff to do. For example, "Required all sales people to attend refresher courses with nationally recognized management training organization."

4. What were the results of your action? This is where you *quantify* the results achieved (e.g., "85% of the salespeople exceeded their individual quotas, and the department exceeded its overall quota by 35%) or *qualify* them (e.g., "Employee morale was substantially improved").

Again, you should make as many additional copies of this worksheet as are necessary to record all of your achievements.

# YOUR VOLUNTEER/COMMUNITY SERVICE

There's some debate among career experts about the advisability of including information about volunteer and community service (as well as hobbies and activities) in your resume. We'll discuss the pros and cons of this debate in greater detail in Chapter 6. For the moment, suffice it to say that we are inclined toward including such information—on a selective basis. We have accordingly provided you with a volunteer/community service worksheet to enable you to record those activities.

## Personal Achievements

Title of success or accomplishment: _____

_____

_____

Problem or situation: _____

_____

_____

_____

_____

_____

Action(s) I took or directed: _____

_____

_____

_____

_____

_____

_____

_____

Results: _____

_____

_____

_____

_____

_____

_____

_____

Think particularly about activities that are impressive, interesting, and/or relevant to your job search. For example, if you are thinking about a career in physical education and have been a volunteer in a youth program teaching mountain climbing, it would be a good idea to include that information in your resume. Conversely, if you're looking for a job as an accountant, unless you're planning to approach a firm that's situated on a mountaintop, you might choose not to mention it.

At this point in the process of crafting your resume, however, we suggest that you include *any and all* volunteer or community service activities in which you've been involved. Once you have them all down on paper, you can determine which ones are the most appropriate for your career or job search.

The volunteer/community service worksheet is very similar to the one you've already filled out for your career history. Make enough copies to provide information on all your activities.

## YOUR HOBBIES AND ACTIVITIES

**FYI**

*Because it's likely that at some time in the future you'll be looking for another new job (if not launching an entirely new career) you should save all the worksheets you prepare during your current job search. When you have to go through the process again, you'll have already done most of the ground-work.*

As we've already mentioned, despite the debate among career experts about including information on your resume about hobbies and activities, we are inclined to use them. For that reason, we've provided the hobbies and activities worksheet below to help you record them.

Again, whatever hobbies and/or activities you include in your resume should be impressive, interesting, and/or relevant to your career goals. If, for example, one of your hobbies is surfing the Internet and you're thinking about looking for a job with a company that creates Web sites, including a reference to it would be extremely appropriate. On the other hand, if you spend most of your spare time watching television, unless your aim is to find a job in the media, it would probably be best to avoid mentioning it.

However, we again suggest that you *not* limit yourself at this point. Merely filling out the forms may remind you of an interest that you had forgotten which might eventually be turned into a career. And the fact that you've written down information on these forms doesn't mean that you will ever have to use it. As with the other forms, you should make copies of this worksheet to provide information about all of your hobbies and activities.

## FOCUSING YOUR CAREER CHOICE

In the last chapter, you identified one or more types of work that you would *like* to do. In this chapter, you've documented the education and skills that you currently possess. Now that you have all this information,

## **Volunteer/Community Service**

Organization name: _____

Type of organization(mission, activities, etc.): _____

_____

_____

_____

Job title: _____

Dates: _____

Responsibilities: _____

_____

_____

_____

_____

_____

Skills learned or utilized: _____

_____

_____

_____

Achievements: _____

_____

_____

Awards/honors/distinctions: _____

_____

_____

References/contacts: _____

What I liked most about this job: _____

_____

_____

_____

What I liked least about this job: _____

_____

_____

## Hobbies and Activities

Name of hobby/
organization/club: _____

Description: _____

_____

_____

_____

Location: _____

Dates: _____

Title/position (officer, member, etc.): _____

Skills learned or utilized: _____

_____

_____

_____

Skill level (novice, expert, etc.): _____

Achievements: _____

_____

_____

_____

_____

Awards/honors/distinctions: _____

_____

_____

_____

_____

References/contacts: _____

_____

_____

_____

_____

the time has come to determine to what extent what you'd *like* to do is appropriate to what you *can* do, and on the basis of that make some decisions. In considering this, you'll probably find yourself in one of four situations.

First, you may have started this whole process with a good idea of what you wanted to do for a living, and doing these exercises has confirmed that you have the values, education, and skills required to be successful at it—or to at least to get launched in that field. If so, the next step is simply to start putting together your resume. Our suggestions for exactly how to go about doing that begin in the next chapter.

Second, you may have known what you wanted to do but discovered that you don't have the education and/or skills required to get a job in that field. In that case, you have to make a decision. You either have to get the education or skills you'll need or start thinking seriously about the possibility of pursuing one of the other potential careers you identified.

Third, you may have had some idea of what you wanted to do but discovered along the way that there are actually other possible careers that are even more appealing to you.

Finally, you may have been unsure of your interests at the beginning of the process and now find yourself with a number of potential career and/or job possibilities.

If you find yourself in any of the last three situations, there's one more step you have to take before you start thinking about creating your resume. As we mentioned at the beginning of the last chapter, a resume is a means of convincing a potential employer that you may be the right person for the job she has available. But in order to make such a persuasive argument, you must first know what you're arguing for. That is, you have to be sure of the kind of career or job you want to pursue.

The checklist below is designed to help you make that decision. It's essentially an extended version of the checklist we used in chapter 2 to help you determine your goals. Now, however, it also takes into account the extent to which you have the tools you need to achieve those goals.

As you'll remember, the last time you filled out this checklist you listed your possible careers, then rated your interests, dreams, work values, and life values on the basis of how closely those careers fit your criteria for the perfect job. You used a scale of one to five, one being the farthest from meeting your criteria and five being the closest. Now you should go back to that checklist and copy the ratings you included there into the checklist that follows.

The next step is to rate your education and skills on the basis of how closely they meet the requirements of those jobs or careers. Again, you

*"I have learned that success is to be measured not so much by the position that one has reached in life as by the obstacles which he has overcome while trying to succeed."*
—Booker T. Washington, *Up From Slavery* (1901)

can use a scale of one to five, one being those that are farthest from the requirements and five being those that are closest.

Now add up the numbers for each possible career. The careers that have the highest overall ratings will be those it would be most advisable for you to pursue.

We must add a caution here. In determining whether or not you have the education and/or skills required to get a job in any given field, it's important that you take into account how essential those requirements actually are. If, for example, you absolutely *must* have a college degree to get into a particular field, but you have only two years of college, you should rate your education as "1." If you don't rate it that way, regardless of how highly you may have rated the job overall, it would be unrealistic for you to pursue it.

On the other hand, as we mentioned before, even those jobs that ostensibly require certain levels of education or skill may not actually require them. In some instances, employers may *prefer* applicants who have attained those levels, but sometimes, or even often, hire those who haven't.

If, for example, you're interested in a career in which it's considered beneficial but not essential to have a master's degree, but you don't have one, you might rate your education as "3" or "4." Similarly, even if you don't actually have what's "required" for such a job, experience in the field can sometimes compensate for that lack, so you should rate your education and/or skills accordingly.

We're aware, of course, that making a choice about the best job or career for you to pursue is not easy. And we're certainly not suggesting that filling out this checklist is the only—or even necessarily the best—way to determine what your choice should be. However, it should be very helpful in enabling you to determine, based on your desires and your background, which jobs or careers it would be advantageous *and* realistic for you to pursue.

Of course, don't think of this decision as one that you'll have to live with for the rest of your life. It's not at all unusual for people to change jobs, and even careers, several if not many times over the course of their working lives. You have to make a decision *now* based on what you want to do *now* and on what you have the education and skills to do *now*.

The one constant in life is change, so you can be sure that the world will change, the business world will change, and you will change. If at some time in the future you decide that the decision you made today was a poor one or that you'd simply like to do something else with your life, you'll have the opportunity to do so.

In the meantime, you still have to make a decision. And once you have, you'll have to start writing a resume, as we begin discussing in the next chapter.

| Making the Connections | | | | | | |
|---|---|---|---|---|---|---|
| Possible Career | Personal Interests | Dreams | Work Values | Life Values | Education Values | Skills |
| 1. _____ | _____ | _____ | _____ | _____ | _____ | _____ |
| 2. _____ | _____ | _____ | _____ | _____ | _____ | _____ |
| 3. _____ | _____ | _____ | _____ | _____ | _____ | _____ |
| 4. _____ | _____ | _____ | _____ | _____ | _____ | _____ |
| 5. _____ | _____ | _____ | _____ | _____ | _____ | _____ |
| 6. _____ | _____ | _____ | _____ | _____ | _____ | _____ |
| 7. _____ | _____ | _____ | _____ | _____ | _____ | _____ |
| 8. _____ | _____ | _____ | _____ | _____ | _____ | _____ |
| 9. _____ | _____ | _____ | _____ | _____ | _____ | _____ |
| 10. _____ | _____ | _____ | _____ | _____ | _____ | _____ |

# JUST THE FACTS

- Evaluating your education and skills is an important factor in finding a job that you would *like* to do and *have the ability* to do.

- Your work history will be the most important factor taken into account by a potential employer reading your resume, so it's essential that you document it fully and accurately.

- Personal achievements, which are part of your work history, can make the difference between being called in for an interview and receiving a rejection letter.

- Having done volunteer and/or community service—as long as it's relevant to the position or career you're pursuing—can be help interest an interviewer in wanting to learn more about you.

- Pertinent hobbies and activities, particularly if they demonstrate interests that are compatible with a job, can make you more appealing to a potential employer.

- Making a decision about which career to pursue is not an easy one, but it's important to remember that, regardless of whatever decision you reach today, you will have the opportunity to change jobs and/or careers in the future.

# Part II

# Resume Basics

# Chapter 4

# Classic Resume Formats

## Get the Scoop On . . .

- The merits of the three classic resume styles
- Deciding which resume will work best
- Customizing your resume format

As we've suggested, your resume is like an advertisement for you—a letter-sized poster designed to highlight your best features as an employee and to entice a recruiter into interviewing you. You want to construct your resume to do the best possible job of interesting and impressing the potential employers who see it, thereby opening the door that will lead to a great job.

Most resumes follow one of three popular formats. They're popular because they're practical, clear, and well-understood by employers and recruiters; therefore, most job seekers should plan on using or adapting one of these classic resume formats. In this chapter, we'll explain all three, offer samples of each, and help you decide which format is likely to work best for you. In addition, we'll begin demonstrating how you can *customize* any of the three formats to highlight your own unique strengths—a technique we'll explain in greater detail in later chapters.

The three classic resume formats you should consider are

- The chronological format
- The functional format
- The combination format

## THE CHRONOLOGICAL FORMAT

The chronological format is the most traditional and still the most popular of all resume formats. It's built around a listing of your work and educational experiences in reverse chronological order—that is, starting with the most recent positions and working backward to the oldest.

The traditional sequence of information in the chronological resume is as follows:

1. Your name and contact information—address, phone, etc.

2. The *headline*—either your job objective, a summary of your background and skills, or both

3. Your work experience—listing each job you've had, starting with your current or most recent position, with a description of each

4. Your educational background

5. Other information, if relevant, including personal interests and activities, certifications and licenses, honors and awards, professional organizations, speeches and publications, and language skills

In Chapter 6, we'll walk you through each of these resume elements, offering many specific tips on how to organize and present your background in the best possible light. We'll also include suggestions about some unusual elements you may want to include, such as Endorsements from people who know your work—elements that can give you the winning edge over your job-search competition.

For now, notice the following special characteristics of the chronological resume:

- It's very straightforward. The factual data about your career are presented in a logical sequence, making it easy for the reader to reconstruct your history in step-by-step fashion.

- It emphasizes the natural progression of your career from one job to the next—or the *lack* of such a progression, if your career has been marked by several steps "backward" or "sideways."

- It makes the chronology of your life and work history obvious. Thus, periods of unemployment or self-employment are generally easy to spot, and it's usually easy to figure out your age.

As these characteristics suggest, the chronological resume is more friendly to certain types of job seekers than others. This doesn't mean that you should necessarily avoid the chronological format if, for example, there's a period of unemployment in your past. There are ways to mask potential weaknesses in your background, which we'll explain in later chapters. But note that the chronological resume may make such masking more difficult.

Look at Resume 4.1. It's the classic chronological resume used by "Richard V. Rodino, Jr.," a sales manager in the radio advertising business. After Rodino's name and contact information, a brief summary

*"Most recruiters favor the chronological resume format because it's simple and clear. We have one to three minutes to spend on a resume—sometimes less. We don't want to have to solve puzzles or think too much! Make it easy for us by keeping your resume as straightforward as possible."*
—Susan Gordon, President, Lynne Palmer Executive Recruitment

of his experience and skills follows (headed "General/Sales Management, Creative Radio Professional"). This is what we call the headline.

Then Rodino's five jobs are listed, in reverse chronological order, tracing his work history back to 1985. For each job, the dates of employment and the name and location of the employer are listed, followed by a short paragraph describing the work and, in this case, one or more bullets highlighting special achievements by Rodino on the job. Finally, two brief sections list Rodino's relevant educational background and professional affiliations.

It's a clear and simple presentation, which makes it easy for a prospective employer to grasp the story of Rodino's career in a few sweeps of the eye.

Contrast this with Resume 4.2. The resume of "David W. Halsey" is another chronological resume, making it superficially similar to Rodino's. But note the accumulation of subtle differences that give it an overall effect that's quite distinct.

> **FYI**
>
> *It's acceptable to* mildly inflate *the significance of a past job or achievement, provided you never make a statement that's factually incorrect. For example, presenting an unpaid internship so that it* re-sembles *a full-time paid job is acceptable;* calling *it a full-time paid job would not be. Most employers reserve the right to summarily fire any new hire whose resume contains a lie—and yes, it happens.*

Halsey is a psychological counselor who recently graduated from "Anderson College" with a certificate of advanced graduate study in counseling. By closely examining his resume, we can see that Halsey has held only one "real" job in his field—the 1999 job as a family therapist at the Family Reunification System in Athens, Georgia. (This appears to have been some kind of geographical detour in Halsey's life; he's now back in Illinois, where he did most of his schooling.) Is this is an impressive work history? Not really.

Therefore, Halsey has had to make several tactical decisions to customize the traditional chronological format to better highlight his strengths (and de-emphasize his weaknesses):

- Halsey has inverted the order of two elements of the resume—education and experience. By listing his educational background first, Halsey emphasizes it. Since this is his single strongest credential, it makes sense to lead with it.

- Halsey has developed his educational background more extensively than most job seekers will do. (Compare his treatment of education with Rodino's.) In addition to listing the degrees and the names of the schools at which they were earned, he has included his GPA (because it was impressive), academic honors received, and specific achievements in research, counseling, and other activities.

- Halsey has also broken out some of his past activities in such a way as to make them appear almost like full-time paid jobs. First, he has

## 4.1 Chronological Format

### RICHARD V. RODINO, JR.
98 Queen Anne's Lane
Portland, Oregon 89070
Residence: 555-555-5930

**GENERAL / SALES MANAGEMENT**
*Creative Radio Professional*

OFFERING 10+ YEARS OF PROGRESSIVE, HANDS-ON LEADERSHIP CONTRIBUTIONS
TO POLICIES, PROCEDURES, PROGRAMS, ACCOUNT AND PROJECT MANAGEMENT,
HUMAN RESOURCE DEVELOPMENT, BUDGETS, COST CONTROL, AND OVERALL
PROFIT GROWTH

**PROFESSIONAL EXPERIENCE**

**NATIONAL SALES MANAGER**
1995 - Present
KTOI RADIO, Portland, Oregon
> Drive national sales strategy development and implementations, with full accountability
> for pricing, positioning, collections, promotions, sales and programming.  Provide
> leadership in budgeting; initiatives for cost containment are regularly utilized by senior
> executives.

- *Formulated strategic pricing and value-added plans that increased representative firm's market share; successful programs elevated station position to #3, up from #5 in 1994.*
- *Maintained a #1 and #2 power ratio Hungerford ranking each month as station Arbitron rank declined.*
- *Direct training and motivational programs; review and analyze existing policy with a view toward increasing productivity and sales; consistently meet or exceed all targets.*
- *Managed inventory and material distribution; established time frames for purchasing; streamlined procedures and developed effective methods for cost control, ensuring the most efficient inventory management possible while gaining 2 share points per month.*

**LOCAL SALES MANAGER**
1993 - 1995
UNIVERSAL RADIO INC.
Walla Walla, Washington
> Directed organization and development of sales and marketing programs, recruitment of
> qualified sales personnel and specialized staff training.  Evaluated performances and
> created effective motivational programs.  Developed strategies for meeting short- and
> long-term goals.

- *Cultivated relations with Westwood One and the NHL, managing sales and marketing to ensure coordinate for the profitable All-Star and Stanley Cup Finals broadcasts.*
- *Developed policy on local sale space; educated staff in the use of creative marketing tactics; consistently exceeded sales goals.*
- *Researched the competition; conceptualized and put into operation plans that increased the station's competitive standing.*

**Richard V. Rodino, Jr.**

**ACCOUNT EXECUTIVE**
1991 - 1993
WISHBONE BROADCASTING GROUP - WSHB RADIO
Hartford, Connecticut
> Developed results-getting plans and excellent relations with advertising agency personnel to develop account business that represented one of the station's major revenue streams. Managed and serviced all accounts effectively; troubleshot problems with quick, positive solutions.

- *Worked effectively with large retailers on vendor program development and implementation.*
- *Met sales targets and generated creative methods to control costs; recognized by senior executives for achieving all projected budget goals.*

**ACCOUNT EXECUTIVE**
1988 - 1991
WNOV RADIO
Philadelphia, Pennsylvania
> Responsibilities included formulation and execution of strategic sports sales plans, vendor / retailer relations, and various administrative tasks.

- *Launched the first vendor program with a major retailer.*
- *Overachieved sales targets by 120%.*
- *Cooperative advertising program generated substantial new revenue.*

**ACCOUNT EXECUTIVE**
1985 - 1988
WLPC RADIO
Providence, Rhode Island

- *Promoted from an entry-level, untitled position to Account Executive in less than 1 year for outstanding sales achievements--earned #1 in sales of sports packages, leading all other Account Executives.*

## EDUCATION

**BACHELOR OF ARTS: COMMUNICATIONS,** 1985
Dover College - Dover, Delaware

## PROFESSIONAL AFFILIATIONS

NORTHWEST BROADCAST ASSOCIATION · OREGON ADVERTISING CLUB

## 4.2 Chronological Format

# DAVID W. HALSEY

20 Edgemont Road
Springfield, Illinois 43430
(555) 555-1153
email: DWHalsey@ion.net

## OBJECTIVE

A position as THERAPIST / COUNSELOR in mental health clinic or counseling center where formal education, related experience and skills will be fully applied.

## EDUCATION

**1996 - 1998: CERTIFICATE OF ADVANCED GRADUATE STUDY (CAGS), COUNSELING & PSYCHOLOGICAL SERVICES**
MAJOR: MARRIAGE & THE FAMILY THERAPY
Anderson College · Springfield, Illinois

**1993 - 1995: MASTER OF EDUCATION, COUNSELING & PSYCHOLOGICAL SERVICES**
MAJOR: MARRIAGE & THE FAMILY THERAPY
Anderson College · Springfield, Illinois
*GPA:* 3.8 / 4.0 · Summa Cum Laude

**1988 - 1992: BACHELOR OF ARTS IN PSYCHOLOGY**
Lehman College, City University of New York · Bronx, New York
*GPA:* 3.7 / 4.0 · Magna Cum Laude
*Honors:* PHI BETA KAPPA · Psi Chi Honor Society · Lehman Scholar · Golden Key National Honor Society

**Research:** Conducted research project on techniques to improve athletes' performance, 1990 -1991. Assisted in research project examining urban pollution and its effect on minority children learning, 1991 - 1992.

**Counseling:** Served as PEER COUNSELOR to 10 - 15 Psychology Club Members, twice per month, 1991 - 1992.

**Activities:** COORDINATOR - United Way Drive, 1991.

David W. Halsey

## EXPERIENCE

**1999:  FAMILY THERAPIST**
Family Reunification System
Athens Family Center · Athens, Georgia
> Provided intensive (2 - 3 times weekly in-home family therapy, couple therapy, individual, and play therapy to high risk families.  Worked in conjunction with the State of Georgia's Foster Care Unit to help place foster children back with their biological parents.  Supervised bachelor's-level counselors.  Created appropriate treatment plans and performed extensive and thorough family assessments.

## INTERNSHIP

**1997 - 1998: OUTPATIENT THERAPIST**
Springield Mental Health Center · Springfield, Illinois
> Provided counseling services to clients from varied cultural backgrounds on an outpatient basis.  Conducted individual, couple and family therapy, including cases of schizophrenia, depression, marital problems and substance and sexual abuse.  Diagnosed and implemented treatment plans; performed intake assessments and utilized knowledge of external resources, encompassing community, state and federal services such as Welfare and SSI.
> - *Participated in case conferences and consulted with psychiatrists and psychologists to ensure accuracy of diagnosis and appropriate treatment plans.*
> - *Coordinated crisis intervention action plans; utilized knowledge of varied resources to facilitate resolutions.*
> - *Completed a 4-day AIDS education and prevention training course.*

## RELATED EXPERIENCE

**1992 - 1993: COUNSELOR**
Children's Home Away From Home · Rochester, New York
> On a bi-weekly, volunteer basis, provided counseling, support and companionship for child in a residential facility for abused boys.

**1992: COUNSELOR**
Montefiore Medical Center · Bronx, New York
> As a member of the child protection team, worked with children and their mothers who were at-risk for abuse.  Provided counseling and support.

## PROFESSIONAL AFFILIATIONS

American Association for Marriage and Family Therapy - Student Affiliate
American Psychological Association - Student Affiliate

listed his work as a therapist at the Springfield Mental Health Center under the special heading of Internship, and described it in considerable detail. Then, under the heading Related Experience, he has listed two volunteer positions he held which were clearly relevant to the work he is now doing.

*Don't regard any resume format as a straitjacket. Instead, modify the format as necessary to highlight what makes you appealing (and to downplay any weaknesses you may have).*

None of these changes violate either the spirit or the rules of the chronological format. Within each heading, the positions are listed in reverse chronological order, and it's easy for the reader to grasp at a glance just what Halsey was doing at any moment in the past decade. But the subtle organizational choices Halsey has made enhance what he has to offer, much as a photographer can enhance the beauty of a model through the right pose, lighting, and other subtle artistic choices.

While sticking to the traditional chronological format, simply by flip flopping the sequence of sections and adding a couple of special headings, David Halsey has managed to craft a resume that makes his relatively meager work background look fairly extensive—and impressive.

Resume 4.3, for scientist "Susan Winger," provides another variation on the traditional chronological format. Winger has chosen to vary the format by adding an unusual section that highlights one of *her* special strengths—her record of scholarly publishing in her field.

# THE FUNCTIONAL FORMAT

*You'll notice that most or all of the same information will ultimately appear in both the chronological and functional resumes. The difference is in the arrangement and emphasis. You may want to experiment with organizing your personal data according to both formats (something that word-processing computer software makes easy to do). This can help you see which format works best for you.*

The functional format is the second most popular resume style. This format de-emphasizes chronology in favor of a focus on skills—the talents, knowledge, and personal qualities you offer a prospective employer. Your work and educational experiences are listed, but only briefly, and they play second fiddle to a detailed and extensive description of your current job skills. These are often organized by job function (marketing, leadership, administration, technical procedures, etc.); that's why it's called the functional format.

Here's the traditional sequence of information in the functional resume:

1. Your name and contact information—address, phone, etc.

2. The headline—either your job objective, a summary of your background and skills, or both

3. Your job skills, listed under a heading such as "Profile," "Professional Skills," "Notable Accomplishments," or the like

4. A brief summary of your work experience—listing each job you've had, starting with your current or most recent position, but with little or no description

## 4.3  Chronological Format with Publications List

**SUSAN WINGER**
3116 Victory Boulevard · Pittsburgh, Pennsylvania 32400
Residence: 555-555-3866 · Lab: 555-555-2564

**MATERIALS SCIENTIST / ENGINEER**

TALENTED, MULTIFUNCTIONAL PROFESSIONAL
OFFERING 15 YEARS OF ADVANCED EDUCATION, TRAINING AND EXPERIENCE
IN RESEARCH, ANALYSIS, DEVELOPMENT, TEACHING,
LABORATORY MANAGEMENT, BUDGETS AND COST CONTROL.

**PROFESSIONAL EXPERIENCE**

**ASSISTANT SCIENTIST - Materials Processing Center**
1992 - Present
PITTSBURGH STATE UNIVERSITY · BARNES LABORATORY
Pittsburgh, Pennsylvania
Conduct research, perform external service work, and manage all operations within the Scanning Auger Microprobe (SAM PHI 660) Lab.  Oversee R&D activities encompassing project preparation, prioritization of project elements, and management of project execution.

- *Analyze composition and chemical bonding information from the top 2 to 5 monomolecular layers of solid sample over areas as small as 100nm.*
- *Originate new methods and processes in the development of practical applications; provide training in molecular techniques and procedures critical to experimental success.*
- *Appeared on May 1996 cover of* U.S. Science Monthly *for quasi-crystal investigation.*

**DEVELOPMENT ENGINEER - Engineering Materials Department**
1988 - 1992
UNIVERSITY OF COLORADO
Denver, Colorado
Utilizing advanced knowledge of ceramics, superconductors, X-Ray diffraction, and laboratory functions, directed operations of 3 labs, training and managing professional teams in policies, procedures, methods, systems and equipment.

- *Planned and launched Superconductivity lab, and the X-Ray Diffraction lab from start-up.*
- *Identified the epitaxical relationship between 123 Yitozia single crystals.*
- *Maintained full accountability for the research supply budget; monitored expenses and made recommendations for cost containment.*

**Susan Winger**

**METALLURGIST - Mechanical Engineering Department, Materials Branch**
1985 - 1988
PRINCETON RESEARCH LAB
Princeton, New Jersey

Provided leadership in research, analysis and laboratory management; trained and supervised teams of up to 10 personnel. Conducted comprehensive analyses of ferrous and nonferrous alloys, evaluating structure and property relationships.

- *Rapidly troubleshot intricate, complex technical problems; recognized for innovative techniques utilized in defect analysis of coatings at elevated temperatures.*
- *Taught materials science labs, working closely with faculty members in the designs and preparation of experiments that explored underlying and related theoretical concepts.*
- *Furnished expertise and guidance in metallographic analysis that ensured high levels of knowledge and success in fulfilling thesis requirements.*

## EDUCATION

**MASTER OF SCIENCE IN MATERIALS SCIENCE & ENGINEERING,** Expected 2000
Pittsburgh State University · Pittsburgh, Pennsylvania

**BACHELOR OF SCIENCE IN MATERIALS ENGINEERING**
Hobson Technical Institute · Albany, New York
*Scholarship Recipient · Dean's List of Distinguished Students*

## RECENT PUBLICATIONS

Boswell, K.L.; Weis, A. R; Winger, S.T. "Preparation of Quasicrystals for Surface Studies." J. App. Metall. In press.

Boswell, K..L.; Winger, S.T.; Chacon, E. Y. "Neutron Irradiation and Intergranular Fracture." Presented in AMT. 1997.

Gonder, J. U; Franco, J. O.; Winger, S.T.; Martin, J.C. "Degradation Characteristics of Intermetallic Coating on Nickel Base Superalloy Substrates." Materials Science Today. 1995.

5. Your educational background

6. Other information, if relevant, including personal interests and activities, certifications and licenses, honors and awards, professional organizations, speeches and publications, and language skills

Because the functional resume leads off with job skills rather than a listing of positions you've held, it offers several distinct opportunities to the job seeker:

- It allows you to group accomplishments by functional area rather than by job. Thus, if you've demonstrated a particular skill on two or three jobs, you can cluster these accomplishments under the same skill heading for a more powerful effect.

- It makes it easier for you to suggest how skills from one field or industry can be transferred to another.

- It de-emphasizes chronology and career progression in favor of the package of skills and knowledge you currently have to offer.

As you can imagine, the functional format is especially popular among certain specific groups of job seekers, including:

- Recent grads or those returning to the workforce who need to highlight the skills and experience gained in volunteer, part-time, or other informal types of work

- Career changers who need to show how their skills from one industry can be applied to another

- Those with irregular career patterns, including periods of unemployment or self-employment, or job shifts that appear to be steps backward or sideways rather than forward

Resumes 4.4 and 4.5 offer typical examples of the functional format. "Eduardo Tatis," the job seeker who created Resume 4.4, has basically two types of job experience: international sales and operational management. He is interested in combining these two backgrounds in his next job and is seeking a managerial position in international operations. The functional format allows Tatis to summarize, in the profile section of the resume, the various skills he's developed in his last several jobs. The idea is to suggest to a possible employer how Tatis could operate effectively at a high managerial level in an American company that does business in Spanish-speaking countries.

In Resume 4.5, financial executive "Louise Dubcek" has produced a functional resume designed to highlight the general managerial skills she has developed in a series of (seemingly unrelated) jobs over the

## 4.4 Functional Format

*Confidential Resume of*
# EDUARDO TATIS
767 East Jefferson Street · Trenton, New Jersey
H: 555-555-2928 · W: 555-555-2324

## *Electrical Industry* : INTERNATIONAL OPERATIONS

TALENTED, BILINGUAL PROFESSIONAL WITH  RECORD OF ACCOMPLISHMENT AND EXPERTISE IN INTERNATIONAL
SALES & MARKETING SUPPORT, OPERATIONS MANAGEMENT, PURCHASING, SALES AND CUSTOMER SERVICE.

## PROFILE

- **International Sales / Marketing Support:**  Selected by International Power to contribute vision and technical / commercial translation expertise in the areas of administration, sales, negotiations, procurement, transportation, and customer service.
- **Inside / Outside Sales Performer:**  Significantly increased sales of various electrical, industrial and marine equipment for several companies.  Skilled at developing new and existing accounts with refineries, plants and engineering companies.
- **Skilled Translator:**  Provide quotes for International Power's local customers and international businesses from countries such as Venezuela, Columbia, Chile, and Argentine, utilizing excellent bilingual abilities.  Translate commercial / technical information between customers and manufacturers.
- **Analytical / Troubleshooter:**  Established track record for identifying complex problems; resourceful and inventive in developing and implementing creative solutions resulting in increased profitability and sales.  Enhanced sensitivity to cost, efficiency and deadlines.
- **Dedicated / Professional:**  Committed to an ideal of quality; combine resourcefulness with initiative and a drive for achievement.  Reputation for giving better than 100%.  Provide effective leadership, make consistently sound judgements under pressured conditions.

## PROFESSIONAL EXPERIENCE

INTERNATIONAL POWER SUPPLY
Trenton, New Jersey
**INTERNATIONAL SALES / MARKETING SUPPORT**
1991- Present

**Eduardo Tatis**

JVA INDUSTRY SUPPORT SERVICES
Princeton, New Jersey
**OPERATIONS MANAGER**
1990 -1991

UNIVERSAL IMPORT CORPORATION
Galveston, Texas
**PURCHASING AGENT**
1987 - 1990

HOUSTON GEAR AND BOLT, INC.
Houston, Texas
**INTERNATIONAL CUSTOMER SERVICE REPRESENTATIVE**
1986 - 1987

GONZALEZ-MARTIN, S.A.
Panama City, Panama
**INSIDE / OUTSIDE SALES / ASSISTANT TO THE GENERAL MGR**
1981 - 1986

UNITED STATES ARMY
Ft. Bragg, North Carolina
**STOCKING CONTROL / ACCOUNT SUPPLY CLERK**
1975 - 1978

## EDUCATION

**BACHELOR OF ARTS IN ECONOMICS,** 1980
Powell University - Bradenton, Florida

## PERSONAL

Married · U.S. Citizen · Bilingual · Excellent Health
Willing to relocate and perform work-related travel

REFERENCES & FURTHER DATA AVAILABLE UPON REQUEST

past twenty years. The functional format also downplays her six-year period of self-employment—something many employers view rather negatively.

Notice how Dubcek combines accomplishments from more than one industry within each of the listings in the "Professional Experiences and Accomplishments" section. For example, under the heading "Spear-headed Expansion," she mentions expansion projects she managed for "Halliburton & Company" (her present employer) and "Fine Computer"— the latter almost two decades ago. By linking them, Dubcek suggests a degree of continuity that's a bit of an illusion—but an illusion that is favorable to her.

# THE COMBINATION FORMAT

The combination format is a hybrid of the chronological and functional styles. In effect, it weds a skills summary to a chronological description of jobs and educational experiences, offering, at least in theory, the advantages of each of the other two formats.

In the combination resume, your career data will be presented in this sequence:

1. Your name and contact information—address, phone, etc.

2. The headline—either your job objective, a summary of your background and skills, or both

3. Your job skills, listed under a heading such as "Profile," "Professional Skills," or "Notable Accomplishments"

4. Your work experience—listing each job you've had, starting with your current or most recent position, with a description of each

5. Your educational background

6. Other information, if relevant, including personal interests and activities, certifications and licenses, honors and awards, professional organizations, speeches and publications, and language skills

You might think that the combination format offers "the best of both worlds" and is therefore the obvious choice for almost any job seeker. In fact, the combination format is increasingly popular today. However, like the other classic formats, the combination format has both advantages and disadvantages:

■ It allows you both to highlight skills that your next employer is seeking and to demonstrate the logical progression of your career from one job to the next.

## 4.5 Functional Format

*Confidential Resume of*
### LOUISE DUBCEK
11 Mersey Drive · Santa Fe, New Mexico 52082
Residence: 555-555-9630 · Fax: 555-555-4633

#### FINANCIAL AND OPERATIONAL EXECUTIVE

VISIONARY EXECUTIVE WITH A PROGRESSIVE MANAGEMENT STYLE. SKILLED AT DEVELOPING STRATEGICALLY RELEVANT PLANS, GAINING CONSENSUS, BUILDING TEAMS, CHALLENGING ORGANIZATIONS AND INDIVIDUALS TO ACHIEVE SUPERIOR RESULTS THAT CONTINUALLY PRODUCE THE 'COMPETITIVE EDGE.'

#### PROFESSIONAL EXPERIENCES AND ACCOMPLISHMENTS

- **Change Manager:** Accomplished at leading high profile, company-wide initiatives. Uniquely skilled at streamlining business processes, infusing innovation, launching information technology / financial control systems, and championing positive cultural change.
- **High Performance Team-Builder:** Ensured integrity and accountability with cross-functional teams. Professional development / cross training programs consistently produce sophisticated, knowledgeable and versatile teams with exceptionally high morale.
- **Business Performer:** Management and financial control systems supported Carter's rapid 30-40% growth to over $200 million. Innovative work flow / cost models affecting 1000+ bank customers increased cash management product profitability.
- **Spearheaded Expansion:** Crafted business plans, programs and alliances to maximize growth. Managed public debt offering for Fine Computer, resulting in $50 million in capital. Assisted in securing $25 million in equity for clients as member of Hallburton and Company Securities Inc. investment banking team.
- **P&L Monitoring / Analysis:** Customer profitability analysis enhanced Langhorn Mutual Funds revenue by $1 million. Tracked and analyzed program effectiveness; measured the impact of reorganization on the balance sheet and income statements.
- **Cost Control Initiatives:** Launched cost and performance models for Langhorn Mutual Funds Division; financial procedures saved $300,000+ in one year. Inventory programs reduced losses 4% and dramatically improved Carter's customer service. JIT implementation slashed Carter's warehouse inventory 30%; trained staff in cost reduction techniques.
- **Computer Proficiency:** Highly skilled in the use of PCs and Windows 2000. Utilize financial / accounting / spreadsheet applications, word processors, graphics / presentation packages, databases, and various other business-related software.
- **Efficiency / Management System Advancements:** Improved Carter's financial / operational controls; optimally trained staff to manage restructured department. Led centralized financial reporting conversion to $18 million mutual funds division reporting, concurrently improving both service and reporting.

LOUISE DUBCEK

## PROFESSIONAL EXPERIENCE

### FINANCIAL AND OPERATIONS PRINCIPAL
1994 - Present
HALLIBURTON & COMPANY SECURITIES, INC.
Santa Fe, New Mexico

### FINANCIAL CONSULTANT
1987 - 1993
SELF-EMPLOYED
San Francisco, California

### CONTROLLER - AVP / CORPORATE SERVICE
### CONTROLLER - AVP / MUTUAL FUNDS
1984 - 1987
LANGHORN BANK, N.A.
St. Louis, Missouri

### MANAGER OF FINANCIAL ANALYSIS & CONTROL
1982 - 1984
CARTER'S, INC.
Kansas City, Kansas

### CORPORATE ACCOUNTANT
1979 - 1982
FINE COMPUTER, INC
Kansas City, Kansas

## LICENSES AND CERTIFICATIONS

REGISTERED FINANCIAL & OPERATIONS PRINCIPAL · NASD SERIES 27

## EDUCATION

### BACHELOR OF SCIENCE IN BUSINESS ADMINISTRATION
Boston University - Boston, Massachusetts

## INTERESTS AND ACTIVITIES

Travel · Photography · Sailing · Rock Climbing · Field Hockey

- Its relative complexity may make it hard to absorb, demanding significant attention and energy on the part of a reader.

- It may appear repetitive, since some of the same accomplishments and credentials may need to be mentioned in both the skills-summary and the work-experience sections of the resume.

*Don't be afraid to use the buzzwords and technical jargon of your industry in your resume. Virtually all those who scrutinize it will be conversant with the terminology of the field; even outside headhunters generally make it their business to learn much of the language of the industries they serve. Sprinkling your resume with buzzwords that reflect your intimate knowledge of the business reinforces your image as a plugged-in professional who can help an employer from Day One.*

Take a look at Resume 4.6, a classic example of the combination format. It was created by "Joshua Tanenbaum," a mechanical engineer eager to demonstrate not only the impressive development of his career in a series of increasingly responsible jobs but also the array of up-to-date technical skills he has nurtured in those jobs. The combination format makes this possible.

Tanenbaum's resume begins with a skills summary under the descriptive headline, "Mechanical Engineer with State-of-the-Art Engineering Knowledge." Note the simplicity and clarity of the bulleted list of skills. The very brief descriptions here, in some cases nothing more than technical acronyms, may mean little to an outsider but will be very meaningful to potential employers. An executive looking for an engineer with Tanenbaum's credentials will be able to glance at this skills list and notice within five seconds a handful of "hot-button" words and phrases that convey the message: *This is the kind of person I want.*

The skills summary is then followed by a traditional, chronological job listing, each job including a bulleted list of duties and accomplishments. The savvy employer will have little difficulty recognizing how and where Tanenbaum developed and used each of the technical skills listed in the summary after reading these job descriptions.

Resume 4.7 applies a similar strategy to a less-technical field, that of marketing management. "Andy Kelleher" is interested in parlaying his (relatively successful) last two jobs into an even more high-powered international marketing position. In an effort to do this, he has taken a traditional chronological job description and topped it off with an impressive headline summary, "International Marketing Executive. Start-Ups. Turnarounds. Creative Product Marketing. Sales Initiatives," and a skills profile.

Kelleher's hope is that several of the buzz-phrases used in this part of the resume will resonate with a prospective employer because they encapsulate exactly the skills the employer needs.

One interesting detail about the profile section: Note Kelleher's use of all-capital-letter type in referring to his last two employers, "MAM-MOTH" and "GLOBAL COMMUNICATIONS." These two (fictitious) companies are world-famous and highly respected, and Kelleher is deliberately making certain that their names will be noticed by a potential employer; they add luster to Kelleher's own reputation.

## 4.6 Combination Format

**JOSHUA TANENBAUM**
478 East 11th Street · Barnstable, Massachusetts 20890
555-555-2449

**MECHANICAL ENGINEER WITH
STATE-OF-THE-ART ENGINEERING KNOWLEDGE**

- Project Management
- Statistical Process Control
- Design
- Benchmarking
- Layout
- Hydraulic, pneumatic, electric, electronic control equipment
- ASME Y14.5M-94
- Military standards and specifications
- Total Quality Management
- Technical / field support
- Stress Analysis
- Cost estimating
- New Product Development
- Measuring and test equipment
- Hot runner injection systems
- ISO standards
- Customer and vendor relations

**PROFESSIONAL EXPERIENCE**

ZYBEX CO.
Hyannisport, Massachusetts
**DESIGN ENGINEER / CONSULTANT** - Tech Department
1992 - present

- Provide leadership in research and technical analysis necessary to meeting engineering requirements in the development of manufacturing machinery for this industry leader.
- Task and prioritize all project elements including design, stress analysis, estimating, layout, and administering budgets; maintain project progress through key schedule milestones.
- Responsible for extensive customer and vendor contact; develop bill of materials; coordinate internal activities.
- Assign and supervise draftspeople, technicians and junior engineers in all aspects of daily operations; evaluate performances and provide effective feedback.
- Troubleshoot test equipment problems; devise innovative solutions to meet complex and critical technical and quality assurance requirements.
- Utilize automated buckle test station, load / unload and measuring devices.
- See project through to completion from design and prototype to manufacturing stage.

**Joshua Tanenbaum**

EVERSTRONG MFG CORP.
Nutley, New Jersey
**DESIGN ENGINEER** - Engineering Department
1990 - 1992

- Developed and implemented methods, systems and procedures to assure cost efficient manufacturing of machine tools.
- Met with customers, estimated costs, developed conceptual designs, determined appropriate materials and design specifications, prepared bill of materials.
- Maintained full accountability for productivity, reliability, safety, cost effectiveness, scheduling, vendor contact and field support; resolved prototype problems.
- Troubleshot problems with customized vertical and horizontal rotary molding automation machines; clamp, load / unload stations; pick and place units; injection, compression, transfer rubber molds; injection and blow plastic molds; and trimming equipment.

GLOBITE PRECISION MFG. CORP.
White Plains, New York
**QA/QC ENGINEER** - Quality Control
1989 - 1990

- Spearheaded quality operations in the areas of product development, improvement, design and detail for this prestigious manufacturer of military products.
- Analyzed manufacturing processes and methods; determined acceptability / rejectability standards and implemented training programs for inspectors and machine operators.
- Skilled in statistical process control; identified, documented and corrected problems throughout the manufacturing process; improved the reject rate.
- Operated with sensitivity to cost, efficiency and target deadlines.

AUTOMATED MANUFACTURING CO.
Minsk, Byeloruss
**SENIOR DESIGN ENGINEER** - Engineering Division, R&D Department
1980 - 1989

- Selected to oversee departmental functions including design, stress analysis, layout and field support.
- Maintained and troubleshot problems in automatic multiposition equipment with robots, utilized in high-volume machining of workpieces.
- Customized and troubleshot CNC machining centers with ATC magazines.
- Worked effectively with test engineers in resolving prototype problems.

## EDUCATION

**BACHELOR OF SCIENCE IN MECHANICAL ENGINEERING**
Byelorussian Polytechnic Institute - Minsk, Byeloruss

## PERSONAL

Willing to relocate and perform work-related travel.

**REFERENCES & FURTHER DATA AVAILABLE UPON REQUEST**

## 4.7 Combination Format

**ANDY KELLEHER**
1930 Franklin Street
Chicago, Illinois 61187
Residence: 555-555-4547

**INTERNATIONAL MARKETING EXECUTIVE**
*Start-Ups · Turnarounds · Creative Product Marketing · Sales Initiatives*

*Visionary leader and quick study with multimillion-dollar contributions to profit growth of prestigious global firms. Seeking to lead strategic business units into the 21st century as an innovative partner of a world-class management team.*

**PROFILE**
*Translate Industry and Consumer Trends into Market Dominance*

- **Management Style:** Executive with 20 years of marketing management success. Gain consensus for new initiatives; build sophisticated, flexible, cross-functional terms; challenge individuals and organizations to gain the competitive advantage through innovation.
- **Skilled Product/Marketing Strategist:** Assessed MAMMOTH'S position in the market; formulated and directed implementation of strategic product and marketing plans, programs and alliances that opened new markets and reversed downward trend in targeted markets.
- **Spearheaded Expansion:** Developed and drove penetration strategy for MAMMOTH'S start-up operations in Canada, the U.K., Benelux, Germany and South Africa; and for expanding the U.S. operations of GLOBAL COMMUNICATIONS.
- **Change Management:** Led high profile, cross-organizational change for 2 industry giants. Provided organization and motivation to implement plans for growth, infusing cutting-edge change management and leadership concepts.
- **Vast Worldwide Resource Network:** Enjoy excellent professional relations throughout several countries and a profound understand of the marketing, economic, political, and cultural trends. Attained credibility to secure approval and commitment for large-scale joint ventures.

**PROFESSIONAL EXPERIENCE**

**MAMMOTH INTERNATIONAL - Evanston, Illinois**
1990-present

Recruited for exceptional record in recognizing and exploiting lucrative market opportunities, critical to Mammoth's mission of turning around negative trend in product and marketing innovation and awareness. Perform all Director of Marketing functions and increase growth.
- Identified consumer needs; rationalized new products across all market segments; launched international product promotions through internal and external sales / distribution channels.
- Initiated and cultivated strategic relationships with development partners, consultants, analysts and the media; pioneered mutually profitable market opportunities and growth.

**Andy Kelleher**

### Selected Turnaround Highlights:

- *Effective business analysis, management research, product launch procedures and competitive strategies recognized with operational start-up responsibility in 3 continents.*
- *Craft initial marketing plans; recruit top-notch external resources including agencies, printers, graphic houses, audio / visual professionals and freelance writers.*
- *Orchestrate multiple, complex projects simultaneously at the helm of market communications, service and event marketing, sales support and new ventures.*

**GLOBAL COMMUNICATIONS SYSTEMS** - Orlando, Florida
1989-1990

Led a talented marketing team in program conceptualization, design, development and implementation as Marketing Manager. Coordinated London and USA marketing operations encompassing new technologies, branding programs, product roll-out and sales strategies.

- Investigated avenues for, and contributed importantly to growth; rationalized new products and developed marketing programs to the regional telephone operating companies.

### Selected Highlights:

- *Marketing and product strategies captured a large share of the market from leading telephone corporations--identified and exploited niche opportunities for this young firm.*
- *Piloted company to emerging technologies industry expert with creation of original sales support programs; opened 3 new highly profitable vertical markets.*

**LITTLE LEISURE PRODUCTS CO.** - Hackensack, New Jersey
1975-1980

Created strategic growth programs for 150 dealers throughout 32 states as Marketing Services Manager.

### Selected Highlights:

- *Provided oversight to advertising, promotions, trade shows, merchandising, distributor and annual sales meetings; gained skill as public relations strategist.*

**EDUCATION**
MAHANEY SCHOOL OF BUSINESS - Chicago, Illinois
Present
**MASTER OF BUSINESS ADMINISTRATION - INTERNATIONAL BUSINESS**
*Degree expected February 2001*

WESTCHESTER UNIVERSITY - White Plains, New York
**BACHELOR OF ARTS - BUSINESS ADMINISTRATION**

**PROFESSIONAL DEVELOPMENT:**
DALE CARNEGIE COURSES · SULLIVAN TRAINING IN LEADERSHIP COURSES ·
AMERICAN MANAGEMENT ASSOCIATION COURSES · CHANGE MANAGEMENT

# HOW TO CHOOSE THE RIGHT FORMAT FOR YOU

There's an element of personal style involved in picking a resume format. Some people are instinctively more conservative or low-key than others; they are likely to feel most comfortable with the chronological format, which is the most straightforward and traditional type of resume.

Others are a little bolder in style, more ready to take on a veneer of "salesmanship"; for them, a functional format, which provides a somewhat more free-form opportunity to sell your strengths, may feel most appropriate.

Naturally, the combination format falls somewhere between the other two for those who are ready to swing a bit more freely that the chronological types but not as freely as the functional gang.

It's important to pay attention to your personal tastes and preferences. If, in reading the descriptions of the three classic formats, you found yourself strongly drawn to a particular style (or shuddering with horror at another), follow your instincts: They're probably steering you right.

The industry in which you work may affect your decision, too. In conservative fields like banking, insurance, manufacturing, and health care, a more conservative resume style may be desirable, while in advertising, media, the arts, software, or other high-tech fields, a more free-wheeling approach may fit.

On the other hand, if you find you have no strong format preference, you'll want to consider the strengths and weaknesses of each of the three classic formats. Each format tends to favor a particular type of job seeker and job search.

### Consider the Chronological Format If:

- Your career progression is clear and logical and seems to lead naturally to your great next job.

- The skills and knowledge you've developed and used in your recent positions will be readily apparent and understandable to any prospective employer.

- Your recent employers and/or job titles are the single most impressive credential you have to offer.

### Consider the Functional Format If:

- Your career progression includes time gaps, steps backward or sideways, or detours into unrelated businesses.

- You're a recent grad, someone reentering the work force, or a career changer.

- You've developed an impressive array of skills in a series of seemingly irrelevant or unimpressive jobs.

**Consider the Combination Format If:**

- Your career progression includes both powerful elements (such as a great company or title) and apparent weaknesses.

- The link between your recent positions and the great next job you seek is real but less than obvious.

- You have both valuable skills and impressive career experiences to offer as credentials.

In any case, each of the three classic formats can and should be customized to show off your credentials to the best advantage. In the next section, we'll explain how.

# CUSTOMIZING FORMATS TO HIGHLIGHT YOUR STRENGTHS

*In the end, choosing a resume format is more an art than a science. Remember, the purpose of the resume is to entice a recruiter into offering you an interview. The resume you present must be one you'll feel comfortable discussing and explaining in an interview. So make sure you pick a style that "feels like you"—one you'll feel comfortable sending out into the world as your personal advertisement.*

Not everyone finds one of the three classic formats to be a perfect fit . . . any more than the same style of suit has a flattering effect on people with different figures. Fortunately, there are many ways to customize each of the classic formats to highlight your particular strengths and mask or de-emphasize any weaknesses.

Resume customization tactics include:

- Rearranging the sequence of sections to bring forward an area of strength while pushing back an area of weakness

- Expanding the coverage of a strength while reducing the coverage of a weakness—or even eliminating it altogether

- Using typographic highlighting (bullets, capital letters, bold face, italic style, or a larger font) to emphasize key strengths

- Inserting an unusual or unique resume heading to emphasize an area of special strength

Let's look at several resumes that illustrate these and other customization tactics. You may notice a trick or two you'll want to adapt for your own resume.

Resume 4.8 is the chronological resume of "Noelle Colby," a case worker in the rehabilitation field who has worked with troubled youths and is seeking a more advanced job in line with her ongoing education.

Notice two tactics that Colby has used to show off her abilities to advantage. First, she has subdivided her work experience into two categories: "Professional Experience" and "Clinical Experience," highlight-

## 4.8  Chronological Format
## with Emphasis on Training and Breadth of Experience

**NOELLE COLBY**
33 Philmont Road
Reston, Minnesota
(555) 555-0246

### OBJECTIVE
A CHALLENGING HUMAN SERVICES POSITION WHERE EDUCATION, CLINICAL
TRAINING, HIGHLY DEVELOPED ORGANIZATIONAL ABILITIES, INTERPERSONAL
SKILLS AND EXPERIENCE WILL BE FULLY UTILIZED AND LEAD TO CAREER
GROWTH AND ADVANCEMENT OPPORTUNITIES.

### PROFESSIONAL EXPERIENCE

**CASE HISTORIAN**
1996 - Present
Center for Human Development, Community Assessment Program
Reston, Minnesota

>Broad and diverse responsibilities for resident client services, program and
staff development.  Participate in assessment of clients and evaluation at
intake procedure; monitor resident behavior; record and report on progress
throughout the program.  Attend staff meetings and case conferences; work
closely with parents and legal guardians of residents.  Demonstrate technical
proficiency and understanding of its impact in areas of responsibility.
Develop and maintain working relationship with police, state youth services
officials, court personnel, school authorities and health providers.  Foster
cooperation, communication and consensus among groups.  Complete all
government and agency paperwork on each case.

**OUTREACH WORKER**
1991 - Present
The Motherhood Project
Reston, Minnesota

>Worked in specially targeted areas in an effort to reduce infant mortality.
Dispensed nutrition and medical information, counseled mothers-at-risk,
planned and arranged follow-up medical care.  Documented all research and
results.

**OVERNIGHT CASEWORKER**
1995 - 1996
REHAB, Inc.
Danforth, Minnesota

>Supervised resident clients in this community rehabilitative program.
Adhered to all program procedures and documented all relevant case
information.  Conducted routine room checks to ensure the safety and well-
being of all clients.  Recognized and defined issues; analyzed relevant
information; encouraged alternative solutions and plans to solve problems.

NOELLE COLBY

## CLINICAL EXPERIENCE

**INTERNSHIP / CASE MANAGER / INTAKE WORKER**
1995
The Henderson House Transitional Living Program
Danforth, Minnesota

> Fulfilled intake duties and completed all program documentation.  Performed initial assessment; solicited area agencies extolling virtues of transitional program.  Assisted clients in developing their Individual Service Plan according to guidelines and program regulations.  Assisted in research necessary to prepare grant proposals.  Helped implement computer conversion.  Researched available facilities and support programs to ease clients back into mainstream.

**PRACTICUM**
1994
The Binfield Home
Laraville, Minnesota

> Assisted staff with administrative functions and provided direct care support to emotionally disturbed children.  Considered and responded appropriately to the needs, feelings, capabilities and interests of children, relatives and staff; provided feedback.  Adapted style to situations; sought to empower, motivate, and guide others.  Supervised recreational activities to assist in the process of moving through stages of transition and crisis.

## EDUCATION AND TRAINING

MASTER OF EDUCATION PROGRAM IN REHABILITATION, 1996-present
Reston College - Reston, Minnesota
*Degree Expected in December 2000*

**BACHELOR OF SCIENCE DEGREE,** 1995
Reston College - Reston, Minnesota
*Major: Rehabilitation Counseling*

**Relevant courses include:**
BEHAVIORAL TECHNIQUE FOR THE DEVELOPMENTALLY DISABLED · LEARNING DISABILITIES · PSYCHOLOGY OF DISABILITY · INDEPENDENT LIVING REHABILITATION · PARENTS AND FAMILY OF THE DISABLED · INTERVIEWING & CASE STUDY METHODS · ASSESSMENT & APPRAISAL TECHNIQUES · PEDIATRIC REHABILITATION

**COMPUTER SKILLS**
Experienced with IBM and Macintosh · Familiar with a variety of software

ing the former by putting it first. This is because her "Professional Experience" is more directly related to the next job she is seeking.

Second, she has expanded and enhanced the description of her "Education and Training" by including a listing of "Relevant Courses" from her undergrad and grad training. This list resembles the skills summary from a functional resume and suggests to the reader some of the areas of strength Colby would bring to her next job.

In Resume 4.9, "Edward Chen," a civil engineer, has adapted the combination format to emphasize the most impressive engineering projects he has managed.

Note the specific customization tactics Chen has employed. First, immediately after the headline (the section labeled "Consulting Project Management"), in the place where a skills summary might normally appear, Chen has created a unique section labeled "Selected Achievements." In this section, he lists and describes three of his most impressive engineering projects. By putting these up front in the resume, Chen makes certain that employers will notice them right away.

Second, Chen enhances the listing of his present job by including not only a paragraph and four bullets describing his work but also a listing of three "Representative Projects"—another opportunity to explain in vivid terms the kinds of major operations Chen has successful developed.

If you're in any field where completion of important individual projects is a major way of measuring professional accomplishments, consider a similar tactic for your resume.

"George V. Condrescu," the creator of Resume 4.10, is an engineer who has been self-employed for the past eighteen years. Now, for whatever reason, Condrescu is seeking employment. (Perhaps business is drying up, or a family health emergency calls for a job where better health insurance will be available—who knows?)

In any case, Condrescu's years of self-employment, though certainly indicative of initiative and managerial talent, need to be disguised lest they scare off a potential employer.

One strategy for doing this would be to use a functional resume, which would de-emphasize employment history and emphasize skills. Condrescu has chosen not to go this route; he prefers the more conservative chronological format. However, he has subtly masked his self-employment status by listing his last two jobs as "Program Director, 1985–Present" (with *no* employer listed) and "Executive Management, 1982–Present, GVC Technology, Ltd."

## 4.9  Combination Format with Emphasis on Key Projects

*Confidential Resume of*
### EDWARD CHEN, P.E.
310 Old Country Road · Williston, NH 04701
H: (555) 555-1282  O: (555) 555-7100

*Civil / Environmental Engineering*

### CONSULTING · PROJECT MANAGEMENT

DEDICATED, ACCOMPLISHED MSCE WITH 11 YEARS OF PROGRESSIVE
CONTRIBUTIONS IN WATER RESOURCES PLANNING AND EXPERTISE
ENCOMPASSING COMPUTER MODELING, MASTER PLANNING, REGULATORY
PERMITTING, CONSTRUCTION MANAGEMENT, BUDGETING, STAFF SUPERVISION
AND RELATIONSHIP BUILDING

### SELECTED ACHIEVEMENTS

- **Developed a Combined Sewer Overflow (CSO) Master Plan for the city of New Bedford, Massachusetts** including Storm Water Management Model (SWMM) collection system, abatement alternatives, capital costs, and electrical and instrumental design for four wastewater pump stations.
- **Assessed Wet Weather Alternative for a Vermont Wastewater Treatment Plant.** Studied alternatives for handling excess wet weather flows.  Analyzed costs, benefits and feasibility and recommended a four-year construction program mix at $11.5 Million.
- **Executed civil engineering and site design for 12 residential subdivisions** in central Connecticut.  Designed sanitary sewer, storm-water collection and water distribution systems, retention basins, road layout, grading and utilities.  Obtained all regulatory permits.

### PROFESSIONAL EXPERIENCE

**PROJECT MANAGER: Wastewater Division**
1993 - Present
New Hampshire Department of Environmental Protection, Grand Forks, New Hampshire
Spearhead all elements involved in water resources planning, design and construction of storm-water, combined sewer overflow and wastewater treatment facilities, collection systems and water supply projects.  Implement procedures for coordinating technical operations, human resource management and key client relations.
- Coordinate multiple site operations to consistently meet project deadlines, profit objectives, regulatory, quality and client expectations.
- Formulate accurate capital and operating costs for projects.
- Negotiate all project regulatory permitting with local, state and federal agencies.
- Awarded cash bonus for contributions to budget surplus.

**Edward Chen. P.E.**

*Representative Projects:*
- *Headed New Hampshire Regional Underground Storage Facility project involving 200 MGD influent screening / effluent pumping station & control building, 7.8 million gallon storage tank, odor control and HVAC facilities, CSO diversion structures, consolidation conduits and modeling of Storm Water Management system.*
- *Analyzed structural design data, calculated pressure limits and identified weak zones in New Hampshire Water Resources Authority's Farley Aqueduct--the primary conduit of drinking water from the Farley Reservoir.*
- *Reviewed best management practices and designed a Stormwater Pollution Prevention Plan for the 360 MGD Gay Island facility to satisfy NPDES regulations for storm-water discharges.*

**PROJECT ENGINEER · MANAGER**
1985 - 1993
HOGAN & VALENZUELA, INC., Boston, Massachusetts
Provided technical and organizational leadership critical to fulfilling client contracts while consistently meeting deadlines, budgets and quality objectives. Conducted site assessments, designed and implemented water / waste treatment, sludge treatment / disposal and hydraulic designs for residential, commercial and industrial projects.
- Managed site operations and all project elements for land surveying, civil engineering, facilities design and layout, hydrologic and hydraulic studies.
- Made presentations at public hearings, fielded questions from concerned citizens and regulatory authorities and secured all require permits and approvals.
- Trained junior engineers in drainage, roadway and sewer design.

## PROFESSIONAL ASSOCIATIONS

CSO / WET WEATHER ISSUES & COLLECTION SYSTEMS COMMITTEES: New England Water Environment Federation · American Society of Civil Engineers · New Hampshire Society of Civil Engineers

## EDUCATION & TRAINING

NEW HAVEN POLYTECHNIC INSTITUTE - New Haven, Connecticut
**MASTER OF SCIENCE IN CIVIL ENGINEERING,** 1992
**BACHELOR OF SCIENCE IN CIVIL ENGINEERING,** 1986

## LICENSES & CERTIFICATIONS

STATE OF NEW HAMPSHIRE, REGISTERED PROFESSIONAL ENGINEER #107-899

Willing to relocate · Willing to perform work-related travel

## 4.10  Chronological Format De-Emphasizing Self-Employment

**GEORGE V. CONDRESCU**
13 Van Ness Avenue · Lompok, Virginia 34189
*Phone:* (555) 555-7273 · *Fax:* (555) 555-8250
Email: gvcondrescu@logos.net

**ENGINEERING MANAGEMENT**
**New Technologies · Design · Start-Up · Construction**

*Self-starter with proven expertise in strategic planning, technology / logistics assessment, project management, process improvements, re-engineering, system design, quality assurance and team building. Innovative, resourceful and inventive. Able to identify opportunities, 'make things happen' and consistently achieve goals and objectives. Offer consistent record of achievement with ability to develop highly focused teams motivated to achieve ambitious goals.*

**PROFESSIONAL EXPERIENCE**

**Program Director**
1985 - Present
Plan, direct, and coordinate activities for $80,000,000 company supporting design, construction and start-up of new programs to supply assemblies and stampings to major automobile manufacturers. Serve as entrepreneurial business developer and creative consensus builder. Establish realistic long-range goals. Plan objectives; develop organizational policies; establish responsibilities and procedures. Review status reports; modify schedules as required. Resolve engineering design and test problems. Direct integration of technical activities.
- *Complete flexible production line to produce 3 different fuel tanks for passenger cars--generating annual revenues of **$21,000,000**.*
- *Instituted 2 production lines of subassemblies for Lodex Corporation--increasing annual revenues by **$10,000,000**.*

**Executive Management**
1982 - Present, GVC Technology, Ltd. · Lompok, VA
Provided consulting and integration of state-of-the-art R&D strategies and systems for manufacturing companies in area of custom design equipment and production improvements. Identified required resources; planned and coordinated projects with others. Determined time frames, funding limitations, procedures and staffing requirements.
- *Specified equipment and manufacturing methods to meet product requirements and cost objectives; recommended steel wool quality improvement that **propelled sales 20%**.*
- *For another client, developed new welding machine that **increased production 35%**.*

GEORGE V. CONDRESCU

**Chief Engineer**
1979 - 1982, Hydropuro, Inc. · Richmond, VA
Marshalled strong leadership skills for company producing waste water purification equipment. Provided technical and organizational management critical to fulfilling client contracts while consistently meeting delivery deadlines, budgets and quality objectives. Directed Engineering, Production, Purchasing and Administration, with overall P/L responsibility.

- *Demonstrated technical proficiency and championed awareness of its impact; established and developed Quality Assurance program with wide employee participation.*
- *Planned, positioned and promoted importance of cost controls--**grew profits 15%**.*

**Project Manager**
1974 - 1979, Michael Conrad & Associates · Chicago, Illinois
Directed and coordinated planning, organization, control, integration and completion of engineering project. Oversaw budget and schedule. Assigned personnel from all engineering disciplines and construction trades to specific phases or aspects of project-- technical studies, product design, preparation of specifications, testing.

- *Recognized and defined issues; analyzed relevant information; explored alternative solutions; achieved **33% improved efficiency** of client's heat treating furnaces.*
- *Designed, developed and delivered plans promoting expansion and modernization of industrial plants; implementation produced increased profits and enhanced product quality.*

**Previous positions include:**
Design Engineer - Weston Machine Corporation - Cicero, Illinois · 1971 - 1974

EDUCATION

**Master of Science**
1970 · Romania National University
*Focus: Combustion Engines and Machine Design*

**Additional courses, workshops and professional development include:**
Welding Technology · Powder Metallurgy · Industrial Ventilation · Noise Control · Business Management · Engineering

REFERENCES AND FURTHER DATA AVAILABLE UPON REQUEST

Now, "GVC Technology" is a somewhat transparent mask for Condrescu's own consulting firm. (GVC = George V. Condrescu, obviously.) But by *not emphasizing* his self-employment status, Condrescu has accomplished two things: First, he has planted just a seed of doubt in the mind of a potential recruiter—is Condrescu self-employed or not? Second, he has sent the message that Condrescu is not overly proud about running his own firm. Therefore, he is likely to be willing to fit in as a team member.

Accomplishing these two things may be enough to get Condrescu's foot in the door for an interview; and once he is in the interview, he should be able to defuse any further doubts the employer may have about his suitability for the job. Such is the power of a subtle customization of the resume format.

In creating Resume 4.11, "Brenda Allenby Cooke" had several goals in mind. First, she wanted to highlight her application of business skills to the health-care industry. (The great next job she seeks is as a high-level manager—vice president or higher—at a for-profit company in the health-care field.) Second, she wanted to show the depth and breadth of her educational background in both business and health-care management. And third, she wanted to indicate that she is an important part of an extensive network of top health-care professionals in her state.

Notice the customization techniques Cooke used to achieve these goals. First, she chose the functional format, which gave her the opportunity to craft a very impressive skills summary section, headed "Profile with Selected Highlights," that brought out many of her greatest on-the-job achievements. (Note the *numbers* that dot this part of the resume. They stand out from the rest of the text, emphasizing Cooke's bottom-line success and her business orientation.)

Second, she expanded the education section of her resume to include a bulleted list of the executive development courses she has taken. This list includes some famous names from the world of business education, including the Wharton School, Tom Peters, and the American Marketing Association, and Cooke is milking them for all they're worth.

Third, she has included a detailed professional affiliations section, listing not only her memberships in various relevant professional organizations but also noting the groups before which she has appeared as a speaker—another impressive credential.

The overall effect of this resume is to position Cooke as not just a good health-care manager but as an important figure in her profession, one with a fine stock of knowledge and skills and a first-class reputation among her peers.

## 4.11 Functional Format with Emphasis on Business Skills, Education and Professional Affiliations

*Confidential Resume of*
# BRENDA ALLENBY COOKE
311 Philmont Road · Cudahy, Wisconsin 67809
Residence: 555-555-3656 · Fax: 555-555-7393

### HEALTH CARE PROFESSIONAL
*Multidisciplined Manager with 20+ Years Experience*
IN THE AREAS OF PROVIDER / RELATIONS CREDENDTIALING, MEDICARE
PROGRAM MANAGEMENT, NETWORK DEVELOPMENT, CUSTOMER SATISFACTION,
REENGINEERING / PROCESS IMPROVEMENTS, QUALITY, AUTOMATION, COST
CONTAINMENT AND MARKETING.

### PROFILE WITH SELECTED HIGHLIGHTS
*Multimillion-Dollar Contribution to Industry Leaders*

- **Management Style:** Gain consensus for new initiatives , build and train sophisticated cross-functional teams. Boost productivity, quantity and quality of services by empowering and creating an environment teeming with learning and innovations.

- **Provider Credentialing / Regulatory Compliance:** Oversaw approval / disapproval of facilities and home care agencies for Medicare participation. Researched requirements, designed and implemented policies, processes and procedures to assess compliance as standards and regulations changed. Troubleshoot contract, billing and procedural issues; investigated fraud and abuse.

- **Network Development / Management:** Managed subcontracts to maintain quality / service levels. Implementation team for Medicare managed care contract. Innovative database tracks health plans, integrated delivery systems and competitors; and identifies statewide network partners. Directed MIS Dept.; spearheaded mainframe / PC system upgrades, increasing efficiency and reducing costs.

- **Utilization Review / Cost Control:** Managed review of Medicare, BLUE CROSS, and national account claims; saved Medicare $5M annually. Contract negotiations saved BLUE CROSS $3M year one. Chair of the Task Force that laid the foundation for streamlining operations, improving efficiency and management reporting. Negotiated $60,000 insurance cost reduction.

- **Quality:** Sought after for current knowledge of accrediting agencies, managed care, customer satisfaction, and survey design. Designed outcomes-based service grants; implemented and reported on results. Directed Quality Assurance; coordinated accreditation. Developed and implemented quality standards for trademark licenses.

- **Key Programs:** Engineered BLUE CROSS's *first* cost containment initiative for private business. Developed and implemented statewide hospital data quality plan. Directed design and marketed experience-based cost containment program to employers.

- **Management Performer:** Chaired BLUE CROSS task force that created a successful HMO, Wisconsin Health, from *start-up*–co-wrote the Federal qualification application. Liaison to health plans; played an integral role in proposals, presentations, Managed Care planning and team coordination. Handled site selection, negotiated leases and directed relocation of 2 major offices. Established funder relationships and co-secured $500 thousand in capital.

BRENDA ALLENBY COOKE

## PROFESSIONAL EXPERIENCE

AMERIGO HEALTH CARE, Milwaukee, WI
1989 - Present
Director - Administrative Services / Marketing & Development Associate

BLUE CROSS OF WISCONSIN, INC., Milwaukee, WI
1975 - 1989
Manager - Utilization Review, Provider Relations Division / Utilization Review Coordinator /
Utilization Review Specialist / Provider Relations / Customer Service

## EDUCATION

**BUSINESS ADMINISTRATION**
Post Graduate Coursework in Management / Marketing
Milwaukee University, Milwaukee, WI

24 credit hours in Marketing Communications / Graphic Design
Graybar College, Madison, WI

**BACHELOR OF ARTS IN SECONDARY EDUCATION**, 1971
Hunter College, New York, NY

**Executive Development:**
- Management - The Wharton School, University of Pennsylvania
- Management information Systems - University of Michigan
- Personal Computing - Graybar Computer Center, Executrain
- Capitation / Medicare Managed Care - Health Financial Managers Association
- Health Plan Report Cards - Wisconsin State College
- Health Plan Data Quality - Wisconsin Women in Healthcare Management
- Quality Improvement - Tom Peters CareerTrack
- Marketing - American Marketing Association

## PROFESSIONAL AFFILIATIONS

- KEYNOTE SPEAKER: NATIONAL HOSPICE CONFERENCE
- FREQUENT SPEAKER: WISCONSIN ASSOCIATION FOR HOME CARE, WISCONSIN HOSPITAL ASSOCIATION, MILWAUKEE SCHOOL OF PUBLIC HEALTH
- MEMBER: STATEWIDE TASK FORCE ON HEALTHCARE - WISCONSIN INTERFAITH HOUSING & HUMAN SERVICES CORP
- MEMBER: WISCONSIN HOSPITAL ASSOCIATION
- MEMBERSHIP COMMITTEE: WISCONSIN WOMEN IN HEALTHCARE MANAGEMENT (WWHCM)
- MEMBER: AMERICAN MARKETING ASSOCIATION

REFERENCES & FURTHER DATA AVAILABLE UPON REQUEST

Finally, let's consider Resume 4.12, created by "Damien Bragg." Bragg is a "financial engineer," a current term in the business world for an investment professional who helps to create and market complex, hybrid financial instruments—investments that combine the characteristics of stocks, bonds, futures, and options in complicated, hopefully profitable ways. The best financial engineers are very bright (sometimes they're referred to as "rocket scientists") and they can make millions for their employers.

Bragg has customized his combination resume to suggest that he is a potential superstar in the world of financial engineering. Note the subtle and not-so-subtle features of his resume that help to create this effect.

First, Bragg heads his skills profile with the notation, "Member: American Mensa." As you probably know, Mensa is the "genius society" that admits only those with super high I.Q.s. Is this relevant to Bragg's career history? Not really; and if Bragg were working in most other fields, it would be obnoxious for him to include this boastful detail on his resume. However, in the field of financial engineering, where massive intellect is highly respected, it seems appropriate (even if it's still a *little* obnoxious).

*Part of the art of resume writing is knowing the culture of the industry in which you want to work and adapting a style and tone appropriate to that culture. What seems "brash," "cocky," and "abrasive" in some businesses is considered "self-confident" in others. Ask an industry insider or two for a reaction to the tone of your resume, and fine-tune it based on how positive or negative the comments are.*

Second, Bragg has divided the chronological portion of the resume into two categories: "Related Professional Experience" and "Other Professional Experience." The first category includes only his position with "Kawasuna Bank" in Tokyo—which dates back a full eight years. All his other jobs, including his current job, are listed as "Other" experience. The effect is to imply that, despite his job history, Bragg is *really* a financial engineer, whose work at Kawasuna Bank is a more genuine indicator of his talents and interests than his other positions.

Will this tactic work? It certainly won't "fool" an employer into thinking, for example, that Bragg has been working exclusively as a financial engineer for the past decade; the years of employment are there on the resume for all to see. However, it does send the message that Bragg intends to devote himself and the rest of his career to financial engineering, and it may help focus the conversation at an interview on that field and on his experience at Kawasuna.

In later chapters, you'll learn much more about how to customize your resume to highlight your strengths and mask your weaknesses, including a wealth of specific advice related to the problems and opportunities faced by specific categories of job seekers.

## 4.12 Combination Format Highlighting the Best Job

**DAMIEN BRAGG**
313 North Truman · Chicago, Illinois 51346
Residence: 555-555-6446 · Office: 555-555-5580 · Fax: 555-555-7786

### FINANCIAL ENGINEER
*Translate Over-the-Counter Products into Creative, Profitable Structures*
Innovative professional with an in-depth understanding of financial products and a remarkable talent for opening markets and generating multimillion-dollar profits for global industry leaders.

### PROFILE

*Member: American Mensa*

- **Seasoned Professional:** Meet with clients, analyze portfolios, determine risk tolerance and experience. Formulate hedging strategies and original products to meet or exceed goals; deliver sophisticated presentations, skillfully negotiating pricing according to client knowledge level.
- **Global Player:** Clients included government officials, senior executives of large Asian and Australian corporation, global banks and finance companies. Traveled throughout the Asia Pacific Region developing KAWASUNA's deliveratives business from $0 to $1 Billion annually.
- **Unparalleled Knowledge of Financial Products:** Took the initiative in early broker, syndicator and financial management positions to gain product mastery across the financial market spectrum. Utilize comprehensive background to create innovative trade ideas.
- **Spearhead Business Expansion:** Craft strategic plans, programs and alliances to open new markets and maximize growth. Drove Financial Engineering Department start-up; cutting-edge strategies gained KAWASUNA financial risk management market dominance.
- **Customer Value:** Earned a reputation throughout the Asia Pacific Region for ability to develop ingenious financial solutions. Investment returns spurred continued account development. Structured products for Singapore, Cathy, and Pacific Airlines.
- **Technical Proficiency:** Highly skilled in programming and operating PCs. Sought after for expertise in Fixed Income Analytics, Scenario & Sensitivity Analysis, Portfolio Hedging Techniques, Technical Market Analysis, and Option Pricing Modeling.

### RELATED PROFESSIONAL EXPERIENCE

**GENERAL MANAGER / FINANCIAL ENGINEER**
1989 - 1991
KAWASUNA BANK LIMITED, Tokyo
Contributed vision and management expertise critical to the growth of this prestigious bank's derivatives business, at the helm of the Financial Engineering Department with full P&L responsibility. Served as principal in FRAs, Interest Rate / Currency / Commodity Swaps & Options; used derivatives to structure option embedded and inverse floating rate loans, collateralized zero coupon deposits, and amortized aircraft financing schemes. Identified and exploited avenues for market expansion.

**Damien Bragg**

- Utilized legal background to design contracts; created results-getting brochures and proposals; engaging presentations captured major new clients and developed existing accounts.
- Developed policies, procedures, programs and controls to minimize risk and exposure.

## OTHER PROFESSIONAL EXPERIENCE

### PRESIDENT
1995 - Present
PACIFIC FINANCE, INC., Chicago, Illinois

Spearhead business development and P&L performance of this successful business specializing in financial consulting and mortgage banking.  Assess client operational structure, organizational capabilities and financial assets; develop effective strategies to enhance revenue.

- Draw on resource networks in related industries to assist the client in meeting its needs; bring strong financial capabilities, creativity and proven strategic methods.

*Selected Highlights*
- *Drove operations from start-up to a national market presence, handling marketing, advertising, promotions, and all financial / accounting functions.*

### VICE PRESIDENT
1994 - 1995
FRESNO INSTITUTIONAL SERVICES, Fresno, California

Rendered financial, managerial and administrative leadership to this prominent division of California Capital Securities, a leader in derivative securities.

### REGIONAL MANAGER, SOUTHEAST ASIA
1991 - 1992
RAINBOW INTERNATIONAL LIMITED, Singapore

### MANAGING DIRECTOR
1988 - 1989
VAN DYCK SECURITIES (HK) LIMITED, Hong Kong

### INTER-BANK CAPITAL MARKET BROKER
1986 - 1988
HENSON GROUP, PLC., New York / Hong Kong / Tokyo

## EDUCATION

### BACHELOR OF ARTS
ROCHESTER COLLEGE · Rochester, New York

### GRADUATE STUDIES
NORTHWESTERN UNIVERSITY LAW SCHOOL · Evanston, Illinois

# JUST THE FACTS

- There are three classic resume formats: the chronological format, the functional format, and the combination format, which is a hybrid of the first two.

- The chronological format emphasizes the progression from one job to the next, while the functional format emphasizes the skills you've developed in those jobs.

- The choice of a resume format depends on your career background, your strengths and weaknesses as a job seeker, and your personal style.

- Whatever format you choose can and should be customized to emphasize your strengths and to mask or de-emphasize any weaknesses.

# Chapter 5

# Words That Shout "Hire Me!"

---

## Get the Scoop On . . .

- Selling your benefits, not your features
- Turning your disadvantages into advantages
- Using active verbs
- Determining the ideal length for your resume
- Secrets of professional resume writers

---

## ADVERTISING YOURSELF

As we've already said, a resume is like an advertisement for you—a letter-sized poster designed to highlight your strengths as an employee and to entice a recruiter into interviewing you.

The analogy is really quite a precise one. For example, most advertisements on TV or radio or in print publications aren't designed to "close the sale"; it's rare that a viewer will literally rush out the door after watching a great TV ad to buy the product at the nearest store. Instead, most ads are designed to capture your interest and get you to take the next step on the road to making a purchase. The next step might be visiting a product dealer, phoning for a brochure, or going on line for more information. At some point, personal contact with a salesperson will probably take place, and that's when the real deal will be struck.

It's just the same with your resume. The *ultimate* purpose of the resume is to get a job offer, but its *immediate* purpose is to get the reader to take the next step on the road to hiring you. Normally, that's to call you and arrange an interview. Only when the personal contact of an interview occurs will a deal be struck—the offering and acceptance of a great job.

There's another important similarity between advertisements and resumes: *Both must struggle to be heard in intensely competitive environments.*

It's a common complaint of modern life that we're drowning in advertisements. Between the broadcasting media, the print media (magazines and newspapers), billboards, signs, labels, packages, and the Internet—to say nothing of the proliferation of company logos almost everywhere—we encounter literally thousands of advertising messages daily.

It poses a tremendous problem for advertisers. How do you break through the clutter? How do you get people to pay attention long enough to absorb your message out of the thousands competing for their interest? The difficulty of this challenge explains why companies spend millions each year devising advertising, marketing, and promotional schemes as well as billions to buy space in magazines and on billboards and minutes of broadcasting time. It also explains why TV commercials, for example, use every trick in the book, from celebrities' faces, catchy songs, and sexy models to cute kids and sarcastic humor, to grab your attention—often resulting in ads that are more entertaining than the shows they interrupt. Your resume faces the same challenge.

*"As a professional recruiter, I usually receive anywhere from 50 to 100 resumes every day. How much time do I get to spend on each? Three to eight seconds to start with—just enough time to see whether it's clear and logically organized. Then, if it's a good resume, I'll give it a little more time . . . ten to fifteen seconds' worth."*
—Robert Defendorf, human resources manager, Scholastic, Inc.

Yes, today's job market is flourishing, with thousands of great jobs to choose from, some even going begging for lack of highly qualified candidates. Yet the numbers game which job seekers must play remains daunting. For most advertised jobs, dozens or hundreds of resumes are received, which recruiters or employers must sort through and read before even scheduling the first interview.

Even when jobs are unadvertised and remain part of the hidden job market, the same problem exists. When word gets out through the business grapevine that a good job is available, scores of resumes are apt to materialize on the recruiter's desk.

And in today's volatile business climate, hundreds of thousands of people are in a more-or-less constant state of job hunting—preparing for their company's next round of layoffs or just looking for the next step up in their careers.

All this means that, at any given time, millions of resumes are in circulation and the recruiter or employer whose attention you want is likely to have a desk weighed down with at least a few thousand of them.

So one of the central challenges for the resume writer is to find ways to grab the attention of an easily distracted, overly busy, rushed, and harried recruiter who may only have a few seconds (literally) in which to scan and absorb your message. It's up to you to find ways of breaking through the resume clutter.

As discussed in Chapter 4, choosing a clear resume format that highlights your strengths in the most compelling fashion is one step in this process. In this chapter, we'll explain a second step: crafting the language and style of your resume to excite, impress, and entice the reader.

## Selling Benefits, Not Features

One of the basic principles of advertising that's especially applicable to the art of resume writing is the rule: *Sell benefits, not features.* What does this mean and how should it affect the way your craft your resume? Here's an explanation.

A *feature* is any positive quality of a product or service. Relatively simple products may have only one or two features. For example, colas and other soft drinks have these features: *sweetness, wetness, coldness.* Complex products like cars, computers, or furniture may have dozens of features: *automatic sunroof, three-way adjustable seats, 16-inch monitor, built-in high-capacity memory drive, solid oak trim, hand-stitched leather upholstery.*

By contrast, a *benefit* is what the feature can do for you. To put it another way, a benefit is a feature as viewed by the consumer or user of the product or service rather than the manufacturer or supplier. If a cola has *sweetness, wetness,* and *coldness* as its features, then its benefits might be *quenches thirst fast, tastes great,* and *refreshes on a hot day.*

Smart advertisers know that potential consumers are interested in features only because of the benefits they offer. Therefore, effective ads focus on benefits, not features. A good car ad might mention the feature—*automatic sunroof*—but it will stress the benefit that the feature offers the consumer—*enjoy the great outdoors while you drive.*

Describing benefits answers the consumer's "So what?" question; they explain why the feature is important and valuable and what good the consumer will get from it if he or she buys the product or service: "Our car has three-way adjustable seats." "So what?" "That means you'll be comfortable no matter how tall you are, even when driving for hours at a time." "Our computer comes with a 16-inch monitor." "So what?" "It's bigger and clearer than most monitors, making it easier for you to handle several tasks at once without eyestrain or discomfort." "It has a built-in high-storage memory drive." "So what?" "You'll never run the risk of losing hours of work due to a power outage or other problem with short-term memory."

You need to use this same technique when writing your resume. To appeal to the "consumer," that is, the potential employer, you must consciously work to describe your background, achievements, and skills in terms of benefits—good things you can do for the company that hires you. Here are some examples.

**Feature:** Reorganized sales and marketing department at Acme Company.

---

### FYI

*The concept of "selling benefits" shows why it's important to do your homework about potential employers before sending out your resume. The more you know about the companies you'll be applying to—their business needs, plans, problems, and opportunities—the better you can craft your resume to offer benefits that are directly relevant to their interests. That takes research—through reading, networking, and asking lots of smart questions of everyone in the field in which you want to work.*

**Benefit:** Reorganized sales and marketing department at Acme Company, cutting expenses by 30% while doubling sales in two years.

**Feature:** Managed development of tools for measuring divisional quality performance.

**Benefit:** Managed development of quality measurement tools that reduced production cost overruns by more than $200,000.

**Feature:** Designed and implemented in-service training program to instruct teachers on recognizing signs of child abuse in students.

**Benefit:** Designed and implemented teacher training program on child abuse that helped staff successfully resolve three abuse cases in a six-month period with no legal liability.

In each case, the second version of the same resume item, the benefit version, explains to prospective employers exactly *why* they should be impressed with the accomplishment described in the feature version. Note that both versions mention the achievement, but only the benefit version tells the potential employer "What's in this for me?"—how he or she could win by hiring you.

### Turning Lemons into Lemonade

Advertising man James Webb Young, who was famous for his brilliance and creativity as a copywriter, liked to tell the story of how he sold a crop of mail-order fruit with ugly marks of hail damage on them. Into each carton of pre-ordered apples, he inserted a card with the following message:

> Note the hail marks which appear as minor skin blemishes on some of these apples. These are proof of their growth at a high mountain altitude, where the sudden chills from mountain hailstorms which these apples received while growing help firm their flesh and develop the fruit sugars which give them their fine flavor.

Rather than angry customers insisting on returning the blemished apples, Young ended up with happy fruit-lovers intrigued and pleased with their unique "high-altitude" apples.

*"When life gives you lemons, make lemonade."*

This story is a classic example of how to turn a possible negative into a positive by "reframing" it—placing it in a different context (or "frame") and so altering others' perceptions of it. It's a crucial skill for any job seeker whose background contains something that could be viewed as a "problem"—which includes almost everyone.

With a degree of creativity, it's possible to find and emphasize the positive (or, at least, neutral) side of almost every career experience you've had. In Chapter 13, we'll discuss some specific reframing strategies that can be used by job seekers with particular "problems" to overcome—a history of "job hopping," for example. But here we'd like to offer a number of examples of how you can turn apparent negatives into positives through thoughtful reframing.

**Problem:** Your only previous job in your current career field was working for a small company with a less-than-stellar reputation.

**Reframing:** In a small company, it's often true that every employee must take on extra responsibilities, even beyond his or her nominal sphere of duties. If this was true of you, then your small-company experience was probably an unusually rich *learning* experience. Furthermore, if the small company you worked for had a poor reputation (perhaps considered a "second-rate" or "fly-by-night" operation), then any accomplishments you can claim—a sales increase, a quality award, a reduction in costs—can be considered *especially* meritorious, since you accomplished them on your own, with minimal help from your unimpressive surroundings.

**You could say:** Helped division earn designation as semifinalist in competition for the Baldrige Quality Award—first such achievement for any division in the company. (The subtle message—you helped make your part of the company a standout in an otherwise lackluster organization.)

**Problem:** You lost your last job when the department you worked in was folded into another because of declining sales and profits.

**Reframing:** In today's business world, reorganizations, mergers, and other shake-ups are commonplace. If you were involved in such a transition and played some role in helping to make it proceed smoothly, you gained experience and mental toughness that may stand you in good stead in future jobs—and which future employers may appreciate.

**You could say:** During merger of Kitchen Products Department into Plastics Products Division, helped coordinate orderly transfer of database and production process information with maximum efficiency and minimal disruption. (You've shifted the focus from the reason for the merger—poor performance of your department—to the skill with which the merger was handled.)

**Problem:** Your educational background is in an entirely different field than the one in which you now want to work.

**Reframing:** Many organizations today are seeking people who are able to "think outside the box," that is, to bring a fresh perspective and new ideas to the problems and challenges they face. Thus, an interesting background from *outside* the field in which you want to work can be considered a positive if you show how it can help you bring new insights to the lucky employer who hires you.

**You could say:** Eager to apply the unique research and analytical skills developed during grad work in physics to the challenges of marketing consumer products in today's increasingly complex and fragmented marketplace.

Do you see the idea? As you begin work on your resume, consider any apparent weaknesses in your work, educational, or other background—elements in your history that employers may have been worried about in the past. Rather than assume that these weaknesses must simply be hidden or masked in some fashion, ask yourself what strength you may have that's connected to them. (You probably have one; as the philosopher Nietzsche said, "What does not kill us makes us stronger.") Then find a way to reframe the weakness in terms of the strength. You may end up *highlighting* the "weakness" in your resume rather than hiding it!

# SECRETS OF THE WORD SPINNERS

In addition to the general principles we've explained so far (selling benefits, not features, and turning lemons into lemonade) advertising writers, like other professional writers, have developed and mastered over the years a number of specific verbal techniques that help make what they write compelling, interesting, and persuasive. After all, they *have* to be convincing—their livelihoods depend on it. Many of these tricks work in resume writing, too. Here are several of the best.

## Using Active Verbs

*Professional writers know that a sentence built around a forceful verb is more interesting and compelling than a sentence centered on a weak or lackluster verb.*

One of the keys of lively, vigorous, interesting writing is the use of interesting and active verbs to drive sentences. (As you may recall from junior high school, verbs are words that express *action*—words like *go*, *build*, *grow*, *climb*, *lead*, and *improve*.)

Thus, in the following pair of sentences, the second sentence is more powerful (the verbs are highlighted in each):

**Weak:** *Was* a leader of a product development team that *was* able to complete its projects in less time than scheduled.

**Powerful:** *Led* a product development team that consistently *beat* project completion schedules.

Active verbs like *led* and *beat* suggest a more dynamic personality than *was*. Typically, verbs that are forms of the verb *to be* are less compelling and forceful than other verbs—and deserve to be discarded.

Active words and phrases that indicate you are more than a passenger on the train of life should be liberally sprinkled throughout your resume. You'll be surprised at the positive impact this simple writing technique can have on your resume. Each industry has its own special jargon, including specialized verbs that are favored, but many great verbs can apply to a host of businesses.

The following table has a sampling of 101 powerful verbs to help get your own creative juices flowing. See how many can be used to add interest and vitality to your resume.

Take a look at Resume 5.1, crafted by "Howard Hermann," paying particular attention to the use of interesting active verbs. In fact, the profile section of the resume is built entirely around a great list of eye-catching and impressive verbs—highlighted by the use of boldface type. Perhaps you'll want to consider borrowing this technique for your resume.

Resume 5.2, for "Carl P. Dresner," is another good example of the use of interesting verbs. Note the following somewhat unusual formulas in particular:

> "Skillfully *translated* customer requirements into chemical solutions."
>
> "*Cultivate* warm relationships with people from diverse backgrounds."
>
> "*Committed* to an ideal of quality."
>
> "*Diagnose* highly complex technical problems."
>
> "*Spearhead* commodity management programs."
>
> "*Conceptualized, designed, developed,* and *tested* new polymer products and adhesives."

Each of these verbs is just slightly different from those that might have been used in a more conventional, typical resume, not so much as to appear "weird" or to be difficult to understand, but enough to give the resume a fresh and attractive tone.

# BEING CONCISE

*Conciseness* means saying what you need to say as briefly as possible. As the old saying has it, concise writing is like a sexy bathing suit—short enough to be interesting, but long enough to cover everything essential.

## 101 Powerful Verbs to Help You Get Your Creative Juices Flowing

| | | | |
|---|---|---|---|
| Accomplished | Eliminated | Invented | Produced |
| Achieved | Enlarged | Investigated | Promoted |
| Administered | Established | Invigorated | Propelled |
| Advised | Evaluated | Launched | Received |
| Analyzed | Excelled | Maintained | Recommended |
| Assessed | Expedited | Managed | Reduced |
| Assigned | Experimented | Maximized | Repaired |
| Assisted | Facilitated | Minimized | Restored |
| Arranged | Focused | Motivated | Scheduled |
| Augmented | Formulated | Navigated | Secured |
| Boosted | Fostered | Negotiated | Shaped |
| Budgeted | Founded | Nurtured | Sold |
| Captured | Gathered | Optimized | Solved |
| Catalyzed | Generated | Organized | Specialized in |
| Conducted | Guided | Originated | Started |
| Consulted | Handled | Overhauled | Stimulated |
| Coordinated | Honored as | Oversaw | Streamlined |
| Counseled | Implemented | Performed | Supervised |
| Delegated | Improved | Pinpointed | Synthesized |
| Delivered | Inaugurated | Pioneered | Systematized |
| Demonstrated | Initiated | Planned | Tackled |
| Deployed | Innovated | Prepared | Tracked |
| Developed | Installed | Presented | Trained |
| Devised | Instructed | Prioritized | Upgraded |
| Directed | Introduced | Procured | Won |
| Drafted | | | |

In the case of your resume, this means eliminating needless words, phrases, and sentences as well as details that add nothing to the interest and power of your message, while not omitting any fact or idea that may help to capture the imagination of a recruiter or employer.

The word *concise* itself comes from a Latin word that means "to cut," and for most people conciseness in writing is achieved only through cutting—figuratively, that is. After you've drafted your resume and packed it as full as possible with compelling, impressive, noteworthy, and exciting skills, accomplishments, and details, all described as much as possible in terms of benefits (not just features), it'll be time to make sure the resume is concise. This generally means trimming, pruning, condensing, and cutting, using the techniques we'll explain in this section.

Why is conciseness so important? Remember what we said in Chapter 1 about the numbers game in today's fast-paced job market? So many job

## 5.1  Vivid Use of Interesting, Active Verbs

*Confidential Resume of*
# HOWARD HERMANN

1270 Pulaski Boulevard
Columbus, Ohio 65432
(555)-555-9021
*Email:* hermann109@coco.net

## SENIOR PROGRAMMER ANALYST

IBM 3083 • 43XX • 370 • VAX • NCR • COBOL • COBOL II • CICS • TSO/ISP • OLM • MVS IMS •
VIASOFT • DATA DICTIONARY • ROSCOE • IDMS • PANVALET

*Offer proven leadership contributions to internetworking, technology planning, academic computing, computer assisted management and diffusion of new technologies. Turn demand into growth and technology into value for financial, manufacturing, educational and publishing applications. Utilize structured programming design techniques in batch and online environments.*

### SKILLS, ABILITIES AND ACHIEVEMENTS • VALUE OFFERED

- **Analyzed** problems, information and sources.
- **Corrected** errors in documentation and programming.
- **Interpreted** technical information in laymen terms.
- **Monitored** progression into programs and documentation.
- **Programmed** information into computer dialog.
- **Retrieved** information pertaining to programming needs.
- **Scheduled** specific tasks, deadlines, and project release dates.
- **Printed** reports and labels.
- **Repaired** minor and major damages within computer systems.
- **Handled** internal technical support.
- **Handled** system setup.
- **Tested** programs for correct results.
- **Modified** IDMS programs for Legal Publishing applications.
- **Converted** IMS programs from OS COBOL to COBOL II and tested programs using Viasoft.

### CAREER TRACK

**SENIOR SOFTWARE ENGINEER**                                         1998 - Present
Vanderbilt Legal Publishing                                          Columbus, Ohio

Provide leadership in areas of creativity, technical expertise, quality assurance and project management. Apply new technologies to organizational needs. Troubleshoot and repair hardware, software, components and programs; test systems—as for Y2K process—to guarantee technical compatibility and minimal downtime. Ensure staff is trained and capable.

- *Modify IDMS COBOL / COBOL II programs for law publication applications; maintain existing programs and forward enhancements to production.*
- *Resolve issues in previously written programs; research and analyze new and emerging technologies with diverse applications; improve overall staff efficiency and effectiveness.*

**HOWARD HERMANN**                                                                    Page 2

**COMPUTER PROGRAMMER ANALYST**                                              1995 - 1998
Dexter Technologies                                                          Columbus, Ohio

    Contract COBOL/COBOL II programmer with Xanandu Systems for the engineering group.

- *Developed new software and modified existing programs to the clients current specifications in an IMS Database environment.*
- *The operating system environment was performed on an IBM system under an MVS/TSO platform using a Window NT Network.*

**COMPUTER PROGRAMMER ANALYST**                                              1994 - 1995
Nu Era Computer Services, Inc.                                               Cleveland. Ohio

    Contract COBOL/COBOL II programmer at local bank with development of software for banking applications.

- *Developed new software and modified existing programs to clients current specifications.*
- *The operating system was performed on an IBM system under an MVS/TSO platform using Windows 3.1 for Work Groups Network.*

**COMPUTER PROGRAMMER ANALYST**                                              1993 - 1994
Nu Era Computer Services, Inc.                                               Cleveland, Ohio

    Contract COBOL/COBOL II programmer at Systems & Computer Technology Corporation with development of software for SCT's SIS/FAM System.

- *Developed new software and modified existing programs to the clients current specifications.*
- *Development was performed on a VAX system and migrated to an IBM system under an MVS/TSO platform.*

**SENIOR PROGRAMMER ANALYST**                                                1980 - 1993
Bank of Ohio                                                                 Cleveland, Ohio

    Was involved in the design and development of Financial software targeted for the banking industry. Wrote applications for Product Creation, fee and index processing. Was also involved with tape processing for third party sources: Credit Agencies, IRS, and Social Security.

- *Developed software in COBOL Platform was on an NCR system through 1985.*
- *Migrated software to an IBM system in 1986 under an MVS/TSO environment.*

**PROGRAMMER ANALYST**                                                       1971 - 1980
Cincinnati Board of Education                                                Cincinnati, Ohio

    Participated in the design of reports and statistical analysis, and in the conversion of the Grade and Attendance Reporting System for the Cincinnati Public School System.

- *Development was done in COBOL.*

REFERENCES AND FURTHER DATA AVAILABLE UPON REQUEST

## 5.2  Attractive Use of Unusual Verbs

**CARL P. DRESNER**
77 Maple Street · Belmore, Vermont 34004
H: 555-555-4746 · W: 555-555-2825

### RESEARCH / DEVELOPMENT / QUALITY MANAGEMENT

*Talented, creative professional with 18 years of innovative accomplishment.  Expertise in polymer products and adhesives, process chemicals, and silicon substrates utilized in the manufacture of integral circuits and other electronic products and materials.  Advanced capabilities in process development and product yield enhancement.*

### PROFILE

- *Research, Manufacturing / Development Expertise:  Recipient of numerous awards for product innovation at NOVOCON, Inc.  Skillfully translated customer requirements into chemical solutions, devising new methods, operations, and systems at each step of the process.*
- *Management Performer:  Self starter with strong planning, organizing and leadership skills.  Oversee operations of 2 cost centers for AMERICAN EQUIPMENT CORPORATION (AEC); prepare and control annual operating budgets in excess of $3.3 Million.*
- *Articulate, Engaging Public Speaker:  Speak and write with proven virtues of strength, clarity, and style.  Cultivate warm relationships with people from diverse backgrounds; skilled at coordinating a multi-functional, multi-cultural workforce.*
- *Dedicated Quality Engineering Professional:  Committed to an ideal of quality; combine creativity with initiative and a drive for achievement.  Make constantly sound judgments under pressured conditions with a reputation for giving better than 100%.*

### PROFESSIONAL EXPERIENCE

**QUALITY ENGINEERING MANAGER**
1984 - Present
AMERICAN EQUIPMENT CORPORATION - Semiconductor Operations
Brattleboro, Vermont

Recruited for advanced technical knowledge of electronic components / material, chemical process development and yield enhancement.  Recognized for outstanding performance with promotion that encompasses management of engineering quality operations and 2 cost centers.

- *Formulate policy/procedure to ensure maximum quality of precision electro-mechanical assemblies, process chemicals, plastic components and silicon substrates in the IC manufacturing process.*
- *Develop and manage annual operating budgets of $4.1 Million+;  project future requirements; formulate strategies; establish effective cost and resource controls.*
- *Explore and develop new testing methodologies; diagnose highly complex technical problems; reengineer manufacturing and engineering processes as necessary.*

**CARL P. DRESNER**

*Selected Achievements:*
- *Launched and directed the cross-organizational team effort to reduce the defect rates of incoming raw materials; achieved a 0.5% rate, down from 33%.*
- *Initiated automated vision inspection and data collection technologies for complex dimensional measurements; considerably boosted efficiency and reduced costs.*
- *Enhanced profits with program that decreased average inspection cycle times by 50%.*
- *Spearhead commodity management programs and a supplier management process to consistently ensure adequate levels of vital raw materials.*
- *Introduced activity based costing and business process analysis systems that streamlined budget / strategy development.*

**MANUFACTURING AND DEVELOPMENT SUPERVISOR**
1982 - 1984
DISK DRIVE CORPORATION
Lewiston, Maine
> Organized and directed operations involved in the manufacture of magnetic coatings for rigid memory disks.  Oversaw research, development and processing of experimental coating made from state-of-the-art polymers and magnetic materials.

- *Worked in a team effort with engineers to successfully develop and improve manufacturing processes and enhance yields.*
- *Designed and directed experiments that quantified the accelerated wear of rigid media.*
- *Utilized computer system to process data and compile results and to provide extensive documentation of all research, development and process design / improvements.*
- *Prepared and submitted detailed reports with conclusions and recommendations.*

**TECHNICAL SERVICES SPECIALIST**
1980 - 1982
NOVOCON, INC. / POLYMER PRODUCTS DIVISON
Lewiston, Maine
> Conceptualized, designed, developed and tested new polymer products and adhesives used in the electronics components of various products that were marketed to consumers, the military, and the automotive and aerospace industries.

- *Met with key clients; analyzed needs and developed innovative solutions to meet complex and critical technical requirements.*
- *Explored existing polymer products; researched methods and devised new processes / procedures.*
- *Oversaw all facets of product development straight through to volume scale-up; implemented improvements where necessary.*
- *Received several awards for product innovation.*

**EDUCATION**

**BACHELOR OF ARTS IN CHEMISTRY,** 1977
College of Saint Paul · Temple, New Hamsphire

seekers are "in play" for any particular job that most recruiters and employers can afford to spend only seconds on an initial scan of the average resume. As a result:

- A resume that appears wordy, difficult, or time-consuming to read is likely to be tossed or ignored by an impatient recruiter.

- When needless words, phrases, and sentences or unhelpful details festoon a resume, they increase the chance that important, compelling ideas will get lost in the shuffle.

- A verbose resume is likely to convey an image of the job seeker as inefficient, time-wasting, or self-important— impressions that can only hurt your chances for an interview.

How concise is concise? There's no specific rule concerning resume length; we can't dictate a certain number of words, lines, or paragraphs as the "right" length for your resume. As with so much else, it depends on the story you have to tell. The longer and more complex your working history and the more varied your relevant skills, the longer your resume will probably have to be. The trick is to make sure that *every word counts*—you don't want your resume reader to waste time wading through verbiage that adds nothing except length to the story you have to tell.

## The One-Page Myth

Some resume "experts" will tell you that *no resume should be longer than a single page*. But this is a myth. If your background, skills, and qualifications are such that two pages are needed to describe them, that's fine. Virtually no recruiter or employer will reject your resume simply because it flows onto a second page. Here are some ground rules for deciding whether or not a second page makes sense for you and how to handle information so that the sheer length of your resume doesn't become a disqualifying factor.

### If You're a Recent Grad or Otherwise Seeking Your First "Real" Job, Stick to a Single Page

Nearly all candidates with only modest job experience that is both recent and relevant should keep their resumes to one page; more than this is likely to appear slightly pretentious, as though you are trying to inflate your background in hopes of appearing more impressive than you really are. Included in this category would be brand-new or recent grads (less than two years in the job market) and those entering the job market who haven't held paid, full-time positions within the last ten years. (Career changers, including ex-military people, are *not* included in this category.)

**FYI**

*As even the best professional writer will tell you, virtually no piece of writing is perfect as soon as it's drafted. That goes double for resumes. "Good writing is rewriting"—that means you'll need to revise your resume, reread it, and revise it again several times before you can be certain it's as concise and compelling as possible.*

## If Your Resume Runs Slightly over One Page, Try Altering the Style and Format to Trim It Back

**FYI**

*Avoid crafting a resume that overflows just slightly onto page two. A vast expanse of white space on the second page looks unattractive, and a page with only a few words on it is likely to be overlooked, misplaced, or lost when your resume changes hands or is filed.*

If your resume is just a little longer than one page—say, with six lines of type or fewer on page two—you can probably trim it back to one page without sharply cutting the content just by making a few small alterations in style and format.

Simple format changes that can cut from one to six lines of type from your resume include: reducing the point size of the type from 12 to 11; reducing the top, bottom, and side margins slightly (from one inch to .75 inches, or from 1.25 inches to 1 inch); and putting two or more closely related pieces of information on a single line rather than "stacked" in two or more lines. As an example of the latter, consider changing this:

> Production Manager
> Plastic Products Division
> Mammoth Industries

to:

> Production Manager
> Plastic Products Division, Mammoth Industries

If these changes don't save enough space, scan your resume looking for what publishers sometimes call *widows*—single words on lines by themselves at the end of paragraphs. These can often be eliminated, saving a whole line, by very slight rewriting of the paragraph. For example, suppose you have the following three items in a job description:

> Recruited, hired, and supervised staff of fifteen analysts.
>
> Increased departmental profitability by average of 10% annually.
>
> Named "Division Manager of the Year" three times in five years.

A total of four words are taking up three full lines here. If you need to cut the overall length of the resume, look for savings here. In the first item, the words "staff of" can probably be eliminated with no loss of meaning. In the second item, the phrase "by average of" can be dropped with minimal sacrifice in clarity, and the "-al" can be dropped from "departmental," too. And in the last item, you can shorten "three times in five years" to "three times." The items now run three lines rather than six:

> Recruited, hired, and supervised fifteen analysts.
>
> Increased department profitability 10% annually.
>
> Named "Division Manager of the Year" three times.

Naturally, you can use the same techniques to cut your resume from three pages to two if necessary.

### One and a Half Pages Is More Appealing than Two Solid Pages

If you decide that you need to run onto a second page (and if that is justified by the length and complexity of your experience and credentials) don't automatically plan on filling up the second page. Instead, try to keep the resume concise enough so that the second page ends one half to two thirds of the way from the top. A resume of two full pages looks long, even perhaps intimidating (remember how overwhelmed and harassed recruiters often feel); by contrast, a resume of 1½ to 1⅔ pages looks quite manageable.

### Avoid Stretching onto a Third Page

Although we don't endorse the one-page myth, we do agree that for almost every job seeker, three pages of resume is one page too many. As is true for so much about the job-seeking process, psychological reasons are at the heart of this. To a busy, harried recruiter, flipping through the pages of a resume and discovering, after two full pages, yet a third with more information to be scanned and digested simply feels excessive.

If your first draft resume runs onto a third page, use the techniques we described above to trim it back onto two pages.

### If a Lengthy List of Special Details Is Essential, Consider Treating It as an Addendum Rather Than as Part of the Resume Proper

For certain types of job hunters, a detailed list of special credentials is appropriate and necessary. If these were included in the resume, it would run longer than two pages—perhaps much longer. The solution is to craft a two-page resume with all the vital information, including a *reference* to the list of special details. Then present those details in the form of an addendum or attachment, stapled together and inserted in your mailing behind the resume itself. The recruiter or employer can examine the addendum in as much or as little detail as he or she prefers while still having a concise two-page resume for most purposes.

The kinds of special credentials that might be listed in an addendum include:

A list of scholarly articles or other writings related to your field of work

Speeches, seminars, or presentations you've given in your career field

For a consultant, a list of clients or projects you've handled

For a contractor, architect, engineer, or similar type of professional, a list of jobs you've successfully managed

> For a creative professional, a list of films, recordings, software programs, or other works you've helped create

You get the idea.

### In Academia, the Longer CV (Curriculum Vitae) Is Usually Appropriate

The traditional CV is still often used by academic professionals—college professors, scientific researchers, fellows in "think tanks," laboratories, foundations, and similar settings. This detailed biographical statement, which includes complete listings of publications, teaching and research interests, professional affiliations, and other credentials, may run anywhere from two to ten pages, depending on the length of your career.

## Techniques for Achieving Conciseness

In addition to the various streamlining tricks we've described above, there are a number of specific stylistic techniques you can use for keeping your resume crisp and concise.

### Delete Pronouns and Articles

*If you're an academic pursuing a nonacademic opportunity—an IT professor applying for a job in Silicon Valley, for example, or an art history scholar applying for work at a fine arts auction house—don't use your academic CV. Instead, craft a one- to two-page resume following the guidelines in this book, turning the features of your academic career into profit-oriented business benefits.*

Pronouns are words like *I, we, he, she, they, me, my, them,* and *their*—words that take the place of nouns (like the names of people). They're highly useful words in most speech and writing—but they can make a resume feel needlessly chatty, even bloated. When you scan your draft resume, look for pronouns that can be eliminated: most can be.

The same is true of articles: *a, an,* and *the.* In the ultra-concise style that's suitable for most resumes, these can and should be deleted, too, whenever that can be done without making the result unclear or very awkward in tone.

Here are a couple of examples of how pronouns and articles can be omitted for greater conciseness:

> I managed a team of 13 engineers that designed a major water treatment facility in the shortest time on record.

After pronouns and articles are deleted, this reads:

> Managed team of 13 engineers that designed major water treatment facility in shortest time on record.

Similarly:

> My division vice-president singled me out at the annual shareholders' meeting as one of the company's "brightest creative talents."

This can be reduced, with a bit of rewriting, to this:

> Singled out by division vice-president at annual shareholder's meeting as one of company's "brightest creative talents."

In each case, the second version sounds crisper and more forceful.

**Delete Needless Words and Phrases.**

**FYI**

*One way to
search for
needless words
and redundancies
is to read your
resume sentence
by sentence,
looking for
phrases that "feel
a little dull" or
that don't excite
any emotion.
When you find
them, circle or
mark them with a
pencil. Then go
back and study
them carefully.
Chances are good
that these
sentences are
"flabby" ones
whose excess
verbiage makes
them feel lifeless
and dull. Start
cutting!*

Most people, including professional writers, find that the first draft of anything they write contains words and phrases that add nothing to the meaning but simply pad the sentences, making them feel bloated and lifeless. As you scan your resume, examine each sentence looking for words that can be eliminated with no loss of meaning. It takes a bit of practice to recognize these, but it's worth doing.

Here are several examples to illustrate what we mean:

Responsible for founding and operating a leading financial risk-management company.

Phrases like "responsible for," "charged with," "selected to," "assumed task of," and "engaged in" are usually unnecessary and can be eliminated with a little deft rewriting. Drop them and simply say what you did, like this:

Founded and operated leading financial risk-management company.

Sometimes, resume writers simply take five to ten words to say something that can be concisely stated in one word—often by using a single effective verb:

Developed programs that have generated positive national media exposure in *Time, Newsweek,* and other publications.

Six words in this sentence can be reduced to the single word "hailed":

Developed programs hailed in *Time, Newsweek,* and other national publications.

Another enemy of conciseness is "hidden redundancy." Redundancy is repetition—saying the same thing twice. Hidden redundancy occurs when a word or phrase needlessly repeats an idea that is clearly implied elsewhere in the sentence:

Currently ranked as the company's top sales producer in the country.

If the writer is the top sales producer, clearly some sort of ranking process is involved. That means the words "ranked as" are unnecessary. By the same token, "Currently" is unnecessary because, if no time frame is stated (and if the job being described in the present job), then it's understood that the time frame is *now.* The sentence could be trimmed to:

Top sales producer in country.

It takes time and practice to develop an "ear" and an "eye" for needless or redundant words and phrases. But it's an important skill that will improve anything you write—especially your resume.

## 5.3  Concise, Clear, Interesting Presentation

**JOHN K. LAUGHLIN**
1515 Kensington Drive
Louisville, Kentucky 85010
(555) 555-3551
Email: jklaughlin@fusco.net

### ADMINISTRATIVE / OPERATIONS MANAGEMENT

**Corporate Management · Finance / Accounting · Project Management · MIS
Inventory Control · Planning / Scheduling · Contracts · Production**

*Progressive leadership contributions to project finance management in multi-company operations. Innovative, resourceful and inventive with ability to identify opportunities and consistently achieve objectives. Offer multifaceted perspective with excellent understanding of today's business conditions, programs and alliances. Seek challenging opportunity to benefit corporate growth.*

### PROFESSIONAL EXPERIENCE

RTY Global Services, Inc. · Louisville, Kentucky
**ADVISOR / LEAD FINANCIAL ANALYST**
1996 - Present

Combine extraordinary market cognizance with a practiced business sense. Lead financial team for System Integration Division of Utility Industry with revenue exceeding $60,000,000. Oversee Revenue, Cost, Expense, Forecasts, P&L, Resource Tracking, Pricing, Reporting and Analysis. Serve as innovative strategist, aggressive troubleshooter and liaison to corporate community.

- *Stay informed on policies, administrative priorities, trends, special interests and other issues to integrate controls, safeguard assets and coordinate activities of Finance Team.*
- *Recognize and define complex financial issues; analyze relevant information; encourage alternative plans and solutions in timely and cost-effective manner.*

Worthington PLC · Louisville, Kentucky
**CONTROLLER**
1995 - 1996

Contributed vision, plans, and management expertise critical to organizational efficiency and business growth. Directed all administrative and financial records systems. Reviewed performance of new systems; evaluated effects on processing; documented workflow; recommended changes to achieve enhanced capability. Monitored cash flow and liquidity.

- *Implemented new technologies; designed and delivered product cost system to track costs by product type and individual system.*
- *Orchestrated Contract Administration, Inventory Control, Asset Management and Capital Expenditures as well as Accounting, Budgeting, Cash Management and Payroll.*

**JOHN K. LAUGHLIN**

Mammoth Services, Inc. · Frankfort, Kentucky
**ADMINISTRATIVE MANAGER / CONTROLLER**
1994 - 1995

Spearheaded planning, organization and coordination of administrative and financial activities for multi-company operation. Utilized superior networking and communications abilities, consistently building strong staff and client relations. Continually evaluated strategies and tracking systems to enhance profits, ensure quality and reduce operating costs. Identified required resources; structures work with others; monitored progress; evaluated outcomes.

- *Conducted project management of cost accounting system, affirmative action programs bidding and estimating system and invoicing programs for federal and state contracting.*
- *Directed day-to-day activities of Accounting, Financial Reporting, Cost Accounting, Budgeting, MIS, Marketing, Personnel, Contract Management.*

Envirotech Inc. · Memphis, Tennessee
**ADMINISTRATIVE / PROJECT MANAGER -** ENVIRONMENTAL SERVICES
1990 - 1993

Utilized business policy development skills and multidisciplined expertise in strategic planning, operational forecasting and budgeting, manufacturing and project costs and human resource development. Oversaw all contract management. Instituted and integrated results-driven company policies and procedures.

- *Championed management of major $20,000,000 project with Ministry of the Environment in Nova Scotia; attained significant extras to contract; enacted extensive change order system.*
- *Effectively used negotiation, persuasion and authority in dealing with others to achieve goals; fostered cooperation, communication and consensus.*

**GENERAL MANAGER -** CHEMCO PRODUCTS DIVISION
1988 - 1990

Demonstrated strong planning, organizing and leadership skills to set priorities for multiples, simultaneous staff actives and consistently meet manufacturing goals, management objectives and quality performance standards for chemical / polymer company. Applied new technologies to organizational needs. Established long-term business alliances and relationships.

- *Ensured effective selection, training, performance appraisal, recognition and corrective action for staff of 24.*
- *Served as Project Manager for multi-million dollar contract with Defense Department; grew production volume; attracted buyer for business unit at substantial profit.*

**EDUCATION**

**Bachelor of Science in Business Administration**
Tennessee State University · State College, Tennessee

REFERENCES AND FURTHER DATA AVAILABLE UPON REQUEST

## 5.4  Concise, Clear Single-Page Presentation

**WILLIAM J. BENNINGTON**
987 Falmouth Road
Hyannis, Masschusetts 23456
(555) 555-6674

### OBJECTIVE

*A challenging position in Public / Media / Political Relations that will fully utilize highly developed persuasive / communications abilities, media writing, and strong organizational / strategic planning skills.*

### PROFESSIONAL EXPERIENCE

**RESEARCH SYSTEMS ADMINISTRATOR**
May 1996 - Present · State Republican Committee
   Direct and perform varied research projects at state level; update, maintain and secure information systems and an archival database of over 1 million articles and 15,000 quotes.  Download newsletter and 500-1000 articles daily from DataTimes.  "Surf" the Internet for timely information.  Liaison between Research Department and states with similar or compatible databases; help troubleshoot computer problems; train and develop staff.

**FIRST TIER ANALYST**
January 1996 - May 1996 · State Republican Committee
   Assist, support, and create comprehensive informational, key-issue database for 1996 statewide elections.  Broad and varied responsibilities encompass all aspects of researching primary source materials regarding regional and national issues for Committee and state party usage; providing senior staff project support for research and communications departments; and assisting in all areas of interdepartmental functions.

**ACCOUNT EXECUTIVE**
June - October 1995 · Cumberland Associates Public Relations
New York, New York
   Provided expert assistance, research and technical support in the marketing of Delishus Sodas.  Designed innovative materials, provided administrative support, composed briefs and press releases.

**STAFF ASSISTANT**
1993 - 1995 · Congresswoman Susan Wanger
Rochester, New York
   Provided daily assistance to constituents in relations with all areas of the government, encompassing immigration, internal revenue service, military and social security.  Created and composed speeches and related materials for Congresswoman Wanger; conducted presentations to large groups on her behalf as necessary; worked extensively on 1994 campaigns.

### EDUCATION & TRAINING

**BACHELOR OF ARTS IN POLITICAL SCIENCE,** 1991
Pierce College - Clinton, New York
*Dean's List · Contributing Editor & Columnist, Political Section: "The Lighthouse" · Founding Member: College Republicans · President: Student Government 1989-1991*

REFERENCES: FURTHER DATA AVAILABLE UPON REQUEST

## 5.5  Concise, Clear Single-Page Presentation

### MARCUS RASKIN
55 Chastity Drive · Parkinson, Missouri 34567
Residence: 555-555-0810 · Work: 555-555-9002

**FINANCIAL SERVICES MANAGEMENT**
*Equities · Mutual Funds · Fixed Income / Government Securities · Index / Equity Opinions*
SOLID STRENGTHS IN PORTFOLIO MANAGEMENT, EXECUTIVE CLIENT
RELATIONS, PRIVACY AND ASSET PROTECTION, RISK MANAGEMENT,
REGULATIONS, AUDIT COMPLIANCE, COMPUTER SYSTEMS AND HUMAN
RESOURCE DEVELOPMENT.

**PROFESSIONAL EXPERIENCE**

*James T. Mailer & Co., Inc.*
BRANCH / SALES MANAGER - St. Louis, MO
1995 - Present

BUSINESS DEVELOPMENT COORDINATOR - St. Louis, MO
1994 - 1995

FINANCIAL ADVISOR / Institutional Management - St. Louis, MO
1992 - 1994

Spearhead strategic planning, portfolio management, business development, client
relations, sales and service team development.  Formulate policy and procedure,
programs and controls to minimize risk and exposure.  Track and analyze the impact of
policy changes and market trends on P&L; make strategic adjustments within proven
financial management guidelines.

- Personally service high net investment prospects and clients; make executive presentations,
synthesizing research and analysis into a combined product and marketing strategy.
- Engaging investment / educational seminars increase new sales and company name
recognition; target prospective customers and community groups.
- Recognized for outstanding revenue contributions with 3 promotions in as many years;
controlled up to $1 billion to assets; expanded St. Louis asset base 68% and customer base
73% in 1 year.
- Product knowledge and financial planning skill, combined with exceptional ability to explain
complex concepts in easily understandable terms, generates repeat customer business.

**LICENSES**
**Series 8 -** Limited Principal; New York Stock Exchange Branch Manager
**Series 7 -** General Securities NYSE / NASD Registered Representative
**Series 63 -** NASD Uniform Securities State Agent

**EDUCATION**

**BACHELOR OF SCIENCE**
College of Texas - Austin, Texas · 1992
*Concentration: Business Management / Marketing · GPA: 3.2*

The previous three sample resumes are all fine examples of the use of concise, crisp, intriguing language. Note how, in Resume 5.3, "John K. Laughlin," every word is made to count; it's hard to identify a phrase that doesn't provide an important piece of information about a skill, achievement, or accomplishment that the resume writer is proud to point to. Every detail sells.

Resume 5.4, "William J. Bennington," and Resume 5.5, "Marcus Raskin," are both single-page presentations that are skillfully crafted to include a lot of vital information in a concise yet clear format.

# JUST THE FACTS

- Your resume should use language that will allow it to stand out from the flood of documents on every recruiter's desk. The techniques used by professional writers can help.

- Every element of your background should be presented in terms of benefits to a potential employer.

- Use reframing to turn apparent negatives into positives.

- Fill your resume with active verbs that capture your energy, creativity, and talent.

- The ideal length for your resume depends on your background, the jobs for which you're applying, and other key factors.

- To achieve a concise presentation, eliminate needless words and phrases, especially pronouns and articles.

# Chapter 6

# Details That Matter: Your Resume from Top to Bottom

## Get the Scoop On . . .

- What information to include on your resume
- Emphasizing your personal strengths
- Disguising your weaknesses
- Tailoring your resume
- Details that make the difference

In Chapter 4, we looked at your resume from a macro perspective—its overall format and structure. Then, in Chapter 5, we applied a micro perspective, studying tricks of style and language that can make each detail of your resume shout "Hire me!" to a prospective employer. Now, with all these techniques in mind, let's consider your resume section by section in methodical fashion. We'll review the kinds of information that should and should *not* be included and the best ways to present each type of data. (Of course, depending on the specific resume format you've selected, the sections to be included in your resume and their sequence may vary. But the general advice given below will apply to almost any resume, regardless of format.)

## NAME AND CONTACT INFORMATION

Your resume should lead off with your name, address, and other contact information—much like the letterhead on a piece of personalized stationery. Seems obvious? Maybe so—yet some job hunters actually forget to include this vital information, without which the rest of the resume is useless.

Here are some specific details about how to handle this routine yet often-botched portion of the resume.

## Your Name

*Does the idea of using a nickname make you uneasy? It shouldn't; America is an increasingly informal society, even at the top levels of business. A nickname is one generally acceptable way in which to express your personality. After all, it didn't hurt James Earl Carter or William Jefferson Clinton to use "Jimmy" and "Bill" when they were "applying" to the voters for the highest office in the land.*

Give your name in the form you most often use. Remember, the resume is *not* a legal document; you're under no obligation to provide a middle initial or name (unless you customarily use one) or a spelled-out first name (when you habitually use a shortened form). If you usually go by the name "Elizabeth," that's fine; if most people call you "Liz" or "Beth," consider using that instead.

One category of job hunter who should *positively* use a nickname if possible is the person with a first name that is long and unfamiliar to most Americans. If you're in this category, you probably realize it by now; people frequently ask you to repeat your name or to spell it out for them, and they may ask about its origin or comment on its unusual quality. Make life a little easier for potential interviewers by presenting your name in an "Americanized" form they'll find simple to pronounce and remember. If your name is "Rabindranath," try "Rob"; if you're an "Edilberto," use "Ed"; if you're "Madnoje," use "Maddie"; if you're "Jongdeok," consider "Jon." You get the idea.

Don't misunderstand. This has nothing to do with disguising or hiding your ethnic origins, nor do we want to discourage pride in your national or family background. Your objective is simply to eliminate any awkwardness for the interviewer who may feel embarrassed over not knowing how to pronounce an unfamiliar name.

Normally, honorifics such as "Mr.," "Miss," "Mrs.," and "Ms." are *not* necessary and should be omitted from your name on your resume. Exception: If you happen to have a "unisex" name or a name whose gender many find unclear, consider adding "Mr." or "Ms." so that the interviewer can't possibly guess wrong (e.g., when leaving a message: "Please have him—or is it her?—call me back"). Examples include names such as "Kim," "Hilary," "Sam," and "Jean," which are attached to both males and females, as well as names most Americans don't recognize, like "Wladyslawa," "Malik," and "Keiko." (Devising an American-style nickname, as we suggested above, can help to solve this problem, of course.)

What about titles such as "Dr." or "Professor" or initials designating degrees earned or other honors, such as "Ph.D." or "M.B.A."? Normally, omit these. If they're relevant to the job for which you're applying, the details should be provided in the education section of the resume; if they're not, you run the risk of appearing pompous, overqualified, or wrongly qualified.

## Contact Information

The basics here include your home address and telephone number. But this is just the beginning. Today, most people have several other ways to be contacted; and with the pace of business constantly accelerating, it's important to make yourself as accessible as possible. More than one job has been lost simply because the number one candidate couldn't be reached in time, forcing the recruiter to shift focus to candidate number two—whose phone number worked on the first try.

Here are some specifics to consider.

**For Your Home Address, Give a Street Address Instead of (or in Addition to) a P.O. Box Number.**
A box number has the feel of "anonymity" or even "secrecy," as though you're trying to obscure your whereabouts—not the impression you want to convey to a potential employer. And some overnight delivery companies cannot serve a P.O. box address. You want that contract offer with the fancy salary to arrive at your door promptly, don't you?

**If You Are Moving or Dividing Your Time Between Two Homes, Give Both Addresses with Dates**

Students making the transition from school to their first jobs and people in the process of relocating may need to list two addresses and phone numbers on their resumes. We recommend presenting both sets of information at the top of the resume, in side-by-side columns, each clearly labeled with dates or other instructions. For example:

Until June 30, 2000

Weekends from June 1, 2000 through October 30, 2000

**If You Are Located Outside the United States, Make the Contact Data Crystal Clear**
If you're a student who has been studying abroad or anyone who has been living or working out the United States, you'll want to give extra thought to presenting your contact data in a way that can't be misunderstood. This includes: Printing your address line by line just the way it should appear on an envelope (since foreign addresses sometimes include elements U.S. residents aren't familiar with); all postal or other codes; and the international country and city code for your phone, just as it would be dialed from an American location. For example, someone located in London might list their phone number this way:

011-44-171-555-5555

The 011 is the international dialing code; 44 indicates Great Britain; and 171 is the British area code for London. Why not make it very easy for a recruiter to reach you, rather than force him to look up the relevant codes in his telephone book?

---

**FYI**

Never *print your resume (or cover letter) on company stationery— job hunting is a personal activity, not work you're doing on company time. This is true even if you happen to be the company president, a freelancer, or consultant now seeking employment elsewhere. Keep your current work status and the job-hunting process separate, as a matter of both ethics and etiquette.*

---

While you're at it, consider adding a line under your telephone number indicating the time difference, like this:

(5 hours earlier than EST)

Again, the idea is simply to make life as easy as possible for your "customer"—the potential employer.

### If Possible, Provide Both a Home Phone Number and a Daytime (Work) Phone Number

Obviously, most recruiters and employers will want to phone you during normal business hours—hours when, if you're employed, you'll probably be at work. Consider your work situation in deciding whether or not it's safe to provide a work number. Do you have sufficient privacy to allow an occasional, brief conversation with a recruiter—or does everyone in your office hear every word of everyone else's phone calls? Is there a reasonably secure system for receiving phone messages—or will you be embarrassed to hear a receptionist shouting out, "Hey, you got a call from that headhunter about the job you're applying for"? The answers to these questions should tell you whether or not it's safe to list a business number.

If you're able to leave both a home number and a work number, label each clearly, like this:

213-555-6434 (home)
213-555-7201 (work)

Or, if it's more appropriate, use designations such as "daytime" and "evenings," or other times.

Note: *Always* include the area code, even if you share the same code with most of the employers you're considering. As phone lines proliferate, so do area codes, and more and more cities and towns now boast two or more codes. Keeping track even of nearby area codes is increasingly difficult; don't take it for granted that a recruiter will know your code.

More and more people now have cellular or mobile phones. If you do, list that number as well. Why not give employers as many ways of reaching you as possible?

Whether you provide one, two, or more phone numbers, try hard to ensure that there's some form of message-gathering capability on each line. An answering machine, voice mail service provided by your local phone company, or a "live" answering service are all fine, so long as they're reliable and you check your messages religiously—preferably twice a day or more.

Don't rely on a friend or family member unless you know they can be counted on to pass along a message promptly and accurately. And if you use voice mail or an answering machine, record an up-to-date and businesslike announcement.

### If Possible, Provide a Fax Number

Nowadays, many companies routinely send messages via fax, including requests for interviews and job offers. You may want to invest in a fax machine for your home phone, especially if the only alternative is an office fax shared by coworkers and lacking in privacy. The price of fax machines has fallen in recent years, and it's not usually necessary to install a separate phone line; most faxes and answering machines can be set up so as to "bounce" messages to the appropriate device automatically.

### If Possible, Provide an E-mail Address

More and more companies now use e-mail as an alternative to phone and fax. It's virtually instantaneous and very quick and convenient. We'd urge you to set up an e-mail address if you don't already have one and to include the address at the top of your resume following your other contact information.

Is it safe to use a company e-mail address for job-hunting messages? That depends. You should never assume that any e-mail message is absolutely secure; the electronic transmission system of the Internet, which involves passing every message through many computers, is easy to crack. So messages whose secrecy is crucial shouldn't be sent electronically.

In addition, courts have held that companies have the legal right to examine the e-mail their employees send on computers provided as part of their working equipment. So, in theory at least, it's quite possible that your boss *may* read any e-mail you receive from a recruiter or potential employer. If you work at a company where job hunting is regarded as "disloyal," you should think twice about using your company e-mail address for job-hunting purposes.

However, at most companies, e-mail is a fairly secure communications medium. (The sheer volume of e-mail most of us receive is one reason: even if company staffers *wanted* to monitor employees' e-mail, who would have time?) If you receive only one or two e-mail messages per day regarding your job search, and if you check and respond to them promptly and then *delete* them from your computer's memory, the chances are good that no one will ever see them. It's a judgment call you'll have to make.

---

**FYI**

*Don't include music, a wacky joke or skit, or any very long or highly personal message on your answering machine. That's fine for friends and family, but in a business context it may make you seem flaky or immature.*

---

**FYI**

*Set up your job-hunting e-mail account with a businesslike or neutral-sounding address. "STHarkness," "Michael145," or "WMurphy" sets a better tone than "LuvGoddess," "Bullsfan," or "SurfDude."*

---

# THE HEADLINE: OBJECTIVE OR SUMMARY

After your name and contact information, your resume needs a "headline"—a succinct statement that quickly describes who you are and where you are headed in your career. Its function is the same as that of the headline in a newspaper or magazine article or an ad: to grab the reader's attention and convince her to read further.

There are two common approaches to the headline: the objective and the summary. We'll explain both.

## The Objective

This is a brief (two- to fifteen-word) description of the kind of job you're currently seeking. It may be very straightforward if you're applying for a job with a traditional title, clear and well-understood duties, and an obvious list of required credentials. In other cases, it may be necessary to craft a more open-ended, even slightly vague objective; for example, if you're not sure about the exact type of job you're seeking or if you're seeking work in a field where functions, titles, and backgrounds vary widely.

Your objective would appear on a line of its own in the resume, preceded by the heading "Objective" in bold, italic, or underlined type. Here are a few examples of objectives, ranging from the highly straightforward to the more open-ended:

> Executive assistant
>
> Psychiatric nurse practitioner specializing in acute care for high-risk adolescent patients
>
> Financial manager for a not-for-profit social service agency or foundation
>
> Business-to-business telemarketing specialist
>
> Marketing position in the software industry

The first of these examples, "Executive assistant," is obviously very brief. This is because the requirements, duties, and responsibilities of an executive assistant are fairly standardized and well-known. No detailed explanation is necessary, and we can assume that the job seeker in this case would be willing to consider an assistant's position in a wide variety of organizations (since no restrictions are specified).

The second example, beginning "Psychiatric nurse practitioner," is much more detailed. Clearly, this job seeker has a rather specific type of position in mind, based on her personal set of educational credentials, interests, and work experience.

The final example, "Marketing position in the software industry," is fairly vague. No specific marketing function (e.g., research, planning, media) is specified, and the industry preference is quite broad. This type of objective might be used by a recent grad who is seeking her first job in business and is open to a range of possible positions.

If you use an objective as the headline of your resume, you'll need to spend some time carefully honing an objective that casts the right size net: one that's neither too broad for your interests nor too narrow. If you've outgrown a particular job level and are unwilling to take a step backward, make this clear in your objective: use a phrase like "Senior public relations manager" rather than the more vague "Public relations professional."

What if you are interested in two or more distinctly different types of jobs? Craft two or more objectives, each accurately tailored to a particular job, and use these to head two different versions of your resume. *Don't* try to save time and energy by devising an *extremely* broad objective that covers all your interests. Chances are such an objective will be so vague that it really says nothing:

> Professional position requiring communication and
> managerial skills.

It's worth the effort to devise separate headlines for each job type you're pursuing. An objective that closely fits the specific job you're applying for sends the message that you and the job are right for each other, suggesting that (if you're hired) your commitment will be solid and your interest level high. Too broad an objective suggests that you are looking for "any old job" and have no real idea what you want to do.

Two other tips about developing an appropriate objective.

**The Objective Should Describe Your *Next* Job, Not Your Dream Job**
Many people, particularly those in the early stages of their careers, have an idea about where they'd like to be five or ten years down the road. In the broadest sense, this is your "career objective." However, the objective on your resume should not indicate the job you hope to have someday but the job you hope to land today. So, for example, if you're a recent grad seeking an entry-level job in a publicity firm, hoping to make it a stepping stone to a job as a publicity director, your objective should read something like this:

> Administrative assistant in a small- to mid-sized publicity or public
> relations firm

Don't worry that this objective will seem "unambitious," as though it implies no greater long-range goals. If your interviewer asks you, "Where do you hope to be ten years from now?" (one of the standard, classic interview questions), you'll have an opportunity then to hold forth about your long-term dreams. To describe your ultimate career goal in the objective section of your resume would imply that this is the job your currently expect to be offered, which would make you seem unrealistic or naïve in your expectations.

**Omit Obvious Qualifiers Such as "Challenging" and "Responsible"**
For some reason, the objective section seems to evoke a host of clichéd and needless qualifying words and phrases from resume writers:

> A challenging position in a dynamic, fast-paced firm where my outstanding managerial and administrative skills will be fully utilized

> A position with potential long-term career growth for a responsible, hard-working individual

Most of the words in these two samples are fundamentally meaningless.

> "A challenging position"? *Any* job may be more or less challenging, depending on your abilities and how much you want to accomplish.

> "A dynamic, fast-paced firm"? Today, almost everyone in business seems to be under intense time pressure; this phrase seems to suggest that you're afraid of not having enough work to stay busy, which will almost surely *not* be the case!

> "Where my skills will be fully utilized": again, this is really up to you.

> "Potential long-term career growth"? No employer can promise what will happen to you in the long term; if your work is outstanding, career growth (i.e., promotions and raises) will happen—if not, it won't.

> "A responsible, hard-working individual"? Of *course* you're responsible and hard-working; if you weren't, you wouldn't even be under consideration for a job. (Would anyone ever describe themselves on their resume as "irresponsible and lazy"? I don't think so.)

Avoid using such clichés on your resume. Instead, describe *specifically* the kind of work you'd like to do and the job for which you're applying. If it matches what the employer has to offer, then the objective has done its work.

### The Summary
Instead of an objective, some job seekers prefer to use a summary statement as their resume headline. The summary is a brief paragraph, 50 to 100 words long, that quickly and enticingly describes your

background, skills, and accomplishments. It may be preceded by the word "Summary" in bold, italic, or underlined type or by a three- to five-word header that ties the information together.

Here are examples of what a summary may look like:

### Summary

Manufacturing manager with 18 years supervisory experience in the chemical and pharmaceutical fields. Managed successful startup of new $30-million plant for world's third-largest chemical company; improved productivity at major pharmaceutical plant by 65% over three years; spearheaded process re-engineering program that halved costs while tripling efficiency in an 18-month period for a leading international consumer products firm.

### Human Resources Professional

Ten years of diverse experience in benefits management, training, and employee development. Created and implemented training programs hailed as among the most innovative in the industry, improving service quality dramatically while reducing turnover and increasing employee job satisfaction by 50%. Skillful management of controversial downsizing program following company merger minimized transition costs and legal fees; praised by company president as "The secret weapon who made this merger work."

Notice how these summaries provide highlights of your finest career achievements, which will be placed in context and explained more fully later in the resume. They also suggest succinctly what special skills and personal qualities you have to offer, making it easy for recruiters or potential employers to picture how you might be able to help them.

Notice, too that these summaries have been written with a minimum of fluff: relatively few adjectives of self-praise ("skillful" in the second example is one of the few exceptions), no vague boasts. Instead, a handful of concrete, specific accomplishments are mentioned, drawn from various phases of your career, with a few impressive statistics and, in one case, a third-party endorsement ("The secret weapon" quote) to enhance the vividness of the picture painted. This kind of style is crucial to making a summary effective.

Finally, notice that in each sample summary, the job objective is strongly implied, though not directly stated. It's pretty clear that the first applicant is interested in a job running a manufacturing plant for either a chemical or a pharmaceutical company while the second applicant is looking for work in the human resources department of a large company, probably one undergoing some kind of major transition or change. As you craft a summary statement, keep in mind the kind of job for which you're applying; word the entire statement so that the qualities you highlight sound clearly applicable to the job you seek.

The psychological advantage of starting with a summary is simple: by focusing at the very *start* of the resume on what you have to offer the employer, you're following one of the basic rules of selling and advertising: emphasizing what's in it for the other guy. By contrast, the objective focuses on what *you* want, which is necessarily of less interest to the person reading the resume. A well-crafted summary can be a powerful enticement that makes the recruiter eager to learn more about you.

## Objective or Summary—Which Is Better?

As with many elements of the resume, there's no hard-and-fast rule as to whether the objective or the summary is preferable. Here are some guidelines to consider.

**Consider Using an Objective . . .**
- If you're a recent grad or have scant work experience.

- If you're on a clear, direct career track where one job leads naturally and inevitably to the next.

- If you're a career changer seeking a specific job as an entry point to a new field.

**Consider Using a Summary . . .**
- If you're a seasoned veteran with an impressive list of accomplishments that anyone in your field will recognize and respect.

- If you're in an industry where a similar background may be applied to a wide range of specific positions.

- If you're a career changer exploring a variety of job options as you seek an entry point to a new field.

When in doubt about which approach is better for you, try both. Draft a job objective and a summary statement and then decide which reads and looks better based in part on the reaction of a trusted friend or mentor, if available.

Beyond this, our recommendation: *If you can craft an impressive summary statement, use it.* This is still a relatively under-used resume tool, one that most job seekers eschew—perhaps because it requires greater thought and creativity than the more conventional objective. Therefore, its potential impact on recruiters is quite powerful. Tap into it if you can.

---

**FYI**

*If you choose to use a summary as your resume headline, try writing it last— after you've crafted the rest of your resume. You'll then be in a good position to take a step back and select the handful of achievements that best summarize what makes you uniquely valuable. (If you try writing the summary first, you'll probably forget some points that really belong there.)*

---

# WORK EXPERIENCE

For most job seekers, this is the next section of your resume. (As we'll explain later, new grads may want to flip-flop this section with their educational backgrounds, leading with schooling rather than work experience.) You'll list the jobs you've held in reverse chronological order, with the most recent job first.

The entire section would be headed, preferably in bold type (and, if you like, all in capital letters), **WORK EXPERIENCE**, **POSITIONS HELD**, or **PROFESSIONAL HISTORY**. (John Bakos of The Bakos Group suggests a fresh fourth alternative: **CAREER TRACK**. It's a nice change from the other, more commonplace phrases, and it has the advantage of suggesting a rational progression to your job choices rather than a merely random collection of positions held.)

For each job, you'll include the following:

### Dates Employed
Provide starting and ending dates, giving either the month and year or simply the year; for example:

> March, 1992–July, 1995

> 1992–1995

Month-and-year dates are generally preferable. However, if you've changed jobs infrequently and have just a few jobs to show with long tenure (three years or more) at each, year-only dates are fine.

### Company Name and Location
Generally, give the full, formal name of the company for which you worked, unless for some reason this would be confusing or misleading. In some cases, for example, the name of a company division is better known, more prestigious, and more widely used than that of the corporation as a whole, which may be considered more of a "holding company" than an operating business. If so, use the better-known name.

On the other hand, in some cases the parent organization is far better known than the division or department, even though employees may rarely refer to it internally. If so, give both the division name and the overall name—for example:

> National Museum of American History, The Smithsonian Institution, Washington, D.C.

For company location, street addresses and similar details may be omitted; the city and state or city and country (if outside the United States) will suffice. In fact, in many cases the state and country may also

*You can use year-only dates to disguise a period of downtime—several months without work, either because of a lengthy job hunt or just because you took some time to chill out between gigs. Naturally, if you're asked in an interview for more specific dates, you should respond honestly. But in an interview, you'll also have the chance to explain in person how and why you knocked off work for a time, an opportunity not afforded by the resume itself.*

be safely omitted; everyone knows where New York, Chicago, San Francisco, London, and Paris are. (If you worked in Paris, *Texas,* however, that's another matter.)

If you worked at two locations, list both; if you worked at three or more, winnow the listing depending on your length of stay, the importance of your accomplishments, and the prestige of the location. For example, suppose you're a financial markets professional whose previous job included stints in Frankfurt and Tokyo as well as several locations in the United States (New York, Dallas, Nashville, Cleveland). Your international experience is interesting, important, and impressive—probably more so than your stops at various American cities. Your company line should read:

> Mammoth Securities, Inc., New York, Frankfurt, Tokyo.

### Title(s) Held

If you held just one job at each company where you've worked, it's obvious how to handle this; each job listing will include a single employer name and a single job title. However, if you changed jobs (hopefully through promotions) while working for one company, you'll need to make a decision as to how to show this on the resume. The options are as follows:

- Combine all the jobs you held at the same company into a single listing.

- Break out the separate jobs under a single company heading.

- Break out the separate jobs under separate company headings.

Suppose you worked for Mammoth Chemicals, Inc. for nine years, holding three positions during that time: research assistant (two years); associate research coordinator (five years); and senior research coordinator (two years). Here's how that same job progression might appear using each of the options we've mentioned.

### Option 1

1990–1999 Mammoth Chemicals, Inc., Princeton, N.J.
> Research assistant, associate research coordinator, senior research coordinator.

### Option 2

Mammoth Chemical, Inc., Princeton, N.J.
> 1990–1992 Research assistant
> 1992–1997 Associate research coordinator
> 1997–1999 Senior research coordinator

**Option 3**

1990–1992 Mammoth Chemicals, Inc., Princeton, N.J.
   Research assistant

1992–1997 Mammoth Chemicals, Inc., Princeton, N.J.
   Associate research coordinator

1997–1999 Mammoth Chemicals, Inc., Princeton, N.J.
   Senior research coordinator

You'd choose among these alternatives based on several factors:

How crowded or skimpy does your resume look? (Obviously the third option takes up the most space, while the first option takes up the least.)

How many other positions do you need to list on the resume?

How important and impressive is each of the jobs? Are there significant accomplishments to describe for each? (If not, consider lumping them together; the cumulative effect is likely to be more impressive than a piecemeal listing.)

And, finally, how closely related are the jobs? (If all the jobs are in basically the same career track, you may want to combine them; if they are very different, say, one job in finance and another in marketing, it makes more sense to break them out.)

> **FYI**
>
> *Of course, this is not a suggestion that you lie or mislead in your resume. Just the opposite: it's a strategy for making sure that your resume* accurately *reflects what you did on a previous job,* despite *what a misleading job title may suggest.*

Another issue that arises regarding this portion of the resume is the question of how to list a job in which you held a title that was inaccurate or misleading. The short answer is: *Don't* feel obliged to reproduce a job title that doesn't clearly describe what you did. (Again, remember: the resume is *not* some kind of legal document!) Instead, either title yourself more accurately (if you can do so without provoking ethical questions) or define your job duties instead of using a title at all.

Here are a couple of examples. My own first job after graduate school was working for a family-owned, for-profit educational company. Although my work actually involved the writing and editing of course materials, my job title (for reasons lost in the misty depths of company history) was "researcher." Later, when I applied for jobs that required skill in writing and editing, I simply listed my job this way:

1982–1984 Little Educational Company, writer and editor

I felt safe in doing this because I knew that my supervisor, whose name I was giving as a reference, would be happy to describe my work as writing and editing—since that was, in fact, what I did. At a larger company with stricter rules and procedures, I might not have felt comfortable doing that.

Here's a different example illustrating another strategy. Suppose you've held a job titled "department secretary" which in fact involved duties that would normally be held by an "office manager": ordering supplies and furniture, collecting and recording employees' timesheets, dealing with inspectors from government agencies, etc. It would be technically correct to list your job title as "department secretary," but it would also be inaccurate, requiring a lot of explanation to convey what you *really* did—if your resume ever got you that chance.

If you knew that you couldn't get away with quietly changing your job title, consider a listing like this:

1993–1995 Little Real Estate Company, office management

Notice the subtle shift here from a *job title* to a *functional description*. You're not claiming to have held the title "office manager," but you are claiming—truthfully—to have performed functions in "office management." This is an effective way to handle the problem of "job mistitling"—a more common problem in U.S. business than many people realize.

### Job Highlights: Duties, Scope, Accomplishments, Honors

For each job listing, after giving your dates of employment, job title, and the company name and location, you'll provide a job highlights section, which describes the work you did and some of your outstanding achievements on the job.

An attractive way to present this information is in the form of a short paragraph (10 to 50 words) describing your duties and the scope of your work, followed by two to five *concise* bullets listing accomplishments and honors you received. Here's a sample:

1993–1995 Counseling supervisor, Village Counseling Center, Smallville, IN

Hired, trained, and managed staff of 9 social workers and psychologists providing family, substance-abuse, and marital counseling in government-funded local clinic setting.

- Administered $1.2 million budget, improving agency's financial performance three consecutive years

- Worked closely with HMO, Medicare, and Medicaid administrators to significantly increase reimbursement approval rates

- Named Smallville's "Outstanding Local Civic Leader" for 1995.

Naturally, it's important to give significant time and thought to selecting your most outstanding and impressive achievements and to describing them vividly. If you haven't already done so, read Chapter 3 and work your way through the worksheet exercises described there. They'll help you unearth the most noteworthy elements of your career experience. And the suggestions in Chapter 5 will help you find the most concise yet powerful ways of describing them.

One more suggestion concerning the work experience section of your resume. If you've pursued two (or more) distinctly different career tracks, consider grouping your jobs, using appropriate subject headings to distinguish the separate portions of your career.

For example, suppose you spent several years in the music industry as a concert promoter, then switched to work in financial management. Now you are seeking a job that will allow you to combine both interests—perhaps by working as a financial manager for a record company. Thus, both career tracks are relevant to your current job hunt, and both need to be equally highlighted. You might group your job listings like this:

**Financial Management Experience**
> 1996–present Job 5, Company E
>
> 1990–1996 Job 4, Company D

**Music Management Experience**
> 1988–1990 Job 3, Company C
>
> 1984–1988 Job 2, Company B
>
> 1982–1984 Job 1, Company A

Note that, within each grouping, the jobs are listed in reverse chronological order, as always. The advantage of this format is that it makes the overall shape of your career crystal clear at a glance and emphasizes the dual nature of your work experience—which is a significant plus for you as a candidate.

# EDUCATIONAL BACKGROUND

In this section, you'll list your educational experiences in reverse chronological order, starting with the most recent degree or program and working backward. For each listing, include the name of the school, its location (unless it's very well known), the subject(s) you majored in, the degree you earned, and the date of that degree.

Include high school if that's your highest level of education or if you're a recent grad. If you've completed college or have been in the workforce for five years or more, you can omit any reference to high school or earlier.

For job seekers with any significant career history, this section should follow work experience. By the time you've been in the workforce for two years or longer, most employers will consider your work history more significant and relevant than your schooling.

However, you should probably flip-flop the two sections if you fall into one the following categories:

### A Recent Grad With Little or No Work Experience that Is Directly Relevant to the Job You're Seeking

Note that a recent grad with significant directly relevant work experience may want to lead with that rather than with education. For example, if you're a recent grad looking for a computer programming job and have two years of impressive part-time work experience with a well-known software company, put this ahead of your educational credentials.

### A Career Changer Who Has Just Completed an Educational Program Directly Related to the New Field.

Suppose you have five years' experience as a restaurant manager but you've decided to become a medical technician and have just earned an associate's degree in that field. Put this credential first since it's more impressive to prospective employers than your years running Cap'n Frank's Seafood.

You should also allot greater space and detail to educational credentials when these are directly related to the job you seek, especially when your work history is of marginal relevance.

Define "education" broadly. College and graduate degrees, of course, belong in this section; but so does any other kind of training or learning that helps to prepare you for the work you're doing or hope to do. Remember to consider all of the following:

- Continuing education programs
- On-the-job seminars, workshops, and training programs
- College or university classes that you audited or attended on a not-for-credit basis
- Classes for professional certification or licensing
- Long-distance, Internet, or correspondence school programs

Any and all of these types of training *may* be appropriate for your resume, depending on their relevance to the job you seek.

Your age and amount of work experience should play a role in your decision about how much resume space to devote to schooling. Educational credentials fade in importance as time passes—particularly in technical fields. Computer training that's five years old is probably no longer relevant and can be safely omitted. And if you've been out of school for ten years or more, you should limit the details you give about your college education; the name and location of the school and the degree earned will suffice.

Here are some other suggestions for maximizing the positive impact of your educational credentials:

### Include any Honors that Reflect Academic Excellence or Other Outstanding Achievements

Like most people, recruiters and potential employers are impressed by brains, so make the most of any truly impressive academic awards or accomplishments you can claim. Each can be listed as a bullet item following the college data, like this:

- Member, Phi Beta Kappa

- Class valedictorian

- Elected president of student body

- Perfect 4.0 grade-point average

- Portion of master's thesis published in *Journal of Comparative Literature* (June 1996)

As with every section of the resume, however, be selective. One or two really powerful credentials will appear more impressive than several lukewarm items.

If you had a college or graduate school GPA below 3.5, don't bother to list it; anything lower than this isn't particularly outstanding. (But consider: if your overall GPA was 3.2, perhaps your average in your major was 3.8. If so, list *that*.)

### If You Lack a Degree, De-Emphasize the Fact
If you attended college for just one or two years, and earned no degree, you should list your college with the years you attended, like this:

Fordham University, New York, 1991–1993.

It'll be obvious to any recruiter that you didn't complete your degree; if it's important for the job you seek, you'll be asked about it.

If you attended college for three years or more (especially if, for health or other reasons, you came close to a degree but failed to finish) you can indicate this in a variety of ways. Here are some suggestions:

Fordham University, New York. B.A. program, completed 108 credits, 1995.

Fordham University, New York. 12 credits short of B.A. degree, 1995.

Fordham University, New York. B.A. degree to be completed next spring.

You can use this last version if you intend to complete the necessary credits within the next year—even if you haven't yet enrolled or are uncertain exactly when the courses you need will be available. If you're offered a job contingent upon your completion of the degree within a given period of time, you'll make it your business to take the needed courses.

### If Your Degree Is Irrelevant, De-Emphasize the Field

In most cases, your educational listings should include the major field of study. However, it's sometimes better to omit that info. If the major is completely irrelevant to the job you're seeking—and particularly if it might make you appear uncertain of your true interests or likely to jump ship as soon as an opportunity in your "real" field becomes available—then simply leave it out.

For example, one recent grad we know (call him Matt) earned a Bachelors degree in chemistry from a prestigious college—then decided to pursue an unrelated career in advertising. Matt's resume says simply:

Bachelor's degree, Williams College, 1998.

But think carefully about whether or not your major field is truly relevant or irrelevant. If Matt were interested in pursuing a job in the advertising department of a pharmaceutical company, then his knowledge of chemistry would be a highly relevant credential.

Furthermore, certain fields have significant prestige even outside their areas of immediate relevance. In the financial world, for example, degrees in the "hard" sciences are highly regarded. (Some of the most brilliant minds on Wall Street are referred to as "rocket scientists"—and some of them literally *were* rocket scientists in a previous career.) So if Matt were pursuing a job as a stock analyst, he might want to list his seemingly irrelevant chemistry degree.

It's a matter of judgment, obviously; get to know the values and biases of the field you're interested in working in and tailor your resume to match them.

## OTHER INFORMATION: WHAT TO INCLUDE, WHAT TO OMIT

### Personal Interests and Activities

There's controversy among career experts over whether or not to include nonwork activities on your resume—hobbies, sports, civic, community, or religious activities. The arguments pro and con run like this:

**Pro**

- No one except the dullest workaholic is defined completely by his or her job. Mentioning some of your personal activities helps the recruiter to get a feeling for the kind of person you are.

- An interest you share with a recruiter may spark a feeling of kinship or camaraderie that can help generate an interview—or provide an opening for ice-breaking small talk on the day you meet.

- Your outside activities may be interesting or impressive, suggesting personal traits that can help boost your candidacy.

- An intriguing item in this heading can help you break through resume clutter on a recruiter's desk.

**Con**

- Most outside activities are not work-related and therefore are likely to serve as more of a distraction from your strengths than a reinforcement of them.

- Your outside interests may alienate a recruiter who doesn't share them.

- If your outside activities sound *too* interesting or time-consuming, they may suggest that work takes a back seat to fun in your life.

- With space at a premium in most resumes, inches devoted to outside activities would be better devoted to more directly relevant information.

The arguments on both sides are sound, as far as they go. Where do we come down on this one? We lean toward the pro side. A section devoted to personal interests and activities can make a positive contribution to your self-marketing effort—*if* it meets certain specific criteria:

- The activities you list should suggest positive personality traits: intelligence and analytical skills; physical and mental discipline; leadership; communication skills; creativity; or social and civic concern.

- The activities should be coupled with *achievements* of some kind.

- The activities should be interesting, unusual, or surprising in some way.

- The activities should not be controversial from any mainstream political, ethical, or religious point of view.

Here are some examples of outside activities that could help strengthen the appeal of a resume.

Nationally ranked backgammon player

*Don't underestimate the importance of boredom in influencing how recruiters will read your resume. After scanning two hundred resumes that seem almost identical, a recruiter may find a seemingly irrelevant, even flaky detail an eye-catching relief from tedium. Just choose carefully so you don't offer any information about yourself that weakens your image as a smart, committed professional.*

Skill at a board game like chess, *go,* or, in this case, backgammon shows analytical skill. Earning a national ranking suggests competitiveness and diligence—qualities valued by many employers.

Climbed Mt. Hood, second-tallest peak in the 48 contiguous states.

Many recruiters are impressed by athletic prowess, which suggests a job candidate who is physically strong, self-disciplined, and psychologically aggressive.

Private airplane pilot with over 300 hours of flying time.

Slightly exotic and challenging sports like hang gliding, scuba diving, and auto racing are likely to intrigue and impress recruiters.

Single-handedly built a 2,500-square-foot log house in the Adirondack Mountains.

Successful completion of a project like this shows remarkable management skills.

Directed two favorably reviewed musicals produced by community theater group.

This accomplishment suggests people skills and creativity.

By contrast, here are some personal activities that probably *don't* belong on your resume.

Hobbies: Video games, surfing the Internet, watching TV.

Although millions of people do indeed spend lots of time in activities like these, listing them on your resume makes you sound like a slacker or a couch potato.

Active in local Democratic [or Republican] party committee

Why run the risk of alienating a recruiter whose political allegiances are opposite yours?

Media spokesperson for local chapter of the American Civil Liberties Union

The ACLU is considered controversial; again, you run the risk of needlessly alienating a recruiter whose views oppose yours. (Similarly controversial: the Christian Coalition, Greenpeace, the National Rifle Association, Planned Parenthood.)

Vestry member, St. John's Episcopal Church

Although the Episcopal Church is about as mainstream as you can get, *any* religious affiliation may be deemed controversial. Your recruiter may be prejudiced against Episcopalians—or against members of any religious group, for that matter.

# OTHER ELEMENTS TO INCLUDE OR OMIT

There are many other items some people choose to include on their resumes. We'll simply run through these and offer our recommendations as to when they are or are not appropriate.

### Certifications and Licenses

*Yes* . . . if you're in a field where these are a customary or essential sign of professional competence, such as health care, engineering, informational technology, law, or accounting. It's not necessary to attach copies of the actual certification documents; simply list your relevant credentials under an appropriate heading near the bottom of your resume.

### Honors and Awards

*Yes* . . . if they're relevant to the job you seek *or* clearly indicate a personal quality that casts you in a favorable light. If you're applying for a job as a writer, for example, and you've received one or more awards for the quality of your writing, you should obviously list them all. On the other hand, you'd list nonwriting honors only if they "worked" according to the same criteria we discussed above in regard to personal interests and activities.

### Professional Organizations

*Yes* . . . if they're relevant to the job you seek. Most businesses have one or more organizations, associations, or clubs, and membership in these indicates that you're active in the field and eager to stay in touch with current trends. If you've ever served as an officer, even at a local level, mention that, like this:

> Member, AICPA; secretary, New York City chapter, 1992–1994

As we discussed earlier, you'll want to avoid listing memberships in groups that are controversial or out-of-the-mainstream. Use your best judgment in deciding which organizations fit this description.

### Speeches, Presentations, Publications

*Yes* . . . if they're at all related to your work or the job you seek. Recruiters and employers are impressed by those who have the guts and talent to speak in public or to publish their writings. If you've done either of these on a handful of occasions, list them under an appropriate

---

**FYI**

*Using a separate attachment is a simple way of providing more information about yourself without making your resume proper appear over-long. It's also considerate, since it gives the recruiter the option whether to spend time reading the additional material.*

---

*Don't exaggerate wildly, but don't undersell your skill level, either. After all, if it turns out that a foreign language is essential to success in a particular job assignment, you can always attend a two-week immersion course to get your (rusty) skills back up to full strength.*

heading near the bottom of your resume. If the list is long (six items or more, say), include it as a separate attachment that you refer to on your resume like this:

Speeches and publications

Over twenty professional presentations and published articles (see attached list)

**Language Skills**

*Yes* . . . if they are relevant in any way to your field of work. In today's increasingly globalized world, foreign language skills are becoming more and more important. Don't assume that the language you studied in high school or college is irrelevant to your next job; the odds are growing that you'll have some opportunity to use it one day, either at home or abroad.

Don't feel you must be completely fluent in a language before listing it. There are many phrases you can use to define accurately your degree of proficiency. For example, consider these options:

Conversant in Italian

Familiarity with German

Working knowledge of Spanish

Basic skill in Japanese

**Personal Data**

*No* . . . unless relevant to the job for some highly specific reason. Such items as your age, your marital status, the number of children you have, and your health status should all be omitted. They *don't* directly affect your ability to do the job; they're nobody's business but your own; and they may trigger prejudices on the part of recruiters, which can only work against you. (Note: in most instances, it's actually *illegal* for employers to consider any of the above in making a hiring decision—a further reason to omit them.)

*Every rule has its exceptions. One recruiter tells of an applicant—a woman returning to the workforce—who, when asked what she'd been doing for the previous ten years, replied, "I raised three husbands." At the recruiter's suggestion, she added this line of "personal data" to her resume, where it provoked many chuckles—and probably garnered a couple of interviews she otherwise might not have gotten.*

If, for some reason, one of these items is actually a relevant, positive factor in your job application, find an appropriate way to mention it either on the resume or in your cover letter. For example, if the fact that you are young, single, and not tied down to a family could be an asset for a particular job, you might include a sentence like this in your cover letter:

I'll bring a youthful energy and enthusiasm to your firm, and for the right assignment I'd be willing to consider relocating anywhere in the country.

Otherwise, simply leave personal data off your resume. For similar reasons, don't attached a photograph of yourself (again, unless your looks are directly relevant to the job—you're applying for work as a model or actor).

### Salary History

*No* . . . by providing this information on your resume you can only provoke a premature salary negotiation, which does *not* work in your favor.

What if you're responding to a job advertisement that specifies "Include salary history"? In that case, you *must* provide the information asked for. However, include salary data in the cover letter, not on the resume itself, and couch it so as to maximize your past and current earnings. For example, mention only the *last* (presumably highest) salary you earned at a particular employer, and include the value of bonuses, stock options, a company car, and other any dollar-value perks as part of an overall "compensation package" figure. This will put you in the best possible bargaining position once a job offer is made.

*You have the greatest leverage to negotiate a good salary offer when you know that the employer wants to hire you. It's to your benefit to avoid discussion of salary until you reach that point.*

### References

*No* . . . generally, these are provided *after* a successful interview, as part of the follow-up process leading to a job offer. Don't include references on the resume or in an attachment; instead, have the names and phone numbers in reserve and be ready to provide them after you pass the interview hurdle.

Is it necessary to include a line on the resume stating "References available on request"? Not really; that references are available is a universal assumption in the world of job hunting. But many job seekers include this as the final line of their resume, almost as if to indicate "This is the end of the resume." If you want to include it, fine. But it's not essential.

## ENDORSEMENTS

Endorsements or testimonials from credible experts who know and like your work are a fabulous way to enhance your resume. This is one of the most underused yet powerful self-advertisement strategies we know. We urge you to try it.

Here are some samples to illustrate how a third-party endorsement may look:

> Described by Mammoth Industries' CEO Jay Barker as "our company's single most effective salesperson . . . an incredible dynamo."

> "Manager of the Year" citation read, in part, "Developed the most innovative marketing management program in the history of our industry."

Senior vice-president Susan Vaughan wrote, "Your work on the Richmond account probably doubled the value of a $10-million project."

Note the features that make these endorsements work. The sources are credible, respected individuals—known, if not by name, at least by company and position. And a few key words or phrases are quoted—if necessary, linked by ellipses (. . .) , just as you see done in movie ads or on book jackets ("Five stars . . . a blockbuster!").

Naturally, you'll need to request the permission of the person you want to quote. (All it usually takes is a phone call.) And cite that person's words precisely, within quotation marks, as shown above: a verbatim quote is far more impressive and powerful than a paraphrase.

In search of endorsements to use, cast your mind back to any laudatory letters or memos you've received, speeches or awards ceremonies in which your work was praised, articles in company newsletters or magazines that mentioned you, or even any memorable off-the-cuff comments your boss may have made at a staff meeting. Gather two or three great quotes about yourself from sources like these and include them on your resume, either in a separate section at the end (headed "Endorsements" or "Testimonials") or as bulleted items under the relevant job headings.

It's no accident that ads for everything from laundry detergent to political candidates make frequent use of third-party endorsements. They're a powerful persuasive tool. Make use of this technique on your resume if you can.

# JUST THE FACTS

- Each section of your resume should be carefully planned, written, and edited to have the maximum positive effect on recruiters and employers.

- Organize the facts about your work history and education to emphasize your strengths and disguise or obscure your weaknesses.

- In deciding whether or not to include specific details about yourself, always ask: Does this fact strengthen or weaken my image as a talented, dedicated professional?

- Consider quoting third-party endorsements to enhance the luster of your skills and accomplishments.

# Chapter 7

# Effective Resume Design

---

## Get the Scoop On . . .

- Using your word-processing software to craft an attractive resume
- How to select the best fonts for your resume
- Designing your ideal resume
- Selecting the best paper and printing techniques

---

How your resume looks is important—though not for aesthetic reasons. Unless you're a graphic artist, no potential employer is going to expect a work of art from your resume. Instead, the look of your resume is important because of the subliminal message it sends about you. A resume that's attractive and easy to read conveys the message that you are well-organized, logical, and smart—the sort of impression you're eager to make.

Fortunately, the principles of effective resume design are simple to learn and apply. We'll explore them in this chapter.

## DESIGN THAT COMMUNICATES

The purpose of your resume, of course, is to attract positive attention to your job qualifications—to serve, as we've said, as a powerful advertisement for you. Thus, the single most important criterion of good resume design is *clarity of communication*. Your resume must:

- Be pleasant and easy to read.

- Contain sections that are clearly separated from one another.

- Visually highlight the most important elements of your background.

- Capture key concepts in concise, easy-to-grasp paragraphs.

- Convey your strengths as a job candidate in a single glance.

The specific tips and strategies that follow are all designed to help you achieve these goals.

## Using Word-Processing Software

A resume produced on a computer is today's standard. The typewritten resume, acceptable just a few years ago, no longer makes the grade: it suggests that the job seeker is out of touch with current technology, a disqualifier for most contemporary careers.

If you're a recent grad or have held an office job in the past few years, you're probably familiar with computerized word processing and may have a favorite software package—Word, Word Perfect, or another choice. But if the computer revolution has somehow bypassed you, now is the time to catch up. Find a word-processing class at your local high school or college or hire an expert for an hour or two of tutoring. It's an important skill, not only for creating your resume, but for most careers today.

If you don't own or have access to a personal computer, you may be able to use one at a local office service center or stationery store; many Kinko's™ locations, for example, will rent you the latest equipment by the hour. College and public libraries sometimes offer similar services.

However, it's not enough to type your resume on a computer. You need to know how to use the formatting and design tools that are built into virtually all word-processing software packages. We're not talking about the sophisticated techniques that graphic artists use for desktop publishing, but such basic yet important techniques as:

- Choosing an appropriate style and size of type for each element of your resume.

- Using the flush left, flush right, and centering commands to position lines of type.

- Using italic, boldface, and small-cap type variations to emphasize key words or phrases.

- Knowing how to delete, insert, copy, and move blocks of text.

- Changing margins, inserting page breaks and page numbers, and using other basic formatting commands.

- Using global search, search-and-replace, spell-check, and other automatic editing techniques.

- Previewing the appearance of the printed document on your computer screen.

If you're unfamiliar with any of these word-processing techniques, you ought to learn them. If you don't, you may find creating your resume with your computer more frustrating, difficult, and time-consuming than with an old-fashioned typewriter. For example, if you aren't aware of the centering command, you may use the spacebar to place a heading approximately in the middle of the page. But if you later decide to rephrase the heading, you'll have to recenter by hand—a frustrating waste of time.

If you master the techniques we've listed, you'll find that you can save hours while producing a highly attractive and reader-friendly document. Break out your word-processing manual, check out your program's "Help" feature, or buy one the dozens of commercially published computer guides available at any bookstore. The time you invest in your software education will be a good investment.

# TYPE STYLES AND SIZES

The computer revolution has given every amateur typist the ability, once reserved to professional designers, to choose from a variety of type styles and sizes. When creating a resume, this flexibility is helpful in several ways. If you're short on space, a small, tight type face can help you squeeze a lot of information readably onto the page; conversely, a more expansive type style can help disguise a slightly skimpy resume. Computerized design can also help you craft a resume that matches the style of the job you're seeking: modern, classic, elegant, offbeat, creative, conservative, or what-have-you.

## Choosing a Type Face

*Originally, a font was an assortment of metal type all of one size and style, from which the old-fashioned typesetter would select letters by hand, one at a time. The word* font *comes from the Latin* fundere, *"to pour"; at one time, molten lead was poured into a mold to create each letter of type.*

Most word-processing programs offer a wide range of type faces, often called *fonts*. Many are not appropriate for resumes—they're better suited for use in newsletter headlines, on posters, in greeting cards, or in other contexts. But most word-processing programs offer at least six to ten fonts that are attractive and appropriate for resumes.

There are two main categories of fonts, known as *serif* and *sans serif*.

A *serif* font is one which has little slash marks, called serifs, at the end of each letterstroke. This book is set in a serif font. Look at a letter like capital I or T, and notice the small horizontal line at the base of the large upright stroke; that's a serif. Most of the other letters in a serif font are marked by similar strokes.

Traditionally, serif fonts have dominated graphic design, and to this day most texts are set in serif fonts, including most books, newspapers, and magazines. If you work in a conservative industry (banking, medicine, brokerage, government, or insurance, for example), or if you want your resume to convey a sense of "classic" style, use a serif font.

The word *serif* comes from the Dutch *schreef*, meaning "stroke," which in turn comes from the Latin *scribere*, "to write." The use of serifs originated in imitation of the finishing strokes made by wood and stone carvers when incising letters on plaques or walls; they continue to be used today because of custom and for aesthetic reasons.

As we'll discuss in more detail later in this book, many employers and recruiters today use computer scanners to absorb and analyze the contents of resumes. Therefore, one consideration in choosing a font for your resume is the relative ease and accuracy with which various fonts may be scanned. Serif fonts that scan particularly well are Garamond and Bookman. Both have well-spaced, standardized letters that rarely touch or overlap. Times Roman and Courier are also fairly easy for scanners to read. Here are samples of each of these fonts:

- Garamond
- **Bookman**
- Times Roman
- `Courier`

Each of these fonts has its own style. Garamond, for example, is rather literary or artistic in feeling; Times Roman has a clear, functional, and businesslike appearance, appropriate for use in a serious newspaper (the purpose for which it was originally designed); and Courier strongly resembles the printing produced by an old-fashioned typewriter. You'll want to look at sample documents printed in each of these fonts to determine which may be closest to your style and that of the industry in which you wish to work.

A *sans serif* font is one that lacks the end slashes. (*Sans* is French for "without.") Here are some examples of popular sans serif fonts:

- Arial
- Century Gothic
- Trebuchet MS
- Verdana

As you can see, sans serif fonts have a cleaner, more modern look than serif fonts, and the graphic designers who first made serif fonts popular in the twentieth century considered their "streamlined" style appropriate to our fast-moving age.

You'll find sans serif fonts in dozens of applications today, including billboards and posters, traffic signs, packaging labels, and TV or Internet graphics, as well as in the headlines and chapter titles of books, magazines, and newspapers. However, sans serif fonts are still rarely used for lengthy texts.

One reason is that studies show most readers find sans serif fonts harder and slower to read than serif fonts. This is apparently due partly to the greater familiarity of serif fonts (most children learn to read using primers set in traditional serif fonts) and partly due to the fact that the serifs help give the individual letters more distinctive profiles, making them easier to grasp at a glance.

Our advice: When in doubt, choose a serif font for the main body text of your resume. It's a conventional choice, but one that is safe and generally acceptable, whereas sans serif fonts are slightly harder to read and strike some people as ugly.

## Mixing and Matching Fonts

As you've undoubtedly noticed, most publications, including books, magazines, and newspapers contain more than one font. You can also mix fonts in your resume—to distinguish sections, to set off headings, to create a varied texture that is aesthetically attractive, and to highlight key words, phrases, and sentences.

However, matching fonts can be tricky; it's easy for an amateur designer to cobble together a computerized document with several fonts that looks jumbled, confusing, and inelegant. We refer to this as the "ransom-note syndrome."

Nonetheless, it's important to spend some time experimenting with fonts to find a look that expresses your personality appropriately. Here are a few specific tips to guide your experiments:

- For design purposes, distinguish between your resume's *body text* and the *headings*. Headings include section titles and your name at the top. It's appropriate to handle these in different styles.

- Pick one font for the body text and use it consistently throughout your resume.

- Consider using a serif font for the body text and either a serif or sans serif font for the headings.

- Use **bold face,** *italic,* and SMALL CAPS variations of your body text for headings.

- Avoid underlining, which often produces lines of text that are hard to read and may not scan accurately.

- Try using bold face to highlight key words (such as impressive company names or dollar amounts linked to accomplishments), like this:

    Developed a divisional reorganization plan that saved **General Electric** over **$30 million.**

## Choosing Type Sizes

Word-processing programs generally use the traditional typesetter's point system for measuring the size of a font's printed letters, or type. In this system, 72 points is equivalent to one inch on the printed page; the most common type size for business correspondence and reports is 12 points—one-sixth of an inch in height.

You may find that you need to make the body text of your resume somewhat smaller than 12 points, particularly if the contents are lengthy. Here's our recommended procedure for making smart choices about type size:

- Start by formatting the entire resume using 12-point type. (You should be able to do this using a single command in your word-processing software.)

- Set the page margins at one inch (top and bottom) and 1.25 inches (left and right). Use one blank line to separate resume sections (e.g., to separate "Work Experience" from "Educational Background").

- Use your word processor's preview feature to see how the resume will fit into one or two pages.

- If you are crafting a two-page resume, be sure to insert your name and the page number at the top of page two. Also make sure the pages break at a natural division—for example, between two separate job listings.

- If the resume runs long, try reducing the left and right margins to one inch.

- If it still runs long, try reducing the type size to 11 points. (Again, a single command should do this.)

- If it still runs long, look for ways to trim words and phrases to eliminate extra lines of type (as suggested in Chapter 5).

- If the resume still runs long—and if you can't find any way of cutting the contents to achieve your desired length—try using 10-point type.

SMALL-CAP TYPE, AS SHOWN IN THIS SAMPLE, IS RELATIVELY LITTLE-KNOWN AND UNDERUSED. *As the name suggests, it's made up of capital letters slightly smaller than normal caps. A heading combining ordinary initial caps with small caps has an attractive, slightly unusual appearance.*

If you do use 10-point type, print out and study a sample to make sure it's easily readable. Whether or not 10-point type works will depend on the specific font and on such other variables as the average length of the words and lines of type you use. Never use type smaller than 10 points.

In the (less likely) event that your resume runs short, try for a balanced-looking full page by inserting extra space between sections. Don't switch to a type size larger than 12 points; larger letters tend to resemble those in a children's book, which undermines your attempt at an impressive professional presentation.

So much for the body text of your resume. For the headings, you may want to stick with the same type size as for the body text, only in a bold face, italic, bold italic, or small cap variant.

For your name at the very top of the resume, use a larger type size. If the body text is 12 points, consider using 14 or even 16 points for your name, with your contact information (address and phone number) in normal body text size. Here's a sample, using 16 point bold for the name and 12 point type for the contact information—all in the serif face known as Garamond:

# Colin B. Hennessey

38–19 Bay Boulevard
Flushing, New York 11109
555-555-5620

Use the centering command to position these lines of type in the middle of the page. That's the preferred design treatment for your name and contact material, and other headings often look best centered, too.

You'll notice that we've used the word "experiment" several times. A major benefit of the computer as a resume-crafting tool is the ease with which you can test different design decisions: larger and smaller type, differing fonts, the use of bold and italic, and so on. Take advantage of this feature

Resumes 7.1 and 7.2 illustrate two successful approaches to the font choices you'll face.

Resume 7.1, "Pedro Anastazio," is a clear and attractively designed resume using a single sans serif font (known in Microsoft Word as Arial). Notice how clean and modern the sans serif text looks; it's an appropriate design decision for Anastazio, who works in the high-tech field of medical technology sales.

The sans serif font also works in this instance because the resume consists almost entirely of relatively short phrases, most of them bulleted. If the resume included full paragraphs of text, the sans serif font might be somewhat uncomfortable to read.

The body text is in 11-point type—necessitated by the relatively large amount of information to be included. Anastazio's name is in 14-point bold; the profile heading "INTERNATIONAL MEDICAL SALES / SALES MANAGEMENT" is 14-point regular; and most of the other headings are in 12-point type. By using a mixture of bold face and a *very* limited amount

## 7.1  Clear, Attractive Use of Sans Serif Font

### PEDRO ANASTAZIO
900 Grove Street, Tuscany, FL  33333
Home: (555) 555-3898  Cellular: (555) 555-6780  E-mail: panastazio@pedro.com

## INTERNATIONAL MEDICAL SALES / SALES MANAGEMENT
Territory/Account Development...Market Expansion...Product Introduction...Strategic
Planning...Relationship Building...International Relations...Distributor Networks...
Inventory Control...Training...Supervision...Presentations...Policies & Procedures

### Value Offered

- Trilingual in English, Spanish, and Italian
- Extensive sales background in anesthesia, critical care, monitor systems, prosthesis, and cardiovascular disposable products with impressive record of accomplishment
- Provide hands-on product instruction and guidance to O.R. physicians during surgical procedures
- Certified X-ray and Lab Technician
- Develop and conduct in-service training seminars for medical professionals and para-professionals in large hospitals
- Build excellent rapport with customers and distributors, as well as loyal customer base
- Manage multiple tasks and responsibilities simultaneously and effectively
- Excellent problem-solving, decision-making, planning, analytical, organizational, communication, and follow-through skills
- Work well independently or as part of a team

### Professional Experience

### AREX, INC.--Miami, FL
**Latin American Sales & Marketing Manager**                     1994 to present
- Responsible for one-half domestic and one-half foreign markets
- Held best record of performance in the region with 3 out of 4 objectives being achieved
- Achieved largest syringe pump sale of the year
- Southeast's #1 "Sales Star" Award - 1998
- Transitioned floundering territory into profitable one
- Grew Latin America into important business segment for the company
- Received "Superior" performance summary rating

Pedro Anastazio                                                page two

**LABCO, INC.--Ft. Lauderdale, FL**
**Territory Manager**                                          1990 to 1993
- Ended 1993 at 165% of sales objective
- Sales and promotion of cardiac monitors to cardiovascular surgeons and anesthesiologists
- Provided in-services to OR-ICC and CCU-ER personnel
- Trained employees from Central and South America

**FUTURA MEDICAL, INC.--Atlanta, GA**
**Territory Manager**                                          1984 to 1990
- "Sales Representative of the Year" - 1986
- Member, President's 100% Club 5 out of 6 years
- #1 in nation in sales, 1988-1990
- Conducted in-services to O.R. personnel (ICC, CCU)
- Trained anesthesiologists and cardiovascular surgeons in the professional utilization of cardiovascular products
- Trained dealers' employees

**Education/Training**

**BACHELOR OF SCIENCE DEGREE**
Union University, Plains, GA
Major: Psychology  Minor: Business Administration

**CERTIFICATES OF COMPLETION**
Biscayne School of Medical & X-Ray Technology, Miami, FL
Biscayne School of Medical Technology, Miami, FL

Internship, O.R. and ICU Training, Jackson Memorial Hospital

**Xerox Learning Systems**
Account Development Strategies ; Professional Selling Skills II

**Professional Memberships**

National Latino Business Board
Florida Biomedical Association
Miami Chamber of Commerce

of underlining, Anastazio clearly sets apart the headings and the various sections of the resume while retaining an overall feeling of design unity.

Resume 7.2, "Dominique Lindisfarne," attractively blends two fonts—one sans serif, the other serif. The body text is set in 11-point MS Sans Serif, while the headings are set in two different sizes of Times New Roman bold—mostly 12-point, with 14-point for Lindisfarne's name at the top. Remember, two fonts are generally all you should try to blend in a single resume; adding a third font to Lindisfarne's resume would probably push this design over the edge into the ransom-note syndrome.

# OTHER ELEMENTS OF RESUME DESIGN

*Experienced graphic designers know that the single most crucial element in creating clear and readable documents is* blank space. *Try this experiment: pick from your shelf any book you find attractive. Select a page, and use a ruler to measure its height and width. Then measure the height and width of the area covered with type. Finally, calculate the area of the page and the type area by multiplying the height by the width of each. You'll probably find that the page is almost* half *blank space! Be generous with blank space in your resume, too.*

## Separating Resume Sections

As we've already seen, it's important to separate the sections of your resume clearly. (Among other benefits, this makes it easy for a reader to quickly find any topic he or she is interested in.) One way of doing this is through careful choices—using a second font or a variation of the body font to create distinctive section headings.

Another tool for separating the sections of your resume attractively is the use of blank space between sections. In fact, blank space, though seemingly "wasted," is actually an important factor in the overall appearance of your resume.

Start by leaving a line of blank space between sections—simply skip a line as you would when typing. If you find you're short on space, you can reduce the size of the blank space. If you reduce several blanks from 12 points to 4, 6, or 8 points, you can fit an extra two to three lines of text onto your resume page with no loss of clarity.

By contrast, if you find that you have more room than you need, try widening the gaps between sections. Giving your resume "air to breathe" will make it more attractive.

Borders made up of lines, rules, rows of dots (periods), or other symbols can also be used to separate sections of the resume. If you go this route, keep it simple. Use the same style of border throughout the resume, and make sure it's not so bold or heavy as to visually overwhelm the lettering above and below. The simple double rule below the name of "Diane Halsted" in Resume 7.3 is a good example of an attractive device that's not heavy-handed or overdone.

## Some Sample Resume Layout Ideas

The Diane Halsted resume (Resume 7.3) also illustrates one slightly unusual but quite effective layout technique: presenting *all* the

## 7.2  Blend of Sans Serif and Serif Fonts

### Dominique Lindisfarne
1117 Fountainbleu Street
Santa Barbara, California 60000
(555) 555-8023
pager: (555) 555-1024

#### Objective

Network Specialist

#### Summary

3 + years consulting experience in the information technology fields, providing businesses with technical expertise in the areas of  Network administration, installation, configuration and troubleshooting of Windows NT and Novell servers. Energetic and dependable contributor with strong problem solving abilities and able to respond to a changing environment and maintain a focus on business values and customer satisfaction.

#### Certifications

Cisco Certified Network Associate · MCP + Internet
Novell Netware Administrator · A+ Computer Technician

#### Professional Experience

**Third Level Technical Support**
1998 - present
California Merchants' Bank · Santa Monica, California
**Responsibilities included:**
- Supported a 7,000 End User environment, performed installs and upgrades to Windows NT
- Installation and configuration of Netscape Navigator and Internet Explorer for Internet access
- Configured TCP/IP, DNS, WINS settings, troubleshoot connectivity problems
- Installation and configuration Shiva Remote communication software on laptop computers
- Installation, configuration and troubleshooting of  Rumba mainframe Software
- Installation, configuration and troubleshooting of Lotus Notes

**Technical Support**
1997 - 1998
Peoples' Bank · The Pelham Agency · Locopoco, Inc. · Santa Barbara, California
**Responsibilities included:**
- Peoples' Bank - Focused on Y2K Software testing; installed testing tools on client PC's; instructed End Users on how to remediate their mission critical Excel spreadsheets and Access databases for any potential Y2K date related issues.
- The Pelham Agency - Scheduled backups and restoration of data using Arcserve, monitor network utilization.
- Locopoco, Inc. - Assisted clients  with the successful migration of Novell Netware servers to Windows NT.  Troubleshoot technical issues in a multi-platform environment, Intranetware, Novell Netware, Windows NT and Lotus Notes, MS Exchange.

Dominique Lindisfarne                                                                          Page 2

**Technical Support**
1996 - 1997
Computer Tech, Inc. / Googol & Company / Friendly Information Services · Santa Clara,
California
**Responsibilities included:**

- Computer Tech, Inc. - Trained students in A+ computer repair, Windows 95, MS Office,
  Internet basics.
- Googol & Company - Supported a 1,000 user environment, logged in trouble calls, order new
  equipment and software for Users.  Help desk support in Windows 3x, Windows 95,
  Windows NT. Troubleshoot hardware and software issues,  provided  installation and
  configuration of multi-media kits, hard drives, floppy drives.  Performed upgrades and
  software installation.
- Friendly Information Services -  Respond to Users trouble calls, the installation and repair of
  various hardware components, hard drives, mother boards, CD-ROMs, sound cards, set up
  network printers. The maintenance of computers, printers and peripherals. Performed
  software Installs and upgrades.

Freelanced Administrative Services · Santa Cruz, California
1993 - 1995
(CTI, Ecco, Word Smith)  Providing Administrative, and Word Processing Support
Services to businesses, which includes medical, legal, banking and corporate firms.
Benton, Barton, Burstein and Bailey, Inc. · Santa Rosa, California
1985 - 1993
Word Processor
Generated correspondence and reports.  Updated computerized files, heavy telephone contact.

## Technical Knowledge

**Software Installed and Configured:**

- Windows 98, Microsoft Office 97, Lotus Notes, Shiva, Rumba, PC anywhere
- Norton anti-virus, McAfee, Service Packs, Drivers, Diagnostic utilities

**Hardware:**

- Cisco Routers setup skills, working knowledge of hubs, switches, Ethernet and Token ring
  environments. Installs of  NIC and cabling components, Cloning with Ghost

**Installed and Configured:**

- RAS, Configure dial-up networking on laptop computers

**Operating Systems:**

- Windows NT Workstation and  Server 4.0,  Internet Information Server 4.0
  Intranetware 4.11, Novell Netware 3x, Windows 95, Windows 3x, MS-DOS 6.22

## Education

Computer College of the West · Santa Felipe, California
**Specialization**: Cisco Certified Network Associate training
Cisco setup skills, configuring WAN protocols, frame relay, ISDN,
FDDI, ATM, routing protocols, OSPF, IGRP, RIP IP

Computer Training Center · Santa Fe, New Mexico
**Specialization**: PC Technician w / Hewlett-Packard laser repair

Northern Training Institute · Santa Claus, Minnesota
**Specialization**: LAN administration, technologies and protocols

## 7.3  All-Bullet Design

### DIANE HALSTED, M.P.A., R.R.A.

505 West 39th Street · Billings, Montana 78909 · 555-555-0876

**PROFILE**

19 years experience in health information management in the following academic medical centers: Montana Methodist Hospital, St. Joseph's Hospital, Evanston Medical Center, Mount Morris Medical Center, Windy City Hospital Center, Seven Oaks Hospital and with Medico System's Strategic Services Group.

**ACCOMPLISHMENTS**
- *Enhancing revenue through DRG Reviews and reducing accounts not final billed.*
- *Maintaining compliance with JCAHO Information Management Standards.*
- *Implementation of health information continuous quality improvement programs.*
- *Conducting medical record department computerization assessments.*
- *Reengineering processes to improve morale, productivity and customer service.*

**PROFESSIONAL EXPERIENCE**

**Montana Methodist Hospital** · Billings, Montana
DIRECTOR OF MEDICAL RECORDS · 9/98 - Present
- Redesigned workflow processes, cross-trained staff and established productivity monitoring systems.
- Developed an MRD Compliance Program to address OIG issues and APCs.
- Maintained work plans to address HBOC implementation issues.
- Marriott customer service facilitator and hospital-wide trainer.
- Instituted a multi-disciplinary clinical pertinence review process.
- Conducted ambulatory record keeping assessments and standardized operations.

**Medico Systems Corporation** · Billings, Montana
SENIOR CONSULTANT · 4/97 - 9/98
- Project management experience implementing SMS systems and training hospital staff on new methods and procedures.
- Performed operational reviews and cost/benefit analyses to implement SMS Systems.
- Conducted medical record imaging assessments.
- Assessed MPI issues for an enterprise-wide duplicate record number clean-up and implemented policies and procedures to maintain the integrity of the MPI.
- Developed ambulatory care documentation criteria to address NCQA, HEDIS, JCAHO standards and for implementing the ambulatory computerized record.

**St. Joseph's Hospital / Catholic Medical Center** · North Falls, Montana
HEALTH INFORMATION ADMINISTRATOR · 5/95 - 4/97
- Implemented a billing optimization process and the inpatient universal chart order.
- Improved correspondence turnaround.
- Developed an MRD Redesign / Workflow Improvement Plan and improved morale.
- Formulated and analyzed a Medical Records Department's Customer Survey.

**DIANE HALSTED, M.P.A., R.R.A.**                                                Page 2

**Evanston Medical Center - North Division** · Evanston, Illinois
DIRECTOR OF MEDICAL RECORDS · 7/92 - 4/95
- Developed a manual on Computerization of the Medical Records Department.
- Rewrote the MRD's Policy and Procedure Manual.
- Cited by JCAHO Surveyor as an example of excellence with MRD and Committee Standards.
- Implemented a MRD Quality Improvement Program.
- Team Leader for Bed Tracking & $O_2$ Utilization Teams.

**Seven Oaks Hospital** · Chicago, Illinois
MEDICAL RECORDS CONSULTANT · 6/90 - 7/92
- Provided advise to hospital staff on medical records issues.
- Assisted administration with preparation for a JCAHO survey.
- Conducted record reviews and in-service education sessions for medical records staff, medical staff, and ancillary department staff.
- Revised the MRD's Policy and Procedure Manual.

**The Mount Morris Medical Center** · Chicago, Illinois
DIRECTOR OF MEDICAL RECORDS · 7/88 - 12/89
- Managed a staff of 95 bargaining and 30 non-bargaining employees.
- Implemented an MRD Quality Improvement and Performance Appraisal Program.
- Enhanced revenue with a DRG review and education program.
- Prepared for JCAHO and State D.O.H. Article 28 surveys.
- Revised the MRD's Policy and Procedure Manual.
- Assisted the Internal Audit Department to improve the MRD's operations.

**Windy City Hospital Center** · Chicago, Illinois
ASSISTANT DIRECTOR OF MEDICAL RECORDS · 9/82 - 6/88
- Established a concurrent coding and analysis program.
- Improved the Case Mix Index and optimized cash flow.
- Enforced 24 hr. operative report dictation requirement, reducing delinquent records.
- Implemented a Quality Assurance Program and Clinical Pertinence Reviews.
- Coordinated JCAHO, N.Y.S. D.O.H. Surveys and PRO Audits.
- Developed a Coding Manual and revised the MRD Policy and Procedure Manual.

**EDUCATION**

MASTERS, PUBLIC ADMINISTRATION, HOSPITAL POLICY / MANAGEMENT, 1992
Northwestern University, Evanston, Illinois
**Certificate in Financial Management,** HFMA, 1987
University of Chicago, Chicago, Illinois
BACHELOR OF SCIENCE IN MEDICAL RECORDS ADMINISTRATION, 1982
Henthorn College, Chicago, Illinois
**Registered Record Administrator (R.R.A.)** - 1983

**AWARDS**
- Sterling's Who's Who, 1994 - 1995 Editions · Who's Who of Women, 1994 - 1995
- Woman of the Year - American Biographical Institute Inc., 1994
- Who's Who Among Students in American Universities, 1981 & 1982 Editions
- R&R Research Services National Register of Outstanding College Graduates, 1982 Edition

**MEMBERSHIPS**
American College of Health Care Executives · Montana Health Administrator's Association
American Health Information Management Association · National Medical Record Association
Health Information Management Association of Montana · Healthcare Financial Management Association

job-related information in the form of bulleted phrases. The result is a very crisp, succinct-looking resume in which key accomplishments jump out easily at the reader.

Two other points about Resume 7.3. The body text of the resume is set in 10 point type—the smallest type permissible. It's readable, but barely. Notice how the generous use of white space *around* the type helps make the small letters legible; a solid mass of 10-point text would induce squinting and annoyance.

Second, note the use of initial cap/small cap type for Halsted's job titles—"DIRECTOR OF MEDICAL RECORDS" on the first page. It's a subtle, attractive way of emphasizing selected words.

Resume 7.4, "Alison Colby," illustrates a different layout device. Colby pulls out all of her specialized job skills (in her field, they're labeled "Clinical Competencies") and masses them in a special section near the end of the resume. By listing these together in bulleted form, she creates the impression of a large and powerful portfolio of talents—a visual impression that helps to strengthen the reader's image of her credentials.

Finally, consider Resume 7.5, "Craig Saltonstall." Saltonstall believes that the most impressive thing in his professional background is the fact that he has worked for two well-known and highly respected *Fortune* 500 companies. (Our version of his resume calls them "Mammoth Industries" and "Global Airlines.") In order to highlight his association with these two great firms, Saltonstall presents their names ENTIRELY IN CAPITAL LETTERS each time they're mentioned.

Is this how the company names would appear in a newspaper or a company publication? Of course not; but it forces the reader to pay attention to a credential that's important in Saltonstall's career. Try looking for similar opportunities to visually emphasize the most important elements of your background.

## Ruffles and Flourishes

We've spoken often about your need to stand out from the crowd of job seekers, about the numbers game every applicant is facing, and the importance of the resume as a competitive tool.

Considering this pressure, some resume writers reach for ways to be "creative," determined to create a resume that looks different from anything ever seen before. They add computerized clip art, drawings, or photos; they substitute odd symbols to serve as bullets or borders; they devise a personal monogram or emblem and emblazon it across the top of the resume like a company logo; or they choose a weird font for the resume headings (or even its body text).

## 7.4  Job Skills "Massed" for Cumulative Effect

*Confidential Resume of*
### ALISON COLBY
719 Bulkeley Road · Lomax, Maryland 34567
(555) 555-0201
Email: acolby@lomax.net

### HEALTHCARE OFFICE MANAGEMENT
**Strong Nursing Expertise · Communications and Business Talents**

*Energetic performer with 25+ years expertise handling healthcare-related documentation. Skilled in reviewing charts, scheduling and preparing materials for insurance companies and law firms, as well as pain management and critical areas of nursing. Proven initiative, integrity, resourcefulness and analytical / decision-making abilities.*

### PROFILE

- **Management Skills:** Self started with strong planning and leadership skills. Establish guidelines, plans and priorities; identify required resources; coordinate work with others; monitor progress and evaluate outcomes. Improve organizational efficiency and effectiveness.

- **Interpersonal Skills:** Foster excellent working environments and quality staff relations. Employ tact and sensitivity to the needs, feelings, capabilities, interests and motivations of others. Provide counsel to senior management personnel. Able to serve as expert witness.

- **Trusted Professional:** Committed to an ideal of quality; combine resourcefulness with dedication to successful patient outcomes. Consistently promote professional image and attitude; lead by example. Make consistently sound judgments under pressured conditions.

### PROFESSIONAL EXPERIENCE

Pulmonary Associates · Brinker, Maryland
**OFFICE MANAGER / PAIN MANAGEMENT NURSE**
1996 - present

Demonstrate strong planning, organizing and leadership skills to set priorities for multiple, simultaneous staff activities and consistently meet service goals, management objectives and quality performance standards. Interview patients. Ready charts for each day. Assist physicians with patient histories, physicals and medical procedures in office setting, minor surgery suite and operating room.

- *Set up and maintain office, exam room, computer files and appointment schedules; create forms and charts; obtain permissions / release forms, fax records and reports.*

- *Serve as patients' advocate; provid pre- and post-procedure instructions, time schedule reports for condition and pain evaluation, and phone numbers to call at any hour.*

- *Assist physicians with blocks, epidural steroid injections and radiofrequency cryoacupuncture; monitor and update schedule for infusion pumps.*

**ALISON COLBY**, page 2

Mercy Hospital · Baltimore, Maryland
**REGISTERED NURSE -** POST ANESTHESIA CARE UNIT & HOLDING UNIT
1986 - 1996
> Provided care, administered medication and treatments and monitored patient condition, determining course of action based on status or change in condition.  Worked closely with medical, surgical and clerical staff in team effort to ensure optimum patient care and efficient operation of the unit.  Reported, recorded and revised critical information.
> - *Medicated and monitored patients pre- and post-op; supervised conscious sedation; taught patients and families how to administer medications and discussed side effects.*
> - *Instituted PACU holding room sheet to streamline organization and assignment of increasing duties; update, printed and copied 150 computerized schedules daily.*

**REGISTERED NURSE -** INTENSIVE CARE UNIT - CORONARY CARE UNIT
1980 - 1986
> Provided exceptional care for critically ill patients.  Utilized advanced assessment skills, monitored cardiac patients, and collaborated with other healthcare professionals.  Supervised patients, analyzed and interpreted EKG information, performed advanced lifesaving techniques
> - *Monitored patients on telemetry; demonstrated patience and skill in determining different types of arrhythmias.*
> - *Perform careful monitoring of patients on dolontamine / dopamine drips and other cardiac medications via IV administration.*

**Previous positions include:**
MEDICAL SURGICAL UNIT · EYE EARS NOSE & THROAT UNIT · PSYCHIATRIC NURSING EVENT MANAGER for Catering Companies · MUNICIPAL HOSPITAL OFFICER, City of Annapolis

**CLINICAL COMPETENCIES**

- Insertion of peripheral lines; care of and changes of dressing and administration of medications via porta-catheters, central lines, Hickman catheters, Quinton catheters and Picc-lines.
- Drawing blood samples via central venous lines, Quinton catheters and porta-catheters.
- Administration of chemotherapy (non vesicant & irritant agents; taxol); blood products (transfusion); lipid emulsions, IV medications; care of related chest-tubes and bilary tubes.
- Starting therapy of epidural and PCA (patient-controlled analgesic) with use of BARD pump.
- Care and removal of hemovacs, Jackson-Pratt drains, sutures and staples.
- Insertion and care of Dobhoff feeding, naso-gastric, jejunostomy and gastrostomy tubes.
- Administration of medications via IV pushes (digoxin, versed, heparin drips).

**EDUCATION & LICENSURE**

**ASSOCIATE OF SCIENCE IN NURSING**
Annapolis Technical Community College · Annapolis, Maryland
Maryland Registered Nurse · Certified in CPR · Coronary Course Basic · Conscious Sedation

## 7.5  Emphasis on Impressive Company Names

### CRAIG SALTONSTALL
96A West Valerie Avenue · Rochester, New York 15678
Phone / Fax: 555-555-0508 · Email: ctsaltonstall@worldnet.att.net

**FINANCIAL / MARKET RESEARCH & ANALYSIS**
*Talented MBA with Expertise in International Business*

*Self-starter with exceptional analytical, research, computer system and business communications skills. Developed innovative database systems that streamlined report generation; design original reports that facilitate rapid analysis of financial performance by MAMMOTH INDUSTRIES management. Analyzed industry scheduling and proposed improvements that increased GLOBAL'S competitive standing. Technical training programs produce knowledgeable, flexible and sophisticated teams; boost moral by valuing the contributions of all employees. Fluent in the latest version of Windows, Lotus, Word, Excel, various other business related software, and MF database programming.*

**RELATED EXPERIENCE**
*Innovative Solutions for Global Industry Giants*

**RONCO, INC.** Rochester, New York
FINANCIAL ANALYST
1995 - Present

- Develop state-of-the-art information management systems for financial analysis and reporting of MAMMOTH INDUSTRIES Northeastern Area financial performance.
- Conduct research and analysis; create status reports for MAMMOTH management to track and measure the impact of policy and programs on profit and loss.
- Implement training programs on the MAMMOTH Customer Collection Information System; provide the vision for technology utilization and the organization to manage growth.

*Selected Highlights:*

- Accomplished at designing and reengineering processes, infusing innovative technological systems to boost operational efficiency and customer value.
- Analyzed MAMMOTH database system; saved labor costs with development of new queries that streamlined weekly report generation.

**MAMMOTH INDUSTRIES** Albany, New York
FINANCIAL ANALYST
1995

- Performed responsibilities similar to Financial Analyst position at Ronco, Inc.

*Selected Highlights:*

- Established a track for developing creative technical solutions to critical financial problems that resulted in increased efficiency and overall profitability.
- Original queries and Lotus spreadsheets facilitated invoice dispute resolution, which speeded up payments and dramatically boosted customer satisfaction.

*CRAIG SALTONSTALL*

## EDUCATION

**MASTER OF BUSINESS ADMINISTRATION IN INTERNATIONAL BUSINESS,** 1992
State University of New York at Oneonta · Oneonta, New York
Member: MBA Student Association · Graduate GPA: 3.2
*International Marketing · International Economics · Advanced Statistics*
*Advanced Business Communications*

**BACHELOR OF BUSINESS ADMINISTRATION IN MARKETING,** 1990
New York University · New York, New York
Honor Roll · National Dean's List · Undergraduate GPA: 3.2
*Marketing Research · Sales Management · Advertising Management*
*Business Communications*

## OTHER EXPERIENCE

**OTSEGO COUNTY PUBLIC WORKS COMMITTEE** Cooperstown, New York
BOARD MEMBER
June 1997 - Present
  • Appointed by Otsego County Judge Robert Rabinowitz.

**MAMMOTH INDUSTRIES** Albany, New York
ADMINISTRATOR ANALYST
1994 - 1995
  • Specialized in collecting MAMMOTH Accounts Receivable; initiated
    communications; developed strategies to assist customers in meeting obligations;
    improved customer satisfaction.

**GLOBAL AIRLINES, INC.** Albany International Airport
CUSTOMER SERVICE AGENT
1990 - 1994
  • Served as member of the On-Time Committee and the Safety Committee; received
    letter of commendation from the management of this prestigious airline.

## PROFESSIONAL AFFILIATIONS
National Association of Securities Dealers · American Marketing Association

## PERSONAL
Traveled extensively throughout Asia and the United States
In-depth understanding of cultural differences between the United States and Asia

EXCELLENT REFERENCES AVAILABLE UPON REQUEST

Gimmicks like these almost always backfire. Yes, many organizations are looking for people with creative gifts; but the resume is (perhaps unfortunately) not the place for displaying them. The overwhelming impression you want to convey with the resume is one of powerful credentials for the job you seek. That means creative talents *applied in the service of your employer* rather than used to attract attention to yourself.

An offbeat resume may appeal to one employer in ten; to most, however, it will suggest that you are too much of a free spirit to fit comfortably into an organizational setting.

# PRINTING YOUR RESUME

**FYI**

*Use the spell-check feature of your word-processing software as part of the proof-reading process, but never assume that every word in a spell-checked resume is correctly spelled. Spell-check verifies only that the word you typed appears in the dictionary; it can't tell whether it's the word you meant to type. "There," "their," and "they're" will all be approved by spell-check, regardless of which one is correct in the given context. And of course spell-check can't verify the spelling of proper names. There's still no substitute for a careful eyeballing by a human proof-reader.*

Until recently, many job seekers chose to have their resumes professionally typeset and printed—often at significant expense. That's no longer necessary. A well-designed resume created with common PC word-processing software and printed with a good laser or inkjet printer is almost indistinguishable from a typeset resume—and more than adequate for any job seeker.

One absolute on which all career experts agree: *A typo or spelling error can sink even the best-written, best-designed resume*. A document as crucial as your resume deserves to be proofread and corrected at least three times before it's sent to the printer. Any errors that slip through will mark you in the minds of many recruiters as careless, lazy, or ignorant—not qualities you want to be associated with

Some other things to bear in mind concerning the printing of your resume:

- Don't use an old-fashioned dot-matrix or thermal printer; the quality is unacceptable for resume purposes. If necessary, borrow a laser or inkjet printer or bring your resume file on diskette to a local stationery store for printing.

- Be sure your printer is in good working order. If necessary, install a fresh toner cartridge to make sure the print is crisp, clear, and dark.

- If you decide to photocopy your resume, be sure the photocopies are as crisp, clear, and dark as the original, with no wrinkles, smudges, or stray marks.

- Always print on one side of the paper only.

## Paper Choices

Choose a paper style that will work well with the printer or photocopier you use and that appears attractive and of high-quality, like good business stationery. Ask for paper with a rag (cotton) content of about

25 percent and a weight of 16 to 25 pounds. (And while you're at it, buy enough matching paper for your cover letter.)

The paper you select may have a watermark (a monogram-like maker's symbol that is faintly visible when you hold the paper up in the light) as well as an unobtrusive woven texture, but it should have no background pattern, border, or other printed design. And it should be either white or faintly off-white in shade. Gray, blue, or pastel colors, while appropriate for personal stationery or notecards, aren't right for your resume.

Finally, the paper should also be standard U.S. business size—8½ × 11 inches. (Note that slightly different sizes are common in the United Kingdom and other countries.) Any nonstandard size may prevent a potential employer from filing, scanning, copying, or faxing your resume. And remember—anything that makes life hard for a potential employer may throw up a roadblock between you and the great next job you're seeking.

## JUST THE FACTS

- Be sure to master the basic features of the word-processing software you'll use for producing your resume.

- Choose one or two fonts for your resume that are clear, easy-to-read, and of a style that fits your own.

- Don't use a body text type size smaller than 10 points; 11 or 12 points is preferable.

- Use a larger type size, boldface, italic, or small caps to create headings and to highlight important elements in your resume.

- Ample blank space makes a resume clearer and easier to read as well as more attractive.

- Be sure your resume is printed crisply and clearly on high-quality white or off-white paper of standard size.

# Part III

# *Resumes for the Online Job Search*

# Chapter 8

# How the Online Job Search Works

## Get the Scoop On . . .

- The Web-based job market
- Using the Internet to research companies, jobs, and industries
- Posting your resume on the Internet
- Internet job-search scams and dangers to beware of

No matter how great a technophobe (a fancy word for "computer hater") you may be, you've surely heard about (and probably been affected by) the explosion of the Internet. It's one of the most significant technological developments of the past century, one whose revolutionary potential some commentators are likening to the invention of movable type by Gutenberg.

That may be a stretch. But there's no doubt that the Internet and the technologies that have blossomed in its wake have already begun to revolutionize the job-search process. In this chapter, we'll explain why and how. But the basic truth is this: because the Internet makes it possible for millions of job seekers to contact thousands of potential employers virtually instantaneously, it's inevitable that the Internet should become the dominant medium by which job connections are made.

In some fields, that's already true. In many others, that day is rapidly approaching. No matter what your current career field, you need to know something about the Internet and the online job-search technology it makes possible. You may or may not find your *next* job online. But the odds are great that, before your career is over, you'll meet a future employer online.

## JOB HUNTING COMES TO THE INTERNET

The modern era of online job hunting can be dated to 1994, when a young Boston-based advertising executive named Jeff Taylor founded an Internet site called the Monster Board. Taylor's Web site was designed to provide services to both job hunters and employers. Job hunters could post their resumes on the Internet and search a database of available jobs, while employers were able to search the resume listings for candidates and post electronic help wanted ads. The service was free to job hunters, while employers paid a fee to participate—and it took off.

Today, Taylor's creation is known as Monster.com, and it's the leading online job-search site, boasting over two million visitors, one and a half million resumes, and a quarter of a million job openings—figures that continue to grow rapidly. Monster.com has also become the template for an entire industry. Nearly 30,000 Web sites of various kinds now offer job-posting services, and the online search has become a crucial part of job hunting for millions of working people.

*The Internet is a global network of computers carrying data and making the exchange of information possible. The World Wide Web is a collection of interlinked documents that work together on the Internet using a specific protocol that lets computer users travel easily from one to another. The Internet can exist without the Web, but not vice versa. However, in common usage, the words* Net *and* Web *are often used almost interchangeably. That's how we'll use them.*

Possibly the best thing about an online job search is that it can work while you sleep, go out for groceries, or work at your current full-time job, as well as while you're working it in real-time. It simplifies the task of making contact with employers in wildly different time zones. Thanks to the Internet, there's no more need to be tethered to your desk or carry a cell phone everywhere to ensure getting all invitations to interviews and job offers.

An online job search can work for local jobs, part-time jobs, full-time jobs, temporary jobs, ordinary jobs, and extraordinary jobs. It can help career changers find out what's out there, giving them the insider's line through job-search "gossip columns." It can help those who want the real scoop about a company they think they'd like to work for.

An online job search can even allow job seekers to create their own job opening by sparking an employer's imagination with a great resume posting or through the direct approach of offering skills the company is not currently seeking and may not know it needs—until you show them.

## What Kind of Job Seeker Can Use the Web?

Any kind. Every kind. And, as of July 1, 1999, 2.5 million (at least) were using it. That's the count, from *Fortune* magazine, of resumes posted; some job seekers don't post resumes, but merely answer ads, so that figure is probably on the low side. And, of course, by the time you read this page, the number has surely ballooned still more.

## What Kind of Employer Uses the Web to Hire?

All sorts of employers use the Web to hire, from the venerable United Parcel Service (a century-old company that prides itself on its quickness to adopt new technologies) to new-millennium firms, and thousands in between.

Unsurprisingly, technology-based businesses have been among the most enthusiastic users of online recruiting. Thousands of jobs in the computer, software, and e-commerce arenas have been filled via the Internet, and other technology industries—engineering, chemicals, pharmaceuticals, electronics, and the like—aren't far behind. Cisco Systems, the computer networking company, reports that fully two thirds of their new hires now come via the Internet.

More remarkably, even some of the most hidebound and traditional American businesses have begun recruiting via the Internet. As a case in point, consider the publishing industry, one of the most change-resistant businesses anywhere. (Long after most freelance writers had become computerized, most of the publishing companies to whom they sold their work had not.)

*"Digital resumes, digital employ-ment advertising, digital resume searches—it's a rebuilding of the infrastructure. It's almost following e-mail in its growth."*
—Andy Grove, Chairman, Intel Corporation.

Today, however, all the major U.S. publishers of books, magazines, and newspapers, and most of the minor ones, have flourishing Web sites that include job postings and e-mail facilities for receiving computerized resumes and applications. Recruiters for publishing jobs now routinely use the Internet—along with such traditional means as newspaper advertisements—to seek out likely candidates.

Remarkably enough, there are even Web sites devoted to jobs for writers, such as these:

www.newslink.org/joblink.html

www.newsjobs.com

www.freep.com/jobspage

www.sunoasis.com

www.bloomberg.com/fun/jobs/bbcareers.html

www.jaws.org/jobs

www.asne.org/kiosk/careers

www.journalism.berkeley.edu/jobs

www.csne.org/jobs/postings.html

www.copyeditor.com/scripts/jobfile.cgi

www.daily.umn.edu/~mckinney

As one might expect, nontechnical job seekers are now migrating to the Internet in large numbers. A poll conducted by Weddle's, an online newsletter and e-recruitment Web site, revealed that 65 percent of net job seekers are from nontechnical professions.

According to *Fortune* magazine, as of January 1998, 17 percent of the international firms listed in the so-called *Fortune Global 500* were actively recruiting online. Just a year later, that percentage had mushroomed to 45 percent! With the amazing rate of increase in job boards on the Net, more and more large companies are using the Net to hire as well as an increasing number of mid-sized and even smaller corporations.

The list of job sites for journalists shown above can be replicated for many other businesses. There are enormous numbers of niche sites serving almost everyone in the job market, from those just entering the workforce at close to minimum wage to those whose last job paid six figures—or who want their next job to pay that amount or more.

### How Many People Have Gotten Jobs Through the Web?

There probably is no way to develop a precise figure on how many people have found jobs through a Web search. *The New York Times* cannot tell you how many people got jobs through its classifieds; why should resume boards and job-search sites be able to tell you how many people were successful through their job portals?

Indeed, it may be even tougher to quantify Net searches than searches using traditional means; using the Net means becoming a mountain goat, jumping from one peak possibility to the next, following links to here and there and, in the end, who knows exactly which search site got you to exactly which job? There is exclusivity of postings, of course, just as some companies exclusively place ads in just one newspaper. But there is overlap, as well.

It's clear, however, that the Internet has come into its own as a vital part of today's employment marketplace.

## STARTING YOUR ONLINE JOB SEARCH

No matter who you are or what you do, there's a Web site you can use to search for employment. You're a truck driver? Try www.Layover.com. Want a job on a cruise ship? Try these sites:

> www.shipjobs.com
>
> www.cruiselinejobs.com
>
> www.intergate.bc.ca/business/jobship
>
> www.jobsinparadise.com
>
> www.ncna.com/cruise.html

For something more esoteric, how about a job in Singapore? Try these sites:

> www.jobasia.com.sg
>
> www.9to5.com.sg
>
> www.pceservices.com
>
> www.asiadragons.com/singapore/employment

There are many more career-specific niche sites that can serve as useful starting points for your online job search. Just by entering the keywords "job banks" in the search engine Infoseek.com, you can quickly gain access to listings of job banks in the following categories:

| | |
|---|---|
| Academia & science | Human resources |
| Arts & design | Insurance |
| Automotive | Journalism |
| Aviation | K–12 education |
| Biotechnology | Law |
| Business & finance | Law enforcement |
| Christian | Library & information science |
| Clerical | Marketing & advertising |
| Computer science | Military |
| Consulting | Multimedia & Web technology |
| Cruise ship | Nonprofit |
| Engineering | Outdoor |
| Entertainment | Sales |
| Environment | Social work |
| Fitness | Sports |
| Government | Summer |
| Health Care | Translation & interpretation |
| High-tech | Truck driving |
| Hospitality | Writing |

Infoseek is not the only Internet search engine through which to begin your quest. Snap, Lycos, Netscape, Excite, GoTo—all will grant you entry to the cyber job mart.

There are monster job-search sites as well. The aptly named Monster. com, whose founding we mentioned before, is currently the largest. Other large sites include CareerPath.com and CareerMosaic.com.

There are also dozens and dozens of general-purpose Web sites—Web sites that act, look, and feel much like the familiar classified sections in your daily newspaper. Indeed, many of them originate with the ads in the daily paper. For example, Careerpost.com, offered by *The Washington Post* displays its own local ads but also accepts national job listings from various sources. Most major newspapers today have similar sites.

Aside from letting you avoid "newsprint hands" from thumbing through the paper for hours, the Net classifieds offer you some added value. Most of them, even those supported by print media, offer additional information, articles about job hunting, etc., that you'd have to pay to have access to through such publications as *National Business Employment Weekly.*

And, unlike newsprint classifieds, you can select specific companies, find out about them, and find out about what jobs they have available—a far neater, more targeted approach than eyeballing columns of tiny newsprint. Thus, the Internet can be a powerful tool both for the job search and for company research, with the two processes often overlapping in unexpected ways.

For instance, at CareerPath.com, a large site that covers a broad range of industries, you can search for jobs by title, or you can search for industries by profile. From a pull-down menu, you can select industries and geographic areas, and you can add key words to farther define your search. Many reputable employers use several kinds of sites, including general-interest job boards, niche sites, and their own company Web sites, to look for the best job candidates. All can be information sources for you.

## RESEARCHING EMPLOYERS ONLINE—A CASE STUDY

Motorola is a sort of combination old way/new way firm and is one of dozens of companies using CareerPath.com as part of their recruitment endeavors. Motorola, which a lot of Baby Boomers associate first with televisions, is also in space and biotechnology today and has stood the test of time without apparently getting decrepit.

What kind of career information can you gather about a firm like Motorola by using the Internet? Its Web site—which you can reach through a link from CareerPath.com—offers a toned-down version of techno/New Age career inducement:

> "Think globally. Hear different perspectives. Learn something new. Invent something even newer. Use your imagination. YOU CAN DO THAT AT MOTOROLA.

> "It's no secret. Technologies are converging. Traditional barriers are falling. The rules of communications are being redefined. And it's happening in the blink of an eye. There's never been a better time to build your career at Motorola."

If you're interested in applying for a job at Motorola, the company site allows you to build a personal profile, including a cut-and-paste of your Web-friendly resume (see Chapter 9, "The Web-Based Resume"). It takes, truly, no more than 10 minutes. And working there sounds great: "Imagine the possibilities. Explore a future with unlimited potential. You can do that at Motorola."

Can you *really*? Possibly. Of course, you'll want to do some further research to learn more about Motorola (or any other company whose profile you have chosen). And you can do it on the Web. For example, each company in the *Fortune* 500 is also profiled, in brief, on the *Fortune* Web site, at www.pathfinder.com/fortune/fortune500/~search.html.

At this site you can gather such facts as these: In the 1999 *Fortune* 500, Motorola came in at number 34, down a few notches from number 24 in 1997. Its current profile ranks it number 93 among global corporations, and its "most admired" ranking is 225. That doesn't sound great, until you start breaking it down, and *Fortune*'s Web site offers the means to do that, too. To rank companies for a total of 55 industry-specific lists, *Fortune* relies on "insider" opinions gathered by surveyers Clark, Martire & Bartolomeo in a survey of more than 10,000 executives, directors, and securities analysts.

If you're looking for a job that will let you use your creativity, the fact that Motorola's "innovativeness" ranking was 109, a good score, would probably be of interest to you. Its quality of management, though, ranked somewhat lower, at 331. Its talent ranking was 190, pretty good. Its investment value, in case you're wanting to invest in the company you're helping to achieve its goals, is only 278. But for another factor important to increasing numbers of employees, Motorola ranked quite well in social responsibility, 95.

*Most online job seekers find they get inquiries from places they would never have access to without the Web. A company headquartered in a distant state may need to fill a job in your home town, and it is easier and cheaper for them to find you where you are than to hire someone where they are and move the employee. So don't limit your geographic search too strictly because the job board may post a listing by headquarters location rather than job location.*

Overall, Motorola ranked about in the middle for its industry, according to *Fortune*. But it has a lot of specialties to offer, from the expected engineering and manufacturing career paths to marketing communications and technical writing to sales. And it makes a point, on that Web site, of telling potential employees that the company is "employee friendly."

Motorola offers examples of its "employee-friendliness":

> "Our total benefits program, called "LifeSteps," is a strategic initiative that implements many of the recommendations made by our employees, including an expanded U.S. Company-wide work-life-wellness initiative, and health-care benefits that focus on education and prevention as well as treatment."

Motorola offers profit-sharing, child care—even the hot new child-care area, care for children who are sick. It offers adoption assistance, two weeks' paid vacation in year one, plus 80 hours of paid holiday time. Basically, that's a month, virtually the same amount of time off Europeans are used to. Oh, yes—and stock purchase plans.

This may sound like an advertisement for Motorola, but it's not. We've provided this information to illustrate the sort of information you can find out about companies that interest you—or that might be interested in you—by conducting a Web-based job search.

You might want to do more than review single-source information on your target companies. Check them out through www.vaultreports.com to get an insider's view, or a bit of gossip, or even a complete current snapshot (what vaultreports calls a "profile") of the company's prospects, culture, and current direction.

About Motorola, vaultreports.com says:

> "Motorola is the world's leading manufacturer of cellular phones, beepers, and two-way radios . . ..As the first manufacturer of two-way, hand-held radios, as well as a pioneering maker of semiconductors and car stereo equipment, [it] has over the years earned 1,016 patents; 403 of these were registered between 1991 and 1995. The company is one of the top three patent holders in the country."

But:

> "Over the past three years . . . Motorola has not performed well. In February 1998, Prime Communications L.P, a wireless-phone service owned by Bell Atlantic, U.S. West, and AirTouch Communications, canceled a $500 million contract with Motorola after persistent failures with the company's cellular network equipment and software . . .."

There's more, all of which helps to explain Motorola's slippage in the *Fortune* 500 list over the previous two years. To be sure you're looking for jobs in all the right places, you'll need to find information about any company that interests you through more than one source. Then create your own snapshot of how the company is doing and what its status might mean to you. If you're looking for a six-figure marketing job, a situation like Motorola's might be the ticket to your success.

If you're in engineering or production, the following information might, on the other hand, be sobering and send you for a look at other firms. Says vaultreports.com:

> "In June 1998, Motorola officials announced a sweeping restructuring and consolidation plan, laying off 15,000 employees (10 percent of its workforce), closing numerous factories, and taking a $1.95 billion charge to pay for the plan."

The analysis says a weak Asian economy contributed to the maneuver but that Motorola is still aggressively pursuing Asian markets.

The site advises applicants to direct their resumes to the appropriate one of the company's highly decentralized locations. Despite its innovations, the site says, Motorola uses a traditional brand-management structure.

All this is valuable information for job seekers. Without the benefit (and marketing hype) of traditional headhunters, applicants can assess their true level of interest in working for a particular company and they get some help determining whether it is likely to be a good fit from their point of view.

Vaultreports.com offers "gossip," too. Here's an example:

> "One needs to be very mindful of managing his or her career [at Motorola]. The advice to find a mentor is freely and amicably given, but there is no real process to make sure one actually finds a good mentor."—Motorola insider

There's also a meter, on a scale of 1 to 10, with 10 being the best: Pay: 6; Satisfaction: 6; Prestige: 8.

# WORKING THE NET IN SEARCH OF JOB OPPORTUNITIES

**FYI**

*Beware "vapor openings." Often recruiters will list imaginary openings in hopes of getting re-sponses and resumes that they can then sell to bona fide recruiters. How can you tell a vapor job? There's no sure-fire way. But if you see the same reply information repeatedly and you don't receive any "Thanks for the resume" replies after sending a e-mail, begin to suspect.*

Before the advent of the Internet, job searches meant a lot of phone calls, a lot of pavement pounding, a lot of real-time effort. An online job search can be significantly faster and easier, with less physical wear and tear.

There is also serendipity in Web searching for a job. Something you read on one site may spark your imagination; you start a search engine looking for something and before you know it, you've ended up in a site about, say, historical musical instruments and find that a dealer in those historical musical instruments is looking for a sales manager through her own Web site and in the end, that manager turns out to be you.

It's also possible, of course, to use the Web in a focused, deliberate search for specific job opportunities. You can simply target companies you'd like to work for, pull up their Web sites, see which jobs they are posting, and apply, by Web or otherwise.

Here's an example of how the process can work. You may have heard that W. L. Gore, the synthetic fiber manufacturer, is a great company to work for. Gore is 40 years old. Most people know it for its breathable synthetic fiber, GoreTex, which has made all sorts of outdoor sports more comfortable, durable, and protective. Hiking jackets are not all it produces; fluoropolymers (the stuff of GoreTex) are its industrial strength, but innovation is its management forte.

Gore has pioneered an unusual employment technique: As a prospective employee, you "bid" on your job, proposing what you will do for Gore and what you want them to pay you to do it. If necessary, to reach agreement, you can add more functions to your proposed job description until you reach a mutually agreeable plan and salary figure.

Neat. Innovations like these may be one of the reasons W. L. Gore is ranked as one of the "100 Best Companies to Work For in America" by *Fortune* magazine.

If you're interested in researching job opportunities at Gore, your first online stop will probably be Gore's Web site, which is understated and informational:

> "Challenge, opportunity and a unique corporate culture are among the reasons to consider a career at W. L. Gore & Associates, Inc. A global, $1 billion enterprise driven by innovation, Gore offers numerous job opportunities at its sites around the world."

Gore employs more than 6,100 people in more than 45 facilities and generates more than $1.25 billion in sales annually. All this you can find out from the Web site. And then you can survey the jobs available, by type and location.

Here's part of a listing for one job available in Gore's Delaware/Maryland region:

> "Expectations: Our Industrial Products Division is seeking a global sales and marketing leader. Global accountability for forecast and performance to forecast. Focus on cross-regional coordination (resource allocation, forecast, and strategy pricing). Responsible for guidance and development of regional leaders. Strong involvement with product marketing and positioning. . . . Qualifications: 10 years marketing and sales experience (industrial experience preferred). BS (Engineering preferred), MBA desirable. . . . Strong written and verbal communication skills. Ability to motivate others. Strategic thinker and planner. Must be able to travel (up to 30% international travel)."

This job description contains enough detail to help you determine whether submitting your application would be wasting your time or not.

Not all job listings on the Web are so thorough. Many, especially those from job boards, are so vague that you need to assume you're wasting your time at least half of the time. That fact alone makes it a better bet for many job hunters to target companies you want and seek them out, individually, on the Web. Even so, not all will give such good descriptions as Gore.

Here's another job description that's not bad, from a different organization's Web site:

> "We are looking for a full-time Assistant Producer to prepare material for publication on washingtonpost.com in our Style Live section.

*To avoid wasting time while hunting electronic or paper files, create a job-search notebook for recording data you discover during your researches. Make a notebook page for every job ad you answer, paper-based or electronic. Behind that cover page, log or print out and add all responses. Be sure to date everything, of course.*

*Some higher-level jobs are never advertised in print or listed on the Web because the employer doesn't want it to get out that a key position is unfilled. So apply for jobs for which you may be slightly overqualified; your resume may be kicked up to the level you are seeking.*

"Position Responsibilities: Editing and writing articles and supervising the work of freelance writers. Preparing HTML pages for publication. Producing entries for a calendar of events.

"Qualifications: Excellent research, writing, and editing skills; experience in a newsroom is a plus. Experience with production for the World Wide Web, including knowledge of HTML; knowledge of Java and multimedia production techniques for the Web are a plus. Broad knowledge of the Web. Good knowledge of the cultural scene in the Washington, DC area and familiarity with current trends in the arts in general. College degree.

"We are committed to diversity in the workplace and promote a drug-free work environment."

Here's another example, this one from the section of CareerPath.com that posts descriptions of jobs that also appeared in any of a large number of respected newspapers nationwide:

"MEDIA RELATIONS SPECIALIST

"A seasoned pro at securing regional and national media coverage for variety of industries: retail, legal, health care, Internet, etc. Must demonstrate off-line and online media experience. Great salary, benefits, colleagues, and working environment at expanding DC-area PR shop. Fax letter and bio to . . ."

Almost all positions that first appear (or also appear) in newspapers are similarly devoid of detail. Why? Because in a newspaper ad, the employer is paying by the word, which encourages brevity, even at the expense of thoroughness.

Conversely, job orders that go directly to CareerPath and appear only electronically tend to offer more detail. Here's one of those:

"Editorial Producer

Job Status: Full-time

Job Category: Writing, entertainment, publishing

Experience: 4 years

Contact E-Mail: . . .

Location: Chicago, IL

Date Posted: 06/23/99

"Complete Listing: Editorial Producer

"Supervise conceptualization, reporting, editing, and production of content for ____.com. Will create new content areas and oversee sections of the ____.com site, assign and supervise freelancers, conduct research and reporting as needed. Must also identify, assess, and acquire third-party data, content, and tools. Assess vendors and products. Provide support for launch of affiliate sites. Supervise assistant producers in their editorial and production tasks. Develop new approaches for interacting with Web users and customers.

"Requirements: Journalism, English, or Liberal Arts degree and 4 years publishing experience required. Familiarity with HTML, PhotoShop, database publishing, and other tools of the Internet trade preferred. Reporting experience and ability to work creatively with multiple media are pluses. Automotive experience a big plus. Sample URL's preferred."

## MINING INTEREST-SPECIFIC WEB SITES

**FYI**

*Once you've posted a resume on a job board, those that come after your resume will push it toward the bottom of the list. Avoid that by updating your resume every few days. All it takes is changing one item—adding your full middle name instead of an initial, adding the month you left a recent job to the year, and so on. When you've made the change, your resume rises to the top again.*

If you are changing careers or changing emphasis in your current career, it will be to your advantage to regularly visit Web sites devoted to your new interests.

Let's take a slightly esoteric example. Cathy has been working in marketing, but she's also been a competitive rider of horses and has decided that she'd like to combine those pursuits in the second half of her professional life. Where in the world might she find such a combination?

On the Web, of course. A trip through equine (i.e., horsemanship) sites reveals www.equijournal.com. That leads to www.GoNetWide.com/EEO/viewad_e.html, where this job listing appears:

"BUSINESS OPPORTUNITY: Facility Operator/Partner—New facility in S/W Pa. with indoor, outdoor, trails, turnout, viewing room needs a trainer and/or instructor that is willing to commit and knows how to market a facility. 35 miles south of Pittsburgh and 20 miles east of Wheeling WV. 1 mile from interstate 70 . . ."

Is this the perfect career opportunity for Cathy, our marketer/horse lover? Maybe, maybe not; she'll need to investigate and explore the possibility face-to-face with her prospective partner, just as in the old pre-digital days. But she might never have discovered this interface between her business and avocational interests without the quick and easy research capabilities of the Internet.

## PASSIVE SEARCHING—PROS AND CONS

As we've noted, you can post your resume on virtually all job-search sites—in most cases, for free. The best bet for most job seekers is to post resumes both on big general sites (CareerPath.com) and on those more targeted to their specialty. "Passive" job searching by posting your resume for employers to read can actually be psychologically advantageous. When employers find you, they may feel they have to court you because your resume spoke so well to them. And they may naturally assume that many other companies have also seen your impressive credentials and are pursuing you—or are likely to do so at any time. Use this leverage to gain the best compensation, benefits, and working conditions package you can.

**FYI**

*Consider paying a fee to get your resume posted on the first page in your category with search sites that offer this special service. Will this make you look too hungry? Not to most employers; it will make you appear willing to go the extra mile to get what you want—just as very reputable firms pay to have their listings placed up front to attract the best job candidates.*

When you post your resume, be aware that there are some unscrupulous recruiters who will grab it from cyberspace and submit it everywhere, looking for a fee. What's so bad about that? Employers may have seen your resume for something you didn't want and decide you were too "hungry" when something you do want comes up. And there's always the chance that your current employer will be sent your resume, raising questions about your "loyalty" to the job you now hold.

You can avoid some of this by stating in your resume exactly what positions you are interested in. Remove your resume when you've gotten a job, at least for a while. And, if absolute confidentiality is important to you, consider restricting yourself to the for-fee resume sites. These generally allow you to control who receives your resume by requiring that you give specific approval before your data is released to an employer.

A good many job boards are beginning to offer notification services, using "intelligent agents" to search new job postings for ones that meet your criteria. These services will e-mail you when they receive job orders you're likely to be interested in. CareerMosaic.com offered this service by early 1999; CareerMart.com, another big site, was preparing its own notification service in summer, 1999, and others will surely follow. To locate the current job-search services that offer notifications, enter "e-mail agent" or "job scout" on your computer's Internet search engine.

## USING YOUR "EXPERT" STATUS TO GET RECOGNIZED

Almost everyone knows a lot about something. And it is nice to be headhunted without sticking your neck out as a publicly identified job hunter. You may be able to arrange a job—or the recognition that can lead to a job—by signing on an as expert in a particular field with one of the many Web sites that offer free advice to inquiring visitors.

One of these Web sites is allexperts.com, which maintains a stable of experts in every imaginable field. Every few days, the site rotates the experts to answer queries from the public. So for a couple of days a week, you'll have to answer e-mail with questions in your chosen field. The queries may come from private individuals, but some are likely to come from companies that are seeking help in a particular field or from members of the media looking for a quote or a tidbit of advice. Either way, your fame as a maven will spread.

Remember Cathy, our horse-loving marketer? She arranged to be listed as an expert in the field of equine sports. Within a month, she'd fielded two inquiries from publications for horse lovers asking her to write columns for them.

# CASE STUDY: TERRI'S ONLINE JOB SEARCH

**FYI**

*If you've posted your resume on several of the free job sites and find that you are not getting the responses you want, consider a paid site. Example: Execunet (bizwiz.com), for people earning more than $75K annually. Even if you decide not to join, such sites are worth visiting. Many offer useful freebies, such as guides for calculating how much your job skills are worth in today's market.*

Terri Garnet conducted her first successful Net job search in 1998, landing a six-figure position through an online posting. She's engaged in a second search as we write. Terri lets the Net work while she snoozes. "I posted resumes, putting up a couple of different versions, one targeted to sales, one to sales training," she says:

> The next morning, I checked my e-mail and got a reply like this: "Regarding the professional sales trainer position: we recently received your e-mail and resume for the position we posted on Monster.com." It was not an offer—yet—but it's nice to know that your materials have been received, and that happens more often with the Web than with mailed or faxed resumes.

It's not only nice to know, of course. It lets you make decisions about whether and when a second approach is in order. That's usually harder to do in old-style, off-line job searches.

Garnet is now responding to listings for sales management and sales training jobs that meet her salary/benefit and location requirements (she's contemplating a move to the Pacific Northwest):

> I've replied to some, and my resume is out there, posted. I expect it to work like last time; the employers will find me. Then I'll have to determine whether they are legitimate companies for my purposes; that means no multilevel marketing, which I don't want to do. It is often hard to tell through the information in the listings, so I expect some of the replies will be multilevel marketing. I'm learning to evaluate the listings, though, to cut down on the multilevel opportunities I would spend time replying to without knowing.

## USING THE WEB TO SUPPLEMENT OTHER JOB-SEARCH STRATEGIES

*"When I find an e-mail address [for a company with a job opening] is not working, it does not bode well. Generally, I don't go to the Net white pages and try to find them. If they have given no other way to contact them, I will delete the entry and say goodbye."*
—Terri Garnet, successful online job seeker

Don't forget there's life beyond the Internet and outside newsprint. Despite the explosive growth of online recruiting, the Internet today accounts for only about 2 percent of all job-related advertising—a growing fraction, but still a relatively tiny one.

Therefore, in addition to posting your resume and searching print and electronic classifieds, don't fail to network, network, network. Some companies still want to do things the traditional way, through the age-old grapevine of "friends of friends" that connects people to organizations. Don't lock yourself out of those opportunities by focusing too single-mindedly on any one job-search medium. Besides, after long hours at the computer screen, you'll probably need some human contact.

Not all jobs that appear in newspapers will appear on the Web somewhere; conversely, some Web postings will never show up in print. If you're serious about your job search, it is still a good idea to subscribe to at least the Sunday edition of newspapers from cities you'd like to work in. Sure, you can generally pull up the paper's classifieds on the corresponding Web site. But thumbing through the paper itself will also give you a feel for the area, including some valuable factual knowledge that you can use in an interview or cover/follow-up letter to suggest that you know something about the company, its competitors, local business, economic conditions, and so on.

> **FYI**
>
> *You can save time in the long run by first determining which of the general sites cater more to your specialty than others. Although it's a general site, Headhunter.net, for example, caters more to sales and training than other general sites, says Terri Garnet.*

Why not do that through the Web? Because the paper's Web site will be edited slightly differently from the physical newspaper, and you'll miss the bulk of the advertising (which gives insight into lifestyles) and the relative importance the readership (apparently) or the editors (for certain) attach to various subjects.

And there's another reason to consult an old-fashioned newspaper from time to time. Says Terri Garnet, "Lately, I've found no matches for the print classifieds in the online *Baltimore Sun*. They probably haven't updated their listings. Somewhere in their chain of information, something didn't flow."

Thus, the Internet should supplement your use of other job-search methods, not replace them. In the next chapter, we'll provide specific advice and guidelines for making sure that your resume is written, edited, and designed to work efficiently in the electronic environment of the Internet.

## JUST THE FACTS

- Web-based job searching is a rapidly growing industry—one you needn't own a computer to participate in.
- A wealth of information about prospective employers can be easily and quickly researched on the Internet.

- You can use the Internet to niche-market your skills or offer them to a mass market, or both.

- If you post your resume electronically, be careful to track where your resume goes and remove or change it from time to time to keep it from getting too familiar or too stale.

- Use the online job search as an adjunct to other, more traditional, forms of networking.

# Chapter 9

# The Web-Based Resume

## Get the Scoop On . . .

- Tailoring your resume for the online job search
- Web-based resume designs
- Tips and warnings about formatting your resume
- Using keywords to put your resume ahead of the rest
  As we've seen in Chapter 8, the Internet has become a major source of employment information for both job seekers and the organizations that may hire them. It's a tool you certainly ought to use in your job hunt. But, like most worthwhile innovations, the Internet requires a degree of learning and adaptation by those who want to take full advantage of its powers.
- In particular, there are a number of ways in which you'll need to modify your resume in order to make it most effective for a Web-based job search. In this chapter, we'll provide you with the information you need to turn your traditional resume into a Web-based resume.

## THREE KINDS OF WEB-BASED RESUMES

The term *Web-based resume* refers, really, not to a single type of document, but to three.

- First, there is the traditional hard-copy resume, printed on paper, but designed in such a way that optical character recognition (OCR) software can read it and enter its contents into a recruiter's or employer's database without turning it into gobbledygook. We'll call this the *scannable resume*.

- Second, there is the "de-formatted," visually simplified resume you can send by e-mail with considerable confidence that your entire text will reach a potential employer with no loss of clarity. We'll call this the *plain-text resume*.

- Third, there is the most high-tech form of Web-based resume, which we'll call the *HTML resume*. HTML stands for HyperText Markup Language. It's a programming language that permits you to create a resume that includes sound, film, animation, and graphics as well as text—a virtual multimedia extravaganza. This form of resume is usually used by creative workers—graphic artists,

Webmasters, actors, animators, photographers, interior designers, singers, architects, models, musicians, and so on.

In this chapter, we'll focus on the first two kinds of Web-based resumes—the scannable resume and the plain-text resume. Chapter 14 includes more suggestions about crafting the HTML resume for those who are active in a creative or artistic field.

# HOW THE SCANNABLE RESUME WORKS

Let's consider what you need to do to make your traditional resume suitable for scanning into an employer's or recruiter's database. (Later, we'll add some extra considerations that go into creating the plain-text resume specifically for e-mail transmission.)

An optical character recognition system (OCR), or scanner (as it is commonly called), is much like a photocopier. Your printed resume is fed into it. When the OCR software "sees" the characters on the page, it creates a text file by recognizing the characters. However, its powers of recognition are limited by comparison to even the least sophisticated human reader. In some fonts certain pairs of letters may overlap (or appear to), while other letters may be shaped in slightly unconventional ways. For these and other reasons, the OCR software may fail to read them accurately.

Furthermore, the OCR won't record **boldface** or variations in type size. It simply loads each character into its memory, and creates its own text file from those words, effectively removing any formatting or design from your original resume.

The value, to a recruiter or employer, of reducing your resume into a standardized text file, is that it is easy to search electronically. When your resume is one of thousands in a recruiter's database, it's easy for a prospective employer to search for resumes containing keywords that denote specific skills, characteristics, or experience. *M.B.A., Java, project management, benefits administration, Web site design* . . . any of these may be a keyword for a particular job, depending on the needs or interests of the hiring decision-maker. Later, we'll provide much more information about how to identify keywords for the jobs you're interested in and incorporate them in your Web-based resume.

The application of this document scanner technology to human resources is called *electronic applicant tracking*. It offers tremendous advantages for both employers and job seekers. Your resume can be scanned into a computer system and kept active for years; no one has to hunt for it in dog-eared paper files. They need only enter the keywords for any current job opening and virtually instantaneously retrieve all the resumes that contain those words.

Which employers are using this technology? It's surprisingly widespread. Because electronic scanning and database systems currently cost up to $100,000, you might assume that few small employers would use them. But like most of the large companies—those which generally offer the best benefits, geographic choice, advancement opportunities, and stability—they do.

In fact, you should assume that most employers will scan your resume, even though some are nominally too small to do so. Many employ service firms, headhunters, or consultants who handle some of their recruiting chores and who will certainly use scanning technology. You can't *hurt* your chances for a job by making your resume scanner-friendly; you can only help it.

The workings of OCR and database technology lead to the three main principles for preparing a scannable resume:

- Use a font and type size that's easy for the OCR to read.

- Keep the layout and format of your resume as clear and simple as possible.

- Load your resume with keywords related to your industry and focused on the specific strengths you'll bring to an employer.

We'll outline more detailed rules in the rest of this chapter. All grow from these three simple principles.

**FYI**

*When in doubt whether a scannable or plain-text resume is needed by a particular employer, call and ask—even if the recruiting ad says "No Phone Calls." This common warning is intended to discourage attempts at telephone interviews; it doesn't mean you can't inquire of the human resources receptionist or operator how they would like to receive resumes.*

# BASIC STEPS TO A SCANNABLE RESUME

Following are the most important things you must do to create a scannable resume.

### Choose a Font That's Easy for OCR Software to Interpret

OCR systems recognize most sans serif fonts more easily than most serif fonts. (As we explained in Chapter 5, serif fonts—like that in which the text of this book is set—feature small cross-lines at the end of each letter stroke. Sans serif fonts do not.) A standard sans serif font, such as Arial, Helvetica, or Century Gothic, is generally a safe choice for the scannable resume.

However, you may choose to use a serif font instead, especially if you intend to send the same resume to companies that scan and those that don't. Serif fonts are more traditional and familiar, and most people find them easier to read than sans serif fonts. Most standard serif fonts,

including Times Roman, Courier, and Century Schoolbook, are acceptable for scanning purposes, provided you follow the other design rules
we'll outline here.

### Choose a Type Size Between 10 and 14 Points

Twelve-point type is most commonly used for the main text of a resume.
Twelve points is large enough for both human and computer eyes to be
comfortable with; fourteen-point type looks bulky, while ten-point type
is on the small size and should be avoided unless you absolutely need to
squeeze extra information onto the page. (Some word-processing
packages offer eleven-point versions of some fonts, which can be a good
compromise.)

### Don't Use the Ten-Point Version of Times Roman

The letters tend to touch too frequently in most versions of the font
(they vary slightly from one software package to another), which may
cause whole words to be misread.

### Set the Length of Your Lines at 80 Characters or Less

If your lines are longer than this, you may get peculiar word wraps,
making the scanned document difficult to read. Here's an example of
how the scanned version of a resume typed in such a format could look:

Over-the-Hill Painting Services, New Haven, CT. 1984-1993
Job Costing and Planning Coordinator. Met with clients to
help determine whether
their projects would be manageable for teams of octogenarian
house
painters
restricted to buildings of no more than one and one-half
storeys,
preferably
with handholds every two feet along each wall, as well as
block-and
-tackle
safety harness equipment installed under roof soffits.

You can see that the herky-jerky line breaks make this document
unpleasant and difficult to read.

Also set your page margins at 1.25 to 1.5 inches on each side, to ensure
that all your words appear within the field the scanner will "see."

### Use Ragged Right Margins

Most word processing programs can be set to justify lines of type—that
is, to print them with straight margins on either the right- or left-hand
sides, or both. (The lines of text in this book are full justified—meaning

that both the right- and left-hand side of the text are straight.) This effect is achieved by variable spacing between words and even between letters within words.

Many people like this effect, but for your scannable resume, avoid it. Justified margins may make it harder, or even impossible, for the scanner to read some words of your text. Use uneven or "ragged" right margins instead.

### Avoid Using *Italics*, <u>Underlining,</u> **Boldface, or any Eccentric or Highly Unusual Font**

In general, fancy text treatments don't respond well to the OCR treatment. Of the three specific styles mentioned above, boldface is the most likely to scan well, but its heavier lines could make letters appear to touch, which would cause the scanner to misread or ignore that word.

Script and other nonstandard fonts are usually not readable. And avoid shading or graphic elements—for example, your initials in a fancy monogram or logo at the beginning of your name and address. The effect may look super on paper, but if your resume is scanned, it will come across as garbage, if at all.

### Use Words PRINTED ENTIRELY IN CAPS to Identify Sections or Headings

All-cap headings make a reasonable substitute for boldface or italics. Also, consider using more white space than you would in a traditional, non-scannable, resume; the extra space will make it easier for the scanner to read and also helps clearly separate sections of your resume.

### Avoid Separating Sections with Vertical or Horizontal Lines

Under scanning, such lines often come out as a string of zeros or other odd symbols. If you do use them (perhaps assuming that your resume will be read by human eyes only), be sure to use lots of white space on both sides of the line.

### Don't Use Vertical Columns

In a traditional resume, a visual effect like this one works fine:

| | |
|---|---|
| 1992–<br>1994 | Dispatcher, Speedee Delivery Service<br>Managed staff of fifteen truck drivers and<br>bicycle messengers [etc.] |

The columnar set-up shown here won't work in a scannable resume, however. When scanning, the computer could juxtapose words from one column with words from the other and produce some very interesting—not to say weird—job listings.

### Use the Best Available Printing Method

Use a high-quality ink-jet or laser printer set to its highest-resolution, so as to produce very crisp, sharp-looking copy. If your printer is old or unreliable, bring a diskette with your resume file to the local mega-copy shop for printing. It's important to have the best possible document for employers to scan.

Never use a dot-matrix printer, which prints using tiny blobs of ink and is likely to produce letters that appear to be touching or overlapping; the space between those little blobs will also confuse many OCRs.

### Always Send Originals Rather Than Photocopies

If you have your resume professionally printed, be sure to get all the copies you think you'll need. The incremental cost of an extra 100 copies is less than the cost of having a second or third batch made on a later visit.

### Use White or Light-Colored Paper with Not Very Visible Grain

So-called *laid paper* is better than linen, because its texture is less pronounced and therefore less likely to complicate the OCR's job. Always print on one side only; if you use two sides, print may show through and confuse the OCR.

### Don't Let Your Resume Get Battered

Mail your resume unfolded and unstapled in a white 9 × 12 envelope. Insert a sheet of thin cardboard to keep it stiff and write on the outside of the envelope—on both sides—PLEASE DO NOT BEND. If your resume arrives at the employer's office with many deep creases, the OCR may not recognize letters in the creases.

## CHOOSING AND USING THE RIGHT KEYWORDS

As we've explained, part of the rationale for the scannable resume is the use of OCR and database software to extract information from your resume, starting with the basics: name, address, phone number, job titles, and so on. Keywords are an important part of this process. To make it easy for recruiters and employers to link you to the right jobs, you need to use the keywords they're likely to be seeking. Each appropriate keyword is like a magnet that will draw the attention of employers to your resume: the more numerous the keywords, the more powerful the attraction.

Start by using common headings for your sections, as the scanner will be looking for at least some of them. These include:

| | |
|---|---|
| Accomplishments | Personal |
| Additional (Experience, Awards, etc.) | Positions Held |
| Affiliations | Presentations |
| Appointments | Professional Affiliations |
| Certifications | Publications |
| Education | Qualifications |
| Employment | References |
| Examinations | Skills |
| Experience | Strengths |
| Honors | Summary |
| Internships | Technical skills |
| Licenses | Training |
| Miscellaneous | Volunteer activities |
| Objective | Work History |
| Papers | |

The electronic applicant tracking software will also search for keywords describing the essential qualities of the successful applicant for a particular job. The more of these words your resume contains, the more likely you are to be called in for an interview.

There are two kinds of keywords: *general keywords*, naming qualifications many employers in various fields are seeking, and *industry-specific keywords*. Let's take a closer look at each.

General keywords may describe:

- Skills related to management, human relations, communication, and organization

  Examples: budget, P&L, training, administration, project planning, outsourcing, schedule, writing, presentation, strategy

- Educational credentials

  Examples: Bachelor's degree, M.B.A., certification, continuing education, credits, license, seminar

- Professional experiences and achievements

  Examples: downsizing, startup, expansion, reorganization, compliance, negotiation, re-engineering

- Other credentials, such as foreign languages required, specific companies worked for or positions held, geographic location, and years of experience

  Examples: Spanish, Russian, Microsoft, military background, chief information officer, vice president of marketing, Northeast, Austin, five years

Industry-specific keywords, of course, vary by the field as well as by the details of your background and the job you're seeking. In general, they will be words like those you'd find in employment ads or job descriptions. Here are some examples.

- **Marketing keywords:** research, statistics, brand management, product management, marketing plans, catalogs, promotions, packaging, competitive strategies, focus groups, trade shows

- **Financial management keywords:** analyst, investment, forecasts, liquidity, cash flow, expense management, budgeting, securities, treasury, risk management, debt, credit

- **Human resources keywords:** interviewing, staffing, benefits, recruiter, EEO, training, retention, employee relations, compensation, exempt/nonexempt, stock options, succession planning

- **Sales keywords:** prospect development, inside sales, customer tracking, business-to-business, cross selling, contract negotiations, account management, presentations

- **Internet keywords:** e-commerce, Java, site traffic analysis, HTML, Webmaster, broadband, intranet, Photoshop, C++.

Do you get the idea? Keywords like these are the words that are likely to jump out at you from the pages of a newspaper's classified advertising section; when you spot an add that contains several keywords that apply to you, you're apt to clip that ad and respond to it. In the online world, it's important to make sure that your resume contains the corresponding keywords. If it does, employers will be apt to grab your resume off the Web and call you up for a chat.

Despite what your fifth-grade English teacher may have told you, you *should* use jargon, buzzwords, and acronyms (i.e., words formed from initials) when crafting your Web-based resume. Acronyms are often important parts of the language of a business, especially in technical and professional fields, and you should use them whenever they're relevant to your work. Examples include:

| | |
|---|---|
| CPA | (certified public accountant) |
| ESL | (English as a second language) |
| HR | (human resources) |
| IT | (information technology) |
| LAN | (local area network) |
| RN | (registered nurse) |
| TQM | (total quality management) |

*Don't confuse scannable keywords with the active verbs that are crucial to reaching and impressing human interviewers (as we discussed in Chapter 5). Keywords are usually nouns (names of people, things, or qualities), not verbs (action words). All the keyword examples we have given you are nouns (or noun phrases), and they're typical of the kinds of words sought by applicant tracking software.*

If you've worked in a particular field for some time, you're probably well-versed in its peculiar lingo; be sure it's scattered appropriately through your scannable resume.

If there are two words in your industry that describe the same function or position, use them both. For example, use both human resources and personnel management, physician and doctor, account executive and sales representative. This way, no matter which term is programmed into an employer's resume search, your paperwork will be pulled up.

If you're uncertain about the keywords you ought to be highlighting, review job descriptions in your field. Focus particularly on descriptions of jobs you'd like to qualify for (pulled from the Internet or from the classifieds) and the descriptions you've written for your own former jobs. Pick out the most specific and descriptive nouns from these descriptions.

Here's an example of a job description with the appropriate keyword nouns underlined:

COMMUNITY RELATIONS DIRECTOR, LITTLEVILLE PLAYHOUSE

Public liaison for nonprofit regional theater

Obtained sponsorships for theatrical performances; created and edited newsletter; hosted press events to introduce each new season; served as liaison with actors' unions and other craft unions; submitted quarterly reports on status of sponsorships and press coverage; defended budget twice yearly before board of directors.

If a resume scanner were looking for someone who could perform high-level management duties in a nonprofit agency, the words *sponsorship, budget,* and *board of directors* would be particularly important.

Here's another example:

SALES MANAGER, MIDWEST REGION, MAMMOTH INDUSTRIES, INC.

Introduced the concepts of team selling to new associates; monitored progress during training; evaluated improvement of sales techniques of new associates; provided remedial training as needed; outplaced new associates who could not meet sales quotas within six months; replaced outplaced junior team members; managed mentoring of stellar performers to promotion to sales management positions in other branches.

The keywords in this description reveal that the applicant knows about and has used various sales management techniques and has managed a sales force, with responsibility for both sales quotas and staff development (keywords *training, mentoring*).

**FYI**

*One of the quickest ways to gather keywords is by visiting jobdescription.com. The site offers current job descriptions for a choice of sample professions, from the ordinary (admissions director) to the unusual (motorcycle racer.) There is a charge for regular use of the services offered by the site, but you can test its usefulness through a free trial run.*

# FROM THE SCANNABLE RESUME TO THE PLAIN-TEXT RESUME

There are a few more things you must do before you can consider your resume not only scannable but e-mailable. Here they are.

Make a digital copy of your scannable resume and store it as a plain text (or ASCII) file. (Generally, this involves using the suffix *.txt* after the file name; for example, you could name your resume file *resume.txt*.)

Now bring this plain-text file up on screen and edit its format as follows:

- Switch from any font with proportional (i.e., variable) letter spacing, such as Times Roman, to a "typewriter-style" typeface in which all the letters are the same width, such as Courier.

- Fix any odd-looking line lengths by using hard returns (by pressing the Enter key) at the end of each line of text. *Don't* use the usual "word wrap" feature of your word-processing software, which will probably producing odd line breaks when your resume is e-mailed. Also eliminate tabs; insert spaces instead.

- Eliminate any signs or symbols not found on the conventional keyboard—they probably won't translate properly. Substitute words or letters as best you can.

You've now created a plain-text resume that can be sent and received via e-mail with no loss of clarity or accuracy. It's not pretty, but it's easy to read or scan, even after being sent and received via e-mail. Store this plain-text resume for e-mail use.

# HOW MANY RESUMES?

Experience shows that your attachment may be difficult or impossible to open at the other end, no matter how sophisticated your equipment and theirs may be. And some employers refuse to open attachments lest they unleash a computer virus into their system. Thus, your attached resume has at best a fifty-fifty chance of reaching its recipient.

You will want to have at least two resumes: one for scanning and one for e-mail. They should contain the same information in the same order, but the e-mail resume will contain even less graphic design (how is that possible?) than the scannable one—like something that might have issued from an old typewriter thirty years ago.

Many job hunters also opt to create a third resume—an eyes-only version, formatted and designed attractively, to be used strictly for non-electronic sharing. Print a batch of good-looking resumes in this form and carry a folder-full when you go out on interviews. Hand them out to the people you meet (who are likely to have misplaced your electronic resume, anyway) to help drive the conversation in the directions you want it to go.

By equipping yourself with the proper resume for *every* medium of communication, you're maximizing your chance of winning attention for your credentials when the job of dreams becomes available.

# JUST THE FACTS

- Today, most businesses are using electronic means of storing and searching resumes; your resume needs to be adapted for the Internet age.

- A visual style that works for your eyes only may not produce a scannable resume. Follow the rules to make sure a computer can read and digest your story.

- Keywords are essential to make sure your resume is chosen for further action.

- Study job descriptions and ads in your field to uncover the keywords you need to highlight in your resume.

- Create a plain-text version of your resume especially for use in e-mail transmission.

# Part IV

## Resumes
## for Special
## Circumstances

# Chapter 10

# The Recent Graduate

- Developing an effective resume for the recent grad
- Defining an appropriate objective for your first "real" job
- Discovering your relevant skills and experience
- Presenting your skills and credentials effectively

As a new or recent grad (two years out of school or less), you face some special challenges in crafting your resume.

Your work experience is probably limited, which may make it difficult to develop a resume that doesn't look slightly skimpy. To compensate, you'll want to provide details about your educational background, part-time and volunteer work, and other non-full-time work credentials. Yet these may appear irrelevant to the kind of job you're now seeking. This can feel like an awkward bind to be in.

Furthermore, this may be the first time you're writing a resume—meaning that you're starting from scratch rather than updating, revising, or improving an already-existing document. As most writers can attest, there's no sight quite as intimidating as a perfectly blank sheet of paper waiting to be filled.

So developing a powerful resume may not be easy for the recent grad. But the picture isn't all bleak. If you're concerned that your work credentials may seem sparse, remember that you are probably competing for jobs mainly with others in the same situation—your fellow recent grads. No employer will expect you to boast the track record of a 40-year-old.

There's also a positive flip side to your relatively brief work history. You haven't had time to accumulate the problems some more-experienced job seekers have to disguise or overcome in their resumes—career gaps, jobs from hell, firings, and big steps backward. Your more brief personal history is something of a blank slate, which many employers actually find appealing; they can view you as a bundle of potential waiting to be developed rather than as a collection of set-in-stone habits they may or may not like.

And finally, as of this writing, you and your fellow grads are entering one of this century's best job markets—an environment especially hospitable to those launching new careers. All in all, the positives in your situation are at least as significant as the negatives.

There's your pep talk, if you need one. Now let's get started with tackling some of the specific challenges you'll face as a new grad in crafting an outstanding resume.

# DEFINING YOUR CAREER OBJECTIVE

As a new grad, you may or may not have a clear and natural career objective. If you just earned a degree in accounting, speech therapy, or hotel management, for example, the basic career track you hope to follow may be obvious. In other cases, however, defining a career objective may be a real challenge. You may be uncertain as to the type of job you're seeking; you may be worried about defining your objective in terms so broad they're almost meaningless, while at the same time you don't want to define it so narrowly that you'll eliminate yourself from a job you might love.

These are valid concerns. Here are some pointers that can help you handle this first resume-writing challenge.

### Write an Objective that Defines Your Next Job, Not the Job of Your Dreams

Fortunately, a career is developed one step at a time, not all at once. And many of the most successful and rewarding careers involve surprising detours no one could have predicted. You may envy fellow grads who appear to have a complete career track mapped out at age 22, but such people are the exception, not the rule—especially in today's rapidly changing work world, where entire industries can mushroom and collapse within a decade or two.

So if you're uncertain where you want to be five years from now, that's fine. The objective described on your resume can be a short-term goal, not a long-term one. You may feel, for example, that you're interested in sales and marketing, but have only a vague sense of where you'd like to go with that interest. Will your ultimate goal be to run your own marketing consulting firm? To be a corporate vice president with a *Fortune* 500 consumer-goods company? To be the superstar salesperson for a commercial real estate developer? To be marketing director of an upstart e-commerce firm?

The beauty of being a new grad is that *all* these goals are possible for you. And right now, your resume objective needn't distinguish among them. You might devise an objective that states simply:

OBJECTIVE: A position in sales or marketing with a growing firm in which my outstanding abilities to communicate, persuade, and energize others will be utilized and challenged.

An objective like this defines where you hope to be one year from now—and that's far enough in the future for your present purposes.

### Don't Be Afraid of the Word "Entry-Level"

Some recent grads are so worried about appearing "too young," "too inexperienced," or "wet-behind-the-ears" that they try to disguise or obscure the fact that they are new to the world of full-time work. It's not necessary—and probably futile, anyway. If you're seeking your first "real" job (or your first job in a particular industry), don't be shy about describing it as such. That's why they invented the word "entry-level."

Clearly defining your objective as an entry-level position will serve several purposes. It helps a potential employer envision you as a candidate for one of several traditional starting gates (which exist in virtually every industry). It signals that you are realistic about your background and willing to start your career at an appropriate level. And it suggests that your main objective is a job with opportunities to learn, grow, and make significant contributions over time.

Everyone is an entry-level employee at least once. If this is your turn, don't try to hide it.

### If You're Open to Jobs in Several Industries or Functional Areas, Say So

*For the recent grad, there's greater danger in an overly-specific objective than in one that's too broad or general. Pigeonholing yourself too precisely can narrow the opportunities for which you'll be considered and project an image of rigidity, both of which are likely to needlessly prolong your job search.*

Another advantage of describing the job you seek as an "entry-level position" is that it implies what is usually the case for most recent grads—willingness to consider more than one possible career path. Most employers will find such openness a desirable trait; it means you are flexible about the jobs you'll consider and may even be willing to take on assignments that involve shifting from one functional area to another, as business needs dictate. These are plusses for you as a job candidate.

Does this sort of flexibility mean that your objective must sound hopelessly broad and vague? Not necessarily. Here are a couple of examples of objectives that are open-ended yet suggest a clear underlying direction:

OBJECTIVE: An entry-level position in sales, marketing, or promotion in a small- to mid-sized consumer products company, where my communication, planning, and quantitative skills may be used to help foster strong customer relationships and business growth.

POSITION SOUGHT: An entry-level position in the media or publishing industries, either in editorial, marketing, or publicity, with an opportunity to learn the business while using my organizational, writing, and speaking abilities to contribute to the organization.

Both of these sample objectives define the job sought within broad parameters (type of company, industry, and a selection of business functions) without narrowly limiting the possibilities you'll look at. They invite a recruiter to call with the question, "We have a great job that *might* be right for you. Have you considered . . .?"

### Consider Using a Summary in Place of an Objective

As we've explained, it's not always necessary to have a separate objective or career goal listed in your resume. If your resume and cover letter describe you clearly and accurately, your current career stage and appropriate next step are likely to be obvious. Thus, the separate objective listing may simply take up space that could be better devoted to selling your credentials.

For an example, look at Resume 10.1, crafted by recent grad "Benjamin H. Snyder." This resume contains no separate "objective" listing. Instead, it leads with a "Career Summary" paragraph which defines what Snyder has to offer a prospective employer: "B.A. in Government, minor in legal studies, and additional course/lab experience . . . ," etc.

The paragraph does contain a sentence that takes a bow to the traditional job objective: "Seek a challenging position that will offer opportunities for career advancement and professional growth." But notice how open-ended this description is. It gives the recruiter a chance to define for herself the types of jobs Snyder may be suitable for, based on his background—most likely, jobs in the public policy or legal fields, especially those related to environmental concerns. The rest of the career summary section then describes personal qualities of which Ben Snyder is particularly proud and that he wants to call to the reader's attention.

In short, Snyder's career summary section *implies* a job objective while focusing mainly on *advertising* his credentials and strengths as a potential employee. You should consider a similar strategy for your resume.

**FYI**

*With a bit of thought, it's often possible to combine your objective with a summary that defines your background, education, and skills, advertising your credentials while you position yourself for a specific job or jobs.*

# DISCOVERING YOUR RELEVANT EXPERIENCE

The second major concern of most new grads is the difficulty of coming up with relevant, interesting, and impressive background experiences to list and describe. Feeling they've "never done anything," some grads are

## 10.1  Recent Grad With Part-Time Work Experience

# BENJAMIN H. SNYDER

90 Avenida de Cortez
Los Angeles, California 11354
*Phone / Fax*: (555) 555-1954

### CAREER SUMMARY

*Offer B.A. in Government, minor in legal studies, and additional course / lab experience on water filtration and purification underscored by solid knowledge of laboratory standards and procedures. Seek a challenging position which will offer opportunities for career advancement and professional growth. Characterized as a quick study and willing contributor. Possess a natural ability to work with others. Establish excellent rapport with co-workers, professionals and staff at all levels. Respond appropriately to the needs, capabilities and interests of others. Committed to ideals of quality which combine resourcefulness and initiative with a drive for success. Coordinate work effectively with exceptional time management skills.*

### LEARNING CREDENTIALS

**BACHELOR OF ARTS - Government and Political Science**                 1999
University of California                                    Los Angeles, California

*Minor*: Legal Studies

*Additional Courses, Seminars, Workshops*:
Studied closely under distinguished environmental scientist and toxicologist,
Dr. Edward Fenster, Ph.D.  Lab work on water filtration and purification systems.
Extensive knowledge of laboratory safety standards and procedures.

### EMPLOYMENT HISTORY

**ASSISTANT RESERVE LIBRARIAN**                                      1998
George Pratt Library                                       Los Angeles, California

- Reserved reading materials for professor's courses
- Handled access to reserve reading room and staff mailing room
- Worked closely with students during the difficult summer session

**LOADING DOCK ASSOCIATE**                                          1993
Guffman Luxury Goods                                       Beverly Hills, California

- Managed shipments of clothing
- Supervised loading dock crew
- Handled waste and refuse management

### INTERESTS

Reading  /  Rock climbing  /  Classical music
Tutor in College English Writing Lab

REFERENCES AND FURTHER DATA AVAILABLE UPON REQUEST

so intimidated by the prospect of crafting a resume that they resort to exaggerating or fabricating their personal histories.

Don't give in to this temptation. Stretching the truth on your resume is always a mistake; if discovered, it can be cause for automatic disqualification, even for dismissal after you've landed the job. (Yes, it does happen.) Furthermore, it's not necessary. With some thought and creativity, almost any grad can unearth sufficient background information to develop a resume that's fully competitive with those of your peers. Here are some specific tips for doing so.

**List Virtually all Your Work Experiences, No Matter How Humble**
In the early stages of your career, *any* job you've held is relevant, whether or not it has anything to do with the kind of career you now hope to launch. That includes part-time work, summer jobs, and temp assignments that may have lasted only a few weeks. It also includes "scut work" of all kinds, from baby sitting and camp counselor jobs to burger-flipping, newspaper-routes, grocery-store stock-clerk jobs, and routine office work—filing, photocopying, and the like.

You may feel slightly embarrassed about a job like one of these, especially if it's the only work for pay you've ever done. Don't feel that way. Most of those who read your resume will have held a job or two like these during their own teenage years (and many have a sneaking fondness for being reminded of what they now consider "the good old days").

*Many employers are especially impressed by recent grads who worked to finance their own educations: it's felt this shows qualities of independence, responsibility, drive, and determination that are valuable in later life. If your part-time and summer jobs helped pay your tuition bills, mention this explicitly on your resume—it's a plus.*

Furthermore, all competent work for pay displays personal traits employers value: self-discipline, endurance, willingness to take orders, ability to work with others, some degree of organizational skill, detail-orientation, patience, etc. If you've *ever* held down a job successfully, you've demonstrated one or more of these qualities, which is a major step toward showing an employer that you're now worth considering for a somewhat more difficult and responsible job.

**Look for Work-Related Learning and Experience Hidden in Your Educational Credentials**
You may have taken a number of high school and college classes that are obviously applicable to the work you want to do. Business-related courses such as accounting, economics, statistics, management, and marketing are examples. You may even have graduated from a program that's completely career-oriented. If so, more power to you. Describe your educational credentials in loving detail on your resume; they'll go a long way toward placing you in the first job on your career ladder.

However, even if your educational background isn't obviously relevant to the job you seek, the chances are good that you've developed one or more work-related skills in the college, graduate-school, or even high-school-level courses you've taken. These deserve to be mentioned and described in your resume.

For example, suppose you've graduated from college with a degree in Spanish, and now want to seek work in the financial world—perhaps in banking, brokerage, or investment management. Although your degree isn't obviously related to the work you want to do, there are almost certainly relevant skills to be unearthed from your college experience.

Of course, you'll accurately describe your Spanish-language proficiency, using whatever appropriate phrase you choose: "Fluent in Spanish," "Good working knowledge of Spanish," "Basic skill in speaking and writing Spanish," or whatever. But as a Spanish major, you probably also developed:

> Research skills—as illustrated by the most impressive library or online research project you undertook

> Communications skills—as demonstrated in any lengthy or unusual writing assignment or oral or computerized presentation you created

> Computer skills—using word-processing, Internet, database, or other software

> Organizational ability—perhaps as an officer of the campus Spanish club or helping to plan the summer study-abroad program

> Teamwork—as shown by projects you successfully completed with other students or under the auspices of a faculty member

> Ability to lead, persuade, and influence others—as demonstrated by your success in helping to orchestrate a sales drive for the campus Spanish-language magazine

These are just examples, of course; but similar examples can be drawn out of whatever educational program you've experienced, whether in your major field of study, a minor concentration, or even a course or two far outside your main areas of interest.

No matter what you've studied, you can probably find several skills you developed in and around the classroom that deserve to be mentioned and highlighted on your new-grad resume. Not only will this help to demonstrate your ability to hold down a job successfully; it will also show employers that you are already thinking in business terms and are prepared to make an effective transition from the mindset of a student to that of an employee.

**FYI**

*For many recent grads, educational credentials are more relevant, impressive, and important than work experience. If that's the case with you, try* inverting *the usual resume sequence: List your educational experiences before your work experiences rather than after them. Rule of thumb: Always lead with your single most impressive credential, whatever that may be.*

- Extracurricular, civic, volunteer, and entrepreneurial experiences may be highly relevant.

Don't consider only job and classroom experiences when developing your recent-grad resume. Also examine everything you've done in the light of the work-related skills, knowledge, and personal traits it may have helped you develop. Remember to consider experiences involving community groups, charitable and religious organizations, political and civic societies, and campus organizations, clubs, teams, and publications.

You may also have "entrepreneurial" work experience in your background that you've almost forgotten about, but which is worth noting on your resume. One young woman we know started and ran a successful business planning and hosting birthday parties for small children—when she was twelve years old. Ten years later, this entrepreneurial experience earned a mention on her new-grad resume. Although her earnings from this venture were small (a few hundred dollars), it exhibited her traits of creativity, diligence, reliability, and ambition at an early age—and was certainly an unusual item that helped her resume stand out from the crowd in an appealing fashion.

### Don't Understate Your Achievements

Recent grads have a tendency to undersell themselves—to use excessive modesty when describing their achievements. Fight this tendency. Modesty is an appealing trait in personal relationships, but it's a mistake when you're job hunting.

Look again at Resume 10.1, focusing this time on Ben Snyder's employment history. The two summer jobs listed here aren't specifically relevant to the kind of work Snyder is now seeking, nor are they "impressive" jobs by most standards. But rather than simply listing them, Snyder has added bullets spelling out some of the responsibilities involved. These make it clear that, in both positions, Snyder developed and used organizational and personal skills that are likely to be useful in future jobs.

For another example, consider Resume 10.2, "Judith Gallagher." Gallagher has held several part-time jobs, all basically unrelated to one another, and is now working full-time as a clerk at an auto supply store. She's hoping to use her newly printed English degree as a stepping stone to more responsible and interesting work.

To maximize her chances, Gallagher has used several strategies. She has listed all of her jobs, demonstrating the fact that she has worked steadily for several years (suggesting diligence and motivation). She has added descriptive details about the work, especially for her current job, which help to bring out the job skills she has developed and used in

---

**FYI**

*If some of your relevant experience involves political or religious groups or organizations that some may consider controversial, disguise or downplay their identities so as to avoid needlessly alienating a potential recruiter. The (Roman Catholic) Knights of Columbus can be described simply as "a national fraternal organization"; the county Republican party can become "a local political organization"; the American Civil Liberties Union can be listed as "a civic association."*

## 10.2  Recent Grad with Checkered Job History

### JUDITH GALLAGHER
3 Old Farm Road · Park City, Utah 06033 · (860) 657-9879

### CAREER SUMMARY

*Offer 3+ years of diverse experience in business and service environments complemented by a degree in English and Communications. Background includes writing, planning and organizing skills underscored by excellent interpersonal abilities. Use tact and sensitivity when dealing with customers; consistently meet business or service objectives and quality performance standards.*

### EDUCATIONAL CREDENTIALS

**BACHELOR OF ARTS IN ENGLISH AND COMMUNICATIONS,** 1998
Bradford College - Bradford, Colorado

*National English Honors Society · Sigma Tau Delta*

### CAREER HISTORY

**CUSTOMER SERVICE / ACCOUNTS PAYABLE**                 1999 - Present
Solomon's Auto Supply                                              Park City, Utah

Provide prompt and courteous service to customers. Respond to inquiries with accurate and timely information. Process orders quickly and efficiently including all insurance matters. Utilize superior communication skills to increase customer awareness, satisfaction and respect.
- *Designed and developed an Employee Guideline Manual for all six store locations.*

**WAITRESS**                                                      1998 - 1999
Rising Phoenix Cafe                                           Bradford, Colorado

**TUTOR**                                                              1997
Homeschool Education Board                        Breckenridge, Colorado
- *Instructed home school student in basic English composition.*

**CHILDCARE PROVIDER**                                               1996
Black Bear Day Camp                                        Bear Creek, Colorado
- *Provided all-day organized activities for a large group of twelve-year-old children.*

### SKILLS, ABILITIES AND ACHIEVEMENTS · VALUE OFFERED

- *Computer skills including Microsoft Word and Excel.*
- *Training and time management skills.*
- *Motivational, organizational skills and teamwork.*

REFERENCES AND FURTHER DATA AVAILABLE UPON REQUEST

each position. And she has summarized these credentials in her career summary under the broadly descriptive rubric, "3+ years of diverse experience in business and service environments complemented by a degree in English and Communications."

By packaging her collection of credentials under this general description, Gallagher is positioning herself to be considered for any service position in which communication skills are important, for example, a job working with customers in a bank, a travel agency, or an insurance company.

Yet another example of presenting modest credentials in the most impressive and appealing light can be seen in Resume 10.3, "Clarisse Okuje." This resume belongs to a recent college grad who completed her degree while holding down a job at a local bank and now hopes to shift into the field for which she has been trained—computer information systems. Note how Okuje has designed her resume to highlight her strengths. After an attractive personal summary (headed with the name of the field to which Okuje hopes to move), she leads off with her educational background (headed "Learning Credentials"). Okuje's degree is the credential most directly relevant to the work she hopes to do now.

Then, Okuje breaks down her job at Bay Colonial Bank into three listings, showing her progression from one position to the next and emphasizing the growth in responsibilities she has enjoyed. She describes the jobs—especially the current job—in terms that emphasize the business, management, information, and people skills required. The overall impression created by the resume is that of a person with a strong (through fairly brief) working background who has now completed a business-oriented college degree and is ready to launch a new career building on both strengths. Okuje has made a (relatively) little look like a lot.

# STRIKING THE RIGHT BALANCE

As you've seen, a recent grad's resume needn't appear skimpy or unimpressive. Most grads can draw upon part-time or summer jobs, educational experiences, and community or volunteer work to present skills and credentials that demonstrate the ability and willingness to handle a responsible full-time position—even if it's their first such job.

At the same time, avoid creating the impression of "overkill." Don't exaggerate or stretch the importance and degree of responsibility of your past jobs (and, as we've warned, you should certainly never tell an outright lie). As a new or recent grad, you're part of the pool of young

## 10.3  Recent Grad with Experience at One Employer

*Confidential Resume of*

# CLARISSE OKUJE

56 Crestridge Road
Newton, Massachusetts 15429
(555) 555-6280
*Email:* cla_oku@flash.com or okujec@JobGroup.com

---

### COMPUTER INFORMATION SYSTEMS

**Forward-Thinking, Results-Oriented, People-Focused Facilitator**

*Energetic, organized and dependable contributor with strong bilingual communications skills, recent business degree and leading-edge computer systems training. Innovative and resourceful. Able to identify opportunities and consistently meet goals and objectives. Persuasive, persistent, pragmatic. Possibility thinker with untiring initiative and enthusiastic commitment. Seek challenging position where training, organizational / sales abilities, interpersonal skills and client service experience will lead to career growth opportunities.*

---

### LEARNING CREDENTIALS

**BACHELOR OF BUSINESS ADMINISTRATION**, 1999
Boston College - Boston, Massachusetts

*Computer Information Systems*
*Major GPA: 3.44 · Overall GPA: 3.295 · Dean's List: 1998*

**ASSOCIATE IN APPLIED SCIENCES**, 1997
Minuteman Community College - Quincy, Massachusetts

*Maintained 3.5 GPA while working 35-38 hours per week*
*Dean's List: 1995 - 1997*

---

### COMPUTER SKILLS

MS Word · Excel · Access · PowerPoint · Lotus Notes
Web Page Design · Windows 95 · Windows NT

Languages: C++ · HTML · Cobol · Java · Dbase III

---

**CLARISSE OKUJE**

## CAREER TRACK

BAY COLONIAL BANK · Cambridge, Massachusetts

**CUSTOMER REPRESENTATIVE / SALES ASSISTANT** 1997 - Present

Utilize superior communications abilities and computer facility to assist customers in making prompt and accurate account transactions including transfers, deposits and withdrawals. Provide general information; promote special products; answer inquiries in courteous manner. Exercise knowledge of bank automated systems, policy and regulations. Refer high profile clients to financial consultants. Foster and develop excellent staff and community relations.

- *Demonstrate ability to coordinate multifunctional, multicultural workforce; ensure effective training, supervision, performance appraisal and recognition for staff of 6 tellers.*

- *Recognize and define complex issues; develop and implement creative alternative solutions to maintain customer satisfaction and continued loyalty, and lead to increased sales.*

- *Generate customized marketing and presentational strategies to exploit and maximize account development opportunities with the largest customers; meet or exceed sales goals.*

**SERVICE ASSISTANT / CUSTOMER REPRESENTATIVE JUNIOR** 1995 - 1997

- *Responded to customers' written and telephone requests using Client/Server Metrolan.*
- *Maintained and operated ATMs, faxes, printers and copiers.*
- *Supervised 6 tellers.*

**TELLER** 1994 - 1995

- *Conducted daily transactions in excess of $20,000.*

## AWARDS

Top Service Representative Nominee, 1998
Top Fraud Buster, 1998

## VOLUNTEER WORK

Actively involved as a French Translator and Prison Pen Pal

REFERENCES AND FURTHER DATA AVAILABLE UPON REQUEST

(or youngish) working people whose career, interests, and personalities are still being formed. There's no shame in that, and it's not necessary to try to hide it.

Thus, creating the effective recent-grad resume is a matter of striking the right balance. Being too diffident about your accomplishments can be harmful; so can being boastful. Finding the line between the two takes tact and judgment.

A useful rule of thumb is this: If you can document an accomplishment with a specific statement of factual detail, it's probably a valid achievement worth highlighting. If not, it's more likely to be a vague assertion that may come across as pretentious or overblown.

Here's an illustration. Suppose you worked for two summers as an assistant manager at a local diner. You'll surely want to list this job on your new grad resume. But the more specifically you can describe your managerial responsibilities, the more genuine and impressive they'll appear.

> **Broad, vague:** Managed personnel, financial, administrative, and production functions at local restaurant.

> **Specific:** Scheduled and supervised work of two cooks, four waiters, cashier, and busboy during evening and weekend shifts at local diner serving over 400 customers per day. Balanced register receipts, managed opening and closing routines, handled bank deposits, and responded to emergencies.

You'll run little risk of writing a resume that seems overblown and pretentious if you back up every achievement with specific details like these.

Here are some other tips for achieving balance between overselling and underselling yourself in the recent-grad resume.

### One Page Is Often Sufficient—But Not Always
Depending on the breadth of your background, a one-page resume may be long enough. If you've never held a full-time job, stick to a single page. However, if you've held one or more full-time jobs that are at least somewhat relevant to the kind of work you're seeking, you may need a second page. If so, don't hesitate to use it.

### Let Your Personality Show
As a recent grad, you don't have a lengthy track record of work accomplishments to offer a potential employer. Instead, you're selling potential—an elusive quality whose definition is inevitably somewhat subjective. The candidate perceived as having potential is often simply the person whose resume (and interview) contained some spark that

---

**FYI**

*When an experienced professional from the field you want to work in agrees to meet for an informational interview, one question to put on your agenda is, "What do you think of my resume?" A candid comment or two about the tone, style, and content of your resume from a person with years of experience in your field can be very helpful in fine-tuning your message.*

ignited a feeling of recognition, compatibility, and excitement on the part of the employer—a sense that the "chemistry" is right for a connection between the job and the candidate.

Does all this sound a little "touchy-feely"? It is; but that's the reality of how jobs get filled. Hiring the right people is more art than science—more a matter of chemistry and "vibes" than of logic.

To increase the chances of sparking the right kind of chemistry, don't be afraid to let your personality show on your recent-grad resume. Include interesting information about your interests, hobbies, sports, favorite reading, and unusual accomplishments. Even minor awards, honors, publications, and presentations may be worth mentioning: "Second-place prize in Engineering Department's annual Dune Buggy Construction Derby"; "Authored series of three interviews in campus newspaper with state political leaders."

Such facts should probably be dropped from your resume within two to five years, but now (at the start of your career) they may help you to stand out from the other recent grads and could provoke enough interest on the part of a recruiter to make an interview possible.

### Your Best Job Perk Will Be the Opportunity to Learn

In searching for your first "real" job (or your first job in a career that you hope will be a long-lasting, varied, and successful one) you'll be seeking to strike a bargain with an employer that's a little different from those that will come later in your work life.

As is always the case, you'll be offering your talent, knowledge, and hard work in exchange for a salary and benefits on the assumption that the value you'll create for your employer will be worth at least as much as the income you'll receive. But in addition, as a recent grad, you'll also be offering an extra measure of enthusiasm, energy, and dedication in exchange for the opportunity to learn and grow on the job. In effect, your first job should be, in part, an extension of your education—an opportunity to apply what you already know in a real-world situation and to develop brand-new skills and knowledge with the help of colleagues, bosses, clients, and the business environment in which you'll work.

This second part of the job bargain is unwritten and usually unspoken, but it's widely understood and accepted by both recent-grad job seekers and employers. Keep it in mind as you craft your resume and cover letter and during the interviews and other parts of the job-search process. You'll want to find an employer willing to accept the inevitable limitations of a recent grad—and willing to support you in outgrowing them.

*An important aspect of researching the industries in which you're considering working is to investigate what forms of training are generally available and how new hires can qualify for them. In some businesses, formal training classes are offered, sometimes comparable to college or grad-level courses; in other businesses, entry-level employees are thrown into the deep end of the pool and must find their own learning opportunities. Ask people with experience in the field what you can expect, and proceed with your eyes open.*

## 10.4  Recent Grad with Full-Time Work Experience

# CYNTHIA LASTAKOS

51 North Street,  Philadelphia, Pennsylvania 37554
*Phone*: (555) 555-4575   *Beeper*: (555) 555-9795
*Email*: Cindy22@ami.com

### CAREER GOAL

*To secure employment that will fully utilize my experience and skills as an administrative assistant. I wish to join a challenging workplace that offers opportunities for advancement and growth. I am adept at coordinating people and processes. I offer more than 6 years of proven business experience in an international environment. I am able to recognize and define problems and have demonstrated resourcefulness in implementing timely and effective solutions. I coordinate work effectively with excellent time management skills and respond appropriately to the needs, capabilities and interests of others. I enjoy being part of a team.*

### PROFESSIONAL EXPERIENCE

J.P. COSTANZA, INC. · Philadelphia, Pennsylania
*International Sales and Marketing Organization*
**ADMINISTRATIVE ASSISTANT / OEM SALES ASSISTANT**                    1993 - Present

Support company executives in all aspects of daily operation. Answer, screen and route calls. Type and word-process documents and correspondence involving extensive data entry and order entry from locations worldwide. Maintain sales and quotation information. Prepare purchasing documents. Appropriately file all documentation, memorandum, reports and office records. Monitor levels of office materials and maintain adequate supplies. Organize and implement effective operating and management systems; utilize knowledge of computer functions to continually upgrade systems.

- *Assist sales / marketing personnel in prospecting, merchandising, collections and records maintenance.*
- *Perform extensive customer service in responding to inquiries, confirming order quotations, and resolving problems.*

### EDUCATION & TRAINING

**BACHELOR OF ARTS - English**, 1999
University of Pennsylvania, Pennsylvania

*Fully employed while completing all academic requirements.*

**Computer Skills:**
Windows 98 · Netscape · WordPerfect · Microsoft Network · Microsoft Word
Internet Research · United Parcel Online Service

REFERENCES AND FURTHER DATA AVAILABLE UPON REQUEST

## 10.5  Recent Grad with Full-Time Work Experience

*Confidential Resume of*

### ANDREW L. WATERSTON

1774 Hermes Avenue
San Jose, California 95773
*Home:* (555) 555-9603 · *Work:* (555) 555-3500
*Email:* alwaterston@flash.com *or* alwaterston@JobGroup.com

*Computer Hardware / Software*

## OUTSIDE SALES

**Forward-Thinking, Results-Oriented, People-Focused Achiever**

*Energetic and dependable contributor with technical prowess, proven leadership, strong communication skills and years of sales experience. Innovative, resourceful and inventive. Fast-track, goal-oriented and disciplined. Offer sound planning abilities and understanding of today's business conditions, programs and alliances to customize and integrate state-of-the-art strategies and systems. Seek challenging position where degreed training, organizational / sales abilities and interpersonal skills will be fully utilized and lead to career growth and advancement opportunities.*

### CAREER TRACK

**SENIOR MARKETING REPRESENTATIVE**                                    1979 - Present
Network Software                                                San Jose, California

Coordinate business development, fulfillment, administrative and marketing activities for company recycling and reselling computer equipment and components. Utilize superior networking and communications abilities; consistently foster strong client relations. Focus on defense industries, utilities and universities. Generate customized marketing and presentational strategies to exploit and maximize account development opportunities with the largest customers. Oversee deinstallation and shipping. Propel product and service matrix.

- *Bought, sold and leased new and used IBM and Control Data mainframe computer systems and peripherals to multinational and Fortune 500 firms throughout U.S. and Europe.*

- *Built list of clientele to include Atlantic Rim Power, DATEX / Horn Pacific, Interprol Systems, Hart Data Coporation, Mobile Research Corporation, Gillet & Danforth.*

- *Perform troubleshooting of delivery and quality issues; achieve outstanding customer satisfaction through high operating efficiencies, reliability and quality performance.*

**ANDREW L. WATERSTON**                                                    page 2

### LEARNING CREDENTIALS

**BACHELOR OF BUSINESS ADMINISTRATION IN MARKETING**                          1999
Stanford University                                                Palo Alto, California
*Graduated Summa Cum Laude*

**ASSOCIATE OF ARTS & SCIENCES IN BUSINESS**                                   1997
Claremont College                                                  Claremont, New York
*Graduated with Distinction*

### HONORS & DISTINCTIONS

Delta Mu Delta - National Honor Society in Business Administration
Alpha Chi - National Honor Society
Pi Alpha Sigma - College Honor Society
Alpha Beta Gamma - International Business Honor Society
Dean's List - Claremont College

### INTERESTS & ACTIVITIES

Reading / Travel / Outdoor activities

### PERSONAL

Eager to perform work-related travel

REFERENCES AND FURTHER DATA AVAILABLE UPON REQUEST

## 10.6  Recent M.B.A. with Unrelated Work Experience

*Confidential Resume of*

# MELISSA C. PRICE

75 Bloom Street, Suite #233
Montpelier, Vermont 11623
*Home*: (555) 555-5861   *Work*: (555) 555-6375
*Email*: mcprice@JobGroup.com

### CAREER SUMMARY

*Offer excellent educational credentials including MBA in Management and BA in Social Science complemented by 5+ years of diverse experience in insurance, banking and teaching. Characterized by strong communication abilities and superior interpersonal skills. Creative and resourceful with proven ability to identify opportunities, and consistently achieve goals and objectives. Recognize and define problems; implement timely and effective solutions. Articulate and persuasive, write with clarity, respond appropriately to the needs, interests and capabilities of others. Committed to ideals of quality which combine initiative with a drive for success. Coordinate work effectively with exceptional time management skills.*

### LEARNING CREDENTIALS

**MBA - Management**, 1999
Vermont Business College - Manchester, Vermont

**BACHELOR OF ARTS - Social Science**
Middlebury College - Middlebury, Vermont

### CAREER TRACK

**CUSTOMER SERVICE REPRESENTATIVE**                              1998 - Present
SomniCom Universal Insurance                                 Montpelier, Vermont

- Assist policy holders, their employees and medical providers with quotation of benefits and claim status
- Address payment of claims in coordination with claims examiners
- Handle eligibility issues that arise concerning medical coverage
- Document all information on line through Call Tracking
- Train new representatives on use and update of system files
- Key and process claims

MELISSA C. PRICE                                          Page 2

**BRANCH OPERATIONS TELLER**                             1996 - 1998
GREEN MOUNTAIN BANK                               Montpelier, Vermont

- Received and processed deposits, withdrawals and loan transactions
- Managed a cash drawer daily and bank vault monthly, alternating with other tellers
- Balanced and replenished ATM funds
- As a team member, assisted in branch balancing procedures
- Maintained proper files using on line terminal
- Cross-sold products and services to new and existing customers

**SUBSTITUTE TEACHER**                                   1994 - 1997
MONTPELIER SCHOOL DEPARTMENT                       Montpelier, Vermont

- Substitute teacher for grades kindergarten through eighth
- Prepared and taught lesson plans as required
- Extended positions for teachers on leave of absence

REFERENCES AND FURTHER DATA AVAILABLE UPON REQUEST

## 10.7  One-Page Resume for a Young Professional

### STEVEN K. RADCLIFF
421 Harlow Place · Potterville, Ohio 45750
555-555-4849

**FINANCIAL INDUSTRY**
A HIGHLY EFFICIENT AND DISCIPLINED ACCOUNTANT, INCISIVE IN IDENTIFYING
COMPLEX FINANCIAL PROBLEMS, IMAGINATIVE IN FINDING AND IMPLEMENTING
CREATIVE, COST-EFFECTIVE SOLUTIONS.

**PROFESSIONAL EXPERIENCE**

**STAFF ACCOUNTANT**
1994 - Present
UBU MUTUAL OF MIDAMERICA · Cleveland, Ohio
- Plan and execute daily accounting / financial functions for two companies; maintain general ledgers
- Perform monthly budget variance analyses and updates; investigate expense / expenditure fluctuations; provide summaries of variance reports to senior management.
- Evaluate year end financial results; research and assess financial risk; develop and present reports with recommendations.
- Prepare corporate tax documents and financial statements for outside auditors utilizing knowledge of current accounting policies and reporting protocols.
- Execute research on bank charges; employ various cost reduction / savings / avoidance strategies.
- Maintain computer systems, generate spreadsheets and various business documentation and reports utilizing Lotus 1-2-3, Excel, WordPerfect and MicroTSP; serve as office computer liaison.

**STAFF ACCOUNTANT**
1993 - 1994
WORLDWIDE BUREAU OF COMMERCE · Chicago, Illinois
- Proved and updated daily cash register.
- Reviewed accounting work prior to general ledger entry.
- Prepared budgets and forecasts.
- Directed registration for Professional School of Development.

**SALES REPRESENTATIVE**
1987 - 1992
MASTERS & MISTRESSES · Oberlin, Ohio
- Worked in upscale clothing store to finance college expenses.

**EDUCATION**

**MASTER OF BUSINESS ADMINISTRATION IN CORPORATE FINANCE,** 1993
Columbus State College - Columbus, Ohio

**BACHELOR OF ARTS IN ACCOUNTING,** 1990
Oberlin College - Oberlin, Ohio

**COMPUTER SKILLS**
Knowledge of PC, Lotus 1-2-3, Excel, WordPerfect, MicroTSP

REFERENCES & FURTHER DATA AVAILABLE UPON REQUEST

At the same time, on your side of the bargain, you'll need to be willing to "pay your dues"—to spend some time doing work that's mundane, routine, uncreative, perhaps even unpleasant: making photocopies, ordering supplies, dealing with complaints, running errands, answering phones, etc. The payoff should come in the form of gradually increasing knowledge and the responsibilities that go with it.

Employers that hire significant numbers of new grads understand this trade-off and are looking for job candidates who understand it, too. Show this by the language you use in your resume and cover letter and by the attitude you strike during your interview.

### More Sample Resumes for Recent Grads

Resumes 10.4 through 10.7 illustrate a variety of other recent-grad situations. Note how the organization, style, and tone of the resumes varies depending on the breadth and depth of the job seeker's work background, how closely it's related to the work they're now seeking, and the relative importance of their educational credentials.

## JUST THE FACTS

- As a recent grad, you have to develop relevant and impressive credentials from a limited work background. With thought and creativity, almost anyone can do it.

- Define your job objective broadly, not narrowly—or combine it with a career summary instead.

- Consider school-related, extracurricular, volunteer, and other activities as sources of job-related credentials.

- Allow your personality to shine through your resume—as a recent grad, it's one of your most important credentials.

- Never forget the unique employment bargain that the recent grad is seeking—one with an emphasis on the value of learning.

# Chapter 11

# The Seasoned Veteran

## Get the Scoop On . . .

- Challenges facing the seasoned veteran in today's job market
- Strategies to help the older person get the job
- Camouflaging your age in your resume
- Overcoming any bias against older job applicants during the interview

## PROSPECTS FOR TODAY'S OLDER JOB SEEKER

It has never been easy for the older employee (over 50) to compete for job openings for two important reasons. The first is that our culture has a bias toward younger people, who are thought to be more energetic, creative, and forward-thinking than their seniors. If you spend an evening watching television, for example, you'll see that most of the characters portrayed are younger people, while very few older people (almost none, in fact) are portrayed in a completely positive light. While in some other cultures the older members of society are revered by the younger members, in ours almost the opposite is true.

*The human resources consulting firm Lowe Barnes Prynn reports that the average worker over the age of 50 who changes employers suffers a reduction of between $3,000 and $4,000 in annual salary. By contrast, the average under-50 worker gets a raise when changing jobs.*

The second reason is that, in keeping with the societal bias, many companies like to think of themselves as being "young" and "dynamic" (even, or perhaps especially, if they aren't). As a result, on the assumption that younger people are more dynamic than older ones, these companies are inclined to hire younger rather than older employees. The middle-aged employee who looks around the office, especially in larger organizations, is likely to notice that he or she has a good number of years on most of the other members of the staff, in some cases even on those responsible for running the company.

In addition to this traditional bias against older employees, there are several specific factors at work today that combine to make it especially challenging for older people to find good positions.

### New Technologies

More than a hundred years ago, when typewriters were first being introduced into the workplace, those prospective employees who were familiar with the then-new technology had an advantage over those who were not. Although to us typewriters may seem simple to understand and use, they certainly wouldn't have seemed so to those encountering them for the first time.

People tend to be wary of new technologies. Your great-grandparents were probably mystified by the use of the telephone, and your grandparents may have been amazed by talking pictures. Your parents may have had a great deal of difficulty learning how to program a video cassette recorder, and you probably remember having to learn to use a fax machine for the first time.

But the impact of these technologies pales in comparison to the impact of the introduction of the personal computer into the workplace. Computers have largely replaced older means of communication and have become an integral part of how we do our jobs. Thus, familiarity with computers is an essential part of any job today, and if you are not familiar with these new technologies, you will find it virtually impossible to compete for many positions with those who are.

## The Baby Boomers

The enormous number of members of the "baby boom" generation (people born between 1945 and 1957) has had an effect on those people throughout their working lives, and continues to have an effect today. The fact that there have been so many people of the same age competing for entry-level, then managerial, then middle-management, and finally senior management positions, has meant that getting into business and moving up through the ranks has been more complicated for the Baby Boomers than for any previous generation. Fortunately, strong economic growth during most of the Baby Boomers' lives has mitigated the problem to some extent.

This difficulty is now being compounded by the additional competition presented by the children of those Baby Boomers, a large group in itself, who are now competing with members of their parents' generation for some of the same positions. And, as a result of our society's bias toward younger people, the children of the Baby Boomers are in some respects more attractive to potential employers than are their parents.

## Financial Issues

The reason the children of the Baby Boomers are more attractive to potential employers has its basis in today's economic realities. In an increasingly competitive business environment, every company is seeking ways to save money. And since the single greatest expense for virtually every company is its staff, one of the most effective ways of containing costs is by spending less in salaries and employee benefits.

As a result, even those companies which recognize that older employees can bring a higher level of experience to their jobs also recognize that those more experienced workers expect higher salaries than younger workers. Although it may not be the wisest choice in the long term, the potential short-term savings on costs to be realized by companies leads many to hire younger, less-experienced workers rather than seasoned veterans with more experience.

### The Middle Management Glut

During the '90s, an estimated half-million middle managers and senior executives lost their jobs as large companies were downsized, reorganized, merged, or re-engineered in search of higher profit margins (or even simple survival). These seasoned veterans constitute a "lost generation" of savvy older workers, too many of whom are chasing too few remaining middle-management jobs. As a result, even those veterans who are able to land new middle-management positions are finding that even matching, much less exceeding, their previous income levels can be difficult.

One of the reasons for this is that many of the older workers seeking jobs have been laid off from positions with large companies attempting to eliminate layers of bureaucracy. Unable to find positions in other large organizations, they often end up signing on with smaller, growing firms that generally pay less.

### The Realities of Age Discrimination

While it is illegal in the United States to discriminate against a job candidate because of his or her age, the fact is that it happens. Because it *is* against the law, and managers know this, only the most foolish, and foolhardy, interviewer will tell you honestly that he or she considers you unsuitable for a position because you're too old. Companies have also learned to avoid such code words for age bias as "youthful," "fresh," and "new thinking" when advertising job openings. Since interviewers are under no obligation to explain their hiring decision to unsuccessful candidates, the chances are that you will never know why you didn't receive an offer, whether it was due to your age or not.

Moreover, there are any number of ways that a company can get around legislation concerning age discrimination. As long as no one can demonstrate that a given company has had a clear and consistent pattern of not hiring older employees, it can probably stay out of trouble even while avoiding 50+ job candidates.

## JOB-SEARCH STRATEGIES FOR THE FIFTY PLUS

Despite all the apparently bad news about the prospects for today's older job seeker, the situation is far from hopeless. There are several

---

**FYI**

*Being a seasoned veteran, if you're turned down for a job, it can be relatively easy (and perhaps tempting) to blame it on age discrimination. But if you're thinking about complaining to a governmental regulatory agency about it, be sure that you have more evidence than your suspicions to present as evidence of discrimination. Bringing an age-discrimination suit against a company, particularly if it's unsuccessful, can make it even more difficult for you to find another position later.*

strategies that you can use to make you more appealing to potential employers, as well as some categories of job opportunities that you may not have yet considered.

## Update Your Skills

*"Is age a problem? In today's market, age is a problem only if the person does not have the right experience and skills."*
—Dennis Inzinna, executive recruiter

One of the most important strategies, in fact an essential one, is to update your skills. We've already mentioned the importance of being familiar with all of the new technology currently being used in companies, but it's of such paramount importance that it can't be stressed enough. Virtually every organization now makes extensive use of computer technology, and if you don't know how to use a computer for such things as word processing, creating spreadsheets, making presentations, sending and receiving e-mail, performing research on the Internet, and other purposes, you might as well retire right now.

Fortunately, although the prospect of learning even the basic operations of a computer may seem daunting, once you've gotten started, you'll find that it's actually quite easy to do. In fact, learning to type is more difficult than learning how to operate a computer. In addition, you'll find that not only does a computer perform many functions better than the tools you used before, but also that, once you've learned the basics, it's not difficult to learn how to use computers in more complicated ways.

Despite the computer's enormous capabilities, it's ultimately just a machine, and once you've learned how to use it, it will do whatever you want. While today's computers and software are much more sophisticated than those of only a few years ago, they are also much easier to use. And, in fact, once you have learned how to use one, you'll wonder how you ever got by without it.

In many industries, other specific skills and job-related knowledge have changed during the past decade or two. As a seasoned veteran, you need to make sure your skills portfolio is absolutely up-to-date. In fact, because of the pervasive bias against older workers, your skills may face more intense scrutiny than those of less-experienced younger workers. If you're in general management, make sure you know the latest leadership buzzwords. If you're in sales, brush up on the most current popular selling techniques and be prepared to explain when and how you might use them. If you're an engineer or in some technology-related field, be current on recent innovations. You get the idea.

## Don't Be Afraid to Ask for Help

If you've been downsized or reorganized out of a job in a large corporation, you may have received outplacement counseling as part of your severance package. If so, take advantage of it. Launching a successful job search is difficult enough under the best of circumstances, but trying to do so while you're coping with the shock of having lost a job is even harder.

A good outplacement counselor can help you re-evaluate your skills (using both detailed self-assessment worksheets and psychological tests), assist you in preparing an effective resume and cover letters, and provide you with means of finding leads for new positions. He or she can also be of enormous psychological help to you in getting through a difficult time in your life.

If you haven't lost a job, or if you have but have not been provided with outplacement counseling, investigate the government agencies, non profit organizations, and private companies that provide employment counseling for older individuals. It's likely that you know some people who have been in your position, so you should ask them if they know of any such organizations or companies. Failing that, check your local yellow pages.

## Look at Small- to Mid-Sized Companies

With so many large corporations today under pressure to cut costs by trimming the staff, one strategy to consider in seeking a new position is that of targeting small- to medium-sized companies. Doing so can be advantageous for several reasons.

One of the most important reasons is that your age may well be considered less of a negative factor in such companies. As we mentioned before, the bias toward younger people seems to be more pronounced in large organizations, so if you target smaller ones you're less likely to run into that kind of bias. In fact, smaller, growing companies often find themselves in dire need of just the kinds of skills seasoned veterans have to offer—especially the ability to organize and make sense of a complicated, quickly changing business.

Another reason for concentrating on smaller companies is that they tend to be less complacent than many larger companies. Although large corporations do sometimes go out of business, small- and mid-sized companies do so much more often. Because smaller companies have a sense of the precariousness of their existence, to some extent they tend to appreciate experience more than their larger counterparts.

Finally, small- and mid-sized companies also tend to be more flexible than larger ones, particularly in their hiring practices. Thus, for example, if you have concerns about particular types of employee benefits or you'd like to be able to work at home on a regular basis, you're more likely to be able to work out an appropriate arrangement with a smaller company than with a larger one.

## Consider Starting Your Own Business

There are more opportunities for older people to launch their own businesses today than ever before. Of course, people have always been able to start their own businesses if they had the start-up money or could find investors willing to back them. In the past, though, starting a business often meant renting office space, buying furniture and equipment, and hiring an assistant or secretary to answer the phone. Today, new technologies have also enabled both older and younger workers to start new businesses with a minimal expenditure of money.

In fact, according to the Bureau of Labor Statistics, a record number of people over 55 are now in business for themselves: 2 million and growing. And where did these people come from? Many of them are the same skilled middle-management executives who lost their positions as a result of downsizing, mergers, and reorganizations. These are individuals with marketable skills who, thanks to low-priced computers, fax machines, telephone services, Internet connections, and all the other new technologies, can set up home-based businesses on a relative shoestring.

Whatever your major area of business experience and knowledge, you may be able to apply it as an independent contractor or consultant. If you are an accountant with experience in financial management, there are many small businesses in need of your knowledge who may be willing to pay you for it. If you're an experienced marketing manager, you can set up shop as a consultant helping small to mid-sized businesses develop marketing plans for their new products or services. If you have some particular technical expertise, you can rent it out, a day or a week at a time, to companies that lack it.

Operating this way has one major advantage over a conventional work arrangement: *employer diversification*. Despite the lack of a steady paycheck, working for (say) 10 different companies, two days per month each, can be more financially and emotionally secure than casting in your lot with a single firm. Downsizing or financial woes at one or two companies needn't cripple you; you still have several other sources of work and income.

So, if you've always wanted to run your own business, can't bear the thought of returning to a corporate environment, or never even considered the possibility before, it might be worth considering the idea of starting a business of your own. There are disadvantages to working on your own, the lack of a steady paycheck and the lack of business companionship being foremost among them. But if you can deal with uncertainty and a little loneliness, starting your own company may be the way to go.

# THE GENTLE ART OF CAMOUFLAGE

**FYI**

*If you haven't already put your resume on a computer, now is a good time for you to do so. You can save a lot of time and effort in making changes in the text and the formatting of a resume if you do it electronically. A computerized resume is also much easier to tailor for specific job opportunities. With a computer, you can effortlessly maintain five or ten slightly different resumes to use with different types of companies or job openings.*

Assuming you do want to find another conventional job, it is essential that you carefully review your resume and revise it as necessary to make you more attractive to potential employers. It's likely that, even in today's excellent job market, you will have several competitors for any job you may seek, and busy potential employers will be looking for excuses to not interview some of those whose resumes they receive. The last thing you want to do is give them such an excuse on your resume.

We are not talking about falsifying your resume in any way but, rather, about "spin"—presenting accurate information in a way that's advantageous to the presenter. Specifically, we're talking about camouflaging certain things that may raise questions in the employer's mind to such an extent that he or she will not call you in for an interview.

Although age is the most obvious factor that you may want to camouflage, there are several others that might seem problematic to potential employers and are accordingly worth thinking about. Among these are jobs with companies with less-than-impressive names, experience in the public sector, periods of self-employment, and job titles that didn't accurately reflect your work. Here are some ways of camouflaging these potential problems.

## Camouflaging Age

If you feel that your age may reduce your chance of being called in for an interview, scan your resume in search of opportunities to delete or downplay any telltale indications of age. Of course, if you do get an interview, as soon as you walk in the door it will be obvious that you're not a recent college grad, but getting the interview is the first step. You'll then have the opportunity to amaze the interviewer with your energy, wisdom, and knowledge of all the latest tricks in business.

The most obvious way of determining someone's age from a resume is by examining the dates of employment and education. If, in the first decade of the twenty-first century, you have jobs on your resume dating back to the late 1960s or early 1970s, it will be immediately clear to potential employers that you've been around the block a few times. This can be remedied by simply *omitting* all but the most recent dates of employment in your resume.

Savvy employers may infer from this that you're a seasoned veteran, but without dates they'll have no way of knowing exactly how old you are. You can do the same with the dates normally included on resumes for college and/or postgraduate education. Resume 11.1,[6970] written by "Adam R. Sydney," shows how a resume can be crafted revealing only the most recent employment dates.

A long list of positions on your resume is another sign that you're a seasoned veteran, and there are a several ways of camouflaging this as well. One way is simply to list, rather than provide full entries for, some of your earlier positions. It's likely that your first jobs were at lower levels and less relevant to your future work than your more recent jobs, so downplaying them will have no appreciable effect on how your credentials are perceived by potential employers—except to allow them to assume that you are younger than you are.

Resume 11.2, belonging to "David Prendergast," provides an example of how this can be accomplished. For an even more powerful age-reduction effect, David could *combine* this technique with the previous one by omitting the dates for all of his jobs prior to 1980, as well as the dates of his schooling.

Another way of reducing a long list of jobs is to condense some of your earlier positions so that the sheer *number* of positions you've held is less obvious—and less intimidating. Let's say, for example, that you started working in a publishing company as an editorial assistant and were promoted over the next 20 years to assistant editor, associate editor, editor, senior editor, and executive editor. Since all of these jobs had similar functions, even though each brought with it higher levels of responsibility, it would be possible to condense them into what will *appear* at first glance to be just one job.

### FYI

*If you do leave some of the earliest positions out of your resume, it's essential that you also eliminate your dates of education or other dates that would make the omissions obvious. If you don't delete those dates, there will be a gap between your education and your (apparently earliest) work experience that will raise a red flag.*

You might, for example, provide detailed information about the most important position, executive editor, and then include the following:

> Prior to becoming executive editor, served as senior editor (1978–1985), editor (1974–1978), associate editor (1972–1974), assistant editor (1970–1972), and editorial assistant (1968–1970).

A third way to camouflage the number of positions you've held is to simply omit your earliest jobs altogether. Remember, your resume is not some sort of legal document. You are under no obligation to include on your resume every job you've ever had, and leaving out the earliest ones will make it appear that you haven't been working for as long as you actually have.

Finally, there is one additional way in which information on your resume can date you. If there is a listing on your resume for a job with a

## 11.1  Camouflaging Age by Eliminating Dates

*Confidential Resume of*

### ADAM R. SYDNEY

141 Cloverhill Lane • Green Springs, Nevada 60565
(555) 555-6472
www.gowork.com/resumes/arsydney.htm
*Email:* arsydney@ami.net

### SALES • MANAGEMENT • MARKETING

**Forward-Thinking, Results-Oriented, Solution-Driven Achiever**

*Offer progressive leadership contributions to new business development, customer retention, management and retailer training, and sales results. Innovative, resourceful and inventive. Insightful and analytical with ability to formulate market-penetrating plans, expand market share and improve profitability. Identify opportunities and consistently achieve objectives.*

### CAREER TRACK

**SALES & BUSINESS DEVELOPMENT**                                    1983 - Present
Silverbeam / Crenshaw, Inc.                                           Reno, Nevada

Combine exceptional market cognizance with proactive, practiced business sense. Formulate and propel mid-range and long-term strategy for manufacturers' representative agency. Consistently review and evaluate existing systems with a view toward enhancing profits, quality, productivity and cost reduction. Identify issues; develop and implement creative solutions leading to increased profitability and sales. Meet deadlines; enhance efficiency.

- *Set **all-time sales records** with M. White & Co. in 1997, Mission Hill Appliance / Kwik Shoppes in 1995, Parker's Department Stores in 1995-97, Holbrook Dairy in 1996-97, Vatco in 1997, Treasure Box Arts & Crafts in 1997, and with Dale Supply in 1996-97.*

- *Won **"Vendor of the Year"** award for Housewares department with volume of $5,800,000 at Parker's, 1995.*

- *Serve such clients as Lewis Powerpad Systems, Millstone, Dexter Home Furnishings, Burke Industries, Spielman, and CleanAir Ventilation Products.*

- *Attend Spade Tools and Valu-Trust dealer shows; help set up booths; sell dealers on drop-ship or pool basis; constructed displays for Luminatrix in Parker's stores.*

- *Negotiated new accounts at Housewares, Hardware, Gourmet Products, and Premium and Gift shows.*

**Positions Prior to 1983**

**DISTRICT MANAGER**
Spielman Inc.                                                      Las Vegas, Nevada

Contributed vision and management expertise critical to organizational efficiency and business growth. Selected and trained high-performing management staff. Managed sales and new accounts. Utilized superior networking and communications abilities, consistently building strong customer relations. Forecasted sales by customer and model. Achieved outstanding customer satisfaction through high operating efficiencies, reliability and quality performance.

*Confidential Resume of* **ADAM R. SYDNEY**

- *Advised and assisted distributors; orchestrated product display and sales at conventions and trade shows; coordinated and directed training seminars for retailers.*

- *Opened major accounts with Megaway and Walsh Pharmacies and Flyer Shops; after others had tried and failed, became first representative ever to sell Lewis Powerpad Systems to Spielman.*

- *Achieved rapid promotion; grew Reno territory over **100%** from $600,000 to $1,250,000+; attained Senior District Manager position in Las Vegas.*

**TERRITORY SALESMAN**
The Polk Company                                                           Evanston, Illinois

Drove development and implementation of market expansion strategies. Fulfilled regional marketing / sales policies and procedures and pursued overall strategy for growth. Generated new sales and serviced existing client accounts. Prospected for new accounts through client referrals and cold calls. Maintained highest possible standards for customer service.

- *Maintained high level of product technical knowledge; kept current with new developments and implications for customer product use; conducted Service Clinics with selected retailers.*

- *Achieved recognition as **#3 producer** out of 25 representatives in Housewares sales for the Chicago Branch, despite having the smallest territory with 22 Midwest counties.*

---

### LEARNING CREDENTIALS

**BACHELOR OF SCIENCE IN BUSINESS ADMINISTRATION**
Northwestern University - Evanston, Illinois

**Additional courses, seminars and workshops include:**
Management Development Program

---

### INTERESTS & ACTIVITIES

Reading / Travel / Outdoor activities

---

### PERSONAL

Willing to perform work-related travel / Willing to relocate

REFERENCES AND FURTHER DATA AVAILABLE UPON REQUEST

## 11.2  Camouflaging Age by Detailing Recent Positions Only

*Confidential Resume of*
# DAVID L. PRENDERGAST
903 Gershwin Street
Dalton, Nebraska 67703
(555) 555-5492
*Email:* dlp24@network.com

## EXECUTIVE MANAGEMENT - FINANCIAL SERVICES
### Multifunctional Strategic Planning and Business Development

*Innovative, accomplished financial executive with progressive achievements in asset-based lending, institutional sales and portfolio management. Established track record for broad technical knowledge, integrity, analytical acumen and relationship-building, · revenue-generating talents. Consistently increase market share and overachieve objectives. Team player, motivator and team builder; creative, insightful and inventive with high energy level; possibility thinker and doer.*

### CAREER TRACK

**VICE PRESIDENT / BUSINESS DEVELOPMENT OFFICER**                    1997 - 1999
Credit Systems of Nebraska                                           Omaha, Nebraska
Allied Services and Management                                       Lincoln, Nebraska

Demonstrate strong planning, organizing and leadership skills to set staff priorities and consistently meet service goals, management objectives and quality performance standards. Establish superior procedures for financial and operational control to manage and conserve resources and ensure data integrity. Continually evaluate strategies and tracking systems to enhance profits and reduce operating costs.

- *At Credit Systems of Nebraska, recognized, negotiated and concluded asset-based deals in telecommunications, high tech and waste management worth $1,000,000 to $20,000,000.*

- *At Allied Services and Management, structured and propelled asset based financial arrangements for chiefly service-industry companies ranging from $2,000,000 to $25,000,000.*

**VICE PRESIDENT / BUSINESS DEVELOPMENT OFFICER**                    1993 - 1996
Lincoln Mutual Bank                                                  Lincoln, Nebraska

Contributed vision and management expertise critical to organizational efficiency and business growth for competitive lender. Spearheaded planning and coordination of administrative and financial activities. Generated customized marketing and presentational strategies to exploit account development opportunities with the largest customers. Utilized superior networking and communications abilities, consistently building strong business relations.

- *Researched, planned and consummated asset-based contract agreements ranging in value from $1,000,000 to $20,000,000.*

- *Maintained a high level of technical knowledge in institutional investments, bonds and related instruments to customize and integrate client-specific financial information and advice.*

**VICE PRESIDENT & CREDIT MANAGER, U.S.A.**                          1990 - 1992
South Dakota National Trust Bank                                     Presswood, South Dakota

Serviced and monitored performance of loan portfolio for nationwide accounts with a book value of $1,500,000,000. Served as financial liaison to corporate community; monitored market and economic conditions for analysis and development of loan plans attractive to new and existing clients in a fast-paced environment.

*Continued*

**DAVID L. PRENDERGAST**                                                                                         Page 2

- *Supervised bank investments and oversaw performance of lenders; ensured that all investment contracts conformed to bank procedure and met all regulatory criteria.*

- *Updated loan policy manuals for Board of Directors; informed President and Senior Vice President of all changes to consumer regulations and likely impact on lending function.*

**CHIEF FINANCIAL OFFICER**                                                                                    1986 - 1990
D. Eubanks Company, Inc.                                                                             Winslow, Washington

Utilized business policy development skills and multi-disciplined expertise in strategic planning, operational forecasting and budgeting, manufacturing and project costs and human resource development. Demonstrated high-level networking capabilities and organizational expertise in day-to-day operations development, risk and growth.

- *Stayed informed on market trends; crafted strategic plans and programs to analyze process impacts on business unit objectives and maximize growth.*

- *Identified more than 100 promising acquisition candidates; closed deals with top 5 firms.*

**VICE PRESIDENT / NORTHWEST REGIONAL MANAGER**                                              1980 - 1986
Mercer Manufacturers                                                                         Mercer Island, Washington

Directed 30 person staff including 15 loan officers. Administered aggregate loan portfolio of $750,000,000. Successfully managed workouts ranging from $2,000,000 to $100,000,000. Continually reviewed and evaluated existing systems with a view toward enhancing operational efficiency, quality, productivity, and reducing expenses.

- *Served as Corporate Training Officer teaching recent MBA graduates the details of financial collateral and credit analysis.*

- *Led due diligence team during Manufacturers purchase of CIT which increased loans outstanding by $500,000,000.*

**Previous positions include:**

SENIOR ACCOUNT OFFICER - Constoll Business Credit, Inc. - Seattle, Washington • 1971 - 1980
ACCOUNT OFFICER - Pacific Mountain Bank - Seattle, Washington • 1967 - 1971
ACCOUNT OFFICER - Island Trust Company - Mercer Island, Washington • 1961 - 1967

---

**LEARNING CREDENTIALS**

ADVANCED INTERNATIONAL CREDIT PROGRAM, 1991
Unified Bank - London

GRADUATE, NATIONAL ASSOCIATION OF CREDIT MANAGEMENT SCHOOL, 1985
Hartwick College - Hartwick, New York

MASTER OF BUSINESS ADMINISTRATION PROGRAM, 1978
Ameritrust - Albany, New York

BACHELOR OF BUSINESS ADMINISTRATION PROGRAM IN ACCOUNTING, 1970
College of the Holy Cross - Connecticut

---

REFERENCES AND FURTHER DATA AVAILABLE UPON REQUEST

company that has changed names, as is so often the case nowadays, using the name under which the company was known at the time you worked for them will make it clear that you are a seasoned veteran. This can be avoided simply by using the name under which the company is *now* operating. Thus, "Bell Labs" becomes "Lucent Technologies," "U.S. Steel" becomes "USX," and "Time, Inc." becomes "AOL Time Warner." (This maneuver also eliminates the need to *explain* the older name to any young whippersnapper of an interviewer who may never have heard of it—and yes, you will encounter people like this.)

## Camouflaging Less-Than-Impressive Company Names

You may also want to camouflage situations in which you worked for a company with a less-than-impressive name: a company in an industry that's not widely respected; a company associated with some well-known failure, fiasco, or scandal; or a company that you're mildly embarrassed about having worked for, for whatever reason.

You can avoid the use of less-impressive names by using initials rather than full names or an official corporate name rather than the better-known company title. Let's say, for example, that you worked for a while as a shift manager at a McDonald's fast food restaurant in Stamford, Connecticut, and you're concerned that a prospective employer may not be impressed with the fact that you worked there. In such an instance, you might be able to use the initials of the corporate name: MFS, Inc., which stands for McDonald's Franchise of Stamford. (The job description that follows would accurately describe your duties and achievements—"Supervised staff of 18 full-time and part-time service employees," etc.—without making it obvious that you were working for Mickey D's.)

Similar strategies can be used in many situations. If you were a staff writer for a disreputable tabloid paper, you could list the corporate owner, "Galaxy Publications," say, rather than the name of the publication. If you ran a division of a business that went bankrupt in a highly public and slightly embarrassing fashion, you could use the name of the parent company, which was barely tarnished by the episode. Or, conversely, if you worked for the one effective division within a lackluster larger corporation, you might choose to list only the division name and omit the corporate name altogether.

## Camouflaging Work in the Public Sector

There is a considerable difference in the cultures of public- and private-sector organizations. The former tends not to be respected by those in the latter because public-sector organizations are perceived as being noncreative, focused on red tape, and not bottom-line-oriented (read "impractical"). For that reason, if you are trying to make a transition from a public- to a private-sector organization, it would be advantageous to camouflage the fact that you've worked in the public sector. Again, the idea is not to pretend something that isn't true but rather to avoid triggering a bias until you have the opportunity to offset it in person, in an interview.

There are two ways of doing this. One way is to translate your descriptions of the functions you performed from public- to private-sector language. Let's say, for example, that you worked as a counselor in a public organization in which you supervised 150 volunteers and carried a caseload of 60 clients. On your resume, you might present this as "Human services manager and adviser."

Another way of camouflaging the fact that you worked in the public sector is to use initials or another abbreviation rather than the full name of the organization. If, for example, your job was to supervise the counselors at the Gandera Counseling Center, you might list the position as "Supervisor, GCC."

## Camouflaging Self-Employment

Potential employers tend to be wary of individuals who have been self-employed for a number of reasons. One is that they are concerned that if you've been self-employed, you may find it difficult to adapt to working as part of a team. Another, is that they think you may be looking for a job only because you've experienced a downturn in your business and will leave as soon as market conditions improve. A third reason is that they may suspect you were self-employed because, for one reason or another, no one else wanted to hire you.

Whatever the reason, it's advantageous for you to camouflage the fact that you worked for yourself, and there are several ways of accomplishing this. One way is to avoid describing yourself as an owner, co-owner, partner, or anything else that suggests that the company is yours.

Another is to find a creative way of simply avoiding the subject. As you will see in Resume 11.3, "Dr. Joseph Micelli," who had been self-employed as a management consultant for many years, did this by listing his major consulting assignments as though they were full-time, permanent positions. One has to look extremely carefully at Dr. Micelli's resume to realize that he was not an employee of any of the companies listed in his resume.

Dr. Micelli also used some of the other camouflaging tricks we've discussed in this chapter. He limited the descriptions of his older job

## 11.3  Camouflaging Self-Employment

**JOSEPH J. MICELLI, Ph.D.**
**DABFET, CPEA, CES, CSE, RPIH**

131-41 Dunn Street, Apartment 7C
Silver Springs, Maryland 34465-4950
(555) 555-5647
www.JobGroup.com/resumes/jjmicelli.htm
Email: jjmicelli@JobGroup.com

### SENIOR EXECUTIVE MANAGEMENT

**Environmental • Occupational Health • Safety • Forensic Engineering-Technology**
**Regulatory Compliance • Facilities Management • Construction**

*Creative, multi-disciplined Profit Center leader with 30-year exemplary record in business planning and entrepreneurial development, operations, project management, finance, marketing, administration and multi-profit center management in the rapid-growth environmental, occupational health and safety, forensic engineering & technology, construction, aerospace and health care industries. Seasoned and consistent. Adept at new ventures and turn-arounds. Innovative, resourceful and inventive. Possibility thinker with tireless initiative and deft influencing skills. Insightful motivator and team builder. Achieved $12,000,000 in revenues with 40+% margins through customized, cost-effective client solutions. A man of integrity and vision dedicated to tomorrow's challenges and rewards.*

### CAREER TRACK

**SENIOR CONSULTANT / ASSOCIATE**                                                1980 - Present
Naturonica LTD. (Senior Consultant)                                              Baltimore, Maryland

**SENIOR CONSULTANT / ASSOCIATE**                                                1990 - Present
Devistar Consulting & Associates                                                 Hedden, Maryland

Combine wide-ranging industry knowledge and regulatory awareness with proactive, practiced business sense. Utilize planning, coordinating, organizing and leadership skills for clientele in need of guidance in the areas of building re-engineering, site rehabilitations, renovations, construction management, forensic engineering and technology with interdisciplinary environmental, occupational health, safety and regulatory compliance. Market and present custom designed solutions and alternatives to maintain, protect, preserve and conserve client environs.

- *Managed 100% revenue growth and structured new innovative services, market segments, groups, organizations, and processes in multi-use structures, sites, diverse projects and other various real estate facilities and entities.*

- *Negotiated million dollar project management contracts.*

- *Directed and supervised activities of over 3500 personnel and 300 managerial staff.*

- *Effectively prevent or eliminate OSHA, EPA, EEO and OFCCP complaints, accidents and frequent audits; downsize corporate liability; integrate proven protocols and procedures.*

- *Manages, consults and offers expertise in forensic engineering and technology management, engineering applications and programs as well as health, safety engineering, environmental, industrial hygiene audits, hazard-risk review / assessment, and building diagnostic monitoring and abatement.*

**SENIOR CONSULTANT / ASSOCIATE**                                                1995 - 1998
Devistar Consulting & Associates                                                 Hedden, Maryland
**DIRECTOR** - SAFETY, LOSS PREVENTION & RISK MANAGEMENT PROGRAMS                 1995 - 1998
**CODE ENFORCEMENT ENGINEER / PRACTITIONER - SENIOR PROJECT MANAGER**
Vialife Safety and Regulation Contractors                                        Baltimore, Maryland

Contributed vision and management expertise critical to organizational safety, efficiency and productivity. Directed and managed programs in safety, loss prevention, risk management and compliance for entire company and all subsidiaries. Developed and conducted site safety programs and audit procedures to identify and correct unsafe working conditions or practices.

JOSEPH J. MICELLI, Ph.D., DABFET, CPEA, CES, CSE, RPIH                          Page 2

- *Stayed informed on laws, policies, priorities, trends and other issues; trained, supervised and audited team of 25 safety engineers, health and safety professional staff.*
- *Managed multi-profit center units increasing margins 18%.*
- *Structured and supervised subcontractor safety standards on-site activities; established emergency response procedures for mishaps, unforeseen incidents and accidents with forensic engineering and technology accountability.*
- *Oversaw environment, health and safety issues for simultaneous construction projects of DEP, Port Authority, BTA, MYTA and other public, industrial, residential and institutional entities valued at over $300,000,000.*

**SENIOR CONSULTANT / ASSOCIATE**                                            1993 - 1995
Devistar Consulting & Associates                                            Hedden, Maryland
SSB Techno-Consulting Services Center                                    Cross River, Maryland

Planned, positioned and promoted total quality management. Served as innovative strategist and insightful change agent. Initiated Quality Action Teams trained for continuous improvement. Developed goals, measurement methodology and feedback loops to ensure systems effectiveness. Established quality control standards, safety systems, programs and procedures.

- *Managed, directed and integrated environmental, occupational health, safety, loss prevention and risk management protocol programs throughout the aerospace system.*
- *Built sophisticated, flexible, cross-functional middle and upper management teams; concluded programs for Department of Defense with ISO 9000 and ISO 14,000 protocols.*
- *Configured Construction Safety Project Management programs with forensic engineering and technology management engineering applications for Avionics, FAA Repair Station, jet engine, fuel and hydraulic test cells for FAA and DOD contracts.*

**SENIOR CONSULTANT / ASSOCIATE**                                            1980 - 1993
Devistar Consulting & Associates                                  Tri-State Area / Metro Baltimore
*Numerous other consulting assignments - Fortune 100-300-500 & 1000 companies including:*

Department of Veterans Administration                                        1990 - 1993
Senior Building & Environmental Project Management Services                  Metro, New York

**DIRECTOR - ENVIRONMENTAL / OCCUPATIONAL HEALTH & SAFETY**
**REGULATORY COMPLIANCE OFFICER / PRACTITIONER**

Designed, developed and delivered campaign to secure long-term contracts for comprehensive environmental management services. Coordinated service offerings related to building maintenance, security, mechanical functions, energy conservation and odor control. Conducted industrial hygiene audits, regulatory inspections, and integrated environmental management.

- *Instituted TQM program; achieved 75% reduction in outgoing defect rate, cut delivery service installation time 30%; grew productivity 25% through health and safety training.*
- *Ensured effective motivation, training, performance appraisal and recognition of QA teams; established quality control standards and safety procedures for ISO 9000 and ISO 14,000.*
- *Integrated Construction Site Safety Project Management Programs with forensic engineering and technology intuitiveness into routine operations.*

---

**Previous positions include:**
GENERAL MANAGER - Arpell Inspectors, Inc. • 1976 - 1980
VICE PRESIDENT & GENERAL MANAGER / SENIOR PROJECT MANAGER / EHS ENGINEER - Certified Metro
Trust Corporation • 1971 - 1976
DIRECTOR OF ENVIRONMENTAL SERVICES / PROJECT MANAGER / ENGINEER -
Bass & Whitman Company • 1969 - 1971
ENVIRONMENTAL SERVICES CONTRACTOR / SENIOR ACCOUNT EXECUTIVE / PROJECT MANAGER
Rosgood Services International • 1963 – 1969

---

**JOSEPH J. MICELLI, PhD, DABFET, CPEA, CES, CSE, RPIH**                    Page 3

## LEARNING CREDENTIALS

MASTER DEGREE IN PUBLIC HEALTH • 1994

Texas A&M University                                                    Stephentown, Texas

*Conferred Honors • 1994 - 1997*

MASTER DEGREE OCCUPATIONAL HEALTH AND SAFETY • 1994
DOCTOR OF PHILOSOPHY IN ENVIRONMENTAL SAFETY AND HEALTH • 1997

University of Chicago                                                    Chicago, Illinois

FOR PROFESSIONAL STUDIES
*Conferred Honors • 1997*

## ORGANIZATIONS & ASSOCIATIONS

Universal Safety Organization • American Society of Standards, Materials, Products, Systems & Services •
National Industrial Hygiene Association • Patriot Society of Safety Engineers • Air & Waste Management
Association • National Safety Council • Entomological Society of America
American College of Forensic Examiners • Association of Professional Industrial Hygienists

## SELECTED CERTIFICATIONS & LICENSES

*Certified Registered Environmental Sanitarian / Certified Registered Food Sanitarian*
*Certified Professional Manager of Buildings and Grounds*
Environmental Management Association

*Certified / Registered Environmental Auditor / Inspector / Engineer*
Environmental Assessment Association
Board of Certified Environmental Auditors

*Certified New York State Integrated Pest Management Consultant*
Department of Environmental Conservation

*Certified Environmental / Occupational Health & Safety Engineer*

*Certified Safety Executive - C.S.E.*
Board - Universal Safety Organization
Licensed / M.Y.S. Dept. of Labor / Work Place Safety and Loss Prevention Consultant

## DISTINCTIONS

*Who's Who in Science & Engineering • Who's Who in the East • Who's Who in America*

Board Member - Legislative & Governmental Affairs, MYS Chapter, Universal Safety Organization
National & International Diplomat and Adjunct Professor for:
Harker University, Brown University and Kingston Law School
Adjunct Faculty Member of U.S. Department of Education
Member of the American Board of Forensic Engineering and Technology
Institute of Forensic Science

## PERSONAL

Willing to perform work-related travel / Willing to relocate

REFERENCES AND FURTHER DATA AVAILABLE UPON REQUEST

positions to brief listings, and he omitted altogether any mention of his early educational background; only degrees he received since 1994 are listed.

## Camouflaging Mis-Titled Jobs

Another problem often faced by job seekers is that their past job titles don't accurately reflect what they actually did on the job. Obviously, if your title makes it appear that you had *greater* responsibility than you actually did, having a mis-titled job will work to your advantage. More often than not, though, the situation is reversed: you actually have more responsibility in your organization than your title suggests.

Without fabricating information on your resume (which will ultimately come back to haunt you), it's possible to present in your resume what you actually did rather than what your mis-titled job suggests you did. For example, if your job title was "secretary" but you actually functioned as an office manager—which is often the case—rather than listing the position as "secretary" you can list it as "office management." (Note the use of "management" here rather than "manager." The latter would smack of dishonesty; after all, you never actually had the *title* "office manager." However, you did in fact perform the *function* of "office management." The subtle change makes the "spin" defensible.)

Similarly, if you have a title that is specific to a particular industry or company, it would be advantageous to change it in the interests of clarity and accuracy. Let's say, for example, that you are a vice president responsible for worldwide distribution of your company's products with the title "Vice President of Wood Products." In such an instance, it would be permissible for you to rephrase the position as Vice President, global distribution." The former title suggests that your expertise is limited to a single, rather specific, even arcane field; the latter suggests a much broader range of knowledge applicable to many industries.

Is this really "camouflage"? We'd argue it's just the opposite—a more accurate and therefore honest portrayal of what your career has really involved rather than the misleading depiction presented by a too-literal transcription of your actual title.

# INTERVIEWING TIPS FOR THE SEASONED VETERAN

As a seasoned veteran, you've probably been through more interviews than you can remember, or perhaps even want to remember, so we're not going to go into a lot of detail about the process here. (However, if you haven't had an interview in a while and feel that you could use a brief refresher, we'd suggest that you take a look at Chapter 18, "From the Interview to the Offer.") Precisely because you *are* an seasoned veteran, though, there are a few aspects of interviewing that are particularly important for you to bear in mind.

As we've already mentioned, regardless of how well you've been able to camouflage your age in your resume, unless you look younger than you really are, as soon as you walk into an interview, it will be immediately apparent that you're no youngster. And, whether it's fair or not, this will evoke preconceived notions about older people that you'll have to make sure to dispel. What you want to communicate to the interviewer is *up-to-date skills and knowledge* and *a high level of energy*. There are four ways you can do this.

## Make Sure You're Up-To-Date

The world changes so fast these days that it's difficult for us to keep up with what's going on, both in general and in our own specific fields. Hopefully you're already making the necessary effort to stay on top of the latest developments in your field, but it's particularly important that you do so prior to going on an interview. One of the preconceived notions about older people is that they don't keep up, and the last thing you want is for an interviewer to think that of you.

Avoid this by staying up-to-date in reading the key publications in your field. You're probably aware of the most important journals and magazines in your industry, you may, in fact, even subscribe to some of them, but sometimes we let periodicals pile up rather than read them as soon as they come in. As long as you have a job you can probably get away with doing that for a while, but when you're looking for a new position, it's particularly important that you keep up on the latest news in your field.

And don't read only the stories that immediately interest you. Make a point of tackling articles that deal with cutting-edge developments, even if you may find some of the details hard to understand or if you disagree with some of the premises. The wider your knowledge of all the latest trends, the better you'll be able to respond to any question or comment an interviewer may offer.

Another way of making sure that you don't appear out-of-date is to use the latest terminology in your field. As you know, every industry has its own lingo, and sometimes that lingo changes, particularly where new technologies are concerned. If you use a term that's out-of-date, it will make you look equally out-of-date. And be ready to comment intelligently on the latest tales of success or failure from your industry and to offer a thoughtful opinion about new developments, referring specifically to companies, people, and current events.

## Avoid Reminiscing

Older people may have a tendency to reminisce to a much greater extent than younger people. (It's probably because they have so much more to look back on.) This is usually harmless, but it can be deadly on an interview. Avoid it.

This doesn't mean, of course, that you can't talk about anything that occurred in the past. Describing your past achievements is, after all, one of the ways you'll convince an interviewer that you're right for the job. But when you talk about the past, make sure it's to provide an example of your experience rather than aimless reminiscing. And, by all means, don't talk about "the good old days" or how things were done "in my day." (Isn't *today* your day, too?)

## Update Your Appearance

The third way to make sure that you appear to be up-to-date is by modernizing your appearance, including both your clothes and your person. While it would be inappropriate for you to dress like a recent college grad, don't be overly conservative in your clothing. Scan your wardrobe and make sure that you have at least two or three suits, dresses, or other outfits that were purchased recently.

It would also be a good idea for you to take a good, hard look at yourself in the mirror. Is your hair graying? Is it worn in an old-fashioned style? Are you losing it altogether? If your answer to any of these questions is "Yes," consider doing something about it.

Many women who are seasoned veterans already color their hair (it's a common practice in our youth-oriented culture), but men tend to be more reluctant to do so. We're not telling you that you won't get a job if you don't get rid of the gray, but doing so can help. If the onset of baldness is your problem, consider getting a hairpiece. If you do, though, it's a good idea to spend the extra money for a high-quality one. A man with a bad hairpiece just looks like a man who is trying to look younger than he is. A good hairpiece is expensive, but you should think of it as an investment in your future.

## Think and Act Young

One of the preconceived notions about older people is that they have less energy than younger ones. Sometimes it's true. But when you go on an interview, it's essential that you appear as energetic and dynamic as possible.

One way of ensuring this is to make sure that you get enough sleep the night before the interview. Researchers say that the *majority* of American adults are routinely sleep-deprived. That is not, however, the way you want to come across in an interview. Making sure you get enough sleep, at least the night before, will help you to avoid that. Only you can say how many hours of sleep you need, but for most people the magic number is closer to eight or nine hours than to five or six hours.

Finally, remember that you've become successful because of your abilities and your experience, and there's no reason to be shy about trumpeting them. The combination of experience, ability, and dynamism *you* have to offer is exactly what smart interviewers are looking for.

# JUST THE FACTS

- Several societal and business factors make finding a job particularly challenging for the seasoned veteran.

- The most effective strategies for older workers in seeking new positions include updating your skills, getting job-search help, targeting small- and mid-sized companies, and—if you don't like the idea of working for someone else anymore—starting your own business.

- To ensure that you get invited for an interview, it's advantageous to camouflage your age as well as other elements of your resume that might impact negatively on your chances.

- Job interviews present special challenges for seasoned veterans which can be met by making sure you're up-do-date, avoiding reminiscing, updating your appearance, and taking pains to appear as dynamic and energetic as possible.

# Chapter 12

# The Career Changer

---

## Get the Scoop On . . .

- Why people are changing careers
- How to identify a possible new career
- Evaluating your past experiences
- Looking more attractive to potential employers

---

A generation ago, changing careers was very unusual. Not only did most people stay in whatever careers they started in, but they frequently stayed with the same companies for their entire working lives, retiring with the proverbial gold watch as a gift from a grateful employer. But much has changed since then.

Today, it's not at all uncommon for people to change careers not once but several times. So if you're thinking of doing so, you're in excellent company. However, common as changing careers may be, it does present special challenges, both in general and more specifically in relation to putting together a resume.

The first challenge you are likely to meet is in defining exactly what you would like to do. Although you may of course already have a specific new career in mind, it's possible at this point that you have only a vague notion that you'd like to do something different.

The second challenge, once you've decided on what you would like to do, is to determine (on the basis of your education, training, and past experiences) whether or not what you have to offer a potential employer is appropriate to the new career you are considering.

The third challenge relates specifically to how you present yourself and your past experience on your resume. While few people attach any stigma to changing careers anymore, unless you are thinking of starting your new career in an entry-level position, your experience is going to be an integral part of any potential employer's decision about whether or not to ask you in for an interview.

And despite the fact that your experience may be quite extensive, depending on how radical a change you're planning, that experience may not count for very much when you're seeking to enter a new industry. On the other hand, it may count for a great deal *if* your experience and skills are translatable to your new career and *if* you can present them in an appealing way.

Although it takes some effort, these challenges can all be met, and in this chapter we'll provide you with the information you'll need to meet them.

# WHY PEOPLE ARE CHANGING CAREERS

*"To improve is to change; to be perfect is to change often."*
—Winston Churchill, in a speech to the British House of Commons, 1925

We mentioned above that there is no longer any stigma attached to changing careers, and there are primarily two reasons for this. The first is that there has been a radical change in the way people think about work, and the second is that the business environment itself has changed dramatically over the past two decades.

The former change is largely a result of the Baby Boomer generation bringing its values into the workplace, and the latter is due to the increasing emphasis on profit in the business world and the resulting changes in hiring practices, among other factors.

## How People Think About Work Today

Recent generations, up to and including that of our parents, tended to see work primarily as a means to an end. You worked because you had to make a living—to pay for clothing, housing, and feeding yourself and your family. It didn't necessarily matter what the job was, as long as it provided you with an income that was sufficient to provide the necessities of life, and perhaps a luxury here and there.

But when the Baby Boomers, who were advised as teenagers to "do your own thing," came into the workforce 25 or 30 years ago, they brought with them some very different attitudes about work. One of these attitudes was a relative lack of respect for tradition. They believed that just because something had always been done a certain way was no reason that it should continue to be done that way. As a result, even if their parents had been satisfied to stay in jobs they didn't like, that was no reason for them to do so.

A second, and equally important, new attitude they brought to the workplace was that of seeing work not only as a means to an end but as an end in itself. That is, they began their careers expecting work to provide them not only with an income but also with a way of fulfilling themselves as individuals. Of course, exactly what constitutes being "fulfilled" varies from one person to the next, but those who did not feel they were getting everything they wanted out of work were as likely as not to seek those things in other careers.

Because those Baby Boomers constituted such a relatively large number of people, all of whom began their careers over a relatively short period of time, the attitudes they brought with them soon began to pervade the workplace. Now, of course, members of that generation are running the business world, and although their attitudes may have been tempered by their exposure to the realities of work and their own changing needs, those attitudes are still valued in the workplace.

## How the Business Environment Has Changed

Not only has the attitude of the workforce changed over the last two decades, but so too has that of the companies that employ them. In the past, many companies, particularly large ones, tended to have paternalistic attitudes toward their employees. They perceived themselves as families and believed that once an employee started working for them, as long as they did their job in an acceptable manner, the "family" would take care of them until it was time for them to retire. Even though many of these companies may have been dysfunctional families, they still took care of their own.

But with today's increasing emphasis on profits, that paternalistic attitude has fallen by the wayside. Companies are now less interested in taking care of those employees they have than they are in bringing in talented new ones who can boost their bottom lines. As a result,many companies expect their employees to be "loyal"—even though they show very loyalty in return.

In addition, there are several societal trends that are having a heavy impact on the business environment:

- The continuing, and worsening, glut of Ph.D.'s is driving thousands out of academia and into careers in industry. For some chemists and physicists, the transfer may come naturally; for others, especially in the humanities, it may be traumatic.

- Dramatic downsizing of the U.S. military with the end of the Cold War has flooded the workforce with former military people now shifting their skills to the civilian labor market.

- The growing power of health maintenance organizations and other adverse social and economic trends are driving thousands of physicians to leave medical practice for occupations in industry.

- The continuing trend toward fiscal conservatism has helped shrink the federal government payroll to its lowest level in years, prompting thousands to seek work in the private sector.

- Numerous business trends, including the advent of new technologies and the deepening interconnectedness of world markets, are shrinking some industries while others explode.

- Thus, if you're thinking about changing careers, not only is it now possible for you to do so, you may even have found yourself in a situation in which it's necessary. Regardless of which position you are in, however, there are several steps you must take to achieve that goal.

# FINDING A NEW CAREER

*"Twenty years ago, it was not unusual to find a Ph.D. in English working as a cabdriver for a living; today, that cabdriver has earned a doctorate from Harvard or Yale."*
—Michael Bérubé
in *The Chronicle of Higher Education*

As we've said, while you may have already decided on your new career, it's also possible that at this point all you know is that you would like to do "something" other than what you've been doing. If you're in this situation, you are in essentially the same position as the recent grad who is still trying to "find himself."

In that case, the first step you must take is to think about exactly what that other "something" might be and see if you can't come up with one or more possibilities. As is true of the recent grad, the best way to start this process is to identify your personal interests, recall your dreams, and determine your work and work-related life values. This is the same process we discussed at length in Chapter 2, so we won't repeat it all here. Essentially, however, you start the process by sitting down and making several lists, including:

1. Your personal interests: People are more likely to enjoy jobs, and do them better, if their work is connected in some way to something they like to do. If, for example, you like to write, journalism might be an appropriate career to pursue. At this point, though, you shouldn't be thinking about how you might apply your interests to a career but simply about what those interests are.

2. Your dreams: The chances are that, as a child or a teenager, you dreamt about the kind of work you would like to do. As you're in the process of beginning a new career, now is a particularly appropriate time for you to recall those dreams. Again, it's more important right now for you to get them down on paper than it is to worry about whether or not they are realistic.

3. Your work values: We all have certain expectations about what we would like to get out of work besides a salary. For some of us, it's the feeling that we're doing something worthwhile; for others, it's that we're being creative or helping others. The extent to which your work values match your work reality can

have a very substantial effect on how happy you are with your new career. Now is the time to think about those values and make a list of as many as you can.

4. Your work-related life values: What you want and expect to get out of life is an important factor to take into account in determining a new career. If, for example, spending time with your family is important to you, you wouldn't want to take a job that would require you to work particularly long hours. Similarly, if you don't relish the thought of making a long commute to work, you'll want to think about careers you can pursue that are close to home. This is the time and place for you to list all those life values that can impact your career decision.

*"Money isn't the only stimulus that brings out that best that's in a man, even in America."*

—F. Scott Fitzgerald, This Side of Paradise

Once you've determined your personal interests, your dreams, and your work- and life-values, the next step is to translate them into potential careers. There are so many possible careers that there is surely one that will enable you to pursue any one of your interests. The problem is simply in finding them.

We included a worksheet in Chapter 2 to give you some ideas about how to do this, but there are also other ways of discovering potential careers. You can, for example, speak with your friends or family about your interest in finding a new career and see if they have any suggestions, based on their knowledge of you. You can also watch television or look through newspapers and magazines, thinking about the kinds of work the people discussed in those media do.

Finally, once you've identified careers that are appropriate to your interests, what you have to do is evaluate those careers in light of your work- and life-values. On the basis of that evaluation, you should be able to come up with one or more potential careers you might think about pursuing.

Again, this entire process is discussed at greater length in Chapter 2. If you are in the process of trying to determine the new direction in which you'd like to go and haven't done the exercises included in that chapter, we urge you to do so now.

## DETERMINING WHAT YOU HAVE TO OFFER

Once you've identified some possible new careers, the next step is to determine what you have to offer a potential employer so that you will be able to evaluate how realistic your chances are of getting a job in those fields.

This process begins with you listing pertinent information about your education and training, your previous work history, your personal achievements, any volunteer or community service you may have done, and your hobbies and activities. Much of this information will eventually find its way into your resume, but it's also important to consider them at this point because some or all of them may have an impact on the likelihood of your finding the ideal position for you. This process is discussed at length in Chapter 3, which also includes worksheets designed to help you record this information.

Once you have all the information about your experience and achievements on paper, the next step is to compare what you have to offer with what a potential employer in your desired new field is likely to want, which is the subject of the next section.

As you will see, because you are changing careers, it will be essential for you to give serious thought to how you can apply the skills you've already gained to a new career. This is an extremely important step for the career changer because it can have a considerable effect on how you evaluate your skills and consequently on determining which new careers would be most appropriate for you. For that reason, if you haven't already filled out the checklist at the end of Chapter 3, we would advise you to not do so until you've done the exercise below.

# REDEFINING YOUR EXPERIENCE

For most job seekers, comparing what they have to offer with what a potential employer will want is a simple task. For the career changer, making that comparison is a different matter. If you were staying in your current field, the chances are that the extensive amount of experience you've already gathered would make you a very attractive candidate for a job. However, since you're planning to change careers, all that experience might, at least at first glance, appear to be more of a hindrance than a help.

What, you may ask, does my experience as a naval officer have to do with serving as a management consultant? Or, what could I have learned as a book editor that would be applicable if I were to go to work for a company looking for someone to help set up and run their Web site? Although it may seem that there is little connection between these jobs, the fact is that there are any number of connections—if you know how to look for them.

The chances are that you already possess many skills that can be easily transferred to other types of work. As a former naval officer, for example, you would have had a great deal of experience managing people—a skill you would be amply qualified to teach others as a consultant. As a book editor, you would not only have writing and editing skills that would be applicable in creating a Web site, but may have also been involved in the design and production of books, another transferable skill.

What you have to do, then, is essentially redefine your skills. Doing so is actually fairly easy, and we've provided a worksheet below to help you do it. The first element of this process, of course, is to figure out exactly what activities, tasks, and responsibilities you performed in your previous jobs. If you've filled out the worksheets in Chapter 2, you've already accomplished this task. If not, we'd suggest you go back to that chapter and fill them out.

We'd strongly suggest, however, that in making a list of your activities, tasks, and responsibilities you make use of all the worksheets you filled out in Chapter 2—not just those on education and training, previous employment, and personal achievements. As we've mentioned before, to the extent that your new career reflects your personal interests, the experience and skills you learned in volunteer and/or community service and in pursuing your hobbies and other activities may be particularly applicable.

The next step is to copy your activities, tasks, and responsibilities onto the worksheet below, and then think about the skills you used to

| Activities and Skills | |
|---|---|
| **Activity/Task/Responsibility** | **Skill Used** |
| 1. _____ | _____ |
| 2. _____ | _____ |
| 3. _____ | _____ |
| 4. _____ | _____ |
| 5. _____ | _____ |
| 6. _____ | _____ |
| 7. _____ | _____ |
| 8. _____ | _____ |
| 9. _____ | _____ |
| 10. _____ | _____ |

accomplish them. We're sure that once you've finished filling out this worksheet, you'll realize that you have many skills that can be applied in the new career you're considering.

# DECIDING ON A NEW CAREER

**FYI**

In listing your activities, tasks, and responsibilities, be careful not to edit them. That is, don't leave something out because you think it's not important: the activity you leave out may be the key to your new career!

Now that you've gathered all the pertinent information about your past experiences, including redefining your skills, the time has come for you to determine which of the new careers you've been considering would be most appropriate for you to pursue. The checklist below is designed to help you make that decision.

This checklist is the same as the one that appears at the end of Chapter 3; so, it's possible that you have already taken this final step. If you did so before redefining your skills, however, we urge you to do it again. Having redefined your skills, you may find that there are more careers available to you than you had originally thought.

On this checklist, you will list your possible careers, then rate your interests, dreams, work values, life values, education, and skills on the basis of how closely those careers fit your criteria for the perfect job. We'd suggest you rate these factors on a scale of one to five, one being the farthest from meeting your criteria and five being the closest. Once

| **Making the Connections** | | | | | | |
|---|---|---|---|---|---|---|
| **Possible Career** | **Personal Interests** | **Dreams** | **Work Values** | **Life Values** | **Education Values** | **Skills** |
| 1. | | | | | | |
| 2. | | | | | | |
| 3. | | | | | | |
| 4. | | | | | | |
| 5. | | | | | | |
| 6. | | | | | | |
| 7. | | | | | | |
| 8. | | | | | | |
| 9. | | | | | | |
| 10. | | | | | | |

**FYI**

*Although it's a good idea to discuss your interest in finding a new career with friends and family before you make a decision, it might be advantageous to do so afterward, too. They may, for example, know people in those fields to whom you could speak to learn more about potential jobs.*

you've rated them all, you should add up the numbers for each possible career. The careers that have the highest overall ratings will be those you should seriously consider pursuing.

Of course, this is not a foolproof way of deciding on a new career. Embarking on such a journey is a serious matter, and there may be other factors that you feel should be considered in the decision. This method should, however, help you determine, based on your desires and your background, those jobs or careers that it would be both advantageous *and* realistic for you to pursue.

As we've mentioned before, however, you needn't think of this decision as an irrevocable one. It's not unusual for people to change careers several, if not many, times over the course of their working lives. You're doing it now because you aren't satisfied with your current career. And if this one doesn't work out for whatever reason, you will have the opportunity to make another change in the future. You do, however, at this point have to make a decision based on what you want to do *now* and on what you have the education and skills to do *now*.

## GETTING IT DOWN ON PAPER

Assuming you have made a decision and settled on exactly which new career you would like to pursue, the time has now come for you to take the next step in the process. This is to put together all the information you've gathered and craft a resume that will make you as appealing as possible to a prospective employer.

The basic difference between the resume of a career changer and that of any other job seeker lies in the way you present your past experience. While those who are seeking new positions in their current fields would want to present their experience in as specific a way as possible, it's essential for career changers to present their background generically. That is, they should emphasize their skills rather than the specific responsibilities of their current or former positions.

In addition, when you are changing careers, depending on how radical a change you are making, it may be advantageous to mask or de-emphasize your previous employer or employers. The last thing in the world you want a potential employer to do is look at your resume and say, for example, "This guy was in the Army! What does he know about logistics management?" By masking or de-emphasizing the name or function of your past employers you will ensure that someone reading your resume will pay more attention to the skills you have to offer than to the names of your former employers.

There are ways of crafting your resume to achieve both of these ends, and we've devoted the remainder of this chapter to showing you exactly how to do that.

## Stressing Skills over Function

**FYI**

*Most industries have their own jargon, much of which is indecipherable to those outside the industry. In presenting your work experience on your resume, avoid using your current (or past) industry's jargon as much as possible.*

As we've said, it's important for individuals seeking new jobs in their current fields to provide as much industry-specific information as possible about what they do and how they do it. Because the function of any resume is to convince the reader of the applicant's ability to do the job he or she is seeking to fill, it's in your best interests to provide those kinds of details.

Let's go back, as an example, to the book editor we mentioned before. As an editor in the reference division of a book publishing operation searching for a new job in his field, the description of his current position might read something like this:

Senior Editor

Acquired trade reference books in a broad range of categories, including history, film, music, child care, literary criticism, and general reference. Major contributions include:

- Acquiring 40 titles over period of 24 months and taking on responsibility for 30 previously acquired titles.

- Managing all aspects of each project, including proposal, contract, and manuscript acceptance; copyediting and production; book and jacket design; and marketing and promotional plans and plan implementation.

Clearly, an editor-in-chief looking for a new member for his or her staff would in all likelihood be impressed by this candidate's experience. On the other hand, if this same editor were applying for a job with a company looking for someone to work on creating their Web site, some of this information would be meaningless to the prospective employer who reads it.

However, there are actually similarities between reference books and Web sites. So if this editor wanted to find a position with a company creating a Web site, the description of his current position may read more like this:

Senior Editor

Selected, developed, and edited reference materials in a broad range of categories, including history, film, music, child care, and literary criticism. Major contributions include:

- Developing and editing 40 new projects over period of 24 months and taking on responsibility for 30 previously acquired projects.

- Managing all aspects of each project, including editorial, design, production, and marketing functions.

If you were looking for someone to come into your organization and create a Web site for the company, which of these two candidates would be most appealing to you? We think the answer is obvious. As you'll see in the resumes that follow, avoiding industry-specific references and presenting your skills generically is one of the best ways of getting a potential employer to ask you in for an interview.

## Masking or De-emphasizing Your Previous Employer(s)

As we've said, when you are changing careers, there is a good argument to be made for masking or de-emphasizing the names of your previous employer or employers. Managers are all extremely busy, so when they are recruiting for new staff members they don't want to spend any more time than necessary interviewing potential candidates. For that reason, when they start to go through the pile of resumes in their in-boxes, they'll seize on any excuse to eliminate all but the most likely candidates.

Obviously, you don't want to give them any such excuse. And when you're changing careers, if a potential employer sees the name of a company on your resume that is clearly in a different industry, that's likely to happen. There are essentially two ways that you can keep this from happening.

The first of these is to mask the name of your current or past employers. Let's say, for example, that you served in the military for many years, in a variety of managerial capacities, and on retiring decided to seek a job in the private sector. While the skills you learned are actually as applicable in business as they were in the service, once a potential employer sees "U.S. Navy" on your resume it may go right into his or her out-box. This was exactly the situation that "Samuel Edward Jones" found himself in.

In order to avoid this problem, when Samuel prepared his resume (Resume 12.1), he masked the name of his former employer by simply listing its initials as "USN"and described his previous positions in such a way that it would be impossible for anyone to know that he had worked in the military.

Again, though, he not only masked the name of his former employer but also emphasized the skills he learned while serving in the armed forces rather than his specific responsibilities. For example, in the description he provided of his job as a plant manager, he wrote:

## 12.1  Masks Name of Former Employer

*Confidential Resume of*
**SAMUEL EDWARD JONES**
22 Hibiscus Circle
Honolulu, Hawaii 99725
*Phone / Fax:* (555) 555-0713
*Email:* samuel.ej@gopher.rpi.net

**MANAGEMENT**
**Human Resources · Electronics · Information Technology**
*Energetic and dependable communicator with noted mentoring skills. Adept in team building and technical research. Exercise leadership, management and planning for operation, maintenance and repair of complex instrumentation and control equipment. Persuasive, persistent, pragmatic. Innovative, resourceful and inventive; 'make things happen' and consistently achieve objectives.*

**CAREER TRACK**

USN · 1979 - Present

**MANAGEMENT / INFORMATION TECHNOLOGY**
1996 - Present
Provide interactive user support and technical assistance. Configure a variety of complex computer applications; troubleshoot and resolve issues promptly. Improve and streamline data handling. Draw on resource networks to inspire possibility thinking. Promote on- and off- site educational opportunities. Develop inexperienced staff into competent, respected technicians.
- *Redesigned Help Desk / Customer Service database to coordinate over 4,000 jobs; reduced trouble call response time 30%; won Outstanding Achievement Award.*

**PLANT MANAGEMENT**
1995 - 1996
Exercised strong planning, organizing and leadership skills to set priorities for simultaneous activities of 6-50 staff to consistently meet goals, objectives and quality performance standards. Directed power-production operations including all aspects of steam and electric plants. Oversaw equipment performance and trend analysis; recommended course of action.
- *Reorganized and led aggressive capital infrastructure program. Upgrading and modernizing 25-year-old, outdated power-production support facilities.*
- *Ensured managers understood effective training and performance appraisal techniques and recognized value of cultural, ethnic, gender and other individual differences.*

**TRAINER / EMPLOYEE DEVELOPMENT**
1992 - 1995
Nuclear Power Training unit
Honolulu, Hawaii
Created active motivational learning environment for Electronics Technician Maintenance School. Restructured and upgraded Nuclear Power Proficiency Phase Training Program to improve maintenance practices. Spearheaded cross-training. Promoted affirmative employment through Equal Opportunity, Rights & Responsibilities and Sexual Harassment courses.

- *Certified over 80 operator personnel trained in state-of-the-art, advanced maintenance practices; taught basic skills to over 500 students in proficiency phase maintenance course.*
- *Designed and delivered advanced electronics troubleshooting course for engineers from Stelling Power Technologies, Morgan Industrial, and power stations.*

## TECHNICAL MANAGEMENT
1989 - 1992

Performed and directed troubleshooting, maintenance and repair of complex electronics instrumentation and control equipment to component level. Coordinated short-term and mid-range planning, training, preparation and service delivery. Utilized positive management strategies. Determined realistic goals and set priorities to meet deadlines.

- *Oversaw preventive and corrective maintenance during 29-month overhaul in demanding environment; achieved recognition for outstanding supervisory and technical performance.*

**Previous positions include:**
REPAIR COORDINATOR · 1987 - 1989
DIVISION SUPERVISOR / TECHNICIAN · 1981 - 1987

## LEARNING CREDENTIALS

DIPLOMA IN PC REPAIR, 1998
ETT Technical College - Surrey Hills, Connecticut

**BACHELOR OF SCIENCE IN HUMAN RESOURCES MANAGEMENT,** 1995
Rutgers University - Rutgers, New Jersey
*Valedictorian · GPA 3.91*

COMPLETED 92 / 139 OF BACHELOR OF SCIENCE IN ELECTRONICS ENGINEERING
Tacoma Institute of Engineering - Tacoma, Washington

**Additional courses, seminars and workshops include:**
*Electronics Mechanic National Apprenticeship Program - 7000 Hours*
Department of Labor

*Master Course in Organizational Behavior and Managerial Communications*
University of Washington - Tacoma, Washington

*Advanced Electronics · Leadership . Management - 4000 Hours*
*Over 70 Training Courses, Schools and Correspondence Courses*

## COMPETENCIES & CERTIFICATIONS
Windows 3.x, 95, 98, NT 4.0 · DOS · WordPerfect 5.1, 6.0 · MS Office
Office 97 · Lotus cc:Mail · MS Exchange
Pursuing Certified Electronics Technician · Certified Quality Manager
Pursuing Certification in Fiber Optics Design and Installation

REFERENCES AND FURTHER DATA AVAILABLE UPON REQUEST

Exercised strong planning, organizing, and leadership skills to set priorities for simultaneous activities of 6–50 staff members to consistently meet goals, objectives, and quality performance standards. Directed power-production operations including all aspects of steam and electric plants. Oversaw equipment performance and trend analysis; recommended course of action.

As you can see, by concentrating on the managerial skills he exercised in running the plant, Samuel was able to mask the fact that he was in the Navy at the time that he ran the plant.

Another individual who was in a similar situation, but who handled it differently, was "Hobart M. Abel." Mr. Abel served in the military for 16 years before deciding to seek a job in the public sector. While in the service, he had become an expert in logistics management, and while he knew that his skills were easily transferable to a position in business, he also knew that specifically mentioning the fact that he'd been in the service might present a problem.

In order to avoid that problem, he simply left the name of his former employer off the resume (Resume 12.2). In addition, he started off with a brief discussion of his skills, and only then went on to describe his specific positions. Although it would quickly become apparent to any potential employer that his work involved the military, at no point did he actually say that he had served in the armed forces.

## How Others Have Done It: Additional Sample Resumes

The resumes that follow were all crafted by individuals who were changing careers and recognized the necessity of stressing the relevance of their skills over their specific functions.

When "Eddie Baker" (Resume 12.3) left the U.S. Air Force, he had been the superintendent of a "nondestructive inspection laboratory" for five years and wanted to find a similar position in the private sector. As you will see, while he did acknowledge that he had served in the Air Force, in the descriptions he wrote of his previous positions he emphasized his managerial skills so it was clear that he would be able to handle the kind of managerial position he was interested in attaining.

"Phoebe Rosenberg" (Resume 12.4) was in a somewhat different situation. She was a funeral director/manager who was seeking a similar position, but whose education and previous employment were unrelated to her current job search. By emphasizing the skills she had acquired in her previous positions, rather than the functions she performed, she showed potential employers that virtually all of her skills would be applicable in the kind of position she was seeking.

---

**FYI**

*If you work for a large, well-known corporation with divisions in a broad range of industries, if you use the corporate name on your resume rather than the division name it will not only make it less obvious that you're changing careers but will provide you with an impressive name on your resume.*

---

## 12.2  Eliminates Name of Former Employer

*Confidential Resume of*

# HOBART M. ABEL

93 Mission Hill Road
Langston, New Mexico 35758
*Phone:* (555) 555-8065  *Fax:* (555) 555-5507

www.RealGroup.com/resumeshmabel.htm
*Email:* hobartmabel@sandstorm.army *or* hmabel@RealGroup.com

---

## LOGISTICS MANAGEMENT

**Forward-Thinking, Results-Oriented, Solution-Driven Achiever**

*Energetic and dependable contributor with technical prowess, proven leadership, highly developed communication skills and years of experience in analyzing, planning and organizing. Innovative, resourceful and inventive in critical situations such as the Grenada and Desert Storm military operations. Self-starter and risk-taker; develop insights and solutions. Guide others to reach goals.*

---

### CAREER TRACK

**LOGISTICS MANAGEMENT SPECIALIST**                                          1992 - Present
Headquarters Aviation and Missile Command

Contributes visions, plans, and management expertise critical to organizational efficiency. Assist in defining mission, goals, and strategies and in developing and propelling timely and effective solutions in inventory, maintenance, and logistics management. Assess and troubleshoot complex problems; streamline existing procedures to meet strict performance measures.

- *As Lead Move Coordinator for the Weapons Systems Management Directorate (WSMD), Headquarters Aviation/Troop Command (HQATCOM), directed and initiated action for the eleven move coordinators in the directorate to use in the movement of personnel and equipment from HQATCOM to Headquarters Aviation/Missile Command (HQAMCOM).*

- *As Chief Retirement Specialist for OH-58A and C aircraft, responsible for the disposition of the aircraft. Under the National Defense Authorization Act FY97, have transferred in excess of 500 aircraft to Federal, State, County, and city law enforcement agencies.*

- *Directed retirement of OH-6A and OH-58A and C aircraft. Provided guidance on removal of spare parts from aircraft for incorporation into Army's Depot System.*

- *Developed briefing package for all levels of management with major command units and Department of the Army agencies and command officers of law enforcement agencies.*

- *Conducted seminars on aircraft retirement for several national law enforcement associations, assisted senior logistician with Army Redistribution Initiative (ARI) program (Force Drawdown), and advised Deputy Chief of Staff for Operations / Deputy Chief of Staff for Logistics (Department of the Army) on aircraft retirement progress.*

*Confidential Resume of* **HOBART M. ABEL**                                                    Page 2

**LOGISTICS MANAGEMENT SPECIALIST**                                                      1990 - 1992
Headquarters Aviation and Troop Command

> Responsible within the Aviation/Troop Command for integrating functions (i.e. Materiel Management, Maintenance Management, and Procurement) and implementing logistics management programs for the Light Observation Office (LOH).
>
> - *Represented the office at executive conferences on logistics covering planning/program resolutions.*

*Continued*

**INVENTORY MANAGER**                                                                     1984 - 1990
Headquarters Aviation and Troop Command

> Responsible for the management of aviation assets for the UH-60 Blackhawk System requiring extensive analysis of unit value, annual demands, mission essentiality, and/or technical complexity of the item relevant to application on the aircraft system.

---

### LEARNING CREDENTIALS

**ASSOCIATE OF SCIENCE**
Crow Hill Community College - Azura, New Mexico
Major: Mid-Management  GPA 3.6

**CERTIFICATE**
U.S. Navy Post Graduate School - Monterey, California
Major: Acquisition Logistics  GPA N/A

**CERTIFICATE**
Defense Management College - St. Louis, Missouri
Major: Acquisition Logistics  GPA N/A

**CERTIFICATE**
U.S. Army Logistics Management College - Fort Lee, Virginia
Major: Supply / Maintenance Management  GPA N/A

*Expert knowledge in the use of Microsoft Office 97 suite*

---

### ACHIEVEMENTS AND HONORS

Superior Performance Award - HQ Aviation and Missile Command, April 1999
Letter of Appreciation - Senate Majority Leader (Senator Michael Kelly), May 1998
Superior Performance Award - HQ Aviation and Missile Command, April 1998
Certificate of Acquisition Level III - HQ Aviation and Missile Command, April 1998

Transfer of 500+ helicopters to law enforcement agencies for counter-drug missions
October 1992 - Present

REFERENCES AND FURTHER DATA AVAILABLE UPON REQUEST

## 12.3 Stresses Managerial Skills

*Confidential Resume of*

# EDDIE BAKER

565 Fox Run
Conway, New Hampshire 78108
H: (555) 555-2847 • W: (555) 555-6688

Email: bakere@amerinet.att.net

## NON-DESTRUCTIVE TESTING & INSPECTION PROFESSIONAL

*More than 20 years of highly successful experience. A self-starter with proven ability to deliver high quality performance from project inception to completion—with safety, on schedule and within budget. Innovative and resourceful with unusual ability to 'make things happen,' and consistently achieve goals and objectives. Skilled in developing highly focused teams motivated to achieve ambitious goals. Establish superior procedures for analysis and operational control. Clearly communicate complex technical concepts. Effectively manage resources and ensure data integrity. Chosen by senior management to develop / execute major special projects.*

### SUPERVISORY SKILLS

- **Received Excellent in Maintenance Award** for developing new nondestructive inspection techniques for C-130 aircraft.
- **Received Excellence in Command Award** for technical writing of Radiation Safety procedures for entire command.
- **Critiqued and proof tested** all new inspection procedures for C-130 aircraft.
- **Researched and designed** the new DVM-1 digital video microscope from Omnia to visually inspect for defects.
- **Meritorious Service Medal** for developing new nondestructive inspection techniques.
- **Advanced knowledge** in Phase analysis eddy current units.
- **15 years professional level systems administration** with PC's, Microsoft Windows 98, spreadsheets, and PowerPoint.

### CAREER TRACK

UNITED STATES AIR FORCE • 1977 - Present

**SUPERINTENDENT - Nondestructive Inspection Laboratory**                    1995 - Present

Combine exceptional technical knowledge and interpersonal / communication skills in effectively managing an 11 person team in all aspects of nondestructive testing. Oversee the operation and maintenance of all nondestructive test equipment, and personally use all equipment, including portable and fixed magnetic testers, fluorescent penetrant, ultrasonic, eddy current, and radiographic test equipment. Perform operator maintenance on oil analysis spectrometers. Prepare / maintain magnetic particle baths for purity and concentration. Develop exposure charts for specialized radiographic techniques. Maintain darkroom equipment including film holders, lead screens, reading lights, and film storage facilities. Perform silver recovery functions and monitor for radiation during radiographic operations. Establish and execute appropriate quality control parameters ensuring the integrity of all processes. Utilize strong planning, organizing and leadership skills to consistently meet or exceed standards. Foster cooperation, communication and a common vision among all staff personnel.

*Continued*

- *Previously served as Fabrication Superintendent with responsibility for 22 personnel monitoring machinist and sheet metal maintenance operations.*
- *Chosen by superiors to develop and write 5 and 7 level skill knowledge specialty tests (Level 2 and Level 3) for the Air Force's nondestructive career field.*
- *Standardized training plan for all new personnel seeking certification in nondestructive testing in the Air Force.*
- *Experienced in nondestructive inspection techniques on a wide range of aircraft including C-5, C-141, C-130, KC-135, Boeing 707, 727, T-37, T-38, OV-110, Learjet and Cessna, as well as HH-1H, CH-1H, HH-53 and Blackhawk helicopters.*

**RADIATION SAFETY OFFICER**

**QUALITY ASSURANCE INSPECTOR**

**HAZARDOUS WASTE MANAGER**

**MAINTENANCE SELF ASSESSMENT CHECKLIST MANAGER**

## LEARNING CREDENTIALS

**ASSOCIATES OF SCIENCE IN METALLURGY & NONDESTRUCTIVE INSPECTION**
Community College of the Air Force

**Additional courses, seminars and workshops include:**

US Air Force Nondestructive principals and applications
12 hours in Human Communication
39 semester hours Quality Awareness course and Quality Assurance
27 semester hours Hazard Communications and Waste Management
Principles of Management • Total Quality Management

**Training**

Nondestructive inspection 7 level course Air University
Applications of advanced nondestructive inspection techniques
Technical writing course • Supervisor training course • Radiation Safety Management
15 hours Covey Leadership management • Nondestructive Task Certifier • Train the Trainer
Awarded Secret Security Clearance

REFERENCES AND FURTHER DATA AVAILABLE UPON REQUEST

## 12.4  Shows Relevance of Other Experience

*Confidential Resume of*
**PHOEBE ROSENBERG**
78 Snowcap Lane
Missoula, Montana 70701
(555) 555 - 0698

**OBJECTIVE**
A challenging position as FUNERAL DIRECTOR / MANAGER where specialized training, highly developed organizational / sales abilities, interpersonal skills and proven experience will be fully utilized and lead to career growth and advancement opportunities.

**PROFESSIONAL EXPERIENCE**

**FUNERAL DIRECTOR / LICENSED EMBALMER**
1994 - Present
Harker Funeral Homes, Inc.
Missoula & Belmont, Montana
> Plan, coordinate and manage all marketing / sales activities and daily funeral service operations. Formulate and present pre-need packages and deal sensitively with bereaved families providing consultation and advice utilizing specialized industry training and knowledge. Develop pricing and effectively present product and service offerings. Process client requests; make financial arrangements. Receive accurate information on deceased; prepare and submit obituaries to local newspapers. Schedule and prepare facilities for funeral services; assign and supervise personnel in organizing, set up and staffing. Ensure total client satisfaction and foster company loyalty. Review and analyze existing policy and procedures with a view toward enhancing sales productivity, efficiency and quality performance. Train apprentice.

- *Initiate and conduct pre-need seminars for church groups, social clubs, sororities and elderly apartment complexes.*
- *Maintain highest possible standards for customer service; reside in apartment above funeral home to assure around-the-clock availability to authorities and clientele.*
- *Supervise and monitor upkeep, maintenance and overall attractiveness of funeral parlor, morgue and grounds.*

**MANAGER**
1990 - Present
Mountain View Trust and Taxes / Rosenberg Spirit Shop (Family Business)
Missoula, Montana
> Exercise planning, controlling and organizing skills to set priorities for continuing operations at this much relied on, family owned income tax office and liquor store serving a medium-sized neighborhood for 35 years. Demonstrate loyalty to family and contribute to area stability by meeting sales goals, management objectives and quality performance standards to sustain the small business. Successfully implement and maintain computer information and inventory management systems. Design vendor programs to lower costs and maximize quality skillfully negotiate beneficial specifications. Actively seek customer input; ensure needs are met; continuously seek to improve quality of services, products and processes.

- *Work with father to recognize and define problems; analyze relevant information; anticipate and seek to resolve confrontation, disagreement and complaints in a constructive manner.*
- *Establish policies, plans and priorities; assume risks when needed; make difficult decisions when necessary.*

**IN VIVO COORDINATOR / QUALITY CONTROL TECHNOLOGIST**
1991 - 1993
Northwestern Medical Laboratory
High Point, Montana
> Combined market cognizance with laboratory expertise and a practiced business sense. Organized and coordinated all surgical testing, clinical, research, and design, and second functional

evaluations.  Collaborated with vendors, the resident veterinarian and such departments as Complaint Investigation, Engineering and Quality Control to schedule lab time, establish product specifications and ensure adherence to quality guidelines.  Fostered cooperation, communication and consensus among groups.  Streamlined processes infused innovation including state-of -the-art technological systems.  Evaluated test data; drew conclusion; submitted results in detailed reports.  Demonstrated exceptional time management.

- *Applied new technology to organizational needs; used Laser (YAG / KTP) and Scanning electron Microscope (SEM); demonstrated experience with various measuring instruments applied statistical formulas to display resulting data.*
- *Developed experimental methods to test new products; performed surgical, functional and dimensional evaluations.*
- *Wrote protocols for product evaluation in surgical and physical labs; trained, motivated and supervised technicians in the testing of in viva and in vitro products.*

**ASSISTANT IN RESEARCH**
1989
Stanford University School of Medicine - Department of Cardiology and Department of Epidemiology & Public Health
Palo Alto, California

Devised and implemented strategies to consistently meet assigned performance goals in these busy laboratory settings. In Cardiology, performed specific tests on albino rats to disclose and establish recovery time from cardiac arrest with increased amounts of saline solution while monitoring subject in an MRI chamber.  Executed specific tests in nuclear cardiology using canine subjects and radioactive isotopes to induce cardiac arrest.  Performed heart bypass surgery.  In Epidemiology, tested for Streptococcus levels for early detection colon cancer.

**CHEMICAL TECHNOLOGIST**
1986 - 1989
TKG / Robins Analysis Corporation

Designed and performed experiments for incorporating laser absorbing dyes into polycarbonate substrates per military specifications; obtained Secret level clearance.  Ensured the integrity of the processes; promoted ethical and effective practices.  Demonstrated technical prowess and an understanding of its impact in areas of responsibility.  Established quality control parameters and production specifications.  Proved proficiency with IR - VIS - UV spectrophotometer.  Effected organic synthesis of dyes under supervision of lead chemist.

**EDUCATION & TRAINING**

**DIPLOMA, 1994**
Harris Institute for Funeral Directors

**BACHELOR OF SCIENCE IN BIOLOGY,** 1985
Pomona College - Pomona, California
*Minor: Biochemistry*

**INTERESTS & ACTIVITIES**
Avid reader of new medical findings  ·  Enjoy Swimming / Dance

**PERSONAL**
Willing to perform work related travel / Willing to relocate

REFERENCES AND FURTHER DATA AVAILABLE UPON REQUEST

## 12.5 Stresses Skills

*Confidential Resume of*

# JENNIFER V. HARRIS

32 North Conley Street   Stonebridge, Maryland 23229
(555) 555-4470

www.RealGroup.com/resumes/jvharris.htm
Email: jvharris@RealGroup.com

## ACCOUNTING / ADMINISTRATIVE PROFESSIONAL
*- more than 10 years of proven and successful experience -*

**Public or Private Sector**

*Energetic and dependable with highly developed organizational abilities and interpersonal skills. Innovative, resourceful, and inventive with a proven ability to identify opportunities, make things happen, and consistently achieve goals and objectives. Offer excellent understanding of multi-million dollar operations, business conditions, programs and alliances, and the inter-relationships of the public and private sectors. A possibility thinker with proven training and influencing skills, analytical savvy, inter-department understanding, technology literacy, and problem-solving ability.*

### CAREER TRACK

BALTIMORE METROPOLITAN DEPARTMENT OF TRANSPORTATION
Baltimore, Maryland   *1986 - Present*

**CHIEF / Revenue & Accounts Receivable**                          1995 - Present

Contribute vision and management expertise crucial to unit functioning and departmental operations. Administer 650 capital projects, totaling nearly $2,000,000,000, and relating to construction and engineering services from numerous FHWA government grants. Serve as liaison to both federal and state agencies and prepare all reimbursements for each project. Monitor payment status, develop monthly financial reports including budgeted vs. actual analyses. Perform bank reconciliation for 13 municipal garage locations, prepare variance reports on 25 concessionaires renting space on government property to ensure that percentage of gross for rental purposes is accurate. Reconcile returned checks for the various revenue producing bureaus. Supervise 14 employees in the Grants, Billing, Auditing and Collections. Perform personnel functions involving the maintenance of confidential employee records. Use Microsoft Excel and Word.

- *Created new procedures for billing and collection of revenue including all aspects of Revenue Analysis and Accounts Receivable.*

- *Key participant in streamlining processes for job analysis, performance evaluation and other areas pertinent to unit operations.*

- *Audit daily reports for the 13 municipal garages to ensure revenue collection by subcontractors.*

- *Manage the Billings unit dealing with highway / emergency / restricted permits for the Bureau of Highways.*

- *Implemented training for the revenue unit to ensure that unit production met assigned targets.*

**DEPUTY CHIEF / Revenue & Accounts Receivable**                   1989 - 1995

Scheduled and supervised 10 employees in the Grants, Billing and Auditing units. Prepared financial statements and schedules for grants, towing and garage revenue. Advised management on issues relating to unit procedures and guidelines. Coordinated work flow for employees within the grants receivable area.

*Continued*

**JENNIFER V. HARRIS**

Consistently developed excellent rapport with associates, outside agency representatives, and subordinates leading to superior operational results. Assisted in the recruitment, selection and training of top notch personnel.

- *Administered local area network (LAN) and mainframe system for monitoring the agency's revenue via the Integrated Financial Management System.*

- *Orchestrated multiple assignments and projects simultaneously, prioritizing the daily activities of the various units within the office.*

**GRANTS COORDINATOR** 1986 - 1989

Continually monitored status of all grants (federal, state, and private) within the department with particular emphasis on supervising the reimbursement processes for millions of dollars each year. Maintained all grant files and prepared all necessary correspondence to each specific federal, state or private grantor (s). Developed inter-office memorandums regarding grant procedures or processes. Demonstrated strong planning, organizing and leadership skills to consistently meet service goals, department objectives, and quality standards.

- *Served as liaison to all outside auditors of grant funds or operations.*

- *Instructed staff personnel on the Data Retrieval System for researching and gathering grants related information.*

- *Served as agency liaison to other city agencies with respect to intra-agency pass-thru grants.*

BALTIMORE DEPARTMENT OF ENVIRONMENTAL PROTECTION
Baltimore, Maryland

**OFFICE ASSOCIATE** June - December 1985

Provided a wide range of administrative support to senior staff. Maintained daily attendance information on timecards for hourly and other sub-managerial employees. Prepared OCR forms for submission to Payroll. Expedited special projects as directed. Reviewed and resolved appeals from employees. Compiled employee time and leave information for the Bureau of Administration. Managed time and multiple work tasks to efficiently meet deadlines and assigned objectives. Promoted rapidly to new position.

## LEARNING CREDENTIALS

**BACHELOR OF BUSINESS ADMINISTRATION** 1984
University of Maryland Baltimore, Maryland

*Major:* Office Administration and Technology

## PERSONAL

Willing to perform work related travel / Willing to relocate
Enjoy fitness activities, reading, the arts, travel

REFERENCES AND FURTHER DATA AVAILABLE UPON REQUEST

## 12.6  Formatted to Emphasize Skills

*Confidential Resume of*
**LAWRENCE A. BARNES**
447 Bolten Street, 25C · Chicago, Illinois 56621
(555) 555-8602


**TEACHING · TRAINING · BUSINESS COMMUNICATIONS**
MA SPEECH AND MASS COMMUNICATIONS WITH PRINCETON MANAGEMENT TRAINING
AND A 16-YEAR BACKGROUND ENCOMPASSING UNIVERSITY TEACHING, PUBLIC
RELATIONS, BUSINESS WRITING, RADIO / TELEVISION APPEARANCES, SALES AND
MANAGEMENT CONSULTING FOR INVESTMENT BANKING AND COMMODITY TRADING
FIRMS


**SELECTED CAREER HIGHLIGHTS**
- **Articulate and Engaging Lecturer:** Creative course design in areas of business, sales, and communications.  Have taught college students, federal employees and corporate professionals including key employees of Omnicom, Thayerweather and other major firms.
- **Media Correspondent:** Experienced source and commentator for both print and broadcast media including *The Great Lake Tribune, The Illinois Inquirer, Coin Collector,* Kensington News Radio, Reading Corporation News, Daily News Show, KLM-TV3 and various PBS stations.
- **Public Relations / Entertainment Industry:** Handled all aspects of advertising, promotion and public relations for Slam recording artist, Shasta McHoney, including US and European tours.  Negotiated contracts and managed recording sales and merchandising.
- **Business & Finance Expertise:** Offer and extensive background in sales, management and profitable management of +$2,000,000 in assets and trade accounts.  Proven market research and analytical skills--assess global climate changes, interests rate trends and capital formation.


**EDUCATION**

UNIVERSITY OF CHICAGO - Chicago, Illinois
**ADMINISTRATION / MANAGEMENT CERTIFICATE PROGRAM**

KALAMAZOO COLLEGE - Kalamazoo, Michigan
**MASTER OF SCIENCE IN SPEECH · MASS COMMUNICATION**
*Scholarship Award*
**Activities:** Assistant Program Director / On Air Personality for KZOO-FM · Audio / Video Producer


**TEACHING EXPERIENCE**

**ADJUNCT PROFESSOR OF COMMUNICATION ARTS & SCIENCES**
CITY UNIVERSITY OF ILLINOIS / EASTSIDE COMMUNITY COLLEGE (1991 - Present)
COMMUNICATIONS AND ADMINISTRATIVE MANAGEMENT INSTITUTE (1985 - Present)
STARLING UNIVERSITY - Chicago, Illinois (1991)
UNIVERSITY OF MASSACHUSETTS - Amherst, Massachusetts (1989 - 1993)
ANSELM COLLEGE - Anselm, New Hampshire (1985 - 1987)
QUINNIPIAC COLLEGE - New Haven, Connecticut (1981 - 1987)
> Develop and teach core subjects to college students; design and present comprehensive training programs to professional in the federal government and in private industry.  Specialize in Communications--speaking and presentation; Business--writing for advertising / public relations and human resource issues; Sales--including developing selling skills, writing and advertising.

Design and administer exams, grade student performance and review results with students offering advice and counseling as appropriate.

- *Lead two to three classes each month for 8 to 50 students including employees of Omnicom, Thayerweather and federal agency officials.*
- *As Interpersonal Communication Specialist at the National Northeast regional Training Center have taught key Department of Defense personnel.*
- *Provide clear explanations, demonstrations and individual attention identifying strengths and weaknesses and targeting approaches to learning which best suite individual needs.*
- *Conceptualized and developed six original programs: "Assertive Communication Skills," "Constructive Conflict Resolution," "Interpersonal Communications," "Creative Problem Solving," "Public Speaking," "Understanding and Managing Human Behavior."*
- *Interact positively with faculty members and administrators regarding educational policy and procedure.*

## RELATED EXPERIENCE

**PUBLIC RELATIONS · ENTERTAINER**
1982 - 1995
SHASTA MCHONEY
Cambridge, Massachusetts

Aggressively promoted appearances in the US and abroad; worked closely with Mr. McHoney's labels, including Slam and Foundling Records. Coordinated publicity campaigns, including advance work for US European tours.

- *Arrange / play lead piano, saxophone. Vocals for live performances and studio recordings. Performed on international tours 1988 - 1991· American Folk Concert Tour, Cambridge Music Festival, Islip Center, Glamour Puss Cafes, etc.*

## BUSINESS EXPERIENCE

**ASSISTANT VICE PRESIDENT**
1993 - Present
WINDY CITY MUTUAL MANAGEMENT
Chicago, Illinois

**BRANCH MANAGER**
1991 - Present
HARPOTH AND COMPANY, INC.
Aurora, Illinois

**BRANCH MANAGER**
1991 - 1992
AMSTAK STOCK COMPANY
Chicago, Illinois

**GENERAL SALES MANAGER**
1976 - 1981
WNOW RADIO
Detroit, Michigan

Provide business leadership and management consultation to 3 investment houses involved in investments banking and commodity trading. Review new accounts; qualify suitability, verify that customer objectives maintained throughout investor relationship. Assist reps with selling skills, handling rejection, difficult personalities. Conduct intensive market research and analysis;

develop and implement strategies to maximize financial performance.  Review new and existing accounts for compliance issues.

**LICENSES & REGISTRATIONS**
GENERAL SECURITIES PRINCIPAL · SENIOR REGISTERED OPTIONS PRINCIPAL ·
REGISTERED REPRESENTATIVE · COMMODITY PRINCIPAL

**PERSONAL**
Will perform work related travel · Will consider relocation
Journalist · Musician / Piano & Saxophone Teacher / Photographer / Rare Coin Collector

REFERENCES & FURTHER DATA AVAILABLE UPON REQUEST

"Jennifer V. Harris" was in a situation (Resume 12.5) similar to that of Phoebe Rosenberg. Like Ms. Rosenberg, she was seeking a job in her current field, accounting/management, but she had held several jobs in the past that were only marginally related. She accordingly wrote the descriptions of her earlier positions in such a way as to stress the accounting and managerial skills she used in performing those jobs.

Like Ms. Harris, when "Lawrence A. Barnes" launched his latest job search, he had already had several careers, which were reflected on his resume, and he stressed his skills by using a different format (Resume 12.6). As is customary, he opened the resume with some general information about his skills. At that point, however, rather than providing information on his work experience, which was both quite extensive and quite varied, he provided a list of "Selected Career Highlights," which he followed with his educational credentials. Only then did he include more specific details of his previous positions.

And even in recounting his previous employment he used a different format. In order to minimize the number of positions he'd held in the various fields in which he'd worked, he grouped all the positions in each field, and only then provided discussion of the skills he had employed in doing those jobs.

As you can see, revising your resume along the lines we've suggested means more than just adding your latest position to your list of past employers. But because of the special challenges faced by career changers, adapting your resume to reflect your skills rather than your previous jobs is an essential part of getting your foot in the door, which is the first step for every job seeker.

# JUST THE FACTS

- Although changing careers was almost unheard of in the past, changes in the way people view work, as well as changes in society and in the business community, have led many people to seek new careers.

- If you're interested in changing careers but haven't decided on a new one, you must begin the process by determining your interests, dreams, and values.

- In order to determine whether what you have to offer is appropriate for the new career you wish to pursue, it's necessary for you to evaluate not only your education and previous employment but also your volunteer/community service and hobbies and interests.

- Making a successful career change requires you to identify the skills you've employed in the past and redefine them to show how they can be applied in a different field.

- Deciding on a new career can be difficult, but by comparing your personal interests and background against the requirements of the new careers you are considering, you will be able to determine those that are both desirable and attainable.

- As a career changer, in writing your resume it's essential that you stress the generic skills you have rather than the specific functions you've performed in the past, and it's the best way to guarantee your being asked in for interviews.

# Chapter 13

# Resumes for the "Problem" History

*Get the Scoop On . . .*

- Accounting for employment gaps in your resume
- Dealing with too many jobs on your resume
- Making yourself more attractive with little work experience
- Countering the lack of formal education
- Presenting layoffs/firings/scandals in the best light

It would be nice if each of us could graduate from college, find a great entry-level position, then move up from one wonderful job to the next with nary a glitch along the way. But the fact is that it doesn't always happen that way. "Life," as John Lennon wrote, "is what happens to you while you're busy making other plans." Sometimes things don't work out quite the way we expect or would like them to.

It's likely that you've had your share of life's unforeseen and unpleasant experiences, and you've learned to cope with them. But even if you've been able to put those experiences behind you, to whatever extent they impacted on your career, they may come back to haunt you. Unless they are handled properly in your resume, they may represent problems from the perspective of a prospective employer. And since you don't want to provide a potential employer with any reason for eliminating you from serious contention for a job, it's important that you find a way to nip those potential problems in the bud.

These problems take essentially five forms: missing years of work; too many jobs; too few jobs; the lack of a formal education; and those situations in which you've been laid off, fired, or worked for a company in which a scandal of some sort occurred. The first four of these are likely to be reflected in your resume, and in the following pages we'll show you how to present them in as positive a light as possible so they won't prevent you from being asked in for an interview. While the fifth type of problem may or may not be reflected in your resume, depending on the circumstances, the chances are that you will have to deal with it at some point. We'll show you how to do that in a way that will minimize the possibility of its jeopardizing your chances for getting the job you want.

# MISSING YEARS OF WORK

Many people, for one reason or another, have employment gaps in their histories—periods ranging in length from six months to several years or more during which they held no regular jobs. Gaps of just a few months here or there can be easily explained as times during which you were looking for a new job. However, while there may be excellent reasons for any longer gaps on your resume, their mere existence is likely to raise a question in the mind of anyone who's considering you for a job—and might even keep you from being called in for an interview.

You may, for example, have started working right out of school, then taken some time off to raise a family. Similarly, you may have gone to work when you graduated from college, then left to pursue a postgraduate degree. You may at some point have worked for a company that went out of business, found it difficult to find another position, and subsequently been out of work for some time. You may have been caught up in a merger or downsizing in which your position was eliminated. Or you may have taken a year or more off as "down time" to recharge yourself psychologically and physically through travel or self-directed study.

Regardless of the reason, if there is a substantial gap, or gaps, in your resume, the chances are that a potential employer will notice and wonder why you weren't working during that time. For this reason, it's essential that you either camouflage or explain the gaps in the resume itself.

### When You've Been Out of Work and Looking for a Job

<aside>
**FYI**

If, while you are out of work and looking for a full-time job, you do some freelance or consulting work—particularly if it's in your current field—you can include a listing for that work under "Professional Experience" in your resume just as though it were a permanent, full-time position.
</aside>

If there were periods in the past in which you were out of work and looking for a job for more than a few months, regardless of the reason, it would be to your advantage to mask this information in your resume. Even though many people have gone through periods of unemployment and would therefore presumably be sympathetic about the experience, employers still tend to be somewhat suspicious of those who were unable to find jobs quickly.

The best and easiest way to camouflage this information is by providing only the years of employment with each company rather than the months and years for each job. Thus, for example, if you have these two jobs listed on your resume:

Assistant Director, Media Relations, The Rogers Company, October 1992–March 1995

Senior Publicist, Doyle & Watson, Inc., April 1989–January 1992

You can change them to read:

> Assistant Director, Media Relations, The Rogers Company, 1992–1995
>
> Senior Publicist, Doyle & Watson, Inc., 1989–1992

As you can see, by providing the information in this format, the eight month gap between jobs simply disappears, and the potential employer will never even be aware of the fact that you were out of work for a time.

## When You've Left Work for School or Family

As we've mentioned, there may be a gap in your work history because you left the workforce for some reason, perhaps to return to school or to raise a family, and then went back to work. While these are clearly good reasons for not having a full-time job, and reasons that almost any prospective employer would respect, unless there's something in your resume that explains these gaps, a prospective employer is likely to wonder about them.

Such gaps in your work history are also very easily remedied. If, for example, you left work to return to school, you can include that information in either the last job listing before you left, the first when you returned, or both. For example:

> Secretary, Brown & Collier, Inc., New York, N.Y., January 1992–July 1994.
>
> Performed a wide range of secretarial and administrative duties as secretary to vice president Richard Collier, including: drafting letters, making appointments, maintaining schedules . . . . Left to pursue undergraduate degree (B.A., Emerson College, June 1998)

Or:

> Editorial Assistant, Bowden House Publishers, New York, N.Y., July 1998–Present.
>
> Returned to work after graduating from Emerson College (B.A., June 1998), serving as assistant to senior editor Charles Goodyear . . . .

Similarly, if you left work to raise a family, that information can be included in either or both of the appropriate places in your resume; for example:

> Local Sales Manager, KRST Radio, Inc., San Francisco, CA, August 1993–September 1996.
>
> Directed organization and development of sales and marketing programs, recruitment of qualified sales personnel, and specialized staff training . . . Left on birth of first child, September 1996.

Or:

National Sales Manager, KMTV Radio, Oakland, CA, September 1998–Present.

Returned to work after spending two years caring for my first child, taking on responsibility for driving national sales strategy development and implementation . . .

# TOO MANY JOBS

*According to Robert M. Tomasko, principle of Temple, Barker & Sloane, Inc., and author of Downsizing, "In 1985 the average U.S. corporate manager stayed put for only 4.5 years . . . Personnel selection often depends as much on interpersonal chemistry as on track record."*

Another potential problem is one in which you have "too many" jobs on your resume. As we've discussed, "job hopping" no longer carries the stigma it once did. Lifetime employment with a single company, once relatively common, is now a rarity. The average working person should expect to hold five to seven jobs in the course of a 40-year career, and 10 to 12 jobs isn't unusual. So it's not necessary for you to start your job search with a defensive attitude about the fact that you've held several jobs in your life, or even in the past few years; it's very possible the person interviewing you has done the same.

Nonetheless, there is a point at which "several" jobs becomes "a lot of" jobs and at that point, prospective employers begin to ask questions about your sense of commitment, loyalty, and self-discipline. You need to decide for yourself whether, given your age and the industry in which you work, your career history looks too checkered. Compare your track record with the track records of friends and colleagues, especially those whose success you'd like to emulate. If it appears that you've had a substantially larger number of positions than your peers, it's worth considering doing something about it.

Of course, until a time machine is invented, you can't go back into the past to change your job history. But there are ways to craft your resume to mask or de-emphasize the sheer number of positions you've held. Here are some tricks to experiment with.

### When There Are Jobs on Your Resume That You've Held Extremely Briefly

Hey, it happens: At one company we know, the founder and CEO had such an unpredictably explosive temper that about one third of all new hires literally walked off the job the first day, declaring "I can't work for that man!" Long-term employees who'd developed their own ways of coping would compare notes on the newcomers' first days; if they lasted past lunch, they were considered "old timers."

And sometimes, even in a more normal organization, it becomes quickly apparent to the employer, the employee, or both, that the fit between a new worker and his job just isn't right. In such a case, it's surely better to part company amicably after a week or two rather than to stick it out for several increasingly awkward and uncomfortable months.

If you have one or two jobs like this in your background, don't feel that they must be included on your resume. Although this kind of work experience may be unpleasant or even mildly traumatic, most employers would view it as unimportant. (Of course, if this is a frequently repeated pattern in your life, you might want to consider career counseling to explore why so many jobs you've held seem to quickly self-destruct.)

You should consider omitting from your resume any job you've held for three months or less (not counting any summer or short-term jobs you may want to include because they were interesting, prestigious, or important). No one has any way of knowing that you've left something out of your resume (there is no national jobs registry for a recruiter to consult), and if the omission somehow becomes known at a later date (a colleague from the omitted job greets you at your new company), it would generally be considered too minor to regard as deceptive.

Naturally, omitting a job may leave a chronological gap in your career history. This can be dealt with in several ways, as we discussed earlier. In almost every case, the missing job turns into a nonissue. In time, you may even forget you ever held it!

## When You've Had Several Jobs with the Same Company

An easy way to simplify the look of your resume and reduce the appearance of job hopping is by combining jobs at the same company. This may be obvious when the jobs involve a natural career progression. You'd certainly want to change these three listings:

> Assistant media planner, Little Advertising Agency, June 1992–September 1993
>
> Media planner, Little Advertising Agency, September 1993–January 1995
>
> Senior media planner, Little Advertising Agency, January 1995–December 1995

Into this single listing:

> Media planning, Little Advertising Agency, June 1992–December 1995

Note that the generic functional term *"planning"* has been used to accurately summarize jobs at three levels with three different titles. If

### FYI

*If you think that there may be too many jobs on your resume, pay close attention to the reactions, spoken or physical, you get from recruiters and employers when they first hear or read about your job history. Raised eyebrows or disapproving looks may mean you've crossed the line.*

it's important or impressive to get the title "senior media planner" onto the page, throw that into the brief description of your job highlights:

As senior media planner, developed a system that saved $2 million . . .

Using a little ingenuity, you can also combine jobs at the same company even when they are from different functional areas. For example, you might combine these three listings:

Senior media planner, Little Advertising Agency, April 1992–September 1993

Account executive, Little Advertising Agency, September 1993–October 1994

Director of research, Little Advertising Agency, October 1994–January 1996

Into this single listing:

Media/research management, Little Advertising Agency, April 1992–September 1993

Again, note that we've replaced specific job titles with a more generic description of two functional areas. If you've worked in more than one area, which one or ones would you highlight in the condensed listing? Whichever is most directly relevant to the job you're currently seeking!

Similarly, if you held several jobs at different divisions within a single large company, or even at several companies within a conglomerate, consider combining the listings, using the overall company or conglomerate name. For example, an accountant who'd taken advantage of internal networking to hold jobs at *Time* magazine, the CNN cable TV network, and Warner Brothers Pictures, could combine all three under the heading "AOL Time Warner Inc."

## When You've Had Several Jobs in the Same Industry

If you've had the same job, or closely similar jobs, at two or more companies in the same industry, it's relatively easy to combine them into a single job listing. The following two jobs:

Marketing director, Little Software Associates, January 1995–February 1996

Associate marketing manager, Mammoth Software, Inc., February 1996–April 1997

can be combined like this:

Marketing management, Little Software Associates/Mammoth Software, Inc., January 1995–April 1997

**FYI**

*Don't combine two types of work and two different organizations into one listing unless you're sure you'll be able to explain in an interview how they are related. If, for example, a candidate were to combine sales management with communications consulting, he or she would have to be able to say something like: "As a sales manager, I discovered that most of the sales staff lacked basic skills in written and spoken communication, so I began to develop a series of seminars to improve these skills with specific reference to the sales environment." etc.*

If you've had much the same job at three or more companies in the same industry, try this format:

> Marketing management, software industry, January 1995– September 1998

The job description below could break this out into as much detail as is necessary and impressive:

> Directed marketing strategy and implementation at four leading software firms. At Little Software Associates, guided launch of most successful new product in personal finance of 1995. At Mammoth Software, Inc., developed . . .

As you will see in Resume 13.1, "Amelia I. Wiesel" was in such a situation. She had worked as a workshop/seminar organizer and presenter for four different companies over a period of more than 10 years. In order to minimize the number of job listings on her resume, she combined them all into one listing.

Sometimes, you can even combine different jobs at different companies into a single listing, providing there are some commonalities in function or industry between them. John Bakos of The Bakos Group, who has worked with individuals who've held as many as *50 jobs* in the course of their careers, suggests this format:

> Sales management/communications consulting, 1992–1998, Little Corporation, Mammoth Industries

Two different types of work *and* two different organizations are here combined into a single listing. You should, however, use this approach only if (1) you are really under pressure to simplify a resume that is suffering from "job listing overload," and (2) if the two jobs you want to combine have some common elements.

## When You Are Changing Careers

If you are planning to change careers, you may be faced with a situation in which you have not only *too many* jobs but also the *wrong kind* of jobs for the career you are entering. As we discussed in Chapter 12, when you are changing careers, many of the details of your previous work are basically irrelevant to the current job hunt. Therefore, you should feel free to drastically *simplify* the job listings from your former life.

Take, for example, a person who has worked for 15 years as a college linguistics professor and is now shifting to a career in computer programming. (Unlikely? We know someone who did just that, she is now CEO of one of the fastest-growing software firms in the world.) Such a person wouldn't want to list six academic jobs ("Associate Professor,

## 13.1 Condenses Similar Jobs

*Confidential Resume of*

# AMELIA I. WIESEL

887 East Mott Street • Winchester, Massachusetts 18826
*Phone*: (555) 555-3133 • *Fax*: (555) 555-1112
wwwRealjob.com/resumes/aiwiesel.htm
*Email*: aiweisel@Realjob.com

### CAREER SUMMARY

*Expert in patient services, health care standards, and institutional organization seeks a challenging executive management position in the public or private sector. Offer dynamic communication, technical, and leadership talents underscored by integrity, resourcefulness and analytical decision-making abilities. Skilled in identifying opportunities and in integrating marketing / service strategies and alliance building techniques into existing goals and objectives. Communicate effectively with associates and clients at all levels; utilize deft influencing skills; convey complex concepts in a clear and engaging way. Energetic and dedicated; excel in enthusiastic commitment.*

### CAREER TRACK

**WORKSHOP / SEMINAR ORGANIZER / PRESENTER**                              1989 - Present
Boston University Hospital School of Radiologic Technology          Boston, Massachusetts
Harvard University School of Radiologic Technology                Cambridge, Massachusetts
Dotex Management                                                  Worcester, Massachusetts
Hulme & Task                                                      Concord, New Hampshire

Design and present workshops and seminars on a wide range of health care topics including the appropriate Policies and Procedures for specific individualized settings (hospitals, nursing homes, assisted care living facilities) and including a range of departments including Intensive Care Units, Emergency or Trauma Units, Pediatrics, Geriatrics, Orthopedics, Surgery and Outpatient Services.

- *Developed Health Care Marketing Consulting Services, Health Care Workshops, as well as the completion of surveys on health care delivery services.*

- *Assessed health care facilities throughout the United States from Massachusetts, Maine, Wisconsin, Florida, and New York.*

- *Visited health care facilities in Montego Bay, Jamaica and Haiti.*

**MANAGEMENT CONSULTANT / STAFF SUPPORT**                                1988 - Present
Divine Grace Hospital                                              Boston, Massachusetts
Freeman Development                                                Quincy, Massachusetts
Homecare & Respite Care Project                                   New Haven, Connecticut
Women's Health Center                                                Hartford, Connecticut
Jesuit City Hospital                                              New Haven, Connecticut
Boston General Hospital                                            Boston, Massachusetts
Back Bay Diagnostic Center                                         Boston, Massachusetts

Provide a broad range of consultative and direct radiologic staff support to a diverse mix of healthcare institutions. Specific focus of services, to each individual institution, are designed to meet the needs of highly targeted project requests ranging from the development of patient surveys to marketing research and cost of development studies to the specific design of mobile medical units equipped with diagnostic imaging, lab and clinical equipment. Over the years more than 80,000 patients have been surveyed / serviced.

*Confidential Resume of* **AMELIA I. WEISEL**                    Page 2

- *Designed a health care center floor plan to more efficiently manage increased patient encounters.*

- *Developed instruments to Assess Patient Satisfaction in the fields of: Dental Services, In-patient Hospital Services, Out-patient Hospital Services; established minimum standards of care based on the surveys as well as personal experience.*

- *Created a marketing plan for a community health care facility.*

- *Trained and provided temporary radiologic technologists at several local hospitals and imaging centers.*

## LEARNING CREDENTIALS

**BACHELOR OF ARTS - Psychology / Marketing**                    1979
Regis College                                       Lynn, Massachusetts

**DIPLOMA - Radiologic Technology**                              1966
Harvard University Teaching Hospitals / School of Radiologic Technology        Cambridge, Massachusetts

*Additional courses, seminars, workshops, professional development:*
Pursuing Certification - Total Quality Management
Medicare & HMO Benefits for Elderly Care - CARIE Foundation, 1999
Certified Utility Analyst - Public Utility Consultants International, 1997
Strategies for Successful Meetings - Chamber of Commerce, 1997
Certified Utility Auditor - Public Utility Consultants International, 1996
Administrative Certification - Assisted Living Care Facility Training, 1995
Computer Repair and Maintenance - Montgomery County Community College, 1993
Courses in Law - Suffolk Law School, Bedford, Massachusetts, 1980-81

## ORGANIZATIONS & ASSOCIATIONS

National Notary Association    Greater Boston Chamber of Commerce
CARIE Foundation    American Registry of Radiologic Technologists
Public Utilities Consultants International

## PERSONAL

Willing to perform work-related travel / Willing to relocate
Extensive travel throughout the United States, Egypt and the West Indies

REFERENCES AND FURTHER DATA AVAILABLE UPON REQUEST

Linguistics Department, SUNY Binghamton" etc.) on her programmer's resume. Instead, her academic career would be summarized in a single listing headed:

Linguistics professor and communications theorist, 1975–1990

The paragraph following this heading would be written to maximize the relevance of her past work to the demands of her chosen future career. Names of universities that employed her might be mentioned, especially if they were prestigious, but not every teaching job need be cited.

The resume of "Heidi Johnson" (Resume 13.2) provides an example of an individual who changed careers. Although she started working as a sales representative when she graduated from high school in 1995, while she was working she went on to college to study biology. As soon as she had the necessary credentials, she found a job as a research assistant in a medical school, and received a B.S. in her chosen field in 1999.

In crafting her resume, Heidi included her earlier jobs even though they were unrelated to her chosen field, but she provided only limited information about them, and put more emphasis on her credentials as a biological researcher.

It's also possible that you've changed careers at some point, or for some reason took a job outside of your chosen field, and are now interested in returning to your original career. In such a situation, the details of your present position are of less importance than those of your earlier jobs, so it's advantageous for you to downplay your current job in favor of those you've held before.

*"Credentials are not the same as accomplish-ments."*

—Robert Half, President, Robert Half International, Robert Half on Hiring

"Bill Huxtable" (Resume 13.3) is an individual who did just that. He graduated from college with a B.S. in electrical and electronic engineering in 1988, held a few engineering jobs, then moved up into project management. In 1996, though, he changed careers and became a securities trader. Unfortunately, while he was successful as a trader, and the job paid better than his previous positions as a project manager, he wasn't happy, and decided to go back to his original career.

In order to make himself more appealing to potential employers who were interested in hiring project managers, he had to play down the short-lived second career. He did it by listing the jobs from his original career first, and then providing only a brief description of his current position.

"Donel J. Owens" is an individual in a somewhat similar situation. For most of his career, he worked as a teacher and coordinator of educational programs, but in 1998 he took a job as a legislative assistant to a congressman representing Washington, D.C. However, his first love was teaching, and he very much wanted to get back into the field.

## 13.2  Camouflages Career Change

*Confidential Resume of*

# HEIDI S. JOHNSON

39 Foster Avenue • Shrewsbury, New York 02332
*Phone:* (555)-555-7686
www.Jobnet.com/resumes/hsjohnson.htm
*Email:* hj23@mason.com *or* hsjohnson@Jobnet.com

## BIOLOGICAL RESEARCHER

### Dependable Laboratory and Leadership Talents

*Demonstrated initiative, integrity, resourcefulness and analytical / decision-making abilities combined with a capacity for work and achievement. Able to communicate effectively with associates and clients in various disciplines and at all levels of responsibility. Characterized as a high energy, goal oriented and disciplined professional incisive in finding and implementing solutions. Excel in commitment. Seek challenging position in private industry or academic setting.*

### CAREER TRACK

**RESEARCH ASSISTANT**                                                                    1998 - Present
New York Medical School                                                         Valhalla, New York

Perform detailed, technical lab work reliably as assigned. Demonstrate technical proficiency and an understanding of its impact in areas of responsibility. Ensure effective documentation of activities to comply with regulatory and departmental standards. Analyze, assess and control difficulties as they arise. Identify actual and potential problem areas and implement solutions.

*   *Assist with endothelial cell adhesion assay in stroke research laboratory; identify required resources; plan and coordinate work flow with others; evaluate outcomes.*

**LAW OFFICE CLERK**                                                                             1998
Law Offices of Daniel Thomas James                                        White Plains, New York

Processed discovery materials; obtained and assembled documentation per client request for attorney courtroom presentations. Researched, analyzed, organized and compiled precedent case information for attorney reference. Organized and maintained current and accurate computer client database and filing system for interrogatories and depositions.

*   *Exercised strong interpersonal skills; demonstrated natural ability to work with others; established quick rapport; exercised diplomacy and tact.*
*   *Answered, screened and routed calls; filed pleadings; organized billing; coordinated work effectively with exceptional time management skills.*

**RESEARCH ASSOCIATE**                                                               1996 - Present
The Nature Trust of Westchester                                               Peekskill, New York

Analyze verbal and statistical data to prepare reports for variety of individuals, lobbyists, organizations and institutions. Search sources to obtain information. Analyze and evaluate applicability of collected data. Prepare scientific and statistical tabulations, reports, abstracts, bibliographies, graphs and maps. Draft correspondence to answer inquiries.

*   *Establish guidelines and plans and monitor progress; assist with field studies; conduct stream water quality testing using benthic invertebrates.*
*   *Champion effective use of natural resources; planned, positioned and promoted program to conserve natural area in Peekskill, New York.*

Continued

*Confidential Resume of* **HEIDI S. JOHNSON**
Page 2

**SALES REPRESENTATIVE**                                                1995 - 1997
Contracting Specialists, Inc.                                  White Plains , New York

Contributed public relations and sales expertise critical to business growth for home improvement company selling franchises and home improvement services nationwide.  Prospected for new accounts through client referrals and cold calls. Generated customized marketing and presentational strategies; made new sales and serviced existing client accounts.

- *Achieved outstanding customer satisfaction through high operating efficiencies, reliability and quality performance standards.*

- *Won promotion from Administrative Assistant / Public Relations; attained ranking among top sales representatives in company.*

## LEARNING CREDENTIALS

**BACHELOR OF SCIENCE IN BIOLOGY**                                      January 1999
New York University                                            New York, New York
*Coursework included Organic & Inorganic Chemistry, Physics, Calculus, Genetics, Biopsychology, Cell & Molecular Biology, Physiology*

## COMPETENCIES

Laboratory
*Uv-Vis, IR and NMR spectroscopy • Agarose gel electrophoresis • SDS-PAGE
Gas, column, thin-layer and Sephadex chromatography*

Computer
*Macintosh • IBM • Windows • Microsoft Word • Works • Excel • PowerPoint • WordPerfect*

Language
*French • Sign Language*

## ORGANIZATIONS & ACTIVITIES

Alpha Phi Omega - National Service Organization
*Treasurer • Finance Committee Chair • Fundraiser*

New York University Crew Team, 1995 - 1996
*Perfect attendance at 5:00 AM daily practices*

Volunteer - Special Olympics, 1993 - Present

## PERSONAL

Willing to perform work-related travel / Willing to relocate

REFERENCES AND FURTHER DATA AVAILABLE UPON REQUEST

## 13.3 Masks Second Career

*Confidential Resume of*
**BILL HUXTABLE**
47 Mountain Bend · Bosley, Oregon
(555) 555-6620

**PROJECT MANAGEMENT - OPERATIONS & SALES**

**Cable · TV · Utility · Right of Way · High-Tech**

DYNAMIC PERFORMER AND PROJECT LEADER OFFERING ENGINEERING DEGREE AND 10
YEARS OF CONTRIBUTIONS IN DEVELOPING, CONSTRUCTING AND OPERATING FIBER
OPTIC TELECOMMUNICATION NETWORKS

*Progressive leadership contributions to bottom-line profitability and state-of-the-art productivity, turning
demand into growth, technology into value, competition into opportunity, and local presence into global
reach. Innovative, resourceful and inventive with unusual ability to identify opportunities, 'make things
happen' and consistently achieve goals and objectives. Establish superior procedures for operational
control; enhance sensitivity to cost, efficiency and deadlines.*

**SELECTED HIGHLIGHTS**

- **Proven Leadership:** Promoted rapidly and consistently from entry-level engineer to project manager
  overseeing combined budgets of $40,000,000+ and over 70 professional staff.
- **Financial Control:** Analyzed cost of staff, office, permit and franchise procurement, in-house and
  sub-contracted labor and all materials; developed network budgets for $20,000,000.
- **Span of Authority:** Directed design and construction of aerial and underground fiber optic
  telecommunication networks using sonet-token ring architecture in 5 major metropolitan areas.
- **Interpersonal Skills:** Seasoned and articulate speaker; represented MFS at meetings with top-level
  city officials nationwide; establish easy rapport with staff; work well in a team effort.
- **Sales Expertise:** Analyzed and synthesized data and materials; developed insights and solutions;
  fostered innovation; assisted Sales Director with major account sales calls.

**RELATED EXPERIENCE**

**PROJECT MANAGER**
1993 - 1996
OREGON STATE SUBURBAN PHASE IV PROJECT
Mosher, Oregon
> Broke up logjam of costly major delays; identified and developed staff talent; created a shared
> vision; fostered communication, cooperation and consensus; obtained critical right-of-way
> agreements and permits needed to complete fiber optic communication network.
> - *Directed competitive bidding, negotiating, awarding and supervision of sub-contracts;
>   established policies, guidelines and priorities; monitored progress; evaluated outcomes.*
> - *Interviewed and hired top-producing engineering, accounting and administrative personnel.*

SALEM COMMUNITY COMMISSION / SALEM EXPANSION PROJECT
Salem, Oregon
> From start-up, directed $23,000,000 project, largest MFS had undertaken--70 miles of urban
> underground fiber optic installation connecting 100+ buildings in Salem metro area. Built out 3
> central office switch sites and facilities for operations and sales staff. Managed office of 40.
> - *Attained right-of-way from 19 cities and towns that had previously denied permissions to all*

BEND SUBURBAN EXPANSION PROJECT
Bend, Oregon

> Oversaw implementation of 30-mile suburban expansion of downtown Bend Network, an $8,000,000 project. Directed over 20 personnel. Effectively used negotiation, persuasion and authority to procure permits and right-of-way agreements with 15 cities and towns.

**CONSTRUCTION MANAGER**
1992 - 1993
Seattle Expansion Project
Seattle, Washington

> Performed extensive administration and oversight of major project. Oversaw all aspects of design, construction and permit procurement. Met regularly with architects, engineers subcontractors and foremen of all trades, together with senior corporate management. Monitored activity to ensure compliance with blueprints, change orders and fiscal parameters.
> * *Prepared cost estimates, negotiated contracts, directed purchasing; led inspections; modified drawings or specifications if necessary.*

**Previous positions include:**

OUTSIDE PLANT MANAGER - Napa Valley Project · 1990 - 1992
PROJECT ENGINEER - Idaho State Project · 1990
FIELD / BICS ENGINEER - Tacoma Project / Seattle Project · 1988 - 1990

**OTHER EXPERIENCE**

**SECURITIES TRADER**
1996 - Present

> Combine market cognizance with a practiced business sense. Perform equity trades. Provide quality advisory services on economic indicators, market infrastructure and political considerations. Formulate competitive strategies within complex, rapidly changing venues. Cultivate dealer, custodian, institutional investor and trader relations to optimize profit.

**EDUCATION**

**BACHELOR OF SCIENCE IN ELECTRICAL & ELECTRONIC ENGINEERING**
1988
Washington State University
Brillmont, Washington

**Additional courses, workshops and professional development include:**
Philip Sewicky Mable Construction, Inc. Executive Management School
PSM Management Seminar on Project Planning and Team Building
Hargrove Fiber Optic Training Program

**PERSONAL**
Willing to relocate · Willing to perform work-related travel
Enjoy Reading / Travel / Outdoor Activities

REFERENCES & FURTHER DATA AVAILABLE UPON REQUEST

For that reason, when he prepared his resume (Resume 13.4), while he included his most recent position (that of legislative assistant), he emphasized his teaching credentials in the introductory paragraph of his resume as well as throughout the listings of his previous positions.

# TOO FEW JOBS

While some individuals may have a problem because there are too many positions listed on their resumes, having too few can also be considered a problem by potential employers. Of course, there may be a perfectly reasonable explanation for your having held relatively few jobs. You may have worked for one company for a long time, or you may not have been in the workforce for very long. Nevertheless, while employers are often uneasy about job candidates who have held a great number of jobs, they are sometimes equally uneasy about those who have held only one or two. The reasons for this concern depend on which of these two situations the candidate is in.

### If You've Been in One Job for a Long Time

If you've been in the same position for a long time, it's entirely possible that it might not seem like a problem to you. You might think that having done so, particularly in this era of "job hopping," would make you appear to be a particularly stable and therefore attractive potential employee. If so, think again. In today's dynamic business environment, employers are looking for equally dynamic individuals who will be able to learn, grow, and move up in their organizations. If you've had only one job for a number of years it might suggest that, while you were competent in fulfilling the responsibilities of that job, you were incapable of growing and taking on greater responsibilities. While this may not be the case, it is not a message you want to send to potential employers, and it's important that you avoid doing so in preparing your resume.

### If You've Had Only One Job Because You're New to the Workplace

If you haven't been working long and consequently have only one or two jobs on your resume, you're essentially in the same boat, although for a different reason. Although, as we've already discussed in Chapter 11, too much experience can be considered a problem by employers, too little experience can be considered a problem as well. Again, once you're in an interview situation, you'll have the opportunity to provide a potential employer with all the details of your experience, and thereby convince him or her that you can do the job. But unless you have that interview,

## 13.4 Masks Second Career

*Confidential Resume of*
### DONEL J. OWENS

22 Whitney Place
Washington, District of Columbia 43304
(555) 555-4018

www.JobGroup.com/resumes/djowens.htm
Email: djowens@JobGroup.com

## TEACHER • PROGRAM COORDINATOR
### Dynamic Communication and Organizing Talents

*Energetic and dependable contributor with strong interpersonal skills to inspire, motivate and guide others. Innovative, resourceful and inventive. Demonstrate flexibility and teamwork. Introduce programs in a comprehensible, orderly manner, relating skills to each other and to appealing real-life tasks and opportunities. Skilled in behavioral control and mental motivation of pupils, encouraging them to learn and excel. Seek a challenging position as a teacher / program coordinator where training and proven experience in public service, education, and media communication will be fully utilized and lead to career growth opportunities.*

### CAREER TRACK

**LEGISLATIVE ASSISTANT**                                                     1998 - Present
Representative Steven Byrd / District of Columbia                           Washington, D.C.

Contribute management, public relations, organizing and interpersonal expertise critical to constructive, focused strategies and communications with constituents, agencies, committees, the general public, and other legislators. Author statements, advisements, briefings and various correspondence. Organize and promote meetings and other functions. Make recommendations to strategically guide perspectives. Research, write and file legislation for Commonwealth.

- *Boost efficiency and effectiveness; generate outstanding relationships with staff, constituents and other professionals.*

- *Review existing policies, procedures and structures; conceptualize and put new programs into action.*

- *Member of the city-wide Violence Prevention Task Force for Washington, D.C.*

- *Member of Young Democrats of Washington, D.C..*

**PROGRAM COORDINATOR - UNIVERSAL**                                          1995 - 1998
**EDUCATIONAL COORDINATOR - TEACH & PREACH / SHARE TO CARE**
National Educational Service, Inc.                                          McLean, Virgina

Created an active motivational learning environment. Managed on-site program operations at Mary Peters and William Johnson Middle Schools in collaboration with the community based organization NES, with focused emphasis on special education / special needs / at risk students. Performed annual and monthly planning. Recruited, trained, motivated and recognized staff. Gave direction to daily activities. Championed growth and development of youth. Demonstrated creative and flexible approaches and positive reinforcement skills. Oversaw updating of client records.

- *Encouraged appreciation of individual talents, skills and potential through cooperative teaching and learning techniques; enjoyed mutually supportive relationships with parents.*

**DONEL J. OWENS**                                                            Page 2

- *Achieved recognition in regional Virginia Union News, October 3, 1996, as "Role Model at Work" for successful outreach to schools in minority teaching program.*

**PROGRAM COORDINATOR**                                                      1994 - 1995
K Circle Family House, Youth Recreation Club                              Washington, D.C

Directed daily recreational and educational activities for lower-income and inner city residents. Helped children explore a range of familiar and unfamiliar forms, dimensions and experiences. Developed awareness, support and a sense of community. Provided technical knowledge and project management expertise for consistent, client-pleasing results.

- *Promoted variety of board games, sports, reading and communication skill activities; worked with staff to enhance children's capacity for delight, wonder and mystery.*

- *Continually worked to improve the range of opportunities and quality of services offered.*

**RADIO HOST / PRODUCER / WRITER**                                          1988 - 1994
WVIA Radio                                                             Richmond, Virginia

Conceived, researched, planned, coordinated and performed a variety of activities to enhance ongoing operations. Cultivated rich resource network. Conceptualized fresh approaches and undertook challenging themes to capture listener attention and furnish solid newsworthy information. Demonstrated creative approaches, positive reinforcement skills and enthusiasm.

- *Created a shared vision for listeners in Richmond region; prepared formats and proposed current issues and lively topics for hour-long Public Meeting (1992 - 1994) and Youthspeak (1988 - 1991) programs, both F.C.C. licensed.*

---

## EDUCATION

COMMUNITY TEACHERS PARTNERSHIP PROGRAM, 1994-1997
American College - Washington D.C.

BUSINESS DIPLOMA, 1988
High School of Commerce - Charlotteville, Virgina

**Additional courses, seminars and workshops include:**

FACILITATOR TRAINING / CERTIFICATION, 1997
Project LIFE - Lifesaving Information For Everyone

BLACK ALCOHOLISM & ADDICTIONS INSTITUTE - 36 HOUR COURSE CERTIFICATION, 1997
Spelman School of Medicine - Atlanta, Georgia

CPR AND EMERGENCY CARDIAC CARE PROVIDER CERTIFICATION, 1996
Medical Training Associates - American Heart Association

CERTIFICATE - URBAN EDUCATION, 1993
Virginia State College - Welles, Virginia

CO-FOUNDER / BOARD MEMBER , CHILDREN & BRETHEN UNITED, 1987
Richmond, Virginia

it's not going to happen, so you have to make sure that your resume suggests that you have as much experience as possible.

### What You Can Do About It

Regardless of which situation you're in, there is one excellent way of making it clear that, although you may have held only one or two positions, you nevertheless have a good, or at least reasonable, amount of experience. "Rodney Giles" was in this situation, and you can see from his resume (Resume 13.5) how he managed to do just that.

When he graduated from college, Rodney went to work as an agency business manager with the Consolidated Life Insurance Company of Nebraska, and continued in the same job for more than 20 years. But when he decided to look for a new position, he recognized that having only one job on his resume might be a liability.

Had he been preparing a standard resume, he would in all likelihood have provided just one or two brief paragraphs on the responsibilities of his position. However, recognizing a potential problem, he put some thought into it and came up with a different way of presenting his credentials—a way that would make him more attractive to potential employers.

Rather than simply writing a paragraph or two, he wrote one introductory paragraph summarizing his responsibilities, then broke down those responsibilities into their component parts: human resources/administration, accounting, systems administration, and marketing. By doing so he was able to provide more extensive details on his responsibilities in each area. Thus, he provided potential employers with a great deal of information on the full range of his experience and in the process created a very impressive resume.

No matter how simple or complex your present position is, it will be possible for you to do the same thing. First, sit down and make a list of all your major areas of responsibility. Once you've determined those, you can break them down even further into their component parts, creating sub-lists that provide more specific information on each of the various responsibilities of your position.

# LACK OF FORMAL EDUCATION

Another potential problem from an employer's perspective is a lack of formal education (meaning, usually, a college degree). If, for whatever reason, you never had the opportunity to go to college, it can be a real

## 13.5  One Job, Many Skills

*Confidential Resume of*
**RODNEY N. GILES**
10 Ringling Alley · Lincoln, Nebraska 60565
Home: 555-555-9886

**MANAGEMENT**
ENERGETIC LEADER WITH A POSITIVE, HANDS-ON MANAGEMENT STYLE SEEKS TO LEAD
A PROGRESSIVE FIRM AND ITS CUSTOMERS INTO THE 21ST CENTURY AS A RESOURCEFUL,
ANALYTICAL PARTNER OF A FIRST-CLASS MANAGEMENT TEAM.

**SUMMARY**
*Proven ability and work ethic to effectively manage a large office with a major company.  Promoted five
times within the position.  Extensive knowledge of the life insurance industry and its issues, as well as
general office operations.*

**PROFESSIONAL EXPERIENCE**

THE CONSOLIDATED LIFE INSURANCE COMPANY OF NEBRASKA
Lincoln, Nebraska
**AGENCY BUSINESS MANAGER**
1973 - Present

> Contribute vision and management expertise critical to organizational efficiency, business growth
> and financial health for this $7.5 Million agency of this prestigious insurance company.
> Spearhead strategic planning, policy formulation and implementation, business development,
> information management, computer systems, budgeting and expense management.
> **Human Resources / Administration:**
> - Direct and manage all human resource functions encompassing recruitment, interviewing,
>   selection and professional development of marketing support of staff.
> - Utilize networking, newspaper and college advertising to recruit top-notch candidates;
>   supervise up to 28 support staff and management level personnel.
> - Provide career counseling services; implement merit ratings, salary increases, promotion
>   recommendations, disciplinary actions and terminations.
> - Keep current with government, industry and company policies and regulations; administer
>   MONY policy, maintaining compliance with OSHA and EEO guidelines.
> - Function as liaison to Facilities Management, coordinating communications and resolving
>   problems.
> - Troubleshoot policy owner complaints / issues with quick, positive solutions, turning
>   problems into sales for MONY representatives; enjoy a persistency rate of 92%.

**Accounting:**
- Develop, administer and control the $7.5 Million agency budget; investigate expense / expenditure fluctuations; formulate and implement cost containment measures.
- Expert business planning and company automation cut agency expenses in half.
- Examine invoices for appropriate classification and recording; authorize check payments.
- Provide accurate financial reporting services and analysis of comparative financial results.

**Systems Administration:**
- Provide technical expertise and information retrieval; serve as agency computer liaison.
- Handle PC maintenance and repair; update and develop enhancements to word processing and financial software.
- Prepare and present engaging procedural and technical support classes on a quarterly basis; consistently utilize positive feedback to increase comprehension and morale.
- Design and produce effective technical and sales proposals and illustrations.

**Marketing:**
- Develop and implement results getting marketing strategies as Agency Business and Individual Marketing Manager.
- Analyze and forecast markets and make new product proposals; advise on and provide training on product lines.
- Marketing programs include targeted mailings, Estate Planning seminars, Video marketing, advanced planning concepts, recruiting, and newsletters.
- Created a direct mail program in 1990 that currently involves up to 15,000 pieces monthly with a 1/2% response rate; purchase lists and utilize mail merge technology.
- Generate a 2 to 3% response rate with campaign that uses on-line real estate lists.
- Serve as Client-For-Life Manager; obtain an outstanding 21% response rate with annual review letter mailing to existing clients, earning reps $10,000 in annual commissions.

**PROFESSIONAL LICENSES / QUALIFICATIONS**

- REGISTERED REPRESENTATIVE: NATIONAL ASSOCIATIONS OF SECURITIES DEALERS (NASD)
- SERIES 6: INVESTMENT COMPANY PRODUCTS AND VARIABLE CONTRACTS
- SERIES 63: UNIFORM SECURITIES STATE LAWS · LOMA I AND LOMA II

**EDUCATION**

**BACHELOR OF SCIENCE IN BUSINESS ADMINISTRATION**
Perry State University - Omaha, Nebraska

**SKILLS**
Lotus 1-2-3 · WordPerfect · Data Entry · General Accounting · ECTA (Email)
REFERENCES & FURTHER DATA AVAILABLE UPON REQUEST

liability in today's competitive job market. For many positions, in fact, candidates are required to have at least undergraduate, if not postgraduate, degrees.

However, sometimes even when a college degree is "required," it isn't really required at all—if you have sufficient additional experience to make up for it. Of course, if you're thinking of becoming a nuclear physicist or a brain surgeon and don't have a college degree, you'll have to rethink your plans. But there are lots of other jobs which in theory require degrees but in reality do not.

So while it's generally advantageous if you have a degree, if you don't, there is a way to de-emphasize your lack of formal education on your resume and so get your foot in the door. "Liam Conner," an expert in electronics/systems engineering, was someone in that situation and, as you can see from Resume 13.6, he was able to craft a resume that effectively worked around the lack of a degree.

Liam accomplished this in several ways. First, he provided an excellent summary of his skills in the profile section at the beginning of his resume, which he followed with strong, action-oriented descriptions of his various positions. Then, after the professional experience section, he provided a long and impressive list of those areas in which he was technically proficient, followed by another lengthy list of the professional training courses he had attended. The result of all this is that, upon reading the resume, the reader may not even notice that Liam doesn't have a college degree.

## LEARNING EXPERIENCES: LAYOFFS, FIRINGS, SCANDALS

As we've already mentioned, there is one other type of issue that may be perceived as a "problem" by potential employers: a situation in which you were laid off, fired, or employed by a company in which some scandal occurred.

It is neither necessary nor appropriate to provide information about any of these issues in your resume. It may in fact be possible for you to mask the identity of your former employer so that the issue doesn't come up when a potential employer is deciding whether or not to ask you in for an interview. We'll show you an easy way to do that.

But whether or not you are able to mask your last employer in your resume, be assured that these issues are likely to come up when you actually go on an interview. For that reason, it's important that you prepare what you will say about them in advance of any such discussion. We'll provide you with some ideas of how to do that.

## 13.6 De-Emphasizes Lack of Formal Education.

**LIAM MARLIN CONNER**
1210 Powell Street
Albany, New York 27680
Phone: 555-555-6790

**ELECTRONICS / SYSTEMS ENGINEERING**
*Technical Proficiency is Complemented by Outstanding Management Skills*
OVER 10 YEARS OF PROGRESSIVE, HANDS-ON LEADERSHIP / TECHNICAL CONTRIBUTIONS
IN TELECOMMUNICATIONS.  ACCOMPLISHED SELF-STARTER WITH STRONG PLANNING
ORGANIZING AND PROJECT MANAGEMENT ABILITIES.

**PROFILE**

- *Leadership / Communication:*  *Successfully orchestrate multiple simultaneous projects; expertly translate customer requiremenis into high technology solutions.  Articulate, skilled bilingual communicator, fluent in both Spanish and English.  Effective team builder; supervise and motivate technical personnel for OPIA  CORP.  Gymnasium owner / director.*
- *Analytical Troubleshooter:*  *Established track record for identifying technical problems; resourceful in developing creative, logical solutions that result in increased efficiency.  Possess state-of-the-art knowledge of EIA communication standards and interface compatibility issues.  Test equipment pro; highly skilled in circuit analysis and troubleshooting.*
- *Dedicated, Trusted Professional:*  *Granted Top Secret / SCI security clearance.  Committed to an ideal of quality and integrity; combine resourcefulness with initiative and a drive for achievement. Reputation for giving better than 100%.  Relied on to provide effective leadership; make consistently sound judgments under pressured conditions.*
- *Award-Winning Sports Enthusiast:*  *Black Belt in Tae Kwon Do and Full Contact Karate · Licensed Trainer in Kickboxing · 3-Time National Amateur Kickboxing Champion in Spain · 1990 National Semipro Light-Heavyweight Kickboxing Championships in Paris, France · Silver Medallist in 1989 European Kickboxing Championships in Rimini, Italy · 1990 Silver Medallist in the World Kickboxing Championships in Hull, Canada.*

**PROFESSIONAL EXPERIENCE**

OPIA CORP.
Albany, New York
**ENGINEERING TECHNICIAN**
1992 - Present
  Contribute supervisory and technical expertise critical to successful contracts with the U.S. Navy.
  Maintain full accountability for the installation and configuration of networks that include
  10BaseT, FDDI, thick-net; design both secure and non-secure networks.
  *Selected Highlights*
  - *Orient, train and supervise a high-performing technical crew; evaluate performance and provide positive feedback to boost performance.*
  - *Played an integral role in the U.S. Navy / NATO systems installations.*
  - *Maintain uninterrupted power service throughout the site, utilizing a 250 KVA UPS unit.*
  - *Manage PC and peripheral repair, upgrades and maintenance; ensure quick malfunction diagnosis / troubleshooting and optimal performance efficiencies.*
  - *Audio / video systems proficiencies include voice nets, CCTV and satellite TV.*

**FIELD TECHNICIAN**
  Selected to utilize advanced technical knowledge of Naval communications.  Telecommunication
  responsibilities encompassed equipment installations, repair, maintenance and operations.
  Handled various power and distribution, as well as customer technical service functions.

*Selected Highlights:*
- *Worked effectively in a team engineering effort to install and troubleshoot complete Naval Communications Centers.*
- *Installed and tested secure and non-secure phone systems, conduit, cable trays, cabling, power panels and various other electrical equipment and components.*
- *Analyzed customer requirements and relocated equipment, power and signal cables; ensured the highest quality technical and customer relations standards.*

**DEPARTMENT OF THE NAVY**
Clearwater, Florida
**CRYPTOGRAPHIC TECHNICIAN**
1983 - 1987

Performed a wide variety of communication line and troubleshooting operations, serving as liaison between local and distant facilities. Ascertained symptoms related to failure and malfunctions and implemented appropriate repair / replacement / routing actions.

*Selected Highlights:*
- *Ensured maximum communications performance with PM checks and BERT tests on station to station lines, troubleshooting circuitry and setting alternate routing as necessary.*
- *Gained valuable knowledge of communications; maintained detailed, accurate documentation on all projects.*

**CONNER BODYWORKS**
New Haven, Connecticut
**OWNER / DIRECTOR**
1980 -1983

Handle the management and administration of this successful gymnasium; launched operations from start-up. Spearhead strategic business planning, program development, marketing, accounting and human resources hiring, training and performance evaluations.

*Selected Highlights:*
- *Track membership status via computer system, solicit renewals, promote the sale of equipment and clothing, give facility tours.*
- *Interview new members to obtain information on physical condition and goals; design personal programs integrating elements promoting flexibility, strength and endurance.*
- *Troubleshoot complex customer problems; effectuate quick, positive solutions to ensure 100% customer satisfaction.*

**INSTALLATION EXPERTISE**

**TELECOMMUNICATIONS**
Directional, omni directional, parabolic antennas · LSY-5C radio (voice) nets · KG-81, KG-84A, KG-84C, KG-196, KY-57 crypto gear · Statistical multiplexors · Patch panels · Computers and peripherals · Modems · Equipment racks · Telephones · Microphones · TVs · VCRs · Large screen projectors and switching units · Audio / video equipment (audio distribution amps and video distribution amps) · Cables and connectors including multiconductor, telephone, coaxial, fiber optic, and power.

**NETWORKS**
Thick-wire · Thin-wire · 10BasseT · FDDI · Transcievers / Multiport transceivers · Terminal concentrators · Routers / Bridges

**FACILITIES**
Cable trays · Rigid, EMT and PVC conduits · Air ducts · 110 and 220V electrical power units · False ceilings and raised computer flooring · Lighting circuits . Emergency lighting · Fire alarm circuits · Emergency shutdown systems · CCTV / Security systems · Station ground bus · Motorized viewing screens · Environmental monitoring devices

**EDUCATION & TRAINING**
TV / VCR REPAIR · ABCS OF VIDEO TECHNOLOGY · TQL TRAINING · TCP / IP · DATACOM
AND WAN TROUBLESHOOTING · CISCO ROUTER OPERATION · PRINCIPLES OF COMPUTER
COMMUNICATIONS · UPS OPERATOR'S COURSE · MASTER ELECTRICIAN'S COURSE ·
MICROCOMPUTERS AND MICROPROCESSORS · PETTY OFFICER RIGHTS AND
RESPONSIBILITIES · CRYTOGRAPHIC TECHNICAL "A" SCHOOL

EXCELLENT REFERENCES AVAILABLE UPON REQUEST

Part VI of this book provides advice on how to prepare for an interview, so here we will discuss only those aspects of the resume and interview that pertain to providing information about these "learning experiences."

## If You've Been Laid Off

*FYI*

*It's particularly important that you not feel defensive about having been laid off from your position. If you feel defensive, you're going to behave defensively, both in writing and in person, and defensiveness is not the kind of attitude you want to project to potential employers.*

If you've been laid off from a position, the most important thing to remember is that layoffs are extraordinarily common today. With all the mergers, downsizings, reorganizations, and re-engineering that's going on in business today, people are being laid off every day of the year. It's become so common, in fact, that the chances are that whoever will be considering you for a position will probably have been laid off him or herself at some point in the past. So even if your first reaction to being laid off is to feel that you've somehow done something wrong and, as a result, been branded for life, it simply isn't true.

We know, for example, of a middle-management executive (call her "Ruth") whose job was made "redundant" by the merger of two large corporations in a particularly volatile industry. When Ruth started looking for a new position, she was extremely concerned that she would be perceived as some kind of pariah by potential employers and consequently prepared a long and somewhat lengthy defense of herself to use should the need arise.

But once she started interviewing, she discovered that the defense wasn't necessary at all. During interviews, as soon as Ruth began to say, "Well, as you probably know, such-and-such company merged with my company and . . . ," she was invariably interrupted by a dismissive wave of the hand and a comment like, "Oh, I know. I've been there."

Nevertheless, even though your being laid off may have had nothing to do with anything you did or did not do, potential employers are sometimes wary of individuals who are in that situation. For that reason, if it's possible to camouflage on your resume the fact that you lost your job through a layoff it would be advantageous to do so.

One of the best ways of doing this is to mask the name of the last employer on your resume. As you can see in Resume 13.7, "Kevin Gallagher" was an individual who found himself in this situation and was able to accomplish this by using the initials of the company's name rather than the company's full name. Had he used the company's whole name, potential employers might have recognized it as the name of an organization which had recently been downsized and possibly decided against interviewing Mr. Gallagher. As it was, though, they didn't recognize the name, and Mr. Gallagher received several invitations for interviews.

## 13.7  Masks Identity of Recent Employer

*Confidential Resume of*
**KEVIN GALLAGHER**
7 Castle Road
Austin, Texas 01951
(555) 555-3101

**SALES AND MARKETING PROFESSIONAL**
WITH 10+ YEARS OF STAFF DEVELOPMENT AND MOTIVATION, TERRITORY
MANAGEMENT AND MARKET SHARE EXPANSION, CUSTOMER SERVICE /
RELATIONS, AND BUSINESS DEVELOPMENT EXPERIENCE
*Talented, energetic professional with demonstrated communications talents, motivational
speaking abilities, staff training and development acumen, and direct sales skills. Resourceful,
imaginative and aggressive with proven persuasive presentation skills and unusual ability to
inspire employees, and maximize performance utilizing interpersonal dynamics. Insightful
listener and team builder.*

**PROFESSIONAL EXPERIENCE**

**SALES REPRESENTATIVE**
1993 - Present
MJB, Inc. - Austin, Texas
> Broad and diverse responsibilities encompass all aspects of territory development,
> business development, delivering persuasive sales presentation, negotiating prices, terms
> and conditions, and providing superlative customer service and support. Aggressively
> solicit new accounts, penetrate new markets, and establish long-term, loyal customers.
> Duties include promoting sales programs and campaigns, merchandising and enhancing
> product visibility.
> * *Recognized for outstanding sales talents, consistently breaking sales and market
>   share records, increasing profit margins and profitability, and outperforming peers.*
> * *Established reputation for ability to open new accounts, solidifying relationships and
>   improving recurring business.*

**SALES MANAGER**
1987 - 1992
Texas Tire and Auto Body - Stephentown, Texas
> Directed and managed full sales, marketing and customer service functions including
> employees supervision, training, motivation and development, vendor relations,
> scheduling, budgeting and forecasting, and operations. Provided leadership and technical
> advice; ensured quality of service delivery; troubleshoot and resolve problems; and
> prepared reports.
> * *Consistently overachieved monthly sales quotas, reduced employees turnover and
>   maximized sales staff performance.*

**EDUCATION AND TRAINING**
**BACHELOR OF SCIENCE IN BUSINESS ADMINISTRATION,** 1990
Texas Business Institute - Dallas, Texas · **Major: Marketing**

REFERENCES AND FURTHER DATA AVAILABLE UPON REQUEST

## If You've Been Fired

**FYI**

*On some company-provided job application forms, you may find the heading "Reason for Leaving" next to each job listing you're asked to provide. If you have to fill out such a form, use the most neutral sounding explanation possible. If you've been fired, consider offering the two-word phrase "Job fit" as your reason for leaving. (You can explain more fully in the interview.) It's never necessary to list a reason for leaving any job on your resume.*

There's no question about it. Being fired is tough. Because we all tend to derive our identities from what we do for a living, and we all like to think that we do a good job. Getting fired feels like being told that we're worthless. Even if you've lost your job for some reason other than poor performance, and there are many other possible reasons, it doesn't make it any easier.

But even if you were fired because you did do something wrong, that doesn't mean that your life is meaningless or that you're a worthless individual. What it does mean is that you made a mistake, a mistake you'll resolve not to repeat, and that you have to pick yourself up and get on with your life, both personally and professionally.

Potential employers know that there are any number of reasons why someone might have been fired; they may have been fired themselves at some point in their careers and may accordingly be sympathetic to your situation. At the same time, though, if they know you've been fired but don't know why, they may be wary of seriously considering you for a position with their firm. As with the individual who was laid off, it's accordingly advantageous to simply avoid making any reference to being fired in your resume.

## If You Worked for a Company That Experienced a Scandal

You may once have worked for a company that experienced some kind of scandal: a highly publicized lawsuit concerning tax fraud or racial discrimination, or a series of embarrassing financial missteps, for example. In such circumstances, it's best to avoid making any direct reference to it in your resume. Even if you had nothing to do with the scandal, as with individuals who have been laid off or fired, potential employers may be concerned about considering a candidate from a company in which some unpleasant events took place.

As with the other situations, it may be possible to camouflage in your resume the fact that you worked for the company by using only the company's initials rather than its full name in order to mask exactly who it was you were working for. You can also use the less-well-known name of the parent corporation rather than the name of your notorious division, or vice versa.

"Patricia Brady," the subject of Resume 13.8, found that most people knew her current employer (let's call it the Phillips Kindergarten) because of an embarrassing accusation of child abuse leveled at one of the teachers. Patricia had played no role in the scandal—in fact, the alleged incident had occurred several years before she even went to work at the school. Nonetheless, whenever she mentioned the school's

## 13.8  Masks Identify of Recent Employer

*Confidential Resume of*
**PATRICIA BRADY**
17-19 Muscat Street
Kenosha, Illinois 67952
(555) 555-5835
www.JobGroup.com/resumespbrady/.htm
Email: pbrady@JobGroup.com

**EDUCATIONAL FACILITATOR / COORDINATOR**
**Dynamic Communication and Consulting Talents**
*Energetic and dependable contributor with proven leadership, highly developed interpersonal and problem-solving abilities. Empathetic listener. Innovative, resourceful and inventive. Able to empower, motivate and guide others to identify opportunities and achieve objectives. Possibility thinker with indefatigable initiative and deft influencing skills. Effective with people of all ages, aptitudes and backgrounds. Excel in enthusiastic commitment.*

**PROFESSIONAL EXPERIENCE**

**MANAGER / SPECIALIST**
1996 - Present
PKG

Create an active motivational learning environment. Define and demonstrate roles and responsibilities for Special Education staff. Structure, facilitate, and supervise policies and procedures to bring district into full compliance with state and federal regulations. Encourage appreciation of individual talents, skills and potential through cooperative learning techniques. Develop work groups and teams; champion alternative solutions and plans to solve problems.

- *Apply new technology to organizational needs; ensure staff are trained and capable; employ Macintosh and Microsoft Word, ClarisWorks, Quicken and Oracle software as needed.*
- *Serve in peer-review role; monitor program evaluation and student documentation; utilize persuasion and authority to mediate between students, parents, and staff.*

**PEDIATRIC SPEECH & LANGUAGE PATHOLOGIST**
1995 - 1996
BetaCor Laboratories

Assessed and diagnosed speech and language abilities for children and adults. Actively sought client and professional input; identified required resources; developed insights and solutions; fostered training abilities and innovation among staff and clientele of all backgrounds. Adapted leadership style to situations and people. Considered and responded effectively to the needs, feelings, capabilities and interests of others; provided feedback.

- *Demonstrated creative and flexible approaches, positive reinforcement skills, sincerity and enthusiasm; designed, developed and delivered in-service training for hospital staff.*
- *Orchestrated family training sessions; planned and coordinated with others; established guidelines, plans and priorities to meet agreed-upon goals.*

**SPEECH & LANGUAGE PATHOLOGIST**
1989 - 1995
Aurora Unified School District

Planned, coordinated, and implemented school-based activities that addressed various learning styles and abilities. Gathered, analyzed, and interpreted data. Arranged scheduling. Oversaw performance in augmentative communication, oral motor development, feeding development, articulation / phonology, language development, fluency and voice. Assisting in writing grant and project proposals. Fostered cooperation, communication and consensus among groups.

- *Organized programs for Early Childhood, special Education (cognitive and learning disabilities, physically handicapped, autistic) and standard education through 8th grade.*

- *Chaired school and community committees; served on statewide committee examining issues concerning Exceptional Educational Needs (EEN) students.*

**SPEECH & LANGUAGE PATHOLOGIST**
1988 - 1989
Tohasha County Early Intervention Program

Provided leadership, consultation and technical support to case workers, parents, teachers, and specialists. Utilized superior networking and communication abilities, consistently building strong provider and clientele relations. Performed trouble-shooting; recognized and defined issues; analyzed relevant information; encouraged alternative solutions and plans to solve problems. Conveyed and maintained highest possible standards for community service.

- *Facilitated services in areas of oral motor / feeding development, articulation / phonology, language development and fluency to children from birth to age 3.*

**EDUCATION**

**MASTER OF SCIENCE**
1989
**BACHELOR OF SCIENCE**
1987
University of Illinois
Keighly, Illinois
*Courses included Psychology · Sociology · Logic · Philosophy · Statistics · Legal / Ethical Issues in Education*

**Additional courses, workshops, and professional development include:**
Instructing Multi-Ability Classrooms - May 1998
Learning Network Literacy Institute - August 1997
Leadership and Supervisory Skills for Women - March 1996
Treatment Strategies for Infants with Cerebral Motor Disturbances - October 1995
Language Sample Analysis - March 1995
Effective Programming for Students with Autism - August 1994
Effective Interaction Skills with Parents - March 1994
The Fully Adaptive Macintosh; Assistive Technology - August 1993
School Improvement Elementary Educational Institute - 1992 & 1991
Implementing Developmental Thinking Skills - February 1990

**ORGANIZATIONS & ASSOCIATIONS**
United States Speech-Language Hearing Association
Illinois Speech-Language Hearing Association
Midwest Association of Speech-Language Pathologists and Audiologists

**PERSONAL**
Willing to relocate · Willing to perform work-related travel
Enjoy Downhill Skiing / Hiking / Home Computing / Reading

REFERENCES AND FURTHER DATA AVAILABLE UPON REQUEST

name, people thought first of the scandal and sometimes seemed to assume that Patricia might have been involved. In order to avoid triggering this reaction prematurely, Patricia masked the school's identity by using only a set of anonymous-sounding initials to identify her employer.

## When You Have to Face the Music

*"It is safest to employ honest men, even though they may not be the cleverest."*
—Ekken Kaibara, 1630–1714, Japanese scholar and author, The Way of Contentment.

It may not always be possible, or even advisable, to try to mask the identity of an employer on your resume. Many industries are close-knit communities where everyone seems to know everyone else's business, and if something significant has happened in one company, the chances are that everyone else will know about it. Trying to hide the name of a company in such a situation may only serve to make you appear deceptive, which is certainly not the way you want to come across to a potential employer.

For that reason, particularly if you're staying in the same industry, you should be prepared to discuss the layoff, scandal, or other controversial episode when you actually go into an interview. One way or another, the subject is likely to come up, so it's essential that you give some thought to how you're going to present the situation to a potential employer.

The simplest and often the best way of handling such a situation is to be completely open and honest. We know one supervisor in a large company who was recently laid off because his company was experiencing financial difficulties; in order to save money, the firm simply eliminated his entire department. Since this was strictly a financial decision, and in no way reflected on the supervisor's performance, he was able to tell prospective employers exactly what happened without fear of repercussions.

Similarly, we know a senior member of the professional staff of a large corporation who was laid off as a result of a downsizing. "Susan's" supervisor told her frankly that she was being let go because she was a senior member of the staff and that, by eliminating her job, the corporation could afford to retain two lower-level staff members. Again, because this did not reflect on her performance, there was no reason for Susan not to explain the situation to potential employers exactly as it occurred. As with these two individuals, if you feel you can be completely open and honest in an interview, we strongly urge you to do so.

However, your situation may be such that the decision to let you go was more personal. If you left on good terms with your last supervisor, he or she may even have suggested something you can tell prospective employers about why you were let go. (You can even ask about this yourself before leaving.) If that's the case, explaining it will be a lot easier. If not, it would be a good idea for you to put as positive a spin on the situation as you can.

One tried-and-true way of doing this is to refer in an emotionally neutral way to "differences" between you and your supervisor. Because people do move from one job to another so frequently these days, it's not unusual to find yourself working for an individual other than the one who hired you. And while you might have gotten along perfectly well with the person you started working for, you may have run into some difficulties with whoever replaced that individual. Consider using a phrase like "philosophical differences," "a disagreement about personal style," or "a less-than-perfect fit between me and my supervisor." Another possible way of explaining why you lost your job is to say that the company or department was "heading in a different direction than the one in which you wished to go."

Finally, there is the situation in which your company has gone through some kind of scandal. Let's say, for example, that you're a supervisor in a company that's recently been successfully sued for racial discrimination. You're in the middle of an interview, and the interviewer says, "Wasn't your company in some kind of legal trouble a few months back?" What do you say?

Whether or not you were involved in the suit, the best way of dealing with it is, first, to acknowledge that there was a problem. Denying it would not only be pointless but, even more important in terms of your prospects for being hired, possibly damaging.

If you were not involved in the situation, it's obviously to your advantage to say so. Even better, if you were aware of the problem and took steps to do something about it, however successful or unsuccessful those steps may have been, telling a prospective employer about it is likely to make you a more attractive candidate. Finding the right tone for such a statement may be tricky. You want to distance yourself from any wrongdoing that may have occurred, but you don't want to come across as an eager tattle-tale or as disloyal. Keep your comments brief and general, sound regretful, and speak as positively as you can about the company's future prospects, like this:

> Yes, XYZ Company was successfully sued for racial discrimination by several former employees. It was a sad situation that a few of us within the company had previously tried to change, without success. It's unfortunate that it took a lawsuit to bring about positive change, but now, I'm glad to say, the company has instituted new policies to make sure all employees are treated fairly.

**FYI**

*If you and your former supervisor have agreed to an acceptable story that you can tell prospective employers about why you lost your position, stick to it. If you left on sufficiently good terms to use your old boss as a reference, you can be sure that anyone interested in hiring you will ask him or her why you were let go, and it's important that your stories agree.*

**FYI**

*Don't criticize your last supervisor. He or she may have been as big a jerk as you've ever met, but that's not something you want to say to a prospective employer. This is particularly important in a close-knit industry, because the interviewer may not only know, but also be a friend, of your former supervisor.*

On the other hand, if you were in any way involved in the problem, it would be best for you to acknowledge that mistakes were made while trying to downplay your role as greatly as possible:

> Yes, XYZ Company was successfully sued for racial discrimination by several former employees. Unfortunately, my department was one of those involved in the discriminatory actions, and we had to devote quite a bit of work to figuring out where we went wrong and how to prevent similar problems in the future. Now, I'm glad to say, the company has instituted new policies . . .

Either way, avoid sounding defensive about the problem. If you were involved, defending any wrongdoing is not likely to go over very well with a potential employer. And even if you had no involvement, your defensive behavior may create some doubt in the mind of the interviewer.

# JUST THE FACTS

- If there are gaps in your work experience, you can make some of them disappear by providing only the starting and ending years of your jobs, and explain others by providing the reasons for them in the text of your resume.

- When you have many more jobs on your resume than your peers, you can minimize their number by eliminating some jobs and combining or condensing others.

- If you've held very few jobs and are concerned that you may not appear to have sufficient experience, try breaking your responsibilities into their component parts and providing more detailed information about them.

- Although it's advantageous to have a college degree in today's business world, if you don't, you can mask the fact by emphasizing your professional training and the skills you've developed.

- It is advisable to avoid any direct references to "learning experiences" such as layoffs, firings, or company scandals in your resume, but be prepared to discuss them during interviews.

# Part V

# Cover Letters That Open Doors

# Chapter 14

# The Cover Letter: A Great First Impression

## Get the Scoop On . . .

- The role of the cover letter
- The three kinds of cover letters
- Basic cover letter structure
- Fine-tuning your letter to interest a recruiter
- Rules of format, style, and appearance

If you've followed the advice in this book from page one to this point, you've put a fair amount of time and effort into crafting an exceptionally winning resume—one that's intriguing, concise, employer-oriented, vivid, and ready for easy scanning by a recruiter's computer system. Having done all this, you're probably eager to rush on to the next step in the job-search process—broadcasting your brilliant resume to the world and waiting for the exciting interview invitations to come rolling in.

Not so fast. There's one more crucial step you need to take before you have a job-search package that's ready for prime time: developing an equally effective cover letter. You may feel like protesting. "I already have a great resume," we hear you say, "So why do I need a cover letter? Aren't any prospective employers just going to look at my resume to decide whether or not to ask me in for an interview?"

That's a fair question. To be honest, some prospective employers may *not* read your cover letter. As we've seen, in today's increasingly fast-paced business world, virtually every executive is overloaded with work and constantly looking for ways to save time and effort. So it's true that some of those you contact may in fact skip over the cover letter and dive right into the resume.

But some of them won't, and since you won't be there when they receive your materials, you'll have no way of knowing what they may or may not read. Moreover, although you may think of cover letters only as a way of introducing your resume to prospective employers, a kind of written small-talk before the real conversation begins, the fact is that they can also serve a variety of truly vital job-search purposes. For that reason, no job-search campaign is likely to be successful without a good cover letter.

There are essentially three types of cover letters. The first is the kind of letter you use to make initial contact with people—to help you make connections with appropriate people in the industry in which you want to work. We call these *networking letters*.

The second type includes letters that are sent with a resume in regard to specific job openings. This kind of cover letter provides you with a way to introduce yourself, make a sales pitch, and suggest further action all at the same time. We call these *job-tailored letters*.

Finally, there's the kind of letter you send to follow up after you've met with someone, either in a networking interview or in an interview for a job. These letters provide you with an opportunity to thank someone for meeting with you, remind them who you are, and, when appropriate, either suggest further action on their part or promise to take such action yourself. We call them *follow-up letters*.

In this chapter, we'll provide general guidance for all three types of cover letters. We'll not only show you why it's advantageous to write such letters, but also take you step-by-step through each of the basic elements of the cover letter, show you how to draft and edit a letter, and teach you the finishing touches that will make sure your letter is not only read but also encourages its readers to go on to your resume. The chapters that follow will provide more specific information on, and examples of, networking letters, job-tailored letters, and various types of follow-up letters.

# WHY A COVER LETTER?

A great cover letter provides you with a means of accomplishing several things that a resume alone cannot accomplish.

Networking cover letters enable you to tell a prospective contact who you are, why you're contacting them, what your background is, and what steps you will take to arrange for a meeting. A well-crafted networking letter is interesting enough to entice a well-intentioned, but busy, professional into giving you half an hour or more of his or her valuable time for a meeting that may help open career doors for you.

Job-tailored letters allow you to tell a prospective employer who you are, why they should hire you, why you want to work for them, and what you, or they, can do to move the process along. Like the first few bars of music in a brilliantly conceived TV commercial, a great job-tailored letter captures the interest of a prospective employer and entices him or her to turn to your resume filled with curiosity about the story it has to tell.

Finally, the follow-up letter conveys an impression of professionalism, tact, respect, friendliness, and organization—all qualities that any employer seeks in a job applicant. A well-timed and well-written follow-up letter can sometimes make the difference between a positive but fruitless interview and a great job offer.

And there are other advantages to writing cover letters. Here are a few.

## A Cover Letter Can Help You Tap into the Hidden Job Market

*Only about 20 percent of the jobs available at any given time are advertised. The other 80 percent represent the enormous hidden job market—the market you want to tap.*

Recruiters and employment specialists agree that most job openings are never advertised. These below-the-radar openings may be the result of someone leaving a company or being promoted, or an expansion that's about to create an entirely new department and/or job in an organization. Often a company's human resources department doesn't even know that a manager is thinking about hiring someone under these circumstances; the personnel manager may be brought in only at the last minute to handle the paperwork on a new hire that's already a done deal.

A cover letter sent at the right time to the right decision-maker can help you uncover the jobs in this so-called hidden market. Of course, if an opening isn't being advertised, you have no way of knowing that a particular executive is looking for a new staff member, but your cover letter may land on someone's desk at just the right moment. If that person is in fact anticipating hiring someone and your credentials fit his or her needs, a good cover letter will be enormously helpful in getting your foot in the door.

Moreover, good executives are *always* keeping their eyes open for strong potential job candidates. (Many a great job has been landed as a result of a delayed call-back: "This is So-and-so at Company A. You wrote to us five months ago. Are you still in the marketplace? . . .") So even if the individual you contact isn't looking for someone at the time your letter arrives, an effective letter (and resume) can result in an informational interview that may in time lead to a job offer or a referral to someone who does have an opening. At the very least, if you write a good letter, your name will be filed away (physically or mentally) for future reference.

## A Cover Letter Personalizes Your Response to an Advertised Opening

You've worked very hard to prepare a strong and appealing resume. But unless you're looking for exactly the same kind of job you've already held, the emphasis, structure, and strengths of your resume may not be a perfect match for every position you're applying for. (This may be true even when the job is one you know you could excel at if given the chance.) In a perfect world, you could revise the resume for every potential employer—but who has the time?

Enter the cover letter. A good basic cover letter can easily be amended to appeal to a specific manager hiring for a particular position. You can use the cover letter to focus on particular aspects of your experience or education, to mention aspects of the company you're applying to that especially fit your interests, to highlight past achievements that match your potential employer's needs and, in general, to spin your resume so that its best features are emphasized. (Later in this book, we'll show you some examples of exactly how this can be done. It's easy.)

## A Cover Letter Can Open a Headhunter's Door

As you know, many companies, particularly large ones, use headhunters (also known as *personnel agents* and *executive recruiters*) to help them find good job candidates. Although the companies pay a fee for this service (usually a substantial percentage of the successful candidate's first-year salary) doing so benefits them in several ways. Most important, headhunters filter out candidates who don't possess the skills or experience the company is looking for. Since they'll make money only if one of the candidates they refer to a client is ultimately hired, recruiters are very careful about which candidates they recommend. For that reason, it's important to make a good impression when first contacting a recruiter.

Virtually all headhunters want to see resumes *and* cover letters before meeting with a job candidate. Of course, even the best cover letter won't guarantee that working with a recruiter will ultimately result in a job offer; but without a cover letter, you probably won't even have the opportunity to find out.

## A Cover Letter Can Help Overcome Job-Hunting Problems

Reasonable or not, employers tend to perceive some kinds of job candidates as problematic. A skillfully crafted cover letter can be very useful in assuaging such concerns. For example, if you've just finished school and have no "real" work experience, a great cover letter will let you concentrate on communicating what makes you a strong candidate rather than dwelling on your lack of experience.

At the other end of the spectrum, if you're a seasoned veteran concerned about (conscious or unconscious) prejudice against the older worker, a cover letter can help you make your case *before* age becomes an issue. Unlike resumes, cover letters don't normally mention dates of employment. A cover letter gives you a chance to discuss your experience and your accomplishments without making it obvious that either may have occurred some time ago.

Cover letters can also be particularly helpful if you're seeking a job in another city. Prospective employers are sometimes wary of individuals who are moving, because they wonder if there's some reason that they can't find a job in their present location. Of course, there are any number of good reasons why someone would want to move—a new job your spouse has accepted, for example. Whatever your reason, explaining it in a cover letter, where it's more appropriate than in a resume, will go a long way toward laying a prospective employer's concerns to rest.

Finally, although ongoing changes in virtually every industry in the last several years have led many people to change careers, employers still tend to be apprehensive about individuals who are doing so. A cover letter will provide you with the opportunity to show how and why your past skills and experience apply to the new career you seek and to indicate briefly your reasons for switching career tracks.

# COVER LETTER BASICS

**FYI**

*Virtually every industry has its own directory of companies, usually including the names and addresses of senior executives. The reference librarian at your favorite public or university library can help you find the appropriate listing for your business.*

As you've already seen, a cover letter enables you to do three basic things: introduce yourself, provide a modicum of enticing and appealing information about your background and accomplishments, and suggest further action. Generally speaking, these three purposes are accomplished in a letter of three or four paragraphs.

1. The first paragraph is *the opening*, in which you introduce yourself and explain why you're writing. This is essentially the same, albeit with variations, regardless of whether you're writing a networking or a job-tailored letter.

2. The second paragraph is *the pitch*. In a networking letter, this paragraph is where you provide your potential contact with some information about your professional background. The purpose is to show the reader that you're a serious individual who is genuinely interested in hearing whatever advice she may have to offer.

   In a job-tailored letter, you'll use this paragraph to answer the question, "Why me?" Here you present your experience and achievements as a step toward convincing a potential employer that you are someone they ought to meet.

   The job-tailored letter may also include a third paragraph. This paragraph is a continuation of the pitch, and is where you answer the question, "Why you?" That is, this is where you explain why you're interested in the reader's particular organization.

3. The final paragraph is *the call to action*. It suggests a next step—either by the reader or by you. Like the first paragraph, it is essentially the same, regardless of the purpose of your letter.

Of course, the structure we've outlined here isn't set in stone; to some extent, you can vary the format, organization, and content of these four paragraphs. For example, if some recent event at a company has prompted you to write, you might place the "Why you?" paragraph at the *start* of the letter:

> Dear Ms. Lohr:
>
> Congratulations on your company's dramatic plans for expansion, which I read about in this week's *Business Week* magazine. Perhaps my background would make me a suitable candidate for one of the new positions I understand you'll be needing to fill, particularly in the area of international marketing . . .

As a starting point, though, we suggest you create a draft in the standard three- or four-paragraph form we've explained. It works for the vast majority of job hunters, and you can always make changes later on.

We'd also suggest that, for now at least, you not concern yourself with the niceties of letter-writing format, style, punctuation, or even spelling. The most important thing at the start is for you to get a draft of your ideas down on paper. We'll go over how to fine-tune the letter later on in this chapter.

## The Salutation

As with all letters, a cover letter must start with a *salutation*: "Dear Mr. Yardeni," "Dear Dr. Bradley," or whatever. *No* job-search letter should ever be addressed "To whom it may concern." Letters addressed in that manner generally go right into the circular file. If you don't know the name of the person to whom you should be writing, there are several ways of finding out. The simplest, and often the easiest, is to call the company, tell the operator that you want to contact the head of whatever department is appropriate, and ask for the person's name.

As a rule, letters should be addressed using either "Mr." for a man or "Ms." for a woman. A title like "Dr." or "Professor" may be appropriate in a medical, academic, or scientific context, and some government officers, religious leaders, and other officials have other forms of salutation: "Senator Hatch" or "Father Knox," for example. Check any dictionary (most contain lists of proper titles for such specialized situations) or phone and *ask* the exalted one's assistant for advice: "I'm writing a letter to the judge, and I wonder how she prefers to be addressed?"

This kind of greeting may seem overly formal to you, but a first-name salutation will probably seem overly informal to them. There are only two exceptions to this rule. The first is the situation in which you already know the person and normally call them by their first name. In that case, "Dear Jim" is fine. The other is those (rare) situations in which an advertisement for a position includes only the first name of the individual to contact.

## The Opening

In the first paragraph, you'll introduce yourself and explain why you're writing. This is where you tell prospective employers how you heard about them, the job, or the company; who you are; and (in a general way) what you want from them.

Particularly in the case of networking letters, it's important to make a *connection* with your reader if at all possible. Remember, most executives receive an enormous amount of mail and are extremely busy, so your opening should grab their attention and give them a good reason to want to read the rest of your letter. There are several ways to accomplish this.

- **Remind them of a previous meeting:**

  You may recall our speaking briefly at the UCLA Job Fair last week in regard to opportunities in the electronics industry. (I came up after your speech to comment about the statistics you cited concerning global competition.) I am writing now in the hope that we can arrange a meeting to continue that conversation.

- **Mention a referral from someone your reader knows:**

  At the suggestion of Albert Decker, I am writing to seek your advice and counsel. For the past two years I have been an associate editor at the *St. Louis Star*, but due to the paper's recent downsizing I am now exploring new career opportunities. If possible, I'd like to meet you briefly to discuss my background and the directions I should consider.

- **Refer to a news item about the company:**

  When I read the recent article in *Chicago* magazine about the growth your company has experienced over the last several years, and your plans for the future, I was struck by how forward-looking your organization is. I am accordingly writing to ask for your advice.

In the case of job-tailored letters, it's important to get right to the point so the potential employer knows why you are writing.

There are essentially three ways you can learn about open positions: through your networking efforts; through company- or executive search firm-sponsored ads in newspapers, magazines, or on the Internet; or by directly contacting a search firm or employment agency. Your opening paragraph should vary accordingly.

- **If you learned of a job through networking:**

    I am writing you at the suggestion of Henry Metzenbaum, who advised me that you have a position available for a senior teller in your bank. Having served as a teller with Charter Bank for the last three years, I would be interested in meeting with you to discuss the open position.

- **If you learned of a job through a company- or search firm-sponsored ad:**

    I am replying to your advertisement for an editorial assistant in the April 17th edition of *Publishers Weekly*. As a recent college graduate interested in entering the publishing field, I would appreciate the opportunity to meet with you to discuss my qualifications for the position.

- **If you are seeking information about jobs through a search firm:**

    I am writing to you because I am interested in finding a senior editorial position with a major publisher in the New York City area. For the past three years, I have served as an editor with a small publisher in Philadelphia and would be interested in talking with you about any openings in New York for which you are currently recruiting.

## The Pitch

As we've mentioned, the purpose of the second paragraph will vary depending on whether you are writing a networking or a job-tailored letter. In the former case, this paragraph should be fairly straightforward, providing key information on your professional background. In your opening, you've already briefly mentioned your qualifications; now is the time to give them some particulars.

There are two ways this second paragraph can be structured: either as a regular paragraph of text or as a bulleted list. In either case, we

---

**FYI**

*If the person you're contacting has a "unisex" first name like Pat, Jan, Morgan, or Francis, find out whether the person is a male or female. You can usually do so by calling the company and asking the operator. If for some reason you're unable to find out, it's acceptable to address the letter using both first and last names, e.g., "Dear Jan Sterling."*

**FYI**

*The second paragraph of a cover letter is not the place to tell a prospective employer your whole life story. Be careful not to ramble on but, rather, focus on the highlights of your career.*

suggest you start with a brief statement that leads into the information you want to give them, and then go into the specifics. *Don't* try to repeat your entire resume here; instead, provide your reader with the most enticing highlights.

In a networking letter, this paragraph might read like this:

> In addition to my experience at Met Life, over the last twenty years I've also worked as an actuarial assistant with State Farm Insurance, an assistant actuary with New York Life, and a senior actuary with both Allstate and the Beneficial Life Insurance Company. I've received several company-wide awards for excellence and advanced my training through a series of graduate-level seminars.

> In addition to my experience at Simon & Schuster, I've also held positions as an:

> - Editorial assistant with St. Martin's Press
> - Editorial assistant and assistant editor with Macmillan
> - Associate editor with Bantam Doubleday Dell
> - Editor and senior editor with HarperCollins"

In the case of job-tailored letters, this paragraph is the beginning of your sales pitch—the answer to the question "Why me?" Remember that the person reading your letter may receive tens or even hundreds of letters and resumes from other candidates for any single job opening, so you have to say something about yourself that's going to make him or her want to continue reading. And, human nature being what it is, the kind of thing that's going to keep him or her reading is something that you can do for them—the "benefit," as we explained in Chapter 5.

As in the networking letter, there are two ways this information can be presented—either as a regular paragraph or as a bulleted list. Here are a couple of samples:

> I have a number of skills that could be highly beneficial to your organization. I've proven myself to be an accomplished professional who is capable of handling several projects at the same time without succumbing to stress or fatigue. I've also demonstrated my ability to manage a large and diverse staff of professionals and support people, ranging from technology specialists to creative artists to numbers-crunchers. As a result, I have shown that I can consistently meet tight deadlines while keeping within departmental budgets.

> There are a number of skills I can contribute to your organization:

**Research**: My market research and the recommendations I developed based upon it have been used by the president of my current firm in several presentations made to the company's stockholders.

**Analysis**: My analysis of our competitors' pricing led my present firm to reconsider and change its pricing structures, in turn leading to considerably larger profits.

**Presentation**: At the request of my supervisor, I have made numerous effective presentations to the company's board of directors.

## The Pitch Continued

In the job-tailored letter, the third paragraph is a continuation of the sales pitch, and answers the question "Why you?" Even though you may actually be sending out twenty cover letters and resumes, you want every person reading one of your letters to feel that you have chosen to write because you genuinely want to work for *his* or *her* company. In order to do that, however, it's essential to know something about the companies you're writing to. Researching the companies you're considering will enable you to make an informed and intelligent choice about the ones that would be of most interest to you.

There are several reasons why you might want to work for a particular firm. It might be the company (its reputation, its culture, its success), the industry, the location, or the job itself. Whatever your reasons may be, this is the place to communicate them to your potential employer. The more specific and informed your comments are, the better.

- **If you're interested in the company:**

  I am interested in the possibility of working in your company because, as someone who has been in the fashion field for some time, I am well aware of your reputation as one of the premier firms in the industry. Last year's successful rollout of your new ready-to-wear sportswear line was a particularly impressive illustration of your unique combination of fashion sense and marketing savvy.

- **If you're interested in the industry:**

  I am particularly interested in your organization because I have had a lifelong interest in music and would like to put my skills to use in a field in which I have both a personal, as well as professional, interest. As international markets become more and more important for success in the music industry, I believe my linguistic skills (including mastery of four European languages) can be an especially relevant credential.

- **If you're interested in the location:**

I am especially attracted to your firm because I will shortly be moving to the Atlanta area and wish to continue working in a dynamic company in the public relations field. As Atlanta continues to experience extraordinary business growth, it appears that the opportunities for a top-flight P.R. company are almost unlimited, and I'd like to help you take advantage of those opportunities.

- **If you're interested in the job itself:**

My interest in your company grew out of my wish to put my five years of experience as an assistant buyer of camping gear and outdoor equipment to work in a more challenging position. As you plan to double the size of your outdoor goods department, I think I'm well-positioned to help make sure that the latest, best, and most salable merchandise is always available at your store first.

Does it take work, effort, and thought to come up with a unique detail or two about each company to which you're writing? Yes! But it's essential. A cover letter that displays genuine, thoughtful interest in and knowledge about the company to which it's addressed is far more compelling and impressive than a boilerplate letter that could have been sent to a thousand firms—and probably was.

As you embark on a job-search campaign, begin spending a little time each week researching the industry and companies in which you're interested. Use the Internet, your local or university library, and the current business press to keep tabs on the leading companies in the field, as well as the interesting smaller firms. Try to get a sense of what problems the companies are wrestling with, what skills or capabilities they seem to lack, what triumphs they're most proud of, and what future strategies they plan to pursue. Each of these can offer you clues about items to mention in your cover letter (as well as during a job interview).

Result: you'll come across as an informed, "plugged-in" job seeker with a sincere interest in the company you're applying to. This alone can make a huge difference in whether or not you're offered the job.

## The Call to Action

The closing paragraph of your cover letter is your opportunity to do one or both of two things. In the case of a networking letter, it's the place to tell your reader what further action you will take to move the process forward. In this instance, your closing paragraph might read something like this:

In anticipation of our meeting, I am enclosing a copy of my resume. I'll call you within the next week or so to see if we can find a mutually agreeable time to meet.

In the case of a job-tailored letter, it's the place to thank the reader for considering your candidacy and to request or suggest further action. Unless it's impossible for you to make the next move, for example, if you're answering a so-called blind ad, which provides no contact name or company name, it's always preferable for you to take a proactive rather than passive stance in this paragraph. Suggest what *you* will do next to follow up, including a time frame. Thus, your closing paragraph might read like this:

> I am enclosing a copy of my resume to give you a better idea of my background and would very much appreciate your taking the time to review my qualifications for the job. I will call you within the next few days [or next week] to see if we can arrange a mutually convenient time to meet.

**FYI**

*If you have a unisex name, one that either a man or a woman may use, it's a courtesy to include either "Mr." or "Ms." before your typed name so your reader won't be in any doubt as to your gender.*

Give your reader a couple of days to open and read your letter—but then follow up with a phone call promptly. If you wait two weeks or more to call, the chances are good that you and your letter will have been forgotten in the crush of more recent business.

If you have a more specific or urgent time frame within which you need to act, state that in your letter. For example, suppose you are looking for a job in a new location and have a one-week trip planned to make contacts, conduct interviews, and scout out possible neighborhoods to live in. Send out your letters and resumes about a month in advance and give the dates of your planned trip:

> I'll be in Denver April 6–13, and if it's possible, I'd like to meet with you during that time. I already have meetings scheduled for the mornings of the 7th and the 8th, but otherwise, I can be available any other time during the week. I'll call you early next week to find out whether we can schedule an appointment while I'm in Denver.

## The Closing

End your letter in a business-like manner. "Sincerely yours" or "Sincerely" are the most generally accepted ways of doing so. If, however, you are writing to a personal friend or someone you've already met, it's acceptable, even advisable, to close your letter with a slightly more personal phrase: "Regards," "Best Regards," or "Best wishes."

After this closing phrase, skip five lines (to leave room for your signature) and then type your name.

# FINE-TUNING YOUR LETTER

Now that you have a draft for your basic cover letter, it's time to fine-tune it. Put it aside for a day or two if possible, and then reread it. The lapse of time helps you see the letter more objectively and detect "obvious" flaws you somehow overlooked when writing it. Look again at the contents of the letter, think about—and, as necessary, change—the tone and language you've used, and make sure the letter flows smoothly and clearly. Finally, double check your grammar, spelling, and punctuation.

## Reviewing Content

**FYI**

*If you're in doubt as to whether you've made your points with sufficient clarity and vividness, have a friend read your letter—preferably one who knows little or nothing about your field of work. If she reads your letter and can easily and accurately restate it in her own words, chances are good that you've said what you have to say. If she can't, you've probably failed to communicate clearly.*

Once your draft is completed, go over it again to make sure that there is nothing unclear in it. The last thing you want to do is leave your reader unsure about who you are, what your background and credentials are like, or why you're writing. Yet, as any recruiter will agree, many a cover letter leaves one or more of these points vague. Reread each sentence and make sure it says exactly what you intended to say—not just something more or less approximating it.

Here are a couple of examples. Suppose you want to mention your background in e-commerce as an important credential for a job as a Web site manager. You could describe it somewhat vaguely, like this:

> I have experience in developing an online business model for a company in the food industry, which proved to be quite successful.

Better to craft a sentence that includes a couple of impressive, enticing, and *specific* details, like this:

> I launched an online consumer sales program for Aunt Rosa's Pasta company, which became profitable within three months and was listed as one of the 'Top Ten Web sites' in *Food Lover* magazine's April, 1999 issue.

Or suppose you want to explain why you're especially interested in working for a particular health-care facility. You could make the point in general terms, like this:

> I'm interested in Hilltop because of the client population you attract, which is similar to the client base I've worked with in the past and which I've developed a good deal of knowledge about through my academic studies.

Better to explain it in *specific* terms, like this:

> I'm interested in Hilltop because you have the largest facility in our area serving adults with substance-abuse problems. I've worked

with such clients for the past six years and have written three published papers on the latest treatment strategies for this population.

One subject *not* to mention in your cover letter is salary history or salary requirements. These issues are completely irrelevant in a networking letter, and mentioning them in a job-tailored letter could be to your disadvantage. We'll discuss this issue in greater depth in the chapter on letters written in regard to specific openings—including what to do when responding to an ad that *requires* salary history.

## Professional Tone and Language

As in every kind of communication, verbal or written, the tone and language you use should be appropriate to your target audience. You wouldn't, for example, speak to a child the same way you speak to an adult. In the case of cover letters, it's important that your tone and language be professional. Your letter (along with your resume) is part of an effort to convince a potential networking contact or employer that you are a mature, responsible adult who would make a good addition to a company's staff. Thus, slang and colloquialisms, the kinds of expressions you might normally use in conversation with your friends, aren't appropriate in a cover letter.

On the other hand, never forget that you are writing to another human being. Being professional doesn't mean being cold. If your letter sounds as if it was written by a machine, loosen it up by using less formal words and expressions—although without going overboard.

For example, don't hesitate to use contractions, such as "I've," "you'll," and "won't," in place of "I have," "you will," and "will not." (We realize this violates the rule you may have been taught in fifth grade. Can't help that.) A sentence that bends over backward to avoid the use of contractions sounds stiff and overly formal; using contractions where they would naturally appear in speech produces a more friendly, self-confident tone. Look back at the sample sentences and paragraphs that dot this chapter; note how we used contractions in those.

In addition, don't shy away from expressing emotions—especially positive ones. "Professional" doesn't mean "without feeling." If you have a sense of excitement, optimism, curiosity, and eagerness about the work you do and the next job you'd like to have, let it show. Employers are looking for candidates they'll enjoy working with—not "dead fish" devoid of personality. Sentences like these, if you can write them in your own voice with sincerity, add zest and appeal to a cover letter:

I'd be excited about the opportunity to work at a youthful, fast-growing company like yours, and I hope we'll be able to arrange an interview in the near future.

Managing the opening of our company's new Boston branch was challenging, overwhelming at times—and deeply rewarding. I'm proud to say that within a year we built Boston into the second most profitable branch in the entire company.

I've read about your company's plans to develop strategic partnerships with firms in other industries, and I have several ideas in this area that I think could work marvelously well both for you and for the potential partner. I'd enjoy meeting you to begin exploring some of these ideas.

The tone and language should also be appropriate to your industry. Virtually every industry has its own jargon, and using it—correctly, of course!—in a letter to a department or division head will tell the recipient that you're an "insider."

On the other hand, if you're writing to someone in human resources, you should bear in mind that they might not be familiar with such phrases. Keep the jargon to a minimum.

Similarly, modulate your tone and language to match the job you're seeking. If, for example, you're seeking a job as a salesperson, it would be appropriate for your letter to read like a sales pitch, with a high degree of energy, a few superlatives, a rhetorical question or two, and even a touch of hype.

On the other hand, if you are an accountant or an attorney writing to the head of a professional services firm, your letter should have a more sober and serious tone.

This kind of modulation may come naturally to you; the fact that you've chosen a particular career in the first place says something about your personality and style. But give some conscious thought to the person who'll be reading your letter and imagine how he or she is likely to respond to the human qualities it expresses. Adjust your language accordingly.

The point here is that "professional" means different things to different people, and it's important that you thoroughly think about who your reader is to make sure that the tone and language you use in your letter is appropriate to the individual, the industry, and the job.

## Flow

Next, consider the flow of your letter. It should basically read as though you were speaking to someone in person. Read the letter over to make sure that one sentence logically follows another and that there are neither choppy nor run-on sentences.

Be sure, too, that not too many of the sentences start with the word "I." The whole letter, in a sense, is about you; but a string of sentences beginning with "I" sets a tone of self-absorption that your reader is likely to notice, whether consciously or not. This can be a turn-off.

### Grammar, Spelling, and Punctuation

Nothing will turn off a potential contact or employer faster than a letter with grammar, spelling, or punctuation errors. If you're working on a computer, use the spellcheck program—but *don't* rely on it. Spellcheck programs can only check to see that the words in your letter are real words, not that they are the words you mean to use. For example, if, instead of writing, "I am sure I will be able to . . . " you write, "I am sure I wills be able to . . . " the computer won't pick up the error, because "wills" is a real word.

So go over the letter by hand and eye to check for misspellings and, if there are any words that you have *any* doubt about, look them up in a dictionary. If you ever find yourself thinking, "I guess it's right," think again. Check the word to make sure.

Of course, even a computer program doesn't include the spelling of proper names, so you have to make sure that the name of the individual to whom you're writing, the name of his or her company, the street, and the city and state are all spelled correctly. Silly as it may sound, it's even a good idea to make sure that your own name and address are spelled right. Goofy mistakes happen.

Although many people are unfamiliar with the rules of correct grammar and punctuation, possibly even including the recipients of your letters, it's never a good idea to take chances. Don't let anything creep into your letters that could make a reader think of you as ignorant, careless, or indifferent. If you're weak when it comes to grammar or punctuation (and if you are, you probably know it) have a truly knowledgeable friend read and mark up your letters. Correct them, then read them one more time.

Look carefully at the sample letters in the following chapters for the correct way to punctuate your cover letters. If you still have questions, pick up one of the numerous writing style guides available in the reference section of any bookstore or through any of the online booksellers.

Having a copy of William Strunk Jr. and E.B. White's *The Elements of Style* at your desk is always a good idea. This little book is a classic guide to good writing and is itself a joy to read. Mastering its few simple yet powerful rules will improve your letters and everything else you write.

# THE FINISHING TOUCHES

Now it's time for the finishing touches—getting your letter ready to be sent. In this section, we'll cover letterhead, layout, paper, printing, proofreading, and mailing your letters.

### Letterhead

Your cover letter should be printed with a heading that includes your name, home address, phone number, fax number, and e-mail address (if applicable). This information is normally printed about three-quarters of an inch from the top of the page, centered, single-spaced, and in bold face. Professionally printed stationery is acceptable, of course, but so is stationery with a computer-generated heading containing the same information.

If you don't have access to a computer, you can still create reasonably clean, clear, and attractive letterhead using the type face available on your typewriter. This, too, is an acceptable alternative. The same information should be included in either case.

### Layout

A cover letter is, of course, a business letter, and there are basically just two ways to format a business letter: the *block format* and the *indented format*. The samples provided here can be modified somewhat, but while neither one is better than the other, it's best to stick to one of these formats.

Cover letters should always be typed single-spaced in a readable font of no less than 10- and no more than 14-point type. Twelve-point type is fairly standard. Your cover letter should never run onto a second page; if necessary, edit it to fit a single page. The margins should be either ¾-inch or 1 inch at the top, and 1 to 1½ inches at the bottom and on either side. You should know how to set these margins correctly on your computer; if not, your word-processing program's manual will explain.

### Paper

It's always best to use 8½ × 11, 20–25 pound white bond paper for your cover letters. Ivory or cream-colored paper are also acceptable, but you should avoid using shades of gray, blue, or other colors. The relative lack of contrast may make them difficult to read or to photocopy.

## Block Format

**Your name**
**Your street address**
**Your city, state, and zip code**
**Your phone/fax number**
**Your e-mail address**


Date

Recipient's name
Name of organization
Street address
Suite, office, floor or room number
City, state, and zip code

Dear Mr./Ms. _____:

The text starts here, single spaced and justified to the left margin.

Skip two spaces, then begin the next paragraph, and so on.

Closing [e.g., "Sincerely yours,"]


[Your signature—by hand, of course]


Your name [typed five lines below the closing]

Enc. [if you're enclosing your resume]

## Indented Format

**Your name**
**Your street address**
**Your city, state, and zip code**
**Your phone/fax number**
**Your e-mail address**

Date

Recipient's name
Name of organization
Street address
Suite, office, floor or room number
City, state, and zip code

Dear Mr./Ms. _____:

The text starts here, single spaced, and indented one tab (or five spaces).

Skip two spaces, indent, and start the next paragraph, with the remaining paragraphs following in the same fashion.

Closing [e.g., "Yours truly"]

[Your signature—by hand, of course]

Your name [typed five lines below the closing]

Enc. [if you're enclosing a resume]

## Printing and Proofreading

If you're working on a computer, printing your letter is, of course, just a matter of pushing the right button. If, however, you're working on a typewriter, it's important that you be as careful as possible in typing the final version to avoid making mistakes.

In either case, when the letter is completed it is absolutely essential that you proofread it again before you even think about putting it in an envelope. Pay particular attention to the recipient's name, company name, and address. The last thing in the world you want is for someone to receive a letter with his or her name spelled wrong. And the next to last thing you want is to have the letter come back to you because you used an incorrect name or address.

You may be using your computer to generate a series of cover letters with similar contents to go out to five, ten, or more recruiters. (As we explained previously, it's always best to customize your letter with details pertinent to the company you're writing to; but, of course, some sections of your letter may be carried over with minimal change from one letter to another.)

If so, be especially careful about checking the name and address of the recipient. It's easy, when preparing a dozen letters, to accidentally stick the letter addressed to Mr. A at Mammoth Industries in the envelope to Ms. B at The Little Company. And make sure, too, that your letter is internally consistent. It's easy to address the letter to Ms. B, then forget to change the salutation, which reads "Dear Mr. A." Very embarrassing.

Finally, whether you're printing your letter on a computer or typing it, it's always a good idea to save a copy in an appropriately labeled file for future reference. If the recipient phones you and refers to part of your letter, you'll want to be able to remind yourself of what you said.

## Mailing Your Cover Letter

Cover letters (along with resumes) may be mailed, folded in thirds, in standard number 10, $4\frac{1}{8} \times 9\frac{1}{2}$ inch business envelopes. Nowadays, with more and more companies scanning resumes into computer databases (as explained in Chapter 8), many job hunters prefer not to fold their resumes. This is to avoid creases, which may make accurate scanning more difficult. Use an envelope that measures $9 \times 12$ inches, into which your standard $8\frac{1}{2} \times 11$ inch letter will fit easily.

The envelopes should be the same color as the paper on which the letter is printed. If you've had letterhead printed, you may also have had envelopes printed with your name and address on them. If not, be sure to include your name and address in the upper left-hand corner of the envelope.

The recipient's name goes to the right of the middle line of the envelope. If you're working on a computer, it probably has a envelope-addressing function, which will mean you don't have to key in the address again. If it doesn't, or you're working on a typewriter, be sure that the recipient's name, company name, and address are spelled correctly.

Unless you've used extremely heavy paper, these three pages and the envelope will together weigh less than one ounce, so you'll only need the standard amount of first class postage. If you have any question about this, however, weigh the finished letter and envelope on a postal scale, or take it to the post office to make sure it doesn't weigh more. If for some reason it does, be sure to include the appropriate amount of postage on the letter. You neither want the recipient to get your letter with postage due nor have it come back to you for insufficient postage.

# JUST THE FACTS

- Cover letters can be used for three important purposes: to make networking contacts, to apply for open positions, and to follow up on interviews.

- A good cover letter has several basic elements. Most crucial: the opening; the pitch; and the call to action.

- Make sure every cover letter you send contains enough specific information to capture your reader's interest, is written with a professional tone, and is free of errors in grammar, spelling, or punctuation.

- Your cover letter must be formatted appropriately and printed in attractive, standard business style.

# Chapter 15

# Networking Letters

---

## Get the Scoop On . . .

- Networking as a key job-search strategy
- Finding and reaching the most important contacts
- Drafting your networking letter
- Conducting an effective networking meeting
- Following up after the meeting

---

Although it's likely that you've heard the word *networking*, you may not be entirely sure what it means. In the context of a job search, networking means contacting as many people as you can in the hope that one or more of them will lead you directly to a job opening or to someone else who can.

Although some people find jobs through ads in newspapers, in magazines, on the Internet, through employment agencies, or executive search firms, the vast majority find jobs through networking—talking with "a friend of a friend of a friend" until they find themselves, finally, in the right place at the right time.

But building up your own career network isn't easy. In fact, it can be a slow, often tedious, and sometimes frustrating process. However, because it's the best way of finding a job, it's also essential. Moreover, if you approach it with the right attitude, it can be instructive, informative, and even (believe it or not) fun. Not only will you have the opportunity to talk about the kind of work you like to do with others in your field, but chances are, you'll meet a good number of interesting people, some of whom may become friends or colleagues in the future.

In this chapter, we'll show you how to get started in networking, how to make contact with people, and how to adapt your basic cover letter for use as a networking letter. We'll also show you how to follow up on your networking letter, how to prepare for a networking meeting, and how to follow up on the meeting.

## GETTING YOUR NETWORK STARTED

Although you may not know it, the fact is that you actually already have a network of people whom you can call on to help you get a job. If you're planning to stay in the same industry in which you're already working, for example, friends in your present organization as well as other people in the industry whom you've met can be an excellent source of help. If you take a quick look through your address file or telephone book, you'll probably discover that you already know lots of people who could be of assistance in your search.

"But," we hear you say, "I just graduated from college, and I've never had a full-time job before." Or, "I want to move into a different industry and don't know anyone in it." Even so, this doesn't mean that you have no resources to draw on. If you're starting fresh, either in the job market or in a new industry, it's particularly advantageous to tell everyone you know that you're looking for a job. This includes:

- Colleagues at a former employer
- Family
- Fellow volunteers
- Friends
- Members of the clubs you belong to
- Members of your aerobics class
- Members of your church or synagogue
- Neighbors
- Parents of your kids' friends
- Past and present schoolmates
- Teachers and professors

We could go on, but you get the idea. You never know who might know someone who knows someone who knows about a job opening. Yes, this is how it's done!

## How Networking Works

There are several ways in which the people you already know and those you'll meet can help you find your next job. The first is by providing you with information about a career, an industry, or a specific company that you're looking into. For example, suppose you're interested in working in retail, and your Uncle Manny managed the local pharmacy before he retired. He'll be able to give you a wealth of valuable information about store management as a career as well as information about the industry in general (and probably the names of a few friends of his who are still in the business).

Another way people can help is by referring you to other people who may be able to provide you with information or assistance. By continuously asking your contacts who else they could suggest you talk to, you can expand your networking circle until you find someone who is actually recruiting to fill a position.

The third way in which people can help is by providing you with leads for specific jobs. When you sit down for a chat with Uncle Manny, he may say (half an hour into the conversation), "Say, that reminds me—my friend Carmine has a son who runs a bunch of stores that sell sneakers and stuff. Carmine says the stores are doing great and that they're expanding. Why not give Carmine's son a call? I'll bet he's looking for managers."

As far as job-search networking is concerned, there are three important things to remember. The first, as we've already mentioned, is that you never know who might know someone who will eventually lead you to a job. Aunt Sally might have a friend in an advertising agency where you'd love to work. Your brother's girlfriend may know someone who's looking for a car salesman at a Toyota dealership, which is exactly the kind of job you're looking for. The important thing is not to rule out anyone.

The second thing to remember is that virtually *everyone* has been in the same situation you're in now—either in need of a job or looking for a better job. And because they know what it's like, most people will be more than happy to provide you with whatever help they can. The important thing here is to not be afraid or embarrassed to ask for help. You'll be pleasantly surprised to find that the overwhelming majority of the people you approach, even strangers, will respond graciously.

The third thing to remember is that, when you do make a contact, you don't just come out and ask the person for a job. That's the best way to end a conversation—quickly. Most of the people with whom you're networking will understand, of course, that finding a job is your ultimate purpose in contacting them. But coming straight out and asking them for work puts them in an awkward position, and the last thing you want to do with networking contacts is make them uncomfortable.

Later in this chapter, we'll show you exactly how to approach networking contacts in a way that will not make them squirm in their seats.

## How to Find Contacts When You *Don't* Have an Uncle in the Business

Making everyone you know aware that you're looking for a job is an essential step in networking, but it's not the only one. Even before

### FYI

*Keep a record of your networking efforts. As soon as you start your job search, start keeping a list of all those with whom you come in contact, noting the date and content of each conversation. Also set up a file for your correspondence, and, if appropriate, add your contacts' names, addresses, phone, and fax numbers to your address file or phone book.*

you've exhausted all your current contacts, there's another way to find the names of people you should be talking to.

We've already mentioned that virtually every industry has some kind of directory of companies. You can probably track it down at your local or college library. Such directories generally provide the names of companies in the industry, addresses, phone and fax numbers, historical information on each company, and, most important for your purposes, the names of senior executives.

These executives are people you will want to be in touch with. Naturally, a particular person you contact may not have a job opening for which you'd be appropriate at the moment, but he may be able to refer you to someone else who might. And, again, if you can arrange a meeting and impress him sufficiently, at the very least you'll be included in his list of possible candidates for future openings.

Another way of making contact with industry insiders is by going where they go. This means attending conventions, trade shows, seminars, workshops, speeches, and professional meetings specific to your industry. And when you attend, don't be a wallflower. Introduce yourself, ask intelligent questions, and collect business cards. If you feel shy about this, look around—everyone else will be doing it, too!

# MAKING CONTACT

Suppose you've tracked down the name of some industry insiders you'd like to meet. Now you have to decide on the best way to make contact with them. There are essentially four ways you can reach potential networking contacts: by phone, by snail mail (i.e., a traditional letter), by fax, and by e-mail. Which way you choose will depend on whether or not, and how well, you know the person you're contacting and exactly what kind of help you want them to provide. There are advantages and disadvantages to each way, but all four methods require you to put something in writing (yes, even if you're making a phone call). That's where the basic cover letter you've already written comes in.

## Making Contact by Phone

Phoning someone for help may seem like the fastest and easiest way to go about it, and in some instances, particularly with people you already know well, that's exactly what you should do. If, for example, you think that Aunt Rose or Uncle Manny can provide you with some help, calling them would obviously be the simplest and most logical way to do it. (And Mom will be so happy to hear about it from Aunt Rose!)

In Uncle Manny's case, given his background in an industry you're interested in joining, it would make the most sense to call him and ask if he could spare some time to speak with you about it. You might even suggest that you get together for coffee or lunch. Similarly, if your brother's girlfriend can provide you with the name of the person who's looking for a new Toyota salesman, simply calling and asking her for the name would be the most sensible thing to do (if for no other reason than you wouldn't want your brother to think you were trying to move in on his girlfriend!).

But there are other instances in which simply calling someone may not be the easiest or most logical thing to do. This is particularly true when you're trying to contact someone you don't know, even if you've been referred to them by someone you do know. Many people have difficulty making "cold calls," that is, phoning complete strangers.

Moreover, because most business people are extremely busy, it's often hard to get in touch with them. You'll probably have to explain your reason for calling to an assistant or secretary, who may or may not pass you along to the boss. In the end, what you expect to take one call may very well end up taking three or four. And even then you might not get to speak to the person you want to contact.

Nevertheless, if you're comfortable with cold calling, there's no reason why you shouldn't try this method. But bear in mind that, though you may not have to send a networking letter at this point (the person you speak to may subsequently ask that you put something in writing), you will need some kind of script for what you intend to say on the phone. Such a script would include essentially the same things you would say in a letter, which we'll cover later in this chapter.

## Making Contact by Snail Mail

Sending a letter by regular mail is a tried and true method of approaching potential networking contacts. The main disadvantage is that, the mail, being what it is (it isn't called "snail mail" for nothing), will take longer to make contact. The main advantage is that writing a letter and then following up with a phone call makes approaching strangers considerably less stressful. We think it's a easier to write to someone you don't know than it is to call them, so we actually prefer approaching potential network contacts by letter or by fax (although there are some disadvantages to the latter, as we'll explain below).

Sending a networking letter to someone you don't know, and then following up with a phone call, is easier than just calling. When you do call, the person will already have at least some idea of who you are and why you're calling and will be more likely to take your call.

## Making Contact by Fax

*Don't assume your fax will be read immediately. Years ago, when faxes were a new thing, they were used almost exclusively for urgent messages. But in today's fast-paced business environment, people fax letters whether there's actually a need for speed or not. So your fax will probably just be placed in your intended recipient's in-box, along with the letters that arrived via the U.S. Postal Service, FedEx, or other mail deliverers.*

Faxing rather than mailing a letter has one clear advantage—it gets there faster. In fact, these days, cover letters and resumes are faxed almost as often as they are mailed (including both networking and job-tailored letters). Many classified ads or other job listings specifically ask job candidates to fax their materials. In addition, if you have spoken with a potential networking contact on the phone, the chances are good that you will be asked to fax your resume before setting up a meeting.

When you're first trying to make contact, though, sending a fax rather than a letter could be problematic. While faxing is almost instantaneous, it doesn't necessarily mean that your letter will get into your contact's hands faster—or necessarily at all.

Smaller companies or offices may have only one fax machine, in which case, all the faxes come in at the same machine and then have to be distributed to the proper recipients. Larger companies often have numerous fax machines—sometimes more than one on each floor of the building. So the chances of your fax finding its way even to the right floor, much less the right person, may not be great.

For this reason, if you want to fax a cover letter (with or without a resume), the best way to make sure that it will reach the right person is to call the individual's office and ask for the correct fax number. Be sure the name of your contact person appears clearly and prominently at the top of the letter. Then hope it gets delivered promptly!

## Making Contact by E-Mail

As the Internet increasingly becomes a part of everyone's life, sending cover letters and resumes by e-mail is becoming almost as commonplace as using snail mail or fax. (See Chapter 9 for details on how to make sure your resume can be e-mailed with no loss of detail or accuracy.)

The most obvious advantage of sending your cover letter and resume by e-mail is that when your intended recipients open up their electronic mailbox, your letter and resume will be right there in front of them. Delivery is virtually instantaneous. If you want to use e-mail in your networking process, however, there are a couple of important things to bear in mind.

First, it's important that what you put in the "subject" field of the e-mail message be sufficiently interesting to grab the reader's attention. Most of today's executives are inundated with e-mail, and unless your subject looks interesting, the chances are they will delete your message without even opening it.

Second, if you choose to send your materials by e-mail, the best thing to do is write a brief note, then insert your cover letter and/or resume directly into the e-mail message. This enables your recipients to print out your letter and resume, if they choose to do so, in the same format in which you created it.

However, there are reasons why sending cover letters and resumes by e-mail can be problematic. Most industry directories do not yet include e-mail addresses of senior executives, nor do company operators, assistants, or secretaries normally give them out to strangers. So it may be difficult to get the e-mail address for the person you want to contact.

In addition, as we've already mentioned, executives often become overloaded with e-mail and may well take longer to look at something received by that method than to look at a letter and/or resume that arrives by mail or fax. For these reasons, at least at this moment in the history of business technology, we'd suggest using one of the other methods of reaching potential networking contacts.

# DRAFTING YOUR NETWORKING LETTER

**FYI**

*Microsoft Word is the word-processing program now used by most businesses. However, Word 97 is not "backward-compatible." That is, computer users with earlier versions of Word are not always able to read documents written in Word 97. So if you are attaching files to an e-mail message, save them as generic Word files before doing so.*

The basic cover letter you've already written can be adapted for a number of purposes. Networking is one of the most important. As with every other kind of cover letter, the networking letter provides an excellent opportunity for you to make a strong and positive first impression on the people you are approaching for help in finding your next job.

Making a good first impression is especially important in networking letters because, unlike individuals who are actively recruiting to fill open positions in their organizations, the people you're trying to contact for networking purposes are unlikely to have any particular motive for seeing you. Even with the best of intentions, busy people may not be overly enthusiastic about spending an hour of their precious time in an activity that's more likely to benefit you than them.

For these reasons, it's especially important that your networking letter be thoroughly professional, courteous, considerate, and to the point. Remember, you're asking for a favor. Act like it.

Like the basic cover letter, the networking letter essentially serves three purposes: introducing you to the potential contact, making a sales pitch (in this case a subtle one), and suggesting further action. However, because the purpose of a networking letter is somewhat different from that of the basic cover letter, some of the elements of the networking letter are different, as is the organization of those elements.

## The Opening

As in the basic cover letter, you should use the opening of the networking letter to introduce yourself and explain why you're writing. Again, since most businesspeople receive a great deal of mail, make sure your opening paragraph is sufficiently interesting to keep them reading. As with the basic cover letter, there are several ways of doing this:

Mention a referral from someone he or she knows:

> At the suggestion of Noel Boyle, I am writing to seek your advice. For the past four years I have been a senior analyst with Kidder Peabody, but due to the firm's recent downsizing, I am now exploring new career opportunities.

> Alfred Norman, a former colleague of yours, suggested that I contact you because you are one of the key players in the recording industry. I'm writing to seek your suggestions regarding a career move I've been considering. For the last three years, I've been an assistant engineer with Decca Records. I feel I've now sufficiently honed my skills to move up into an engineer's position.

Remind them of a previous meeting:

> I very much enjoyed our brief meeting at the Spielbergs' cocktail party last week. As I mentioned, I'm presently working as a senior executive actuary for the Metropolitan Life Insurance Company, but I am interested in finding a way to make use of my skills in another industry. Accordingly, I am writing to seek your advice.

> You may recall our meeting briefly after your speech at the Plastic Packagers convention the other day. As a recent college graduate interested in joining the plastic packaging industry, I am writing to ask for your advice and guidance.

Refer to a news item about the company:

> I am writing to you because the recent article on your company in *Chicago Business* made it clear that your organization is one of the leaders in the meat packing industry. Having just been discharged from the United States Marines, and being interested in joining the industry, I am writing to seek your counsel.

> I read with great interest the article in the June 15th edition of the *Boston Globe* about your company's efforts to find new ways to market videos for family viewing. As an assistant in a small marketing firm who is interested in finding a position with a larger company, I am writing to ask for your guidance and advice.

### FYI

*If you see an article about a company which reports that it's been accused or found guilty of having done something wrong, don't even think about citing that in the opening of your networking cover letter. A public embarrassment is the last thing in the world an executive will want to be reminded of.*

## The Pitch That Isn't

As in the basic cover letter, the second paragraph of a networking letter is essentially a sales pitch. It is, however, a sales pitch with a difference. Since you're *not* trying to convince the recipient of your letter to hire you but only to agree to meet with you, it is neither necessary nor appropriate to go to great lengths to extol your own virtues.

All you really want to do in the second paragraph of the networking letter is to give your reader a fuller understanding of your background and experience. You want to show that you're a serious individual who is genuinely interested in hearing her advice and has no intention of wasting her time.

As with the basic cover letter, there are two ways this paragraph can be organized: as a regular paragraph or as a bulleted list. Remember, this is not the place to repeat all the information in your resume but, rather, a place to provide your reader with the highlights of your career. Having already mentioned your current work situation in the opening paragraph, this is where you'll mention your other related work experience. Some samples:

> In addition to my experience at General Motors, over the last fifteen years I've also served as executive assistant to a vice president of Chrysler Corporation and to the senior executive vice president of the Goodyear Tire Company.

> Aside from my experience with NBC-TV, I've held positions as:
>
> - Assistant engineer with WKRP Radio in Cincinnati
> - Engineer with KMRI-TV in San Francisco
> - Senior engineer with WNBC-TV in New York

## The Call to Action

The closing of the networking letter is where you specifically advise your reader what you want of him or her, and tell them what *you* will do to help bring it about. We say what *you* will do because, since it's primarily in *your* best interests to move the process ahead, it's your responsibility to get it done.

The closing of a networking letter usually comprises two paragraphs. The first contains a specific request for a face-to-face meeting or, if such a meeting is impossible for reasons of geography, to speak on the phone.

This paragraph must also contain a very clear and unambiguous disclaimer. You must make it perfectly clear that you are *not* asking the recipient for a job and that you won't be asking for one if you have the opportunity to meet. As we mentioned before, although it's possible

**Sample Networking Letter—Block Format**

**Peter Vane**
**3333 Mockingbird Lane**
**Batavia, N.Y. 10577**
**612-666-7760**
**E-mail: pvane@bestweb.net**

July 1, 2000

Ms. Emma Golding
Empire City Media
3387 Capitol Avenue
Albany, N.Y. 10599

Dear Ms. Golding:

At the suggestion of Arnold Brooks, I am writing to seek your advice and counsel. For the last five years, I have served as senior editor of *The Capitol* magazine, but due to the company's recent elimination of a number of editorial positions, including my own, I am now exploring new career opportunities.

Before joining the staff of *The Capitol,* I worked as an editorial assistant and assistant editor on the Albany *Times Mirror*, as associate editor on *Young New York* magazine, and as an editor on *Empire State* magazine. My goal is to find a senior editorial position with a major newspaper or magazine publisher.

I would very much appreciate the opportunity to meet with you briefly to discuss any suggestions you might be willing to share with me regarding my search for appropriate opportunities. Please be assured that I do not expect you to know of any positions that would be open at this time.

In anticipation of our meeting, I'm enclosing a copy of my resume to give you a better idea of my background and experience, and I will call you within the next few days with the hope that we'll be able to find a mutually agreeable time to meet.

Sincerely yours,

Peter Vane

Enc.

**Sample Networking Letter—Indented Format**

**Barbara A. Gordon**
**46 Albermarle Street, N.W.**
**Washington, D.C. 20002**
**202-789-5554**
**E-mail: barbg@capitol.net**

August 14, 2000

Ms. Alana Smith
Smith & Company Public Relations
880 Lincoln Street, S.E.
Washington, D.C. 20014

Dear Ms. Smith:

Your name was given to me at a University of Chicago alumni meeting by Sarah Allgood as someone who might be able to help me enter the public relations field. Sarah mentioned the work you'd done with her in connection with the General Mills account, and she said you were among the most respected P.R. directors in the industry.

I'm seeking an entry-level position, but I already have experience in some of the necessary skills, which I learned as a public relations intern, including:

- Writing product publicity
- Helping to set up press parties
- Writing factual fillers for newspapers
- Researching people the agency wanted to pitch

While I don't expect you to know of any entry-level openings at this time, I would appreciate it if you would meet with me to provide any insight, guidance, or suggestions you may like to share with a recent Chicago graduate.

I am enclosing a copy of my resume and will call you next week to see if we can arrange for a meeting. Thanking you in advance, I am,

Sincerely yours,

Barbara A. Gordon

Enc.

that the person you're contacting may have an open position for which you might be appropriate, you have to assume this is not the case.

Here are a couple of samples of how your first call-to-action paragraph might read:

> I would very much appreciate the opportunity to meet with you briefly to discuss any suggestions you might be willing to share with me regarding my search for appropriate opportunities. Please be assured that I do not expect you to know of any positions that would be open at this time.

> I would be very appreciative if you would be kind enough to meet with me briefly to share any suggestions you may have regarding my search for new opportunities. Of course, I don't expect you to know of any available positions in your organization or elsewhere at this time.

The final paragraph of the networking letter is where you tell your reader what you are going to do to move the process along. If you have a particularly impressive resume—and if it is appropriate—you might want to include it with your networking letter. If so, this is the place to mention it. Whether you do or not, however, it is here that you tell your reader how and when you will contact him or her as a means of taking the next step. For example:

> In anticipation of our meeting, I am enclosing a copy of my resume to help you get a better understanding of my background. I'll call you within the next few days in the hope that we'll be able to find a mutually agreeable time to meet.

> To provide you with a clearer idea of my experience, I am enclosing a copy of my resume, and I'll call you next week to see if we can arrange for a mutually convenient time for a brief meeting.

## If You're Calling Instead of Writing

As you recall, we recommend that when you're trying to contact someone you don't already know, you write a networking letter and then follow it up with a call. However, if you choose to simply call potential networking contacts, you should prepare a script for what you're going to say.

This script should include essentially the same information that you would otherwise put in a networking letter. It is very important, though, that you pay close attention to the language you use in your phone script. To avoid sounding too formal, we suggest that, after preparing a script, you read it out loud for a better sense of how it sounds. Even better, record the script so you can concentrate on just listening to it. If you sound stiff or overly formal, rework your script.

**FYI**

Having done so, however, it's best to stick as closely as possible to the script. That will keep you from omitting key points, rambling, or losing your chain of thought.

# FOLLOWING UP YOUR NETWORKING LETTER

Even the most brilliantly written networking letter won't be of any use to you if you neglect to follow it up with a phone call. Remember that it's you who wants to set up a meeting, not the person you're contacting, so if you don't pursue it, it's probably not going to be pursued.

Whether you've sent your letter by snail mail, fax, or e-mail, it's best to wait at least a few days after you think the recipient has received the letter before calling. The piles of paper in busy executives' in-boxes can be staggering, and the chances are that your letter isn't going to rise immediately to the top of the pile.

When you do call, you may be connected first to a secretary or assistant. If so, say who you are, who you wish to speak to, *and* that you are following up on a letter you sent. One of the reasons people have their assistants or secretaries answer their phones is to screen out calls they don't want to take, and if you say you're following up on something, you're much more likely to be put through to the person you want to speak to.

Once you are put through, you should have a good idea of exactly what you're going to say. Introduce yourself, mention that you're following up on a letter you sent, and recall what your letter was about. (Don't assume your contact will remember your name—and certainly don't act offended if they don't!) Once you're sure that they do remember, tell them that you were hoping to be able to set up a *brief* meeting whenever it would be convenient for them.

Truth is, sometimes you won't even be able to get past the secretary or assistant. And sometimes, even if you get the person on the phone, they may not be willing to meet with you. Our experience, however, is that, as long as they genuinely believe they can be of some help to you, most people will agree to a meeting—especially if you're courteous, friendly, and businesslike when you call.

# PLANNING THE NETWORKING MEETING

Before you go into the networking meeting, there are several things you should bear in mind. Most important is that the person you'll be seeing is probably quite busy and is doing you a favor by agreeing to see you. For that reason, it's essential that you plan an agenda so you don't waste their time—or yours.

There should be four essential items on your agenda:

- Breaking the ice

- Your presentation

- Your questions

- Your final request

### Breaking the Ice

**FYI**

*A networking interview is an opportunity for you to make a potentially valuable business contact. So don't for a minute think that just because it isn't a job interview, you don't have to dress and behave appropriately, that is, the same way you would if it was a job interview. Follow all the usual rules that would apply to any job interview: wear a conservative suit or dress, don't chew gum or smoke, be on time, make eye contact, etc.*

Despite how busy they are, few business people expect anyone to plunge right into the subject of a meeting. After you've both said hello and told each other how nice it is to meet, you should take a few minutes to break the ice.

A good way of doing this, if you've been referred by a mutual friend, is to say something about the friend:

> It was nice of Harriet to put me in touch with you. I've known her for two years—ever since we attended a seminar on patent law together at New York University. I understand you two met when you worked together at 3M?

Another way is to look quickly around the person's office and see if there's something you might talk about briefly. If there's an autographed baseball on the desk, it's a good bet your contact is a baseball fan, and you can ask about that. Similarly, if someone has a photograph of a cat on her wall, you might break the ice by saying something like "I see you're a cat lover," and mentioning your own pet cat.

Don't let the ice-breaking go on too long. Move on to the real purpose of the meeting after a couple of minutes.

### Your Presentation

The person you're meeting with may or may not have reviewed your networking letter and/or resume before the meeting. It's useful to prepare something to refresh his or her memory about why you've asked for the meeting. You can start by saying something like, "As I mentioned in my letter . . . .." Begin with your current position, mention other positions you've held, and explain why you're interested in finding a new position, as well as exactly what kind of new position you're looking for:

As I explained in my letter, I've been in retailing for the past four years, including the last two years as a buyer of women's sportswear for Bloomingdale's in Los Angeles. I'd like to move on to a job at one of the specialty chains, and I'm hoping you'll have a suggestion or two as to how I might get started.

Although this presentation should include the same kind of information you've already included in your letter, it should be more informal and personal. As we suggested with regard to creating a script for making cold calls, practice out loud to yourself beforehand so you can make adjustments if you sound too formal.

## Your Questions

**FYI**

*If you intend to question your networking contacts about their industry, it's best to avoid asking about specific individuals, particularly anyone with a less-than-excellent reputation. You can never tell who they may know, and you don't want to mention anyone with whom they may have battled at some point in the past.*

At this point, you should tell the person that you don't want to take up too much of his time, but that you have a few questions to ask. Before the meeting, prepare three or four such questions, depending on exactly what your situation is.

For example, if you've just finished school or are looking for your first job in a particular industry, you might ask questions about the current state of the industry:

I hear that competition from online marketers is having quite an impact on computer retailers like you. Are you finding that to be the case?

If you are planning to stay in the same industry, you might ask the person what he or she thinks about particular recent developments in the field:

I have a friend who works in marketing for Calvin Klein, and she says that many of her colleagues are worried about the effect that the latest merger of fashion magazines may have on fashion advertising. What do you think?

People usually love to talk about what they do, and the idea here is to give them an opportunity to do so. You should, of course, make comments yourself, that's how they'll get to know something about you, but remember that you've asked them to provide you with advice, not the other way around.

Never ask if they have a job available or if they know of a job that may be available. If you impress them sufficiently, and they do know of something, the chances are they'll volunteer it. Otherwise, don't put them on the spot.

### Your Final Request

In the course of the conversation, it's also possible that they may give you the names of some other people for you to contact. Whether they have or not, now is the time to ask: "Is there anyone [or anyone else] you can suggest who would be a good person for me to talk to?"

Be sure to write down the names to make sure you won't forget them, and, if they don't offer the information, if you can use their name when you contact the other people. Finally, be sure to thank them for their time, their advice, and their suggestions.

# FOLLOWING UP AFTER A NETWORKING MEETING

*What's the greatest compliment you can pay to a networking contact during your meeting? Really listen to them. Think about what's they're saying, ask intelligent questions, add relevant comments, and take notes when they say something interesting or important. The things you'll learn may end up providing clues to where your industry is heading—and where your next job may come from.*

There are several good reasons for you to follow up a networking meeting with a letter.

First, it's simple courtesy to thank someone who's done you a favor.

Second, despite the fact that it's a basic rule of etiquette, many people *don't* send follow-up letters. Thus, if you do take the time to write, it impresses people and helps you to stand out in what may be a considerable crowd.

Finally, a good follow-up letter reminds the people you met with who you are and that you're interested in finding a job. Executives within any given industry tend to know each other, and you can never tell when someone you've met may hear about a possible job from one of his or her colleagues. Sending a follow-up letter will help keep you in their minds.

So follow-up letters are extremely important. They are, however, also quite different from the kinds of letters you've written so far—so different, in fact, that one of our later chapters is devoted exclusively to them.

# JUST THE FACTS

- To get started networking, make everyone you know aware that you're looking for a job.

- Mailing or faxing networking letters is preferable to calling when first contacting someone you don't already know.

- Networking letters are variations of the basic cover letter and easy to adapt for that purpose.

- It's your responsibility to follow up a networking letter with a phone call if you want to set up a networking meeting.

- Before a networking meeting, prepare a presentation as well as several questions to ask.

- Sending a follow-up letter to thank someone for meeting with you is not only courteous, its makes good business sense.

# Chapter 16

# Job-Tailored Letters

## Get the Scoop On . . .

- Choosing the type of cover letter
- How to draft, fine-tune, and check your letter
- Using the cover letter to "spin" your career history
- Maximizing your chance for an interview

A s we've seen, it's essential to develop networking contacts when you're looking for a new job, and doing so will have both short- and long-term benefits. But the ultimate goal of a networking campaign is to find someone with a great job you can fill.

Aside from networking, there are, of course, other ways to find out about job openings. Even while you're seeking potential networking contacts, it's important that you explore those avenues as well. There are two other primary sources of information for job openings. The first is want ads placed by employers in newspapers, periodicals, and Internet job sites. The second is headhunters (also called executive search firms or employment agencies). Such firms often run want ads themselves. When job hunting, it's worthwhile to identify and contact the top search firms in your field.

Regardless of how you find out about a job opening, we suggest you contact the potential employer as quickly as possible. Although, as we discussed in Chapter 1, the job market is currently very good (in many industries and regions of the United States, there are more good jobs available than there are good people to fill them) there are *always* lots of people looking for new positions. Moreover, times change; and the job market invariably changes with them. For these reasons, when you hear about an opening, it's best to get your bid in as soon as you can.

In this chapter, we'll discuss the various ways you can make contact with potential employers and/or headhunters and show how cover letters can help you in this effort. We will also show you how to adapt your basic cover letter to be appropriate for specific jobs as well as how to follow up on job-tailored letters.

# MAKING CONTACT WITH POTENTIAL EMPLOYERS

As with making networking contacts, there are several ways of making initial contact with individuals who have jobs available: telephone, snail mail, fax, and e-mail. Although there are advantages and disadvantages to each method, all of them ultimately require you to write a cover letter. Yes, all of them. Even if you phone first, whoever you speak to will in all likelihood ask that you send a resume as well as a cover letter.

## When You've Been Referred by Someone

**FYI**

*With the growth of the Internet, many companies and industries are advertising jobs electronically. If you're interested in a particular company, check out their Web site as well as the numerous other sites that contain job listings. More details on the online job search can be found in Chapter 8.*

Networking contacts who provide you with job leads are, of course, trying to be helpful. However, they may have been misinformed about openings, or their information may be out-of-date. For these reasons, unless you are sure that someone to whom you've been referred does in fact have an opening, it's best to call first to verify it.

As with networking contacts, before making such a call, you should prepare a short script containing an abbreviated version of what you'd put in a letter (which we'll cover later in this chapter). Don't expect the person on the other end of the phone to immediately invite you in for an interview. The chances are that, even if they like the way you sound, they will ask you to follow up with a resume and, of course, a cover letter, either by fax or by mail.

If you're sure there's an opening (or if you still have a problem with making cold calls to strangers), it's okay to simply mail or fax a cover letter and resume to the person who is recruiting to fill a position. As with a networking letter, you would then follow up with a phone call to see if you can make an appointment for an interview.

## When Responding to a Want Ad

If you learn of an opening through a want ad placed by either an employer or a search firm, follow any instructions provided in the ad. Many ads specifically request that you send a resume and cover letter, either by mail or by fax, rather than calling.

On the other hand, some supply you only with a phone number and the name of the person to contact. In fact, some companies ask people to call so that they can screen out any candidates who are unlikely to be appropriate for the position being advertised. For this reason, if an ad does suggest you call about an opening, a script that'll help you make all your best points is a good idea. If you pass this initial screening, you'll probably be asked to send a resume and cover letter.

## When Contacting a Headhunter

Some headhunters (a.k.a. search firms or employment agencies) handle a variety of industries. However, many specialize in particular fields. So if you're interested in a specific industry, it would be best for you to seek out one that specializes in your industry. Their recruiters develop real expertise regarding industry trends, company reputations, and the job marketplace. They can be truly helpful in identifying the best opportunities for you.

If you are planning to stay in the same industry in which you're currently employed, you probably already know which search firms concentrate on your field. (Chances are good you've gotten a call from one of them.) If not, you can find out by asking networking contacts and/or by looking at the ads the various firms place in newspapers or, even better, industry publications.

If you've been referred by a networking contact to a specific individual in a search firm, it's advisable to call that person first, and then follow up with a letter and resume. However, if you are contacting a firm as the result of your having seen a want ad, you should follow the instructions in the ad. One way or the other, the search firm will at some point ask you to provide both a resume and a cover letter.

Once they've evaluated your credentials, they'll let you know whether they're currently recruiting for any positions you might be appropriate for. Although such firms often just send resumes of prospective employees directly to their clients, it's possible that they may ask you to write an additional cover letter to send with your resume to a specific client.

> **FYI**
>
> *Headhunters only make money when they place candidates in jobs. Therefore, their primary interest is always in trying to fit you into a position at one of their client firms. You* must *always be the one to decide whether a particular job is the right one for you. Don't allow a headhunter to pressure you into accepting a position you feel uncomfortable about.*

## MAKING THE JOB-TAILORED COVER LETTER WORK FOR YOU

As we noted in Chapter 14, job-tailored cover letters offer you two powerful advantages in your job hunt. First, cover letters enable you to personalize responses to advertisements for specific jobs. Second, they can be particularly helpful in overcoming job-hunting problems.

### Using Cover Letters to Personalize Your Applications

By this time, you should have already prepared a strong, appealing, and professional resume. However, unless you're seeking the same kind of job you already have in another company, it's possible that your resume may not be exactly appropriate for the job you want. It may, for example, highlight skills that are important in your current position but not as vital for the kind of job you're now seeking.

Now, you could revise your resume every time you send it out for a different job. But that's a lot of work, and it's really not necessary. Instead, once you have a good basic cover letter, you can easily revise it to appeal to any specific manager recruiting to fill a specific position. We'll explain exactly how to do that later in this chapter.

## Using Cover Letters to Help Overcome Job-Hunting Problems

Cover letters can help put to rest particular issues that dog some job hunters, making it harder for them to get their foot in the recruiter's door.

For example, although it's against the law to discriminate against a person because of age, if your resume shows that you have 15 or 20 years of work experience, you might be worried that a potential employer will consider you too old for the job. In fact, many companies do prefer to hire younger people, partly because they can pay them less and thus keep their payroll costs down.

If you do have such a concern, sending *only* a cover letter rather than a cover letter and resume can be a real advantage, because cover letters don't normally include dates of employment. By doing so you will be able to discuss your experience without making it obvious that some of it was gained years ago.

At the other end of the spectrum, you may have just finished school and not have any actual work experience. Sending a cover letter alone (rather than a cover letter and a bare-bones resume) enables you to concentrate on communicating whatever skills make you a good candidate and downplay your relative lack of experience.

Another potential problem that cover letters can help you sidestep is when you're interested in changing careers and/or industries. Although many more people are doing so today than was the case a few years ago, not all managers are able to clearly see how your skills and experience may be translated from one field to another. Cover letters can help to clarify the connection and thus make you a more appealing candidate.

In Part IV of this book, we provide many more additional tips and strategies for job hunters with various specific issues to address. Be sure to study the chapters in that part of the book which apply to your situation.

# DRAFTING YOUR JOB-TAILORED LETTER

A job-tailored letter is essentially a variation on the basic cover letter you've already written. Like that letter, it provides you with an important opportunity to make a good first impression. It also serves the same three primary purposes (introducing yourself, making a sales pitch, and calling for further action) that are generally accomplished in a letter of four paragraphs.

### The Opening

The first paragraph of your letter is where you introduce yourself and explain why you're writing. Again, you should remember that most businesspeople are extremely busy, so you should make your opening paragraph short and to the point. How this paragraph is structured will, of course, depend on how you found out about the specific opening in which you are interested.

For example, if you learned of a position through a networking contact, you might begin your letter this way:

> I am writing you because Peter Schneider, a former colleague of yours, has told me that you're currently recruiting for a new associate in your law firm. Having just graduated from the University of Texas Law School, I would very much appreciate the opportunity to meet with you to discuss the possibility of my joining your firm.

> At the suggestion of James Moriarty, I am writing in regard to the open position in your department for an assistant manager. I have served as an assistant manager with Holmes, Watson & Company for the last two years and would like to meet with you to discuss my qualifications for the job.

If you learned of a position through a company-sponsored ad, your opening might read like this:

> I am writing in response to your advertisement in the July 18th issue of *The Washington Post* for an assistant buyer. As I am currently serving in a similar position with the May store, I would very much like to meet with you to discuss my qualifications for the job.

> I am interested in the position as an administrative assistant that you advertised in the April 22nd issue of *Plumbing News* and am accordingly writing in the hope that I will be able to meet with you to discuss the possibility of my joining your organization.

If you learned of a position through a search firm-sponsored ad:

> I am writing in response to your advertisement in the September 17th edition of *The New York Times* for an assistant analyst with a large New York-based bank. For the past three years, I've served in the same capacity with a small but very profitable bank in Buffalo and would be interested in discussing with you my qualifications for the opening.

> Because I am interested in the position of assistant vice-president with a large San Francisco-based bank that you advertised in the May 4th edition of the *Examiner*, I am writing to request an interview to discuss my qualifications for the job.

## The Pitch

*Most job seekers err on the side of being too shy about their credentials. Don't be afraid to say positive things about yourself in your cover letter. This is your opportunity to sell yourself, and if you don't do it, no one else will. If in doubt as to whether you've overstepped the line from positive assertion into bragging, ask a trusted friend to read and react to your letter.*

Having introduced yourself and explained your purpose in writing, the next paragraph of your letter should be devoted to the first part of your sales pitch and should essentially answer the question "Why me?" This is your opportunity to tell a prospective employer about your experience and abilities in terms of what he or she is looking for in an applicant.

Don't try to include your complete work history in this paragraph. Instead, just give your reader a few great reasons to invite you for an interview.

As we saw in Chapter 14, there are two ways to structure this paragraph, either as a regular paragraph or a bulleted list. Regardless of which you choose, start with a brief statement that will lead your reader into the information you want to provide.

If you learned of a position through a networking contact or are responding to an advertisement that does not specify qualifications, you might present this paragraph like this:

> I have skills that I believe would be of real value to your organization. Perhaps most important, I've never exceeded a budget or missed a deadline for completion of a project. In addition, I have demonstrated my ability to successfully renegotiate contracts downward with outside vendors, and thus saved my company thousands of dollars on an annual basis.

> Over the past three years I have demonstrated my sales abilities in several important ways:

> - Made up to 100 cold calls every week
> - Exceeded my sales quota by 250%
> - Ranked first out of 14 salespeople in my office
> - Named "Salesperson of the month" more than a dozen times

If you're responding to an advertisement that does cite specific qualifications, try using the bulleted list format for this paragraph. Let's say, for example, that you see an advertisement for a job that lists four specific requirements, all of which you have. Using a bulleted list, you can address the four requirements point-by-point, showing your reader that you do have the experience, skills, or personality traits that he or she is looking for.

> I think you'll find that my qualifications are a good match for the skills you mentioned in your advertisement, specifically:

- Minimum of three years of editorial experience—I began my career as an editorial assistant five years ago and was subsequently promoted to assistant editor, associate editor, and editor.

- A good understanding of the market—In the past two years, three of the books I edited appeared on *The New York Times* Bestsellers list.

- A demonstrated ability to work effectively with authors—Several of the authors with whom I've worked have expressed their appreciation of my work to my superiors, and virtually all have acknowledged my efforts in their books.

- The ability to meet deadlines and work under occasionally stressful conditions—Except in two instances in which manuscripts were delivered extremely late by their authors, all of my books have been published on schedule.

## The Pitch Continued

This second paragraph of your sales pitch is where you explain why you want to work for this particular company: "Why you?" There are, of course, several possible reasons that this company might be attractive to you.

There may, for example, be something in particular about the company that you find appealing. If you're planning to stay in the same industry you're now in, it's likely that you already know something about the companies you're considering; they are, after all, your present company's competitors. If, however, you are changing industries, it will be necessary for you to do some additional research.

Information about companies can be found in industry publications, industry directories such as those we've already mentioned, and, in the case of publicly owned companies, annual reports. Be sure, too, to check out the companies' Web sites, which will often have a considerable amount of useful information (more on this in Chapter 8). If you'd like to work at a particular company because of something about the company itself, your paragraph might read something like this:

> I am particularly interested in pursuing a career with the ASPCA because I would like to lend my skills to an organization whose goals I've supported for many years. When I worked at the Sidney Foundation, one of the nonprofit organizations with which I served as liaison was the ASPCA, I was consistently impressed by the professionalism and dedication of your staff members.
>
> Because of the outstanding reputation your company has in the field, and the many positive statements about it made by your

employees, I am particularly interested in joining your organization. For example, I noted that your aerospace division finished second in the competition for a Baldrige quality award last year, a noteworthy achievement by any standard.

Another reason you might be interested in a particular company is because of the industry of which it is a part. You may, for example, currently be an editor in a book publishing company but would like a job requiring similar skills with a company providing information on the Internet. Or you may be a marketing manager in a fast-food chain who's interested in moving into the music industry. If you are looking for a new position in a specific industry, your paragraph might read like this:

> I am particularly interested in your organization because I have had a lifelong interest in music and would like to put my skills to use in a field in which I have a personal as well as professional interest.

> The possibility of joining your organization is of particular interest to me because it's part of a new and growing industry that I believe will become even larger and more important in the years ahead.

A third possible reason may be the company's location. If you are, for example, a financial analyst with a large metropolitan newspaper but wish to relocate for some reason, you might want to work for another large newspaper in another city. Similarly, your spouse may have received a job offer he or she couldn't refuse but which required relocating, so location is an essential component of your job search. In such a situation, you might write:

> I am especially attracted to your firm because I will shortly be moving to your area and wish to continue working in a dynamic company in the public relations field.

> Your company is particularly attractive to me because, since my wife has recently accepted a position with a law firm in the area, we will be moving to Pittsburgh shortly.

The last, although certainly not the least, reason for your interest in a particular organization may be the job itself. It might be, for example, that you've been working in production in your present company and wish to move into a sales position. Or that you're currently an assistant buyer in a large department store and feel you are ready to move up to a buyer's position. If you are contacting a company because you're interested in the job itself, you might write a paragraph such as:

> My interest in your company has grown out of my wish to put my five years of experience as an assistant buyer to work in a more challenging position.

I am especially interested in joining your company because I have had a lifelong interest in putting my accounting skills to work in a small but growing organization.

## The Closing

The fourth and final paragraph of your job-tailored cover letter is the appropriate place to thank your reader for considering your application and to suggest the next step in the process. Except when you're responding to a blind ad (which does not include the name of a specific individual or company) and consequently cannot know who to contact, it's always best to be proactive in this closing paragraph. Thus, as a rule, your last paragraph should read something like:

I very much appreciate your considering my application for the position. I will call you within the next few days [or "next week"] to see if we can arrange a mutually agreeable time to meet.

If you are responding to a blind ad, the closing paragraph might read:

Thank you for taking the time to consider my qualifications for the job. I hope that we'll be able to meet at some point in the near future, and I look forward to hearing from you in that regard.

## If You're Calling Instead of Writing

As we've already mentioned, if you're not sure that someone to whom you've been referred actually does have an opening, it's a good idea to call first to confirm it. In addition, there may be situations in which a newspaper or periodical advertisement for a job includes only a phone number to call. If you're going to call, for either reason, you should prepare a script for what you're going to say.

This script should be essentially an abbreviated version of your job-tailored letter. If you're calling to follow up on a referral, you should explain who referred you and who you are, and ask whether the person is actually recruiting to fill a position. If they aren't, thank them for their time and ask if you might send a resume anyway. Remember, the more people who know you're looking for a job, the more likely you are to find one.

If they *are* currently trying to fill a position, it's likely that they will ask you something about your background and experience. Similarly, if you're calling to respond to an advertisement, whoever you speak to will probably ask the same kind of questions. Here you can make the same pitch you've already written for your cover letter, including making a suggestion that you get together to discuss the job. While it's possible that they'll agree to set up a meeting on the spot, it's more likely that they'll just ask you to send a resume—with a cover letter, of course.

*Why do companies place blind ads? There can be several reasons. Since you don't know which company placed the ad, the company is relieved of the task of responding to every letter. A blind ad prevents job seekers from inundating executives with calls or notes. And sometimes, when no definite job is available, a company may place a blind ad simply to "test the waters" of the marketplace by seeing what kind of candidates, and how many, respond.*

As we've mentioned before, when you're speaking to someone on the phone rather than writing to them, it's particularly important that you not sound overly formal. By practicing aloud what you're going to say before you call, you'll be able to adjust your language and tone so you can sound both friendly and professional.

# FINE-TUNING YOUR JOB-TAILORED LETTER

**FYI**

*If two weeks pass after you've sent a job-tailored letter in response to a blind ad and you haven't heard from anyone, it's perfectly acceptable to mail or fax a note to the original address or fax number to inquire about the status of the opening and your application.*

Before you put your letter and resume into an envelope and send it on its way (in fact, before you even print it out) make one final check of its contents and style. We've already discussed some of these issues in the chapter on the basic cover letter, but they're especially important when you're sending a letter off to a prospective employer.

As we explained in Chapter 15, there are two standard business letter formats you can use for the cover letter: the indented format and the block format. You'll find examples of each on the adjacent pages.

## Content

After you've finished writing your job-tailored letter, it's important to read it over to make sure that it includes everything that should be included. Thus, you should check to see that in your opening you introduce yourself and tell why you're writing; that the pitch paragraphs explain why a potential employer should hire you and why you want to work for them; and that your closing thanks your reader and suggests the next step in the process.

**FYI**

*Although it is illegal for companies to make hiring decisions based on age, sex, race, religion or other such factors, the fact is that prejudices do exist. By not mentioning them, you can avoid giving potential employers any excuse, reasonable or otherwise, to not seriously consider you for a job.*

In addition, as we've already mentioned, if there is anything in your letter that might be perceived as a problem by a potential employer, you should be sure that it's been dealt with appropriately. If, for example, you are changing industries, you should make sure that you've explained why you're doing so. Similarly, if you're relocating, to avoid the recipient's imagining negative reasons for your moving, you should explain why you are doing so (assuming, of course, that it isn't for some negative reason—jumping bail, for example).

It's also important to make sure that your letter does *not* include anything that it shouldn't. Except in those rare instances in which they would be genuinely relevant to a particular job, you should never mention your age, religious beliefs, marital status, political affiliation, or health (including any handicaps). Nor should you make any reference to your physical appearance, including your race.

The other important subject *not* to mention in your cover letter is salary history or salary requirements. When you're looking for a new job, you

## Sample Job-Tailored Letter—Indented Format

**George Buckner**
**15 Helping Hand Way**
**Cortland, N.Y. 10567**
**914-736-9091**
**E-mail: geobuck@watson.com**

April 12, 2000

Mr. Alexander Corbett
Executive Vice President
New York Finance, Inc.
55 East 44th Street
New York, N.Y. 10022

Dear Mr. Corbett:

At the suggestion of John Watson, I am writing in regard to the opening in your company for a vice-president of marketing. I have served in the same capacity with The Watson Company for the last two years and would accordingly very much like to meet with you to discuss my qualifications for the job.

I have an array of skills that I believe would be of real value to your organization. Since I joined Watson, I've increased the company's gross sales by more than 85% and increased its net profit by 40%. This was accomplished, in part, by devising and instituting new policies that substantially decreased the previously high turnover rate in the marketing department and raised morale to a considerable extent. I also worked closely with the heads of other departments to better coordinate overall company efforts.

I'm interested in the possibility of becoming a member of your team primarily because New York Finance enjoys an outstanding reputation in our industry. Your current plans for growth, as outlined in the recent *Forbes* magazine article, sound exciting and suggest that a person with my history of achievement might fit in well.

I am enclosing a copy of my resume to give you a better idea of my background and experience, and will call you within the next few days to see if we can arrange for a meeting.

Sincerely yours,

George Buckner

Enc.

**Sample Job-Tailored Letter—Block Format**

**Linda Bardwick**
**220 Mockingbird Lane**
**Portland, ME**
**512-650-0510**
**E-mail: lbard@ATT.com**

January 22, 2000

Ms. Alexandra Kennedy
Colco Internet
8282 Stonesong Road
Portland, ME 71555

Dear Ms. Kennedy:

I am writing in response to your advertisement in the *Portland Daily News* for an assistant supervisor in your customer service department. I have been working as a senior customer representative in the customer service department of Daley &; Company for the last two and a half years, and I'd like to meet with you to discuss my qualifications for the assistant supervisor's position.

I think you'll agree that my qualifications closely match the skills you mentioned in your advertisement, specifically:

- "Minimum of two years customer service experience"—I began my career as assistant to the director of customer service four years ago and was subsequently promoted to associate and then senior customer representative.

- "A demonstrated ability to deal with difficult customer problems"—Satisfied customers routinely call or write my superiors to tell them how helpful I was in solving their service problems.

- "A good understanding of computers and the Internet"—I have used a computer at home since I was in high school and minored in computer science in college.

- "Some supervisory experience"—As senior customer representative, I am responsible for managing the department whenever the manager is on vacation or otherwise out of the office.

I am particularly interested in the possibility of joining the Colco Internet staff both because of the considerable growth of your organization over the last several years and because I am interested in moving into a supervisory position.

I am enclosing a copy of my resume and will call you next week in the hope that we can make an appointment to meet.

Sincerely yours,


Linda Bardwick

Enc.

are starting with a clean slate to a certain extent, and you don't want to mar it by providing information about the past that may be disadvantageous.

For example, in the case of salary history, there may have been an instance in which, rather than continuously increasing your income, you took a new job for less compensation than the previous one. A potential employer is likely to wonder why you would have done that. You may have had an excellent reason, but it's not the kind of question you want to raise in someone's mind.

As for salary requirements, suggesting a particular figure, even a range, can place you at a disadvantage with a potential employer. If, for example, you say in your cover letter that you're looking for a position in the $40–45,000 range, and the employer is willing to pay $60,000, if they do make you an offer it's likely to be for less than you might otherwise have been able to negotiate.

Some advertisements do ask for either salary requirements or history. Here's how to handle these.

**FYI**

Don't *simply ig-nore the request for salary informa-tion. If you do, your cover letter and resume may simply be tossed out. The recruiter is eager to avoid wasting time inter-viewing candi-dates who are clearly out of the running based on their current in-come, which is why they may choose to insist on this information.*

- When your salary requirements are requested: Skirt the issue in your letter. Without stating a specific dollar amount, include a sentence to the effect that you are seeking a competitive salary commensurate with your experience and credentials.

- When your salary history is requested: Quote the highest accurate figure you can cite (probably from your most recent job). Include not only base pay but all dollar-denominated perks and benefits, such as bonuses, stock options, incentive pay, club memberships, company cars, etc. (Don't include the value of health insurance or vacation pay, however.) Quote the total value of this compensation package, which may be an approximate rather than a precise figure:

> In my current position at Mammoth Enterprises, I receive a total compensation package, including salary, sales commis-sions, average annual bonus, and stock options in the $75,000–$80,000 range.

## Professional Tone and Language

In reading over your letter, you should check to make sure that the tone and language you use is appropriate to your audience. Remember that you're not writing this letter to a friend but, rather, to a stranger whom you are trying to convince to meet with you and, hopefully, offer you a job. Again, while it's inadvisable to be overly formal, your tone and language should nevertheless be professional and free of slang or other colloquialisms.

Your letter should sound as much as possible as though you were speaking to your reader. As a test, try reading the letter out loud. Doing so will also be very helpful in enabling you to detect any missing information, as well as grammatical, spelling, and punctuation errors. (See Chapter 14 for more tips on tone, style, and language in the cover letter.)

## FOLLOWING UP YOUR JOB-TAILORED LETTER

*In determining how long to wait before following up after you've sent a letter, you should take into account how long it will take your letter to reach the recipient, how long you think it will take him or her to read it, and then add a few extra days. Eight to ten working days, up to two weeks of elapsed time, is a good rule of thumb.*

It's possible, of course, that your job-tailored letter will be so perfect, and make you so attractive to a potential employer, that immediately upon reading it, he or she will pick up a phone and call you to schedule an interview. It's possible, but don't count on it.

In fact, people recruiting for open positions in their organizations rarely read letters and resumes as soon as they arrive. Rather, they are likely to separate out the mail that concerns the job and, when they have time, sit down and go through the job-related letters quickly. In the first run-through, they usually divide the pile into promising candidates, possible ones, and unlikely ones, and then arrange to contact those in the first group to set up interviews.

All of this, however, takes time, more time than you, or they, for that matter, would like it to take. For that reason, you may send a letter and resume and not hear back from someone for weeks. However, as we've said, unless you don't even know who to contact after you've sent a letter, it's best to be proactive at this stage of your job search. Give your reader some time to review your letter and resume, and then call to follow up on it.

You might be told by an assistant or secretary that the person hasn't reviewed any letters yet, or that he or she has just begun to do so, or that a decision was made to hire from within the organization. On the other hand, you might be connected to the person you're trying to reach and be told that they were just about to call you to set up an interview.

If you are told that the letters and resumes are still under consideration, it's all right for you to call again, but you should wait another couple of weeks before doing so. The idea here is to appear to be enthusiastic but not desperate, and certainly not to be perceived as a nuisance.

If you haven't heard from the potential employer for some time (a month or two after your second call) it would be a good idea to call again. Although it's probable that by that point they'll have already hired someone else, not everyone takes the time to get back to every applicant. And, if for no other reason than your own peace of mind, it's better to know if you're no longer being considered for a position.

Hopefully, however, you will hear back long before then and be asked to interview for the job. And when you have, you'll know that all the work you put into your resume and cover letter was worth the effort.

# ONE JOB HUNTER'S TALE: SIX LETTERS FOR SIX JOBS

In today's business world, changing careers is no longer the exception but the norm. Most people develop a portfolio of loosely related skills that they use in a series of jobs, often in a variety of industries.

If this sounds like your career, you'll find the following story instructive. A person we know (we'll call her Wanda Winograd) has a background that includes stints in writing, teaching, and marketing. (The common thread in all three, when you think about it, is *communication*.) Though much of her career has been spent in book publishing, Wanda has held jobs in several other fields as well—based on such factors as where she and her husband were living and on what interested her at the time. So her job history is a checkered one—like many others today.

Over a period of several months, Wanda recently found herself looking for a job. (She'd had a baby and moved to a new city and was now ready to jump back into the workforce.) Interested in, and qualified for, a wide variety of positions, Wanda found herself applying for many different jobs using the same resume, but with various job-tailored cover letters. In the end, she created six different letters, each focusing on and highlighting a different set of skills and experiences. They ended up netting her a host of interviews—and a great job.

As you'll notice, Wanda's cover letters don't always follow our recommended four-paragraph format precisely. That's okay; you, too, may want to experiment with variations on the classic structure. But Wanda's letters are a powerful case study in how one person and one set of credentials can yield an array of appropriate letters, each tailored to a particular industry.

As you read them, notice the subtle (and not-so-subtle) differences in style and emphasis that make each letter uniquely appropriate for the specific job and situation. For example, Wanda is careful to use the jargon of each professional field appropriately within her letters—and to explain any references whose meaning might not be obvious to a particular reader. Her tone modulates from informal (even humorous) when applying for a job in the creative, freewheeling field of advertising to serious and rather idealistic when applying for work in education. And, of course, the specific career achievements she cites in each letter depend on the interests and needs of the reader to whom she's writing.

## Letter 1
## Writing Children's History

**Wanda J. Winograd**
**321 Helicon Avenue**
**Tacoma, Washington 98416**
**253-555-1234**

April 10, 1999

Writer
P.O. Box 99484
Tacoma *Sentinel*
Tacoma, Washington 98416

Dear Sir or Madam:

I am very interested in writing for the children's history project you advertised in the April 7th Tacoma *Sentinel*.

Lively, intelligent writing has always featured strongly in my book publishing career. For instance, I coauthored a popular book for young people on living in group houses. It received high acclaim in several national publications and sold well in bookstores around the country.

As an editor at Mammoth Books and The Little Press, I worked with many authors who were specialists in their fields but not professional writers. I worked closely with them to develop, revise, and, in some instances, rewrite their books. The good reviews, book club adoptions, and special acknowledgements I received from authors are all testimony to my prowess in this area.

In the most recent position I held before relocating to Tacoma, I handled publicity and marketing efforts for both adult and children's books with a strong emphasis on history. I was able to garner significant radio and print publicity for a number of YA history titles, including *Ticket to Freedom: Story of a Runaway Slave* by Ellen Cruz and the *History of Everyday Life* series by John Falmouth.

In short, I am a talented writer who is very familiar with—and interested in—children's nonfiction. I hope we can meet to discuss the possibility of my working on your project.

Sincerely,


Wanda J. Winograd

Enc.

### Letter 2
### Writing Advertising Copy

**Wanda J. Winograd**
**321 Helicon Avenue**
**Tacoma, Washington 98416**
**253-555-1234**

August 1, 1999

Mr. Michael Gagliardi
Creative Director
The Hansen Agency
190 King Street
Tacoma, Washington 98417

Dear Mr. Gagliardi:

If you need copywriting that gets results, I hope you'll consider hiring me.

As a copywriter for Mammoth Books' business and professional books division, I developed advertising campaigns for a wide range of audiences—from tax attorneys and real estate agents to high school football coaches, accountants, teachers, and general consumers. My ability to extract the key selling points for each book and present them in a compelling way served the company well: my mailings and space ads netted $400,000 in sales per year. Enclosed, along with my resume, are some samples of my work, including my biggest winner, a mailing to funeral directors (!) which pulled an 8% response.

My experience, however, is not limited to book publishing (or the mortuary business). I recently completed several copywriting projects for Cobalt and Harrison. There, I've been able to effectively wed clever, snappy headlines to benefit-oriented copy for such clients as National Bank and Sunset Cruises. Also, at C & H, I've gained a reputation as a quick study. I don't need lengthy briefing; I turn copy around quickly, and my copy usually needs only minimal revision.

Perhaps most important, I'm truly excited about bringing my copywriting skills to your agency, whose reputation as one of the most creative in the Northwest is well known. I hope we can meet soon to discuss whether my skills can be of value to the Hansen Agency. I'll call you shortly to see when it might be convenient to meet.

Sincerely,


Wanda J. Winograd

Enc.

**Letter 3**
**Promotional/Editorial Work in Publishing**

**Wanda J. Winograd**
**321 Helicon Avenue**
**Tacoma, Washington 98416**
**253-555-1234**

May 1, 1999

Ms. Deborah Salisbury
Walrus Books
3131 Northern Boulevard
Tacoma, Washington 98421

Dear Ms. Salisbury:

When I spoke with you at the 20th anniversary party for Walrus Books, you recommended that I send you my resume. Here it is. I'm hoping that Walrus can use my book publishing skills and experience.

The areas where I might be of most use to Walrus are in (a) direct mail promotion and (b) substantive nonfiction editing. Regarding the former, I've written direct response pieces for a wide range of audiences—from tax attorneys and English teachers to women's basketball coaches, accountants, and general consumers. My ability to extract the key selling points for each book and present them in a compelling way has served companies well; at Mammoth Books, for instance, my mailings and space ads netted $400,000 per year.

On the editorial side, I have been what Ted Solotoroff once called (in a *Nation* article) a "working editor." As an editor at Mammoth Books and The Little Press, I worked with many authors who were specialists in their fields but not professional writers. I worked closely with them to develop, revise, and, in some instances, rewrite their books. The good reviews, book club adoptions, and special acknowledgements I received from authors are all testimony to my prowess in this area.

While attending the Walrus Books party on Friday, I picked up a strong sense of pride in work worth doing—and work done well. Also, as I told you, setting foot inside your publishing house made me feel more "at home" in Tacoma than ever before. I'd enjoy making another trip to your office to discuss whether my skills might be of value to you. I'll call you next week to see whether we can schedule an interview.

Sincerely,

Wanda J. Winograd

Enc.

## Letter 4
## Marketing Work in Publishing

**Wanda J. Winograd**
**321 Helicon Avenue**
**Tacoma, Washington 98416**
**253-555-1234**

April 30, 1999

Ms. June A. Gracenote
Harborside Publishing
12 Pillsbury Street
Tacoma, Washington 98421

Dear Ms. Gracenote:

As a veteran of a small (four-person) publishing company, I know how much small houses rely on the versatility of in-house "Jills of all trades." I'm writing in the hope that you can use my considerable talents in marketing and promotion.

Initially charged with only publicity and subsidiary rights responsibilities at The Little Press, I soon took on the production of seasonal and academic catalogs, served as managing editor, and worked on book jacket design. It may interest you to know that I obtained rights to use the work of artist Judy Chicago for the cover of Little's *Bibliography of Women's Studies* (see attached copy). In short, the words "that's not my department" are not in my vocabulary, and I believe that the ability to juggle several tasks at once is essential for the staff of growing companies.

Women's interest titles and books by women writers have always held my interest most, and, by all accounts, Harborside has gained a reputation for publishing quality books by and for women. I would like very much to have a hand in your company's continued success, and I hope we can meet soon to discuss whether my experience can be of value. I'll call you next week.

Sincerely,


Wanda J. Winograd

P.S. As a volunteer for the Tacoma Literacy Project, I've recently become proficient at desktop publishing with Pagemaker, another skill that might come in handy at Harborside.

Enc.

**Letter 5**
**Adult Education**

**Wanda J. Winograd**
**321 Helicon Avenue**
**Tacoma, Washington 98416**
**253-555-1234**

June 11, 1999

Mr. Howard Berman
Consortium for Adult Learning
52 Conlon Place
Tacoma, Washington 98423

Dear Mr. Berman:

I enjoyed chatting with you after your speech on Wednesday. When I heard about the Consortium during my work with the Tacoma Literacy Project, I was excited about the vital effort it was making to educate the city's workers. Now I'm eager to be part of this effort.

In my six years at TLP, I relied much more on my own inventiveness, wits, enthusiasm, and resources than on any standard ESL text or rote teaching methods. For this reason, I'm confident in my ability both to establish rapport with adult students and to teach them in ways that hold their interest and relate to their lives. Also, after years of teaching people for whom English lessons are not a luxury but a necessity, I feel particularly sensitive to the needs of Consortium students.

I hope we'll be able to meet soon to further discuss the work of the Consortium and the possibility that I might become part of it. I'll call you next week to see whether we can arrange an interview at a convenient time.

Sincerely,


Wanda J. Winograd

Enc.

**Letter 6**
**Nonprofit Fund-Raising**

**Wanda J. Winograd**
**321 Helicon Avenue**
**Tacoma, Washington 98416**
**253-555-1234**

May 20, 1999

Mr. Paul Carney
Director of Development
St. Helen's College
Tacoma, Washington 98417

Dear Mr. Carney:

If you need grant writing that gets results, then I am a promoting candidate for the Grant Writer position advertised in the May 18th edition of the *Tacoma Weekly.* As a talented writer and marketing professional, I believe I have much to offer St. Helen's College.

Throughout my ten years in book publishing, I've written direct response pieces for a wide range of audiences—from tax attorneys and English teachers to women's basketball coaches, accountants, and general consumers. My ability to extract the key selling points for each book and present them in a compelling way has served companies well; at Mammoth Books, for instance, my mailings and space ads netted $400,000 per year.

My experience, however, is not limited to book publishing. Since relocating to Tacoma in March, I have completed several copywriting projects for Cobalt and Harrison (an agency with $50 million in billings).My work has been highly praised by such clients as National Bank and Sunset Cruises.

Perhaps most important, I'm truly excited about using my writing skills to help obtain funding for St. Helen's. I'm an ardent supporter of education, and my enthusiasm will make my writing that much more persuasive. I hope we can meet soon to discuss whether my experience could be of value. I'll call you next week to see if we can schedule an interview.

Sincerely,


Wanda J. Winograd

Enc.

In short, Wanda does an impressive job of customizing each cover letter to the particular sales situation she faces. You can learn from her example.

## JUST THE FACTS

- There are three ways to find out about job openings: networking referrals; help-wanted ads; and search firms or employment agencies. Each method requires a form of cover letter.

- The basic cover letter can be easily modified to create job-tailored cover letters designed for a specific situation.

- Always double-check your cover letters for the correct content, format, and tone and to make sure they're free of grammatical, spelling, or punctuation errors.

- Avoid salary discussion in your cover letter if you can; if you can't, cite the largest figure you can accurately claim.

# Chapter 17

# Follow-up Letters

## Get the Scoop On . . .

- Writing follow-up letters
- Using follow-up letters to pitch your candidacy
- Following up after turning down a job offer
- Following up after being turned down for a job

Although follow-up letters are in most respects very different from the networking and job-tailored cover letters we've already discussed, there's one way in which they are not only similar but virtually identical. Like networking and job-tailored letters, follow-up letters provide you with an invaluable opportunity to impress your readers with your skills, your background, your professionalism, and your personality.

In this chapter, we'll show you why writing follow-up letters is so important. We'll help you write effective, professional letters for a variety of situations, including letters to follow-up networking and job interviews, letters for when you've been offered and accepted a position, letters for when you've been offered and turned down a position, letters thanking your interviewer even when you've not received a job offer, and letters to follow up with your networking contacts after you've started a new job.

## NETWORKING INTERVIEW FOLLOW-UP LETTERS

It's always appropriate to thank someone, especially someone who doesn't know you well, for taking time out of their schedule to talk to you. And this is true whether they were considering you for a job or not. Although the individual who is actively interviewing potential job candidates obviously has a business interest in talking with you, they're still under no obligation to spend time with you. And people who *aren't* recruiting to fill a position certainly don't have to give you an hour of their valuable time. So thanking these people is courteous, considerate, and appropriate.

## Sample Networking Interview Follow-Up Letter

**Michael Broderick**
**919 Massachusetts Avenue**
**Brighton, MA 07122**
**617-750-9086**
**E-mail: mikeb@bosnet.com**

August 18, 2000

Ms. Corinne Blackman
Nehan, Ross & Blackman
22 Boylston Street
Boston, MA 07125

Dear Ms. Blackman:

I am writing to tell you what a pleasure it was to meet you the other day and to thank you again for taking the time to speak with me.

The information, ideas, and names you were kind enough to share with me will, I'm sure, be extremely helpful, and I appreciate it very much.

I will be in touch with you again to let you know how my job search is progressing. In the meantime, should you hear of any openings for which I might be appropriate, I would very much appreciate hearing from you.

With best wishes,


Michael Broderick

More specifically, in the case of networking interviews, sending a follow-up letter serves the purpose of reminding the reader who you are and the fact that you're looking for a job. Remember, the person you met with may have a job opening in the near future, and if you've sent a follow-up letter they're more likely to remember you. In addition, because executives in any given industry tend to know each other, the person you follow up with may contact you if he or she hears of a position in another company for which you would be qualified.

Like the other types of letters you've already written, the networking interview follow-up letter can be divided into three elements, or paragraphs—in this case, the opening, your comments on the meeting, and the closing.

### The Opening

**FYI**

*All follow-up letters, regardless of their purpose, should be sent as soon as possible after the meeting—preferably the next day, but certainly within the next few days. It's not only courteous, it's a good way to make sure that you won't forget to do it.*

The opening should be a brief, straightforward, one- or two-sentence paragraph in which you thank your reader for taking the time to meet with you, such as:

> I'm just writing to say what a pleasure it was to meet you yesterday and to thank you again for spending some time with me.

> I'm writing to say how much I enjoyed our meeting the other day and to thank you for taking the time to help me in my efforts to find a new position.

### Comment on the Meeting

The second paragraph of the follow-up letter is the appropriate place to make some comment about the discussion you had. Even if the networking meeting didn't result in your actually gaining a great deal of information, it's still appropriate for you to say something positive about it, for example:

> The information, ideas, and names you were kind enough to share with me will, I'm sure, be extremely helpful, and I appreciate it very much.

> Having the opportunity to discuss the industry with you, as well as hearing your thoughts about its future, was interesting, informative, and enjoyable.

On the other hand, the person you met with may have made some particularly interesting comment, given you an especially good idea, or provided you with several names of people to contact. In this case, it would be appropriate to be more specific about the discussion:

> Your comments about recent developments in the industry were particularly interesting and thought-provoking. I had not consid-

ered the impact of gun control legislation on the business and am now beginning to see it in a new light.

Your suggestion that I contact the National Booksellers Association concerning entry-level positions with their member companies was an especially valuable one, and I will certainly follow up on it.

In addition to the other valuable suggestions you made, your providing me with the names of so many people to contact will no doubt be enormously helpful, and I sincerely appreciate it.

Finally, if either you or the person you met with promised to do something in the course of the meeting, this is the appropriate place to do what you promised or (tactfully) remind the other person of his or her promise:

As I promised I would, I'm enclosing the article from the *San Francisco Examiner* about Peter Anderson's new film.

I very much appreciate your offer to contact Steven Ryan at the Ryan Company on my behalf, and I will follow up with him within the next week or so.

### The Closing

The final paragraph of the follow-up letter should include both a promise and a request, for example:

I'll be in touch again to let you know how my job search progresses. In the meantime, should you hear of any positions in which you think I might be interested, I would very much appreciate hearing from you.

I will let you know how my efforts to find a new position proceed. Should you, in the meantime, learn of any positions for which you think I might be appropriate, I would appreciate your letting me know.

## JOB INTERVIEW FOLLOW-UP LETTERS

It's even more important to send follow-up letters after a job interview than after a networking interview. One reason is that, since many job candidates do *not* send them, interviewers tend to more clearly remember those who do. It's always important to find a positive way to stand out in the interviewer's mind; sending a well-crafted follow-up letter is a excellent way to do that.

Writing a follow-up letter after a job interview also gives you an opportunity to remind the interviewer of your skills and experience, as well as of their applicability to the position for which you've been interviewed.

## Sample Job Interview Follow-Up Letter

**Cecilia Arnold**
**5550 Nepperham Avenue**
**Los Angeles, CA 90233**
**206-788-8562**
**E-mail: cece@lanet.com**

March 15, 2000

Mr. Brock Peters
Braintree Publishers
1000 Sepulveda Boulevard
Los Angeles, CA 90256

Dear Mr. Peters:

I just wanted to tell you how much I enjoyed meeting you yesterday and to thank you again for spending time with me. It's clear that Braintree's plans for the future will make it an exciting and challenging place to work, and I would very much like to be a part of it.

On the basis of our conversation, I believe that my experience in the industry, my managerial experience, and my experience and interest in acquiring and developing popular reference books would enable me to make a real contribution to your organization as a publishing director. In addition, I sense that you and I share a common philosophy about publishing and that we would accordingly be able to work well together.

I understand that you are not expecting to reach a decision about the position for some time. If, however, I haven't heard from you within the next two weeks, I'll give you a call.

Sincerely yours,

Cecilia Arnold

As you'll see, there are some similarities between networking and job interview follow-up letters, but one important similarity is timing. Writing *promptly* after a job interview is essential. You have no way of knowing how quickly the interviewer is going to make a hiring decision, so you should always send a follow-up letter within 24 hours of the interview. After all, if the letter is received while the recruiter is still trying to choose a candidate, it could be the thing that tips the scales in your favor.

In certain respects, letters you send after job interviews are like the job-tailored letters you sent to request interviews. Like those letters, the job interview follow-up letter includes three elements divided into four paragraphs: the opening, the two-part pitch ("Why me?" and "Why you?"), and the closing.

### The Opening

As with the networking interview follow-up letter, the first paragraph of the job interview follow-up letter is the place to thank the reader for meeting with you, for example:

> I'm writing just to say what a pleasure it was to meet you and to thank you for taking the time to discuss with me the possibility of joining your organization.

> I'm taking this opportunity to tell you how much I enjoyed meeting you and how much I appreciate your speaking with me about the opening for an assistant manager in your department.

### The Pitch: "Why Me?"

Here is where the real difference between networking and job interview follow-up letters begins. The purpose of the networking letter is basically to thank the interviewer and remind him or her of your interest in finding a new position. By contrast, the purpose of the interview follow-up letter is to make a final argument for your candidacy. In this paragraph you should reiterate the (one or two) best points that you've already made in the interview itself as well as add (one or two) others you may have neglected to mention. A couple of examples:

> On the basis of our conversation, I believe that my experience in the industry, my managerial experience, and my agreement with the goals of your organization would enable me to make a real contribution in your company as an assistant manager. The fact that I've managed a similar operation in a smaller company should also, I think, make me a good candidate for the position.

> As we discussed, the fact that I have managed a similar operation, although in a smaller firm, has provided me with the opportunity

to learn and use the same skills that you are looking for in an assistant manager. In addition, the experience I gained in working directly with customers in my previous position would, I think, be very useful in dealing with the sometimes difficult suppliers you mentioned.

One element of my background that we didn't have time to discuss is the year I spent managing the customer database for Little Industries, my previous employer. The experience I gained in managing information technology would be directly applicable to the business reorganization project you mentioned, and I think it could help me be an effective member of the team charged with implementing it.

### The Pitch: "Why You?"

The third paragraph of the job interview follow-up letter is the appropriate place for you to discuss why you're interested in working for this particular company. Your comments should be based on both whatever you learned about the company during the interview and any information you may have gathered from other sources. If there's been any (positive) "breaking news" about the company, here is a good place to mention it.

From what you told me about your organization, it sounds like a dynamic and exciting place to work. In addition, having heard so many positive things about it from other people in the industry, I believe that it's a company in which I would not only be comfortable but also one in which I would be able to make a substantial contribution.

During our discussion I was particularly impressed with your company's ambitious goals. As we both know, ours is a particularly competitive industry, but I'm sure that with the excellent staff you mentioned you will be able to achieve those goals. On the basis of what you told me, I would very much like to be a part of that effort.

As we discussed, I'm excited about the possibility of working for Mammoth Films. I noted that two of your new releases were among the top ten box-office hits again last weekend—an impressive showing for such a young company. I hope I'll have the opportunity to help contribute to even greater achievements in the future.

### The Closing

The last paragraph of the job interview follow-up letter should be short and sweet. You've made your pitch, given it your best shot, and now you just have to wait for the interviewer to make a decision. (Well, more or less.)

Toward the end of the interview, you should have asked approximately how long the interviewer expects it will take to reach a hiring decision. Thus, you'll have at least some idea of her time frame. Bear in mind, though, that many interviewers say, "We want to move quickly on this decision," and then don't. It's not that they're lying, but, rather, that things always take longer than people expect them to.

Although it's unlikely that anything you do will make her come to a decision any sooner, it doesn't hurt to prod her a bit. So the closing of your letter might read:

> Again, I appreciate you taking the time to meet with me and look forward to hearing from you soon. If I haven't heard from you within the next few weeks, I'll give you a call to follow up.

If it's true, you can subtly suggest that you might be in demand from other employers, which could increase the sense of urgency on the recruiter's part:

> Thank you again for meeting with me. As I continue to explore other potential positions, I'll look forward to hearing from you shortly. If we haven't spoken in two weeks' time, I will call you with an update on my status and to find out how your decision-making process is progressing.

# JOB ACCEPTANCE FOLLOW-UP LETTERS

**FYI**

*Following up with a phone call to an interviewer a week or so after a meeting is acceptable, but calling him day after day is not. Not only is it un-professional, but calling frequently is likely to hurt rather than help your cause.*

While sending a follow-up letter after you've been offered and accepted a position may seem gratuitous (after all, you got the job!) it's still a good idea to do so. Because writing such a letter is both courteous and professional, it's likely to impress and please your new boss. It will help to confirm in his or her mind that they've made a good decision in hiring you, and it'll help you start your new job on a positive note.

The job acceptance follow-up letter is very different from the other types of follow-up letters we've discussed. Since you've already closed the sale, it's neither necessary nor appropriate to include any kind of sales pitch. Your letter should, however, be enthusiastic, warm, and to-the-point.

# JOB TURNDOWN FOLLOW-UP LETTERS

It's entirely possible that you'll receive job offers for positions that you're not interested in accepting. It may be that they're not paying as

## Sample Job Acceptance Follow-Up Letter

**Joshua Kriegel**
**224 Sansom Street**
**Phoenix, AZ 04405**
**602-890-8165**
**E-mail: joshk@aol.com**

February 17, 2000

Ms. Marjorie Simpson
Phoenix Power & Light
2000 Arizona Avenue
Phoenix, AZ 04412

Dear Marjorie:

I'm just writing to tell you how pleased I am that we were able to come to an agreement about my joining your staff at Phoenix Power & Light as a senior planner.

I am looking forward to working with you and helping to find efficient and cost-effective ways of meeting the challenges of the increasing need for electricity in our growing community.

I will be leaving my current position a week from now, and then taking the short vacation I mentioned prior to my starting the job on March 1st.

Sincerely yours,


Joshua Kriegel

## Sample Job Turndown Follow-Up Letter

**Sandra McGregor**
**620 Centennial Avenue**
**San Francisco, CA 90366**
**818-755-0236**
**E-mail: sandymc@sfnet.com**

June 1, 2000

Mr. Albert Decker
White Industries, Inc.
4050 Michigan Avenue
Detroit, MI 86420

Dear Mr. Decker:

I'm writing to thank you again for spending time with me to discuss your need for a market research assistant.

Although, as I told you on the phone yesterday, I am pleased and proud that you are interested in having me join your team, I have been offered and have accepted a position with another firm that I think would be a more suitable match for me at this point in my career.

I sincerely hope, however, that we may be able to work together at some time in the future. In the meantime, if I can be of any assistance to you, I hope you won't hesitate to let me know.

Yours truly,

Sandra McGregor

much money as you'd like, or that you've simultaneously received an offer from another company that you'd prefer working for, or for any number of other reasons.

Whatever the reason may be, in such a situation it's likely that you'll turn down the offer over the phone (since companies extending job offers generally need a fairly prompt response). It is still, however, advisable to write a follow-up letter, for one very good reason.

Most industries tend to be small worlds. That is, as people move from one company to another within any given industry (and they do) they get to know a lot of other people in the industry. Moreover, they tend to run into those people again and again over the years. So the chances are that you may at some time in the future find yourself being interviewed again by, or working with, a person whose offer you rejected. When that happens, it won't hurt if they remember that you turned them down in a graceful and professional manner.

## JOB REJECTION FOLLOW-UP LETTERS

*Being successful in business sometimes really is about who you know, so it's in your best interests to make an effort to stay in touch with highly placed individuals in the industry whom you've met during your job-search networking efforts. Make it your business to call your networking contacts periodically "just to catch up"; invite them for breakfast, lunch, or a cup of coffee once or twice a year; and send a quick note, a relevant clipping, or a bit of news from time to time.*

While it may seem odd to write a letter thanking someone for *not* hiring you, it's a good idea to send follow-up letters even when you *haven't* received a job offer. Hard though it may be to do, writing such letters may well bear fruit at some later date.

For example, although you may have no way of knowing it, you may have been your interviewer's second choice, and just a tad behind his or her first. (You may even have been the first choice of some people involved in the hiring decision, who were overruled by the boss.) If they have another opening in the near future, you'll probably be the first person they'll call anyway—especially if you send a gracious, professional letter thanking them for considering you for the position.

In addition, as we've already mentioned, you never know when you might run into the same interviewer again, and it could well be to your advantage if they remember that you accepted their decision with maturity and class.

A rejection follow-up letter is probably the hardest kind of letter to write. But if you can bring yourself to do it, it may have very positive results at some time in the future. Like the job acceptance follow-up letter, this one should be short, to the point, professional, and infused with as much warmth as you can manage under the circumstances.

## FOLLOW-UP LETTERS TO NETWORKING CONTACTS

It's likely that by the time you've found a new position, you will have spoken with a good number of people, both people you already knew

## Sample Job Rejection Follow-Up Letter

**Howard Seaview**
**777 Pittsburgh Avenue**
**Chicago, IL 66666**
**302-888-0050**
**E-mail: howards@aol.com**

January 17, 2000

Ms. Barbara Harris
Dillon Bank
4406 Finance Way
Evanston, IL 99755

Dear Barbara:

I am writing to thank you again for meeting with me a few weeks ago and for considering me for the position of assistant treasurer with the Dillon Bank.

Although I am of course sorry that you chose another applicant for the position, I enjoyed meeting you very much, and sincerely hope that we may be able to work together at some time in the future.

In the meantime, if I can be of any assistance to you, I hope you won't hesitate to let me know.

Sincerely yours,

Howard Seaview

## Networking Contact Follow-Up Letter

**Dorothy Arnold**
**36 Pleasant Avenue**
**Tacoma, WA 90877**
**704-654-0022**
**E-mail: dottya@ATT.com**

May 14, 2000

Mr. Howard Bean
World Communications, Inc.
666 Fifth Street
Tacoma, WA 90874

Dear Mr. Bean:

You will, I hope, remember your being kind enough to meet with me some months ago when I was in the process of seeking a position in the communications industry.

As I promised to let you know how my job search progressed, I'm writing now to tell you that I have just received and accepted an offer to become an assistant engineer with KBAL-TV here in Tacoma.

Your suggestions for who to contact were extremely helpful, and I just wanted to tell you again how much I appreciate all your help. I hope and look forward to meeting you again, and if there's ever any way I can be of help to you, please don't hesitate to ask.

Sincerely yours,

Dorothy Arnold

and those you met as a result of your networking. It's not only courteous to contact them again, especially if they either directly or indirectly led to your finding a job, it also makes good business sense. Your personal network is a lifetime career tool because keeping those connections strong and positive will pay dividends for years to come.

## JUST THE FACTS

- Networking interview follow-up letters are not only courteous but also help remind your contacts of who you are and that you're looking for a job.

- Sending a follow-up letter after a job interview may make the difference between an offer and a rejection.

- Writing a follow-up letter to someone from whom you've just accepted a job offer will help you get off to a good start on your new job.

- Follow-up letters after you've turned down a job, or been rejected, show style and professionalism and may pay long-term career dividends.

- Once you've started a new job, send follow-up letters to all your networking contacts; you never know when they may be in a position to help again in the future.

# Part VI

# *The Next Steps*

# Chapter 18

# From the Interview to the Offer

---

## *Get the Scoop On . . .*

- Preparing for an interview
- Interview dos and don'ts for making the best impression
- What to do after the interview
- The steps to take after you've heard from the interviewer
- How to negotiate the best deal possible
- The fine art of juggling multiple job offers
- What to do once you've got the job

---

S
o now all that hard work you put into creating an attractive and effective resume and cover letter has paid off: You've been invited in for an interview with one of the potential employers you contacted. Congratulations! You've impressed them sufficiently for them to want to meet with you; you've gotten your foot in the door. The last thing you want to do now is stub your toe walking in. So now is the time for you to do all you can to handle the interview to make sure you get the job offer you're hoping for.

There are essentially seven steps involved in moving from the invitation for an interview to the first day on your great new job. The first of these is preparing for the interview. This means finding out not only what you can about the company with which you'll be interviewing but also, if possible, about the individual (or individuals) who will be conducting the interview. It also means preparing yourself, psychologically and physically, to guarantee that you make the best possible first impression.

*"You've got to be the CEO of your own life, the flag bearer of your own personal brand."*
     —Tom Peters, bestselling business author

The second step is the interview itself. There are lots of dos and don'ts you should know about interviewing, and we'll provide you not only with the basic information you need but also with a few extra tips we've learned to really help you shine.

The third step concerns what you should do after the interview is over. No, you don't just go home and wait for the phone to ring. How you follow up after an interview can make the difference between your getting an offer and getting a "Thanks but no thanks" letter.

The fourth step is getting the job offer. This is not a step *you* take, of course, but rather one that (hopefully) you'll find yourself having to respond to. How you respond can set the tone not only for the final step in the process but, believe it or not, for your entire future with the company.

The fifth step is negotiating the employment deal, and here the possibilities are almost, but not quite, limitless. We'll discuss some of the most common requests you might make of a potential employer, as well as those that are considered unreasonable, and suggest some basic negotiating tactics you can use.

The sixth step is having to juggle two or more job offers that you've received at around the same time. It's not a problem every job seeker encounters, but it's one everyone would like to face. We'll tell you what factors you should take into consideration in choosing among multiple offers, how to weigh them against each other, and how to make a final determination of which job would be best for you.

The seventh and final step concerns those steps you have to take once you've accepted an offer, and we'll give you some suggestions not only about how to celebrate but also about how to prepare for a great start on your new job.

# PREPARING FOR THE INTERVIEW

There are a number of important steps you should take to prepare for an interview, all of which can have an impact on whether or not you receive a job offer. These include not only gathering information about the company and the interviewer but also anticipating questions, preparing responses, practicing for the interview, and dressing appropriately.

## Showing Knowledge of the Company Impresses Interviewers

Interviewers are impressed when job applicants exhibit knowledge of the company. It's a sign to them that you're serious about working for their firm and have done your homework. The chances are that, if you are already working in the industry in which you're applying for a job, you probably already know something about the company. If not, and even if so, there are several easy ways to get more information about the organization.

First, learn the basics. Exactly what does the company do? How successful is it? How long have they been in business? How large is the organization? If you don't already know the answers to these questions, you can find this kind of information in the directories that are available for virtually every industry. Ask your local librarian for help.

**FYI**

*You may know someone who's had a bad experience with the company in which you'll be interviewing. Don't assume that the "nightmare job" was all the company's fault—and conclude that you'll never be happy there. The same company may prove to be a perfect fit for you.*

But you also want to find out *how* the company does what it does, and one of the best ways of doing that is through the network of contacts you've developed. If any of your contacts work, used to work, or know someone who works in the company, call them to see what they can tell you about how the organization operates. Ask such questions as:

- How formal or informal is the company's style?

- How do decisions get made?

- How open is the communication process?

- Is the atmosphere very intense or rather laid-back?

- How do older and younger employees interact? Are women, minority-group members, and the differently abled treated with equal respect?

- How do employees develop and hone their skills? Is there a formal or informal training or mentoring program?

- What accomplishments or qualities does the company pride itself on? In what areas does the company need improvement?

- How good is company morale?

### Tactfully Exhibiting Knowledge about the Interviewer Can Work to Your Advantage

Knowing something about the person who'll be interviewing you can also be advantageous. Your networking contacts may be the best source of this kind of information as well. You should ask your contacts what kind of person the interviewer is, how long he or she has worked for the company, where he or she worked before, and whether there are any things that they know he or she particularly likes or dislikes.

Armed with this kind of information, you can ask tactfully probing questions such as:

I know you worked at the May Company before you came here. How is this place different from that one?

I understand that you helped launch a new product last year that was one of the most successful in the company's history. Is there another new launch in the works now?

I've heard that your former boss was Mr. B., now the president of a rival company. What did you learn about the business while working for him?

But you have to be careful here. Although the information you will solicit should concern only the interviewer's *professional* life, it's possible that you may also learn something personal in the course of your information gathering. Don't allude to anything you've heard that's not strictly business-related. So if you should learn, for example, that the interviewer once had an affair with a coworker that resulted in the breakup of his marriage, it's definitely not a good idea to mention it. In other words, use discretion.

## Anticipating Questions Will Enable You to Provide Better Responses

It's always a good idea to anticipate what will come up in any kind of business meeting, but especially so when preparing for an interview. You've probably been on some job interviews before, either for summer jobs or other full-time positions, so you may already have a good idea of the kind of questions that you're likely to be asked.

Here's a helpful exercise. Spend an hour listing (on paper) a dozen questions you think an interviewer may toss your way and improvise answers to each. You may want to jot down some notes (just a few words or phrases) to remind yourself of important points you'll want to use in response to each of these likely questions. Don't memorize a prepared answer; it'll sound canned, making you seem slightly phony. But the time spent thinking through the questions *before* the actual interview will help you feel and appear more prepared and poised when the real meeting takes place.

It would also be a good idea to look over your resume again to see if there are any questions that are likely to come up about your past work experiences. If, for example, you've switched careers and/or industries, it's likely that you'll be asked about it, and you should be prepared to explain why you did so. Identify potential problem areas in your resume—employment gaps, unusually short tenure at a particular job, backward steps on the career ladder, and so on—and be prepared with brief, honest, and nondefensive explanations.

## Practice Makes Perfect (or Close to It)

*"There are people who interview extremely well and perform poorly. But the reverse is also true. There are lots of people who interview terribly but have done a great job."*
—Paul W. Barada, President, Barada Associates, Inc.

If you've never been through a job interview before, and even if you have, it's an excellent idea to go through a rehearsal interview. Prepare a script for your "interviewer," and ask a member of your family or a friend to play the role for you. Doing so will enable you to work on your answers in a relaxed environment and with someone who has your best interests at heart to provide you with genuinely constructive criticism.

If you have a video camera, you can even tape the interview rehearsal so you can review it later. Seeing yourself on videotape can be a somewhat disorienting, and sometimes eye opening, experience that will provide you with a much better sense of how you come across to others. An honest evaluation of how you look and sound on tape will enable you to be aware of (and avoid) any behaviors that might work to your disadvantage in a real interview: a nervous laugh, awkward and unnecessary gestures, a tendency to ramble, or whatever.

It's essential to have at least one rehearsal interview, but several rehearsals would be even better. If you have more than one rehearsal, you'll probably find that you get better and better with each one, which will provide you with the confidence you'll need when it comes to the real thing.

Rehearsing will also give you an advantage over your competition, particularly if you've never been through an interview for a job before. Most people don't rehearse their interviewing skills, so if you do, the chances are that you'll come across to the interviewer noticeably better than most of the other candidates for the position.

## Clothes Make the Man—Or the Woman

We all know that the way you dress for an interview doesn't necessarily reflect the type of employee you'll be. For this reason, judging a job candidate by his or her dress is somewhat unfair. Nonetheless, the person interviewing you may feel strongly that the clothes you choose reflect your personality, judgment, and character. Furthermore, our reactions to people are always influenced, whether consciously or unconsciously, by irrational factors—including appearance. For these reasons, it's essential that you dress appropriately for any interview.

For men, generally speaking, this means traditional business dress: a suit, or slacks and sport coat, and a tie. While there are some industries in which this type of dress is neither customary nor necessary in the workplace (the film industry, for example), it's still a good idea to dress up for an interview. Look at it this way: Wearing standard business attire can't hurt your chances, but not doing so may. Why take any needless risk?

Be reasonably conservative in your choices of colors, styles, and fabrics as well. A white or pale blue dress shirt is always acceptable. A striped necktie or one with the sort of small, overall pattern called *foulard* looks attractive and pairs with almost any suit/shirt combination. And pick a suit in a dark, conservative shade of gray or blue, either plain or with a subdued stripe to pull the business look together.

Also consider visiting your barber or stylist if your hair has become a little shaggy or unkempt. Longer hair may be appropriate in college, but hair down to your shoulders isn't likely to impress an interviewer. Finally, if you wear a mustache or beard, you might want to think about shaving it off. Facial hair is acceptable in certain industries (communications companies come to mind) but it's rare to see anyone in a bank,

### FYI

*If you don't already have appropriate interview clothes, invest in a couple of outfits. Two or three sets of clothes will be sufficient, but you might be able to get away with just one if you remember to keep it clean and pressed.*

for example, with a beard. At the very least, trim facial hair so that it's extremely neat and "professional" in appearance.

For women, appropriate dress means a two-piece business suit, a dress, or a skirt with a blouse, and low-heeled shoes. It's not necessary to be overly conservative (the '80s "power suit" look has given way to a broader array of options) but if you wear loud colors, a dress with a particularly bold design, or otherwise inappropriate clothing, the interviewer may be more likely to remember what you wore than what you said. And that isn't what you want.

Don't wear more than one or two simple pieces of jewelry—modest-sized earrings and a plain gold bangle, for example. And your makeup and hairstyle should be unobtrusive, attractive, but not particularly alluring. Carry both a small purse for your personal items and a briefcase or portfolio for business papers—extra copies of your resume, for example.

If you're still not sure of how to dress, call the company's human resources department and ask them. You don't even have to give them your name. You can just say that you're scheduled for an interview with the company and would like to know what the appropriate dress would be.

Finally, although you should already know that your clothes should be neat and clean, you might also want to pay special attention to the condition of your shoes. It may seem odd, but some interviewers scrutinize an applicant's shoes, so you should make sure that they're polished and free of holes.

## HOW TO SHINE IN AN INTERVIEW

There are several dos and don'ts to remember when going into an interview, but before we even mention those, there's one very important point you should bear in mind.

While it was your credentials, as outlined in your resume, that earned you the interview, it's the interview that's going to earn you the job. And the fact is that, impressive as your credentials may be, there are probably a good number of people with similar credentials who could do the job as well as you. (Maybe not *quite* as well.) The interview is your opportunity to distinguish yourself from your equally qualified competition—to stand out by impressing the interviewer.

"So how," you ask, "do I impress an interviewer?" You do it largely by projecting a *positive attitude*. This means appearing appropriately confident and self-assured (although never too much of either). It also means making it clear to the interviewer that you want to do your best, that you will do whatever it takes to get the job done, and that you'll be able to handle yourself in any situation that's likely to come up on the job.

You can present this image by using positive language, talking about trying to do your best, and using examples from your past to show your willingness to put out that extra effort to get something done. You can also present this image by obeying the following dos and don'ts.

**Do . . .**

- Shake hands with a firm grip when first meeting the interviewer. A floppy handshake doesn't impress anyone.

- Speak distinctly in a normal conversational tone. If you slur your words, you may not be understood, and if you speak too softly or too loudly it may make the interviewer uncomfortable.

- Stick to the point in your responses to questions, and stop talking once you've finished your answers. (If the resulting silence makes you uncomfortable, try asking, "Have I answered your question?")

- Try to make the interview as much of a *conversation* as possible by asking as well as answering questions. Doing so will make both you and the interviewer more comfortable.

- Ask about the job and its responsibilities. This will better enable you to show how your skills match the job's requirements.

- Make eye contact with the interviewer. If you don't, it may suggest that you lack self-confidence or, worse, that you're not telling the truth.

- Stand and sit up tall. Stand up straight and, when seated, sit so your upper body is straight but not rigid.

- Keep your distance. Remember that some people need more personal space than others, and if you stand or sit too close to an interviewer you may make him or her nervous.

- Be natural. It's normal to be at least a little nervous in an interview, but relax and be yourself as much as possible.

- Toward the end of the interview, ask the interviewer how long he or she expects it will take to reach a hiring decision. Nothing you can do is likely to make the interviewer come to a decision sooner, but at least you'll have an idea of when you might expect to hear from him or her.

- Let the interviewer know that you're interested in the job then the interview is over. Hiring managers will tell you that the distinguishing feature that wins a job offer for one candidate rather than another is often not a particular skill or type of experience but sheer *enthusiasm for the job*. If you feel it, show it!

## Don't . . .

- Talk much about personal matters. Remember that this is a *job* interview, so it's essential that you project a professional image. After a little "ice-breaking" chat, which may involve a personal reference or two ("What a beautiful picture of the beach in Nantucket. I'm fond of the island myself"), get down to business.

- Discuss politics, religion, or other potentially volatile subjects. Even if the interviewer agrees with something you say on one of these subjects, it probably won't help you get the job. And if he or she disagrees, it might hurt.

- Make elaborate gestures with your hands or arms. It may put off some interviewers. Make sure whatever gestures you make are natural and appropriate.

- Criticize your current boss, company, or a former employer. It's a small world, and the interviewer may be friends with your current or former employer. Anyway, complaining may raise the question in the interviewer's mind, "Is this person a chronic troublemaker?"

- Be too casual. It can let an interview get off track and keep you from making the points you want to make about yourself.

- Be afraid to ask for clarification if you don't understand a question. When in doubt, try to rephrase the question to make sure that you know what the interviewer is asking before you answer: "It sounds as though you're asking me whether . . . Is that correct?"

- Discuss salary. Your aim during an interview is to convince a potential employer that you're the right person for the job. You can talk about money when they make you an offer—at which point your leverage to command a larger offer will be greater.

- Let the interviewer provoke you to anger. Some interviewers may deliberately try to create a stressful situation to see how you react under pressure, and it's essential that you stay calm.

- Forget to ask the interviewer if there's anything else he or she would like to know before you leave. This will give you an opportunity to make sure you've answered any lingering questions he or she may have.

- Overstay your welcome. Recognize when the interview is over, thank the interviewer, shake hands, and say goodbye.

There is one last point to remember when you're about to go on an interview: *The sky will not fall if you don't get the job.* If you go into an interview thinking and feeling, "I *have* to get this job," the anxiety you feel will work against you. If you come across as being desperate, the interviewer will sense it, and desperation does not breed confidence.

This doesn't mean, of course, that you shouldn't try your best during the interview. As with so much in life, it's a balancing act: showing your eagerness for the job without overdoing it. Also, try to relax as much as you can so your true personality comes through while letting the natural stress that goes with interviewing provide you with the extra energy and intensity that can help you stay focused. The more you get to practice, the easier it'll be to achieve this essential balance.

# AFTER THE INTERVIEW

There are obviously only two possible results of any job interview—either you receive a job offer or you don't. Of course, it may well take some time, several days or weeks, before you hear from the potential employer. (In fact, inconsiderate as it may seem, sometimes you may never hear back from an employer at all.) In the meantime, though, you shouldn't be sitting at home simply waiting for the phone to ring. There are several things for you to do both before and after you get that phone call.

## Evaluate Your Interview Performance

The first thing you should do after an interview is evaluate your performance. "Performance"? Absolutely! Going on a job interview is a little like auditioning for a role in a movie or a play. Like a performer, you want to impress the interviewer with your abilities, your experience, your intelligence, and your personality so that he or she can easily envision you in the role you hope to fill. Even if you impress your interviewer, you may not get the part, but if you don't, you definitely won't receive an offer.

Go back over the "dos" and "don'ts" listed above and try to remember whether you did the things you should have and didn't do those you shouldn't have. Of course, there's nothing you can do afterward about how well you performed, except for one thing, which we discuss below. But this kind of evaluation can help you to make sure you do what you should the next time you have an interview.

## Write an Interview Follow-Up Letter

The next thing you should do after an interview is write a follow-up letter as soon after the interview as possible, preferably the next day. We've already discussed the form and contents of this type of letter in Chapter 17, but it's worth discussing the reasons for writing a follow-up letter again.

The first and most obvious reason is that it's appropriate to thank the interviewer for seeing you. From an employer's point of view, interviews are something of a necessary evil; they're not something most people enjoy doing. (Believe it or not, most interviewers are as nervous as the job candidates themselves.) If for no other reason, it's simply good manners to thank the person for taking the time and effort to see you.

The second reason for writing this kind of letter is that it enables you to remind the interviewer of your skills and experience, as well as their applicability to the position. And here's where evaluating your performance during the interview can pay off. If you realize in the course of your evaluation that you neglected to make any important points during the interview, writing a follow-up letter gives you the opportunity to make them.

But the third and perhaps most important reason for writing an interview follow-up letter is that, surprisingly, many people don't do it. Bear in mind that you may have been one of a dozen people who were interviewed for a job, and it's not unusual for all those applicants to begin to blur in the interviewer's mind. Thus, it's important for you to find some way of standing out in the crowd, and writing a follow-up letter is a good way of doing that.

Let's say that of all the people interviewed for the job, the manager was most impressed with you and one other candidate. The other candidate doesn't bother to send a follow-up letter, but you do. To which of the two candidates do you think the manager is more likely to offer the position? Of course, sending a follow-up letter may not get you the job, but it may help tip the scales in your favor.

It may also be a good idea to mention in your follow-up letter some personal connection that may have come up during the interview—a shared love of baseball, for example, or a common acquaintance at the interviewer's company. Doing so will not only help the interviewer remember who you are but also help reinforce a bond between you.

## Call to Follow Up on the Interview

If you haven't heard from the interviewer by the time he expected to make a decision, it doesn't hurt to follow up with a phone call. When you call, you should explain that you're following up on the interview and wondering whether he has made a decision yet. Bear in mind, though, that things almost always take longer to do then people think they will, so don't be surprised if you're told that a decision has not yet been reached.

Because not all interviewers advise all candidates once they've made a decision, it's possible when you call that you'll be told that someone else has already been chosen for the position. If that's the case, be gracious, thank them for having interviewed you, and say that you hope you may be able to work together at some point in the future.

If, on the other hand, they tell you that they haven't made a decision yet, it's perfectly acceptable for you to ask again when they think they will and to suggest that you'll call again to follow up.

# WHAT TO DO WHEN THE CALL OR LETTER COMES

As we said before, there are two possible outcomes of an interview—either you receive an offer or you don't. Of course, if you do receive one, it's time to celebrate. Although there are still several steps to be taken before your first day of work, you're certainly entitled to give yourself a pat on the back. But even if you don't receive an offer, you're not quite finished yet.

## If You Don't Receive an Offer

The chances are that if the interviewer is courteous enough to contact everyone she interviewed and has decided on another applicant for the position, you will receive a letter rather than a phone call breaking the news. No one enjoys delivering bad news, and for many people it's easier to do so in a letter than over the phone.

If you do receive such a letter, as we mentioned in the last chapter, it's appropriate to send the interviewer a follow-up letter. We've provided a detailed discussion of a job rejection follow-up letter in Chapter 17 but, again, it's worth reviewing why you should bother to send such a letter.

> **FYI**
>
> *If an employer insists that you accept or reject his job offer immediately, beware. It may suggest a company that has difficulty attracting or keeping employees or one that treats people with little or no respect. Think long and hard before accepting a job under such circumstances.*

The main reason for doing so is that it may serve you well in the future. For all you know, you may have been the interviewer's second choice for the position (out of 20 candidates, or 50). And if the person she hired doesn't work out, or if another position opens up in the near future, having received a gracious letter from you is more likely to incline the interviewer to contact you about the next job. Moreover, because industries tend to be fairly insular, you may well run into the interviewer again, and it won't hurt if they remember you as having accepted their decision with grace and professionalism.

## If You Do Receive an Offer

Even when you do receive an offer, there are two possibilities—either you will accept it or you will turn it down.

There are several reasons why you might reject a job offer. For example, you may have received another offer that's more appealing. Or your current employer may have offered you a big raise and you've decided to stay. Or you may have decided that, upon reflection, you wouldn't be happy working for the person who interviewed you.

Whatever the reason, if you receive an offer you're not interested in accepting, you'll have to tell the interviewer. While you would in all likelihood tell the person over the phone, it's also a good idea to follow it up with a letter, which we also discussed in the previous chapter. As with the job rejection follow-up letter, and for much the same reasons, writing a letter thanking someone for offering you a job and respectfully declining it can benefit you in the future.

On the other hand, if you want to accept the offer, *don't say so immediately.* Instead, you should tell the interviewer that you appreciate the offer and are certainly interested in the position, but would like a day or two to think about it. This is a completely normal request that virtually all employers will accept. You'll agree on a day and time to speak further.

At that point, you have to start thinking about negotiating the deal. Taking a little time to get your bearings, evaluating the negotiations landscape, and setting your strategy is an essential step in preparing for a successful negotiation.

## NEGOTIATING THE DEAL

A classic story that illustrates the role of leverage in job negotiations is told about the circus (one of the world's largest, in fact) that needed to hire a new ringmaster. Ringmaster is a prestigious and important job in the world of circuses, of course, but the management of the circus was determined *not* to pay their new ringmaster a penny more than they had to.

The story goes that, after a series of auditions had narrowed the likely candidates to 10, one would-be ringmaster was selected and invited in to receive a formal job offer. When the lucky candidate arrived at the meeting, his head filled with the tough strategic tactics he planned to employ to get the best possible deal, he was presented with a contract to sign, his name already filled in at the top, reflecting the best possible deal for the circus—and the worst for him.

*"I'll make him an offer he can't refuse."*
—Don Vito Corleone, a character in The Godfather

Here's the kicker: on the desk, right beside the candidate's contract, were nine other contracts, all identical to the first—except filled in with the names of the other nine candidates. The message from management was crystal clear: If you don't sign the deal we're offering, who cares? We've got nine other people in line for the exact same deal!

You can bet he signed. That's what happens when all the leverage is on *one* side of the equation: the options for the guy on the other side shrink to virtually nothing.

Fortunately, this is not always, or even often, the case. In most job negotiations, almost every aspect of the position is negotiable to some extent, although the degree to which this is true will vary. For example, small companies are often more flexible than larger ones, which tend to have more stringent corporate policies; and more experienced, senior employees can often demand more personalized employment terms than entry-level workers.

Nevertheless, since you may have received (or hope to receive) two or more job offers, you will want to know exactly how much you can get from the company to enable you to reasonably evaluate the various offers. Even if you don't have other offers on the table, since the deal that you negotiate at this point can have an effect on the rest of your career with the company, it's a good idea to get as much as you can up front.

A basic principle of negotiating is that the seller (in this case, you) should always ask for more than he or she wants, while the buyer (in this case, the prospective employer) will almost always offer less than he or she is willing to give. Negotiation is the process whereby a fair point of compromise, usually somewhere between the two opening positions, is reached and agreed upon.

### Negotiating Salary

Salary is, obviously, one of the most important issues for you to negotiate with a prospective employer. The trick here is to get the employer to make an offer first, rather than tell them how much you're looking for. Once they've made an offer, they can only go up, but once you've set a figure, you can only go down, and you don't want to put yourself in that position.

As noted above, the employer's first offer will almost certainly be less than the company is actually willing to pay. You should, accordingly, ask for more than you expect to receive. For example, if you would realistically like to receive a salary of $60,000, and the employer offers $55,000, you can ask for $65,000, and compromise at $60,000.

Larger companies usually have salary administration systems with prescribed minimum and maximum salaries for each job. If you can't get the employer to make a specific offer, you can ask what the salary range for the position is, suggest that you'd like a figure close to the maximum salary, and negotiate from there.

With salary negotiations, as well as with other negotiations with a prospective employer, it's best not to make irrevocable decisions in the heat of the negotiation process. Even after you've gotten the best deal you think you can, it's advisable to ask for at least a day to think about it.

**FYI**

*If the employer insists on having your "salary history" as a basis for determining their salary offer, be sure to provide the maximum figure you can honestly cite. Combine base salary, any bonus or commissions, and other dollar-denominated perks, such as the value of a company car or a company contribution to your savings plan, into a single figure that you can call "total compensation." Use that number as the anchor for discussions about your future pay rather than your past base salary alone.*

### Negotiating Bonuses or Incentives

Sometimes a bonus or incentive payment is part of the compensation package. If so, you should ask the prospective employer how the bonus is determined: Is it based entirely on your own performance, on that of the department, on that of the division, on that of the company, or, as is sometimes the case, on a combination of all of these? Is a fixed formula used to determine the bonus amount, or is there a subjective element based on your employer's evaluation of your work? The more fully you understand how the bonus works, the better you'll be able to intelligently negotiate the details.

It is possible that none of the components of the incentive program will be negotiable, but it can't hurt to ask. It may be that there is some flexibility in the percentage and/or the timing of payments. Many companies are open to guarantees that would once have been almost unheard-of, particularly in today's competitive market for top employees. You may be able to negotiate a signing bonus (an immediate payment upon hiring) or a minimum figure for your first year's incentive pay.

### Negotiating Performance Reviews and Future Salary Raises

Don't assume that performance reviews are conducted on a regular basis or that raises are necessarily tied directly to performance. This is usually the case in large companies, but many smaller companies have no specific schedules for performance reviews.

This is the time for you to negotiate with the prospective employer for a specific timetable for such reviews as well as to find out what the range of raises usually is. This may be an important aspect of the job for you, and if you've received another offer, the frequency of reviews and size of raises may tip the balance.

### Negotiating Benefits and Perks

Most large companies, and many smaller ones, have a standard employee benefits package, and you should certainly ask what this package includes. Don't assume, however, that you *must* accept the standard package, as there may be aspects of it that are negotiable, particularly in smaller organizations or for positions at the middle-management level or above.

For example, it may be important for you to be able to have your spouse or children covered under the company's medical insurance. You may know that one of your kids needs braces and will accordingly want to have a dental plan with generous orthodontia benefits. It's possible that the company never offers such coverage, but if it does, particularly if it's important to you, that's something you may be able to negotiate for.

*While you should be able to expect the prospective employer to be reasonable, it's essential that you be reasonable as well. You'll probably be able to sense when your employer has genuinely reached his negotiating limit. If you really want the job, stop pushing at that point.*

Depending on the industry, the company, the type of job, and the level of the job in the organization, a company may offer numerous perquisites ("perks"), and you'll want to know about all of these as well so that you can focus on those that are most important to you. The following list includes some of the perks to be considered and possibly negotiated:

- Annual physical examinations
- Athletic club memberships
- Bonuses
- Company car/gas allowances
- Country club memberships
- Disability plan/insurance
- Executive dining room privileges
- Expense accounts
- Life insurance
- Matching investment programs
- Medical/dental insurance
- Parental leave
- Pensions
- Profit sharing
- Sales commissions
- Severance pay/outplacement services
- Signing bonuses
- Stock options
- Tax/legal/investment counseling
- Vacations

Some of these may, of course, be inappropriate for a particular job. If you've been offered an entry-level job, for example, most of these perks wouldn't be available to you. Ask others who work in the company or in the same industry to get a sense of what's customary, and use your good judgment in determining which perks would be appropriate.

# JUGGLING OFFERS

Sometimes you're fortunate enough to have offers for more than one position at the same time. It's an enviable position to be in. However, it will require you to juggle the offers skillfully until you've made a final choice.

Most potential employers will be reasonable about giving you some time to decide whether or not to accept an offer. Giving you a few days, or even a week, is unlikely to be considered a problem by someone who's decided they'd like you to work for them. And, you can use this time to negotiate the best deals you can from the various individuals who have made you offers.

During your negotiations, in fact, you'll want to tell each of those who have made you an offer that you are also considering other offers. Knowing that other companies are vying for your services will only serve to make you more attractive to them and consequently make them more likely to accede to your requests during the negotiations.

You may even be able to use a single offer as leverage for obtaining others. Suppose you've had good interviews at three companies, all of which promise decisions within a week or so. If Company A calls on Monday with a job offer, you can ask for a few days to consider it, then phone Companies B and C with the news that another offer has come through but that you'd really like the chance to weigh their best offers as well. If the decision-makers at Companies B and C are already leaning toward some *other* candidate, it's unlikely that they'll change their mind just because you're being wooed elsewhere. But if you are at or near the top of their list, they may well say, "Someone else is after her—let's move fast to grab her before it's too late." A quicker positive decision may result.

Eventually, and probably sooner rather than later, you will have to decide which offer is the best. There are several factors to take into consideration and a number of questions you'll have to ask yourself.

## Questions About the Company

- Is the company in a growing industry or one that's stagnant?

- What kind of reputation does the company have?

- What have you heard about what it's like to work there?

- Do you know anyone who works there who has good and/or bad things to say about it?

- Will you be able to get to work easily, or will it require a long and/or difficult commute?

- Does the company produce a product or service with which you would be proud to be associated?

## Questions About the Job

- If you've received offers for more than one type of job, which job seems like a better fit for your personality?

- How great is the opportunity for promotions in this position?

- Is the job something you think you'd like to do for a long time, or would you have to start looking for another job in the not-too-distant future?

- Are there aspects of the job that you don't find appealing and that might cause problems down the line?

### Questions About the Supervisor

- Did you like the person you'd be working for when you had the interview?

- Is he someone you think you would be able to work with?

- Is there anything about the person that you think might cause personality conflicts between you?

- Do you have serious philosophical differences that might cause problems in the future?

### Questions About the Offer

- How does the offer you've received from this company differ from the others?

- Is the salary higher?

- Are there more or fewer benefits offered by the company?

- Does it offer the benefits you consider most important?

- Will the lack of any given benefit cause any kind of financial or other difficulties for you?

### Making a Decision

In making a decision about which offer to accept, it's important that you take all of these factors into consideration. It's also important, however, that you weigh the importance of each factor. For example, if you're a single woman, all other things being equal, a company that offers more money but does not provide medical coverage for dependents might be more attractive to you than a company that offers such coverage but will pay less. On the other hand, if you're a single parent, the opposite trade-off may be preferable.

Your age and station in life are also things you should consider in deciding which offer to accept. If, for example, you're an older person expecting to retire within the next decade and you're relatively unconcerned about advancement, a company with a good pension plan might be most attractive to you. Conversely, if you're a young person just starting out in business, a company offering a lower starting salary but with plausible opportunities for future advancement might be more to your liking.

Thus, it's important that you evaluate all these factors in making your decision. Of course, if for one reason or another the job doesn't work out, you can always start looking for another position. Having just gone through this exercise though, you probably won't want to do it again for a while.

One final factor to weigh is your current job. You might want to consider using an offer or offers you've received to improve your current situation. If you are a valued employee in your present position, it's likely that your employer will not be happy about losing you, and this is something you can use to your advantage.

After you've negotiated the best deal you can from a prospective employer, and before accepting their offer, you can advise your present supervisor that you've received an offer from another company. You can tell him or her, if it's true, that the other offer is very attractive and that you're tempted to take it, but that you would stay if your current employers is willing to make staying equally attractive.

Of course, your current supervisor may simply say, "Good-bye and good luck." On the other hand, if you really are considered a valuable employee, your supervisor may well ask you to give him or her a few days to come up with a counter-offer.

One strategic point to be aware of: You can use the tactic of leveraging a better deal on your current job through an outside offer only *once*. Accepting your company's counter-offer as an inducement to stay means making a tacit commitment to the company. If you try to go back to the same employer a year later saying, "Well, I've received another outside offer, can you up the ante again?" you'll begin to appear opportunistic and slightly disloyal. Of course, you're not locked into a lifetime job, but the next time you're pursued by another company, you'll need to either "fish or cut bait"—accept the outside offer or simply reject it.

### FYI

*If you haven't actually received another offer, don't even think about approaching your current supervisor claiming that you have. Doing so might result in a counter-offer, but it could also result in your finding yourself out of work.*

## YOU'VE GOT THE JOB—NOW WHAT?

So now you've made a decision and accepted an offer. What you do next will depend on your current situation.

If you don't currently have a job, it's time for you to celebrate in whatever way you think most appropriate. Some people take themselves out to dinner, some buy themselves a present—something they've wanted for a long time but couldn't quite bring themselves to buy. However you choose to celebrate, you should certainly give yourself a good pat on the back. You've successfully navigated one of the more difficult passages of your professional life, and you deserve congratulations.

At this point, as we mentioned in the previous chapter, it's also a good idea to write a letter to your new employer formally accepting the offer.

Writing such a letter is both courteous and professional and will probably not only please and impress your new boss but also reinforce in his mind that hiring you was a good decision.

If you currently have a job, you'll have to give your current employer notice. Two weeks' notice is generally considered appropriate and will give you enough time to clear out your office, say your goodbyes, and bring your supervisor up-to-date on your current projects.

Even if your current supervisor is clearly unhappy about your leaving, it's very important that you behave in a professional manner during the brief time you remain with your former company. This means cooperating to the fullest extent in providing your supervisor with whatever information he may request and whatever help in the transition you can reasonably provide. Remember again that it's a small world; you may find yourself being considered for a job by the same individual at some time in the future. And, if so, you'll want to be remembered as someone who handled a tricky process professionally.

You may also be asked by your supervisor to write a formal letter of resignation. If so, keep it short and sweet, simply stating that you are resigning your position effective as of whatever date you've determined. You might also want to add that you've enjoyed working for the company, that you learned a lot during your time there, or any other pleasant parting remarks you can offer. This parting letter is no place for settling scores, complaining about any unfairness you feel you suffered, or gloating about the fact that you're leaving. The letter will probably be placed in your file in the Human Resources Department, and you'll never know who might see it in the future. Why burn a bridge you may someday want to recross?

### And What About That Great Resume?

Finally, don't toss your successful resume into the recycling bin—carefully file it for the next time (there will almost certainly be one). Keeping your resume handy and up-to-date at all times is a basic career strategy for the fast-paced, ever-changing business world of the new millennium.

# JUST THE FACTS

- Properly preparing for an interview can mean the difference between getting a great job offer and going home empty-handed.

- It's important during an interview to not only avoid negative and accentuate positive behaviors but to impress the interviewer with your energetic, enthusiastic attitude.

- Keeping in touch after an interview and evaluating your performance can help you hone your interview skills to land this job and others in the future.

- Negotiate with care once you've received an offer to get more of what you want now and set the right tone for your future with the company.

- If you're fortunate enough to receive more than one job offer, evaluate all the elements of each offer so as to make the wisest possible decision for your future.

- Once you've accepted an offer, it's time to celebrate!

# Part VII

# *Appendices*

# More Sample Resumes

This appendix contains 34 sample resumes, all drawn from real-life job-hunting success stories and representing job seekers with widely varying backgrounds and career histories. The resumes themselves differ greatly as well. They range in length from one to three pages and make use of various formats, styles, headings, and design elements.

No single resume is likely to be a perfect model for you—after all, your skills and background are uniquely your own. However, scanning the resumes here (as well as those in the rest of this book) is likely to give you a number of good ideas for shaping a resume that reflects your strengths and credentials in a highly attractive, powerful fashion.

## Trust and Estate Attorney—Clean, Clear, Professional

### HOWARD KATZENBACH, Esq.

630 East 44th Street
New York, New York 10067
*Phone:* (555) 555-3001 · *Fax:* (555) 555-9597

### TRUST & ESTATE ATTORNEY

*Demonstrated initiative, integrity, resourcefulness and analytical / decision making abilities combined with a capacity for work and achievement. Capable of communicating effectively with associates and clients in various disciplines and at all levels of responsibility. Effective at organizing and coordinating efforts toward the achievement of desired objectives. Strong tax background. Demonstrated capability for motivating personnel and for fostering cooperation, communication and consensus among groups.*

### PROFESSIONAL EXPERIENCE

Law Offices of Richard S. McConnell · New York, New York
**SENIOR ASSOCIATE**
1997 - Present

Handle a broad range of legal issues in this general practice firm but with personal concentration in the areas of estate administration. Exercise planning, controlling and organizing skills to set priorities for simultaneous, continuing staff operations. Counsel Public Administrator's staff in proper estate administration procedures. Recognize and define issues; analyze relevant information; encourage alternative solutions and development opportunities for a divers work force. Select, hire, and train and supervise law clerks and paralegal assistants.

- *Joined firm when it was appointed the new counsel for the Public Administrator of New York County; assisted in organizing the new office.*
- *Apply new technologies to organizational needs; create new estate tracking software systems; ensure staff is trained and capable.*

Beame, Lindsay & O'Hara · Bronx, New York
**ASSOCIATE**
1992 - 1997

Advised and counseled clients and executed administrative, accounting and reporting tasks and special projects for this firm concentrating its practice in the estate administration field, both testate and intestate. Researched and formulated estate plans; drafted wills and interviews trusts. Brought numerous wills to probate; appointed administrators in intestacy. Marshaled estate assets; prepared complex accountings and tax returns. Represented fiduciaries in tax-related matters. Pursued Surrogate's Court procedures in probate, kinship proceeding and litigation.

- *Executed estate planning, administration and litigation as primary attorney for estates ranging in value up to $6,000,000.*
- *Performed considerable work for this firm's then-major client, the Public Administrator of Bronx County, which processed 1,000 estates a year.*

**HOWARD KATZENBACH, Esq.**

**SENIOR LAW CLERK**

Researched and identified laws, judicial decisions, legal articles and related material on estate planning and administration. Drafted pleadings and motions; researched and wrote legal memoranda; prepared information and estate tax returns; drafted tax opinion letters; engaged in corporate legal matters. Conducted discovery and factual investigation of cases. Processed client intake interviews. Assisted attorneys during trials. Planned and coordinated work with others; monitored progress; evaluated outcomes. Developed insights and solutions.

- *Interviewed, hired, trained, and supervised law clerks; developed excellent rapport with business associates, professionals, clients and members of the community.*
- *Networked with, and provided information to, key groups and individuals; appropriately used negotiation, persuasion and authority in dealing with others to achieve goals.*

### EDUCATION & TRAINING

**JURIS DOCTOR,** 1992
Columbia University Law School - New York, New York
*Honors: Hansen Scholar*

**BACHELOR OF ARTS,** 1985
Hofstra University - Hempstead, New York
*Major: Psychology*

### ORGANIZATIONS & ASSOCIATIONS

Lowenstein Center for the Arts, New York, New York
*Trustee and Treasurer*

### COMPETENCIES

Admitted to the Bar
*New York 1993 · Connecticut 1994*

*Advanced Proficiency in Computers, Including Fiduciary Accounting*

REFERENCES AND FURTHER DATA AVAILABLE UPON REQUEST

## Financial Analyst—Chronological with All-Bullet Job Descriptions

Confidential Resume of
**CORINA M. LINKAS**
17 Meadow Street · Bilton, Connecticut 02974
Telephone: 555-555-0614 · Fax: 555-555-6141 · Email: cml@rpi.net

### FINANCIAL SERVICES
*Talented Financial Analyst and Research Specialist*
WITH SOLID STRENGTHS IN DOMESTIC AND INTERNATIONAL FINANCIAL
MARKET RESEARCH, TECHNICAL ANALYSIS, INFORMATION SYSTEMS,
MODELING, FORECASTING, CREATIVE REPORT DESIGN, BUSINESS
COMMUNICATIONS, HUMAN RESOURCE DEVELOPMENT AND MANAGEMENT.

### PROFILE WITH SELECTED SKILLS AND ABILITIES
*Charter Financial Analyst (CFA) Level II Candidate*
Enjoy intensive industry and company research. Adeptness within market application
includes awareness of trends and economic indicators, and an unusual ability to
anticipate future moves. Keep current with exchange, interest and inflation rates, as well
as political and competitive considerations. Measure the impact of market developments
on related sectors. Highly skilled in the use of PCs, the Internet, relational database
system design, word processors, spreadsheets, and various other software for research,
charting and technical analysis. Effectively utilize charts, statistics and computer
modeling to develop decision-making rationale and communicate up-to-the-minute
investment information. Excellent multi-industry reputation.

### PROFESSIONAL EXPERIENCE
*Vast Resource Network of Industry Professionals and Academics*

TRANSIT INTERNATIONAL- THE TRANSPORTATION FINANCE JOURNAL
Harrington, Connecticut
**FINANCIAL ANALYST / MANAGING EDITOR**
1995 - Present

- Render critical financial, technical and managerial expertise in the areas of
  domestic and global company / industry research and analysis, business
  communications and journal production.
- Utilize technical and computer analysis to provide readership with material
  enabling interpretation of market trends and predictions of future impact on
  associated sectors.
- Launched new programs and sections targeted to the investment community;
  initiate relations with industry professionals and academics, secure
  contributions and edit articles.

*Selected Highlights:*
- Enhanced annual ranking issue, reader interest and profit growth with
  financial ratios, comparison tables, and comprehensive company profiles
  offering a plethora of useful data.
- Original reports and articles facilitate rapid market analysis; offer
  recommendations for achieving substantial capital appreciation and superior
  return-to-risk performance.
- Pioneered the popular "Market Watch" section that illuminates international
  market issues and trends; as well as cross-sector and cross-company
  comparative statistics.

CHIPLINK, INC.
Eastham, New Hampshire
**INDUSTRY ANALYST**
1994 - 1995

- Led the organization in research and analysis, identifying and targeting specialized sectors, predicting future developments, structuring the foundations for future growth into new markets.
- Traced and summarized regional and national market data in original, easily understandable reports; formulated strategies and recommendations; provide counsel to senior management.

*Selected Highlights:*

- Developed cutting-edge relational databases and analytical tools, from concept to full implementation, designed and updated client databases.
- Customized an economic model to forecast rates and price moves; created a comprehensive library of documentation for all analytical functions automated.

TEKCRAFT & CO.
Minos, Greece
**ASSISTANT FINANCIAL ANALYST**
1989 - 1990

- Provided technical and financial management advisory services in the areas of international operational analysis, forecasting, export revenue variance analysis and summarization.
- Prepared financial statements, analyzed comparative financial results, submitted management reports, communicated complex financial / market concepts in a comprehensible manner.

*Selected Highlights:*

- Bridged gaps and provided support to multiple departments with innovative reporting systems displaying revenues, expenses and cash flows.
- Assessed competitive standing in the global sector; calculated market variables; observed trends and made recommendations to enhance position in the marketplace.

**EDUCATION**

**MASTER OF BUSINESS ADMINISTRATION - FINANCE AND INTERNATIONAL BUSINESS,** 1993
Adams Institute of Technology - San Francisco, California

**BACHELOR OF SCIENCE - MARINE ENGINEERING,** 1990
State University at Smyrna - Smyrna, Georgia

**PROFESSIONAL AFFILIATIONS**
Member: Connecticut Maritime Association (CMA) · Hellenic Resources Institute (HRI) · International Association of Maritime Economists (IAME)

**PERSONAL**
Enjoy: Travel · Reading · Community Involvement · Jogging and Other Outdoor Activities
Willing to relocate and perform work-related travel

## Information Manager—Impressive Profile and Use of Testimonials

*Confidential Resume of*
**CATHERINE JOHNSON**
1134 West Ingres Avenue · Mariby, New York 12985
555-555-9620

### MANAGEMENT

HIGHLY INTELLIGENT AND ACCOMPLISHED INFORMATION PROFESSIONAL WITH HIGH
LEVEL KNOWLEDGE OF CORPORATE INFORMATION CENTERS AND AN UNCANNY ABILITY
TO CUT COSTS THROUGHOUT OPERATIONS WHILE INCREASING PRODUCTIVITY.

### PROFILE

**Management Performer**
Strong planning, organizing and cooperative leadership skills. Exceptional development and management
of BIG APPLE BANK's Document Center has created an invaluable resource for all divisions and
departments. The Center has been utilized for numerous multi-million dollar deals.

**Effective Team Builder**
Developed and implemented, together with the Research Manager, a program that cross trained Document
Center and Research staff. This has streamlined functions; eliminated duplicity; and created a
knowledgeable, sophisticated and flexible work force with extraordinary high morale.

**Computer Proficiency**
Highly skilled in the use of IBM PCs and peripherals. Utilize DOS, Windows, LAN - Novell, Lotus 1-2-3,
dBase III, Nexis, Dun & Bradstreet, Dow Jones News Retrieval, Laser Disclosure, and various other
business related applications.

**IN-DEPTH KNOWLEDGE OF GOVERNMENTAL FILINGS**
Provided library staff with formal seminars on the use of SEC documents as a source of corporate
intelligence, at no cost to the company. Proficient with numerous SEC related online databases to research
corporate filings and other financial information. Thorough knowledge of numerous governmental filings
and vendors that supply required data.

**ANALYTICAL / TROUBLESHOOTER**
Established a track record for developing creative solutions that result in enhanced profits. Significantly
reduced costs for outside vendor services and Laser Disclosure use with a mass mailing to New York and
American Stock Exchanges. BIG APPLE BANK now receives filings directly. Built a bankruptcy filing
and registration statement collection, again reducing document costs.

**EXCELLENT PERFORMANCE REVIEWS**
"Catherine has played an integral role this year in developing a unified and cohesive library. Additionally,
she can be credited, despite enormous obstacles...with establishing one of the finest Document Centers in
New York. Last year she pretty much single-handedly built the foundation for the Center."

"Through her diligence and work, The Document Center has cut costs in almost every aspect of their
operation. She has addressed the pricing of documents with every vendor she deals with and has
implemented numerous procedures that have saved substantial sums of money. Moreover, she has
implemented these procedures at no sacrifice to the provision of service."

**PROFESSIONAL EXPERIENCE**

BIG APPLE BANK
New York, New York
**DOCUMENT CENTER MANAGER**
1991 - Present
- Contribute management expertise critical to organizational efficiency; assign, train, and direct Document Center and Library support staff.
- Work effectively in a management team effort to formulate strategic initiatives and in the development of the Standard Operating Procedure manual.
- Ensure high levels of knowledge through on-going staff meetings; actively promote staff participation in policy and procedure planning for the department.

ROCO USA, INC.
New York. New York
**DOCUMENTS ASSISTANT SERVICES**
1990
- Responsibilities included updating / maintaining tax, legal and business libraries; providing reference information; coordinating interlibrary loans and controlling material flow.
- Managed filing service updating; prepared and submitted statistical reports to senior management with conclusions and recommendations.
- Monitored and maintained all 10-K reports, prospectuses and various other documentation.

UNITED CITY CORP.
New York, New York
**DOCUMENTS COORDINATOR**
1986 - 1989
- Utilized extensive knowledge of computer systems and databases to obtain financial information, including corporate filings.
- Oversaw all facets of documents library LAN operations; installed and integrated software.
- Gathered statistical data; prepared and submitted reports to senior management.
- Recognized for outstanding performance with promotion from Subscription Coordinator.

**SUBSCRIPTION COORDINATOR**
- Responsible for all aspects of book and periodical requests and subscription renewals.
- Served as liaison to Accounting Dept. and publishers to troubleshoot order / payment problems.

OLIVER & STENSON, INC.
New York, New York
**LIBRARY ASSISTANT**
1981 - 1985
- Researched press releases, newspapers, magazines, and online databases; gathered and compiled historical / statistical data.
- Specialized in retrieval of highly confidential information of research librarians.
- Oversaw the interlibrary loan process.

**EDUCATION**

**BACHELOR OF ARTS**
1980
Mariby College - Mariby, New York

**PROFESSIONAL AFFILIATIONS**
Special Libraries Association
New York Librarians Caucus

REFERENCES & FURTHER DATA AVAILABLE UPON REQUEST

## Financial Analyst—Emphasis on Education

### SOPHIA ERRICO
13 West 98th Street, #7
Dallas, Texas 72041
Home: (555) 555-4539 / Voice: (555) 555-5795
Email: serrico1@bin.com

**LEARNING CREDENTIALS**

MASTER OF BUSINESS ADMINISTRATION CANDIDATE, 1999 -Present
Pawling University - Dallas, Texas
Concentration: Finance
Fulton Press Scholarship Recipient

MASTER OF BUSINESS ADMINISTRATION COURSEWORK, 1997 - 1998
Dewitt University - Reading, Kansas
Concentration: Finance / Marketing
Student Government Association - House of Delegates

**BACHELOR OF SCIENCE IN ACCOUNTING, 1995**
Murray Business College - Sun City, Missouri
Delta Mu Delta Business Honor Society

**CAREER TRACK**

Weekly Political Journal
Boston, Massachusetts
**FINANCIAL ANALYST,** ADMINISTRATIVE SERVICES, FINANCE PROJECTS
1998 - Present
- Assist in developing MBD database for American Journal Corporation directory and internal marketing: identified $10,000,000 expended to minority suppliers in analysis of accounts payable system.
- Help prepare zero-based budget for rent-related P&L through lease obligation review, historical expenditures and analysis of fixed asset system to determine depreciation expense.
- Process billing statements to American Journal Building sub-tenants, communicating functional procedures that verify accurate billing by following, as well as, implementing timely advisory services.

**INTERN** - ADMINISTRATIVE SERVICES, FINANCE
1998
- Reviewed lease obligations and proposed FASB 13 actions: assisted with reconciliation of budgeted expenditures and ensured timely accounting leasehold improvements.
- Identified required resources: planned with others: coordinated balance sheet review process and construction in progress accounts, reconciling over 35 accounts exceeding $12,000,000.
- Worked individually with department heads in verifying and auditing cost management initiatives. Surveyed operating policies, systems and procedures: assisted in all areas of functional responsibility needed.

County Insurance Corporation
Chicago, Illinois
**ACCOUNTING ASSISTANT** - ADMINISTRATIVE SERVICES
1998
- Performed assessment, accounting and audit procedures on cash accounts and subsequent events; monitored routine operations: examined invoices for appropriate classification and recording.
- Researched and traced variety of financial transactions; validated 1998 budget forecasts and general ledger entries: prepared analytical illustrations for management accounts and project development.
- Conducted bank reconciliation; produced retirement plan schedules; completed and monitored payroll expenditure reports for 26 company offices in excess of $5,000,000.

Marrington College
Panama City, Florida
**FINANCIAL ANALYST** - GRANTS & CONTRACT ACCOUNTING
    1996 -1997

- Designed critical risk models; administered special diverse financial operations and assignments and management advisory services. Implemented timely and creative solutions to cost and efficiency needs. Synthesized and submitted reports.
- Identified complex reporting issues; analyzed relevant information; met deadlines; effectively managed $24,000,000 of restricted funds; served as primary contact for service grants.
- Verified and updated journal entries for A/P, general ledger, balance sheet, payroll, budgets, overhead, financial status reports and monthly close

Sun Valley Management
Sun Valley, Idaho
**PAYROLL AUDITOR** - TEAMSTERS PENSION TRUST FUND
1995 - 1996

- Performed accurate, timely, high financial review and reporting of payroll and pension trust activities of companies employing Teamster Union laborers. Provided assessment, accounting and audit procedures. Ensured compliance with trust policy and contract agreements, using GAAP and established research procedures.

**COMPETENCIES**
MS Excel / Word / PowerPoint / Access / Lotus / Qpro / Accounting Systems / Internet

## Consumer Finance Expert—Powerful Profile

*Confidential Resume of*

# PAYNE R. WASHINGTON

1874 Marist Lane
Bancroft, Oregon 88414
(555) 555-1678

## SENIOR MANAGEMENT - CONSUMER FINANCE

*Progressive leadership contributions to new business development market research & analysis, investment management, client / banking communications, project finance management, process improvement and cost control. Innovative, resourceful, and inventive with unusual ability to identify opportunities, effectuate action, 'make things happen' and consistently achieve goals and objectives. Offer multifaceted perspective with excellent understanding of today's business conditions, programs and alliances to customize and integrate state-of-the-art strategies and systems. Establish superior procedures for financial and operational control to manage and conserve resources and ensure data integrity. Excel in communicating complex financial concepts.*

### PROFESSIONAL EXPERIENCE

**SENIOR VICE PRESIDENT - OPERATIONS**      1996 - Present
Greenbriar Utilities

Combine exceptional market cognizance with a practiced business sense. Direct all regional center operations in 9 states. Utilize superior networking and communications abilities. Establish long-term alliances and relationships with other major corporations. Assist in restructuring and redirecting overall operations. Identify required resources; plan and coordinate work; monitor progress; evaluate outcomes. Review performance of new systems; document effects on processing / work flow; execute changes to achieve enhanced capability.

- *Develop and implement a $20,000,000 expense budget; instituted new collection department structure that reduced portfolio delinquency, repossessions and losses.*
- *Direct and advise approximately 170 employees.*
- *Pursue due diligence and purchase of other non-prime auto finance companies.*

**SENIOR VICE PRESIDENT**      1993 - 1996
SUPERCAR
Contributed vision, perspective and technical management expertise critical to corporate efficiency and business growth at this sub-prime auto finance company. Exercised broad and diverse responsibilities encompassing all aspects of operations, financial administration, client relations and cash management. Networked with, and provided information to, key groups and individuals; effectively use negotiation, persuasion and authority to achieve goals. Established guidelines. Developed underwriting criteria for purchasing accounts from automobile dealers.

- *Personally recruited and trained credit department and sales force; ensured effective selection, training, appraisal and recognition for staff of 30+ employees.*
- *Maintained a high level of technical knowledge in institutional investments and related instruments; kept current with developments and implications for business.*
- *Analyzed, researched and executed options; developed portfolio to $60,000,000.*

Continued

*Confidential Resume of*

## PAYNE R. WASHINGTON

**VICE PRESIDENT / NATIONAL SALES DIRECTOR**                                            1989 - 1993
**GENERAL MANAGER** - NORTHEASTERN OFFICE
THE GRANT AND LOAN FOUNDATION

Provided focused business and organizational leadership at a major regional center for this competitive national firm. Coordinated business development, fulfillment, administrative, marketing and public relations activities. Created and administered operating budget. Tasked assignments, determined realistic goals and set priorities to meet deadlines. Demonstrated adeptness within market application across the financial spectrum. Ensured staff was updated on current insurance, banking and regulatory issues, priorities, trends and special interests.

- *Recruited, trained and developed high-performing team of marketing account executives and dealer relations personnel; directed credit, collection and accounting staff; supervised 160 employees.*

- *Negotiated $1,000,000+ purchases of accounts receivable from automobile dealers throughout the U.S.*

**FINANCE MANAGER**                                                                      1988 - 1989
K-AUTO Sales Corporation                                                       Birmingham, Michigan

Marshaled strong planning, controlling and leadership skills at this #1-rated luxury car dealership on the East Coast. Spearheaded Finance & Insurance department. Set priorities for multiple, simultaneous activities to consistently meet sales financing goals, management objectives and staff performance standards. Performed fiscal management, breakeven analysis and rate calculations. Ensured staff was trained and capable.

- *Originated, negotiated, analyzed and presented auto loan and insurance options; worked closely with lenders and sales force to achieve leverage in closing each sale.*

- *Finance department achieved one of the highest profit years in history.*

**Previous position:**

SENIOR MANAGER - Michigan Municipals Corporation, Birmingham, Michigan

---

### EDUCATION & TRAINING

BUSINESS ADMINISTRATION MAJOR
Clarence College - Centerville, Michigan

**Additional courses, seminars and workshops include:**

Finance and Insurance - Greenbay Financial Advisors
Property and Casualty Agent Training

---

### PERSONAL

Willing to perform work related travel / Willing to relocate

REFERENCES AND FURTHER DATA AVAILABLE UPON REQUEST

## Training Specialist—Profile Highlights "Value Offered"

*Confidential Resume of*
# CHRISTINE DIANA LIPNICK

478 Maple Drive
Harrison, Ohio 57704-5306
*Phone:* (555) 555-1331 • *Fax:* (555) 555-0191
*Email:* cdlip@yes.com
www.WorkGroup.com/resumes/cdlip

## INSTRUCTIONAL DESIGN • TRAINING MANAGEMENT
### Dynamic Communication and Organizing Talents

*Energetic, dependable, degreed contributor with strong interpersonal skills to inspire, motivate and guide others. Innovative, resourceful and inventive. Demonstrate flexibility and teamwork in fast-paced environment. Exercise excellent delivery skills; proficient in MS Office and Lotus Notes*

### PROFILE • VALUE OFFERED

❑ **Management Skills:** Strong conceptual and organizational abilities and analytical skills. Innovative strategist, proactive decision maker, artful problem solver, and insightful change agent.

❑ **Troubleshooter:** Recognize and define complex problems; identify relevant information; demonstrate resourcefulness in implementing timely, effective, client-pleasing solutions.

❑ **Management Style:** Gain consensus; build and train sophisticated, flexible, cross-functional teams; challenge individuals and organizations to continually produce at the competitive edge.

### CAREER TRACK

### TRAINING COORDINATOR
#### 1996-PRESENT

Marshall strong planning and leadership skills to set priorities for multiple, simultaneous staff activities to consistently meet program needs and quality performance standards. Supervise provision of training services to clients from varied cultural backgrounds. Promote and propel product and service matrix. Champion quality improvement teams. Served as interim manager for Regional Center and interim Area Field Office Director.

• *Orchestrated proposal and roll-out of training for new contract in 8 states; designed, developed and delivered core curriculum training program; coordinated training of 600+ new hires.*

• *For provider representatives, offered training on cost of care and strategic network development; for Beneficiary Service Representatives, claims research training.*

• *For managers, developed 21 modules including "soft skills" in communication, coaching and interviewing; with Documentation Services, forged Administrative Assistant training.*

#### CONSULTANT
#### 1994 - 1995

Independent Resource, Inc.

Bellevue, Vermont

Contributed vision and management expertise critical to organizational efficiency and business growth for competitive healthcare service providers. Established policies, guidelines and priorities. Identified required resources; planned and coordinated with others; monitored progress; evaluated outcomes. Improved organizational efficiency and effectiveness.

• *Customized system data worksheets; developed macro template for system entry, ready reference guide for Health Care Finders.*

• *Worked in timely fashion across company levels and with outside clients / contractors.*

*Continued*

CHRISTINE DIANA LIPNICK

## ACCOUNT REPRESENTATIVE
### 1992 - 1993

Mountain View Chronicle                                                    Bellevue, Vermont

Utilized superior networking and communications abilities, consistently building strong customer relations. Developed effective marketing and presentational strategies; prospected for new accounts through client referrals and cold calls. Actively sought customer input; developed insights; provided technical information; ensured needs were met.

- *Nearly doubled revenue over initial accounts with new ads and new contracts in a 4 month period.*

**DIRECTOR, SCHOOL AGE CHILDCARE**
### 1990 - 1992

Bellevue, Vermont/ Essex County Community Education Board                   Bellevue, Vermont

Developed, marketed and delivered 8 Before-and-After School child care programs. Motivated, trained and supervised staff of 30+ part-time staff; managed budget of $100,000. Provided environment conducive to learning through active exploration and creative activities. Established excellent relations with staff, parents and children as basis for critical evaluations.

- *Provided support services and encouragement; energized collaborative efforts of schools and university for Volunteers in Public Schools program.*

**Previous positions include:**

COMMUNITY SCHOOLS COORDINATOR - Essex County Community Education Board • 1987 - 1990

---

## LEARNING CREDENTIALS

**MASTER OF SCIENCE IN PUBLIC HEALTH** 1995
St. Francis University                                                      Smithtown, Maine
*Focus: Health Care Administration • Graduate Assistant*

**BACHELOR OF ARTS IN MIDDLE EASTERN STUDIES** 1977
Brooke College                                                     Bently, New Hampshire
*Cum Laude*

---

## CERTIFICATIONS

NEEDS ASSESSMENT • INSTRUCTIONAL DESIGN
Rosencrantz Learning Services
INFORMATION MAPPING

---

## ORGANIZATIONS & ASSOCIATIONS

International Society for Performance Improvement
American Society for Training and Development

REFERENCES AND FURTHER DATA AVAILABLE UPON REQUEST

## Hospitality Manager—Resume Rich in Compelling Details

*Confidential Resume of*

# RICHARD A. DUBOIS

23 Bradley Lane, Still River, Rhode Island 03780
(555)555-4273
Email: RADUB@etco.com

### OBJECTIVE

A CREATIVE AND CHALLENGING POSITION IN THE HOSPITALITY INDUSTRY
WHERE TRAINING, HIGHLY DEVELOPED ABILITIES, INTERPERSONAL SKILLS,
AND INDUSTRY EXPERTISE WILL BE FULLY UTILIZED
TO ACHIEVE PROFITABILITY OBJECTIVES, AND LEAD TO
CAREER GROWTH AND ADVANCEMENT OPPORTUNITIES.

### PROFILE

*Over 20 years of progressive experience in the Hotel / Restaurant / Club industry. Background encompasses supervision and comprehensive knowledge of dining room operations in restaurants and hotels; food and beverage / staff management, budgetary administration. Proven skills in developing and implementing policies / procedures to create standards of excellence in customer service and enhance bottom-line profitability. Excellent communicator, fluent in German, Russian and Czech. Computer literate in several applications and Point of Sale Systems.*

### PROFESSIONAL EXPERIENCE

**GENERAL MANAGER**                                           1997 - Present
The Newport Cultural Club                            Newport, Rhode Island

Direct all aspects of daily operation within an historic 119-year-old, 500 member, club focused on the arts and letters. Provide the highest levels of quality service, productivity, and cost control with respect to budget, building maintenance, staff management, event scheduling, training, and daily hospitality offerings utilizing a main dining room, grill room, music room, library, overnight guest rooms, and several function rooms. Administer a $1,200,000 budget. Design and implement all accounting procedures. Plan club events, art openings, and weddings. Regularly change art exhibits. Ensure an excellent cuisine. Serve as member of the Executive Committee.

♦ *Significantly increased room revenues by 30% through upgrading and streamlining room reservation processes and front desk procedures.*

♦ *Oversaw a major $500,000 building renovation project.*

♦ *Brought annual budgetary figures into "the black" by reducing expenses in all operational areas including the purchase of goods, insurance premiums, and maintenance expenses.*

**CLUBHOUSE MANAGER, FOOD / BEVERAGE DIRECTOR**                    1994 - 1997
Marion Sailing Club                                 Port Marion, Rhode Island

Specialized and key responsibilities for the overall profit and loss performance of this $3,100,000 gross dollar volume member-owned club with $860,000 in annual food sales, $340,000 in annual beverage sales. Planned, directed and supervised all aspects of the food and beverage operation of the formal dining room, grill room, special function rooms, two bars, pool snack bar and 10th tee snack bar. Controlled and administered operating budget for labor, overhead and equipment purchases; oversaw cash operations and accounting, payroll and general ledger maintenance. Established highest possible quality customer service and performance standards.

♦ *Dedicated worker, committed to an ideal of quality; combined resourcefulness with initiative and a drive for success. Coordinated work effectively with exceptional time management skills to create successful well-run club operation.*

♦ *Established, continued and maintained excellent relationship with members, staff and guests in defined tradition of this nearly 100-year old club.*

Continued

**RICHARD A. DUBOIS**

♦ *Successfully and actively marketed club facilities to 650 members and guests.*

♦ *Selected and implemented Point of Sale System to streamline operations, improve accountability, and increase efficiency.*

♦ *Established tableside service in the formal dining room of the club. Designed and installed service bar.*

**ASSISTANT GENERAL MANAGER** 1990 - 1994
Night Star Restaurant Billerica, Delaware

Member of the Executive Committee for this exclusive club and restaurant seating 300 guests with an annual food and beverage sales volume of $4,700,000. Assisted the General Manager with all aspects of operations, marketing, promotions, menu planning and wine selection. Responsible for staffing, including hiring, training and scheduling of two maitre'd and a staff of 60. Oversaw cost control and budgetary objectives.

♦ *Monitored wine and liquor costs to achieve a 1.5% reduction in liquor cost and a $2.5% reduction in wine cost, while continuing to maintain selection and quality.*

♦ *Developed and implemented the formation of full menus and modifications analyzing seasonal food selections, labor costs and profitability.*

**RESTAURANT MANAGER** 1989 - 1990
Newport Square Hotel / Restaurant and Bar Newport, Rhode Island

Directed all operations for the 120-seat full service restaurant and 110-capacity bar with lounge of Newport's luxury Grand Dame hotel. Managed a staff of 50; maintained full budgetary responsibility.

**RESTAURANT MANAGER** 1987 - 1989
Gourmands & Epicureans Salem, Rhode Island

Responsible for inventory control, profit and loss, monthly and yearly reports for this gourmet dining room and function facility. Performed all opening and closing procedures. Hired and scheduled 60 employees.

**CAPTAIN** 1984 - 1987
Harbour Hotel / S & S Restaurant Lawrence Harbor, Rhode Island

Oversaw team of waiters providing tableside service for busy formal restaurant serving hotel and local clientele.

**RESTAURANT MANAGER / MAITRE'D** 1982 - 1983
Hotel Edelweiss Hamburg, Germany

Responsible for banquets, including parties during ski championships, and weddings in this Five Stars Hotel in the German Alps providing French service in an elegant 150-seat restaurant.

## EDUCATION & TRAINING

**BACHELOR OF SCIENCE IN HOTEL BUSINESS MANAGEMENT,** 1978
Vianve Hospitality and Business College - Paris, France
*Major: Hotel and Restaurant Management*

**Additional courses, seminars and workshops include:**
Paris Culinary Arts Institute , Paris, France- *Hotel and Restaurant Service, 1974*
Nice, France- *French Service, 1979*

Harbour Hotel Corporation - Lawrence Harbor, Rhode Island
*Management Program, 1987*

Night Star Restaurant- Billerica, Delaware
*Micros and Remanco Computer Restaurant Systems, 1992*

**ORGANIZATIONS & ASSOCIATIONS**
Member, CMAA

## Systems Manager—Competencies Highlighted

*Confidential Resume of*

# HOWARD SCHLIECHTING

89 Branch Road • Stoneham, Illinois 51195
(555) 555-6920
*Email:* hs1@tvone.net *or* hschliect@realgroup.com
www.realgroup.com/resumes/hschliect.htm

## SYSTEMS INTEGRATOR / COMPUTER SPECIALIST

**Turning Demand into Growth, Technology into Value, Competition
into Opportunity, Local Presence into Global Reach**

*Proven leadership contributions to technology planning and computer assisted management. Energetic and dependable facilitator with highly developed communications abilities, interpersonal and computer skills and years of training experience to empower others. Innovative, resourceful and inventive. Identify opportunities and consistently achieve objectives. Offer excellent understanding of today's options to customize and integrate state-of-the-art strategies and systems. Possibility thinker with persistent initiative and enthusiastic commitment.*

### COMPETENCIES

NT Server (3.x, 4.x) • Novell (3.x, 4.x) • Oracle v7.x • MS-SQL • Windows 95, 98
TCP/IP • OTG (Optical Software) • Optical Jukeboxes

### CAREER TRACK

**SYSTEMS INTEGRATION / COMPUTER SERVICES**
1997 - Present
GKB Network Services      Rain Valley, New Mexico

Contribute vision, plans and knowledge of systems integration critical to client success and business growth. Recent projects include backup and recovery procedures for NT-based Oracle database, and design and delivery of an SAP-output management solution. Employ needs analysis, 3rd party hardware and software evaluation as well as systems integration and testing. Utilize QMASTER print management NT, Oracle and Optical storage.

- *Achieve recognition for extensive, leading-edge knowledge, troubleshooting acumen, systems maintenance expertise, and ability to extract optimum performance within budget.*

- *Designed and installed client server application implementations and SQL databases for such clientele as Remca Corporation, U.S. Trust and Davidson Puskin & Lyette.*

**MANAGER - INTEGRATION SERVICES**
1997
Jacoby Unlimited      Santa Fe, New Mexico

Provided leadership in areas of creativity, technical expertise, quality assurance and project management in development of right-sized system solutions featuring Filemark's COLD and IMAGING product SMARTi. Actively sought prospect and customer input. Researched and analyzed new and emerging technologies with diverse applications. Developed insights and solutions. Collaborated with Sales department to ensure HW & SW needs were met.

- *Responded to customer needs for capacity planning and scheduled implementation; exercised sensitivity to cost, efficiency and deadlines.*

- *Planned and completed work on various LAN-related technology projects including NT-based Optical storage system conversion - migration to new system.*

Continued

### SENIOR INTEGRATION ENGINEER
1996 - 1997
National Technoserve Inc.            (NTI) Harpersville, Kentucky

Demonstrated strong planning, organizing and leadership skills to set priorities for multiple, simultaneous staff activities and consistently meet management objectives and quality performance standards. Designed, tested and installed Defense Logistics Agency (DLA) Documetrix Oracle 7.x databases and NT servers. Orchestrated workflow design. Provided training for customers and staff in configuration, NT, Oracle and Windows.

- *Established databases using tools such as SQL PLUS, SQLDBA, IMPORT and EXPORT; created process to start, stop, export and back up Oracle databases on NT servers.*

- Customized Documetrix SQL database creation scripts and procedures for DLA installation; performed pre-installation audits of target sites; produced plans and specifications.

### MANAGER - NETWORK SERVICES
1994 - 1996
Data Service Corporation            Frankfort, Kentucky

Propelled applications of Windows-based document storage and retrieval product SMARTi. Utilized client server, SQL Database and Optical technology. Coordinated project and reporting schedules; initiated departmental operating protocols. Configured a variety of complex applications. Provided interactive user support and technical services to clients and staff.

- Designed, developed and deployed SQL databases Oracle, Watcom and Sybase on Windows NT and Novell server platforms; explored new hardware and software offerings.

- *Provided pre- and post-sales consulting, design, implementation and troubleshooting; tested systems and ensured technical compatibility and minimal downtime.*

### NETWORK SPECIALIST
1990 - 1994
Southern Investment Management            Nashville, Tennessee
Prime Financial Services            Nashville, Tennessee

Optimized performance of company equipment. Oversaw file server maintenance, software and device installation. Established guidelines, plans and priorities. Identified required resources; monitored progress. Performed troubleshooting of network difficulties and workstation issues. Ensured adequate capacity for new users and efficient use of network resources.

- *At Fidelity, bolstered Unix environment of Sun 630 & 690, 7 Sun and 50+ Next work-stations; supported 300-node LAN with 7 subnets, 5 Novell servers and 300+ stations.*

- *At Prime, coordinated interoperability projects, in-house moves, needs definition and vendor evaluation; supported Ethernet backbone, LANs, 8 Novell servers and 150 nodes.*

**Previous positions include:**
COMMUNICATIONS TECHNICIAN - Prime Financial Services - Nashville, Tennessee • 1985 - 1990

### EDUCATIONAL CREDENTIALS

CERTIFICATE OF PROFESSIONAL ACHIEVEMENT IN COMMUNICATIONS
Southeastern University - Atlanta, Georgia

CERTIFIED NOVELL ENGINEER, 1993

**Additional courses include:**
Oracle 7.x Database Administration • Netware 4.1 Administration • NT 3.51, 4.0 Administration

REFERENCES AND FURTHER DATA AVAILABLE UPON REQUEST

## Human Resources Manager—Education Highlighted

*Confidential Resume of*

# MAREN E. WHITMAN

500 Shorecliff Road
Rye, New York 14359
(555) 555-9695

*Email:* WhitM@resource.com *or* mewhitman@JobGroup.com
www.JobGroup.com/resumes/mewhitman.htm

## HUMAN RESOURCES MANAGEMENT

### Training • Development • Presentation • Compliance

*Progressive contributions to human resource development in both academic and business environments. Innovative, resourceful and understanding. Able to identify opportunities and consistently achieve objectives. Offer multifaceted perspectives with excellent understanding of today's management conditions, programs and alliances. Develop insights and solutions; foster cooperation, communication and consensus; improve organizational effectiveness.*

### LEARNING CREDENTIALS

**MASTER OF SCIENCE IN INDUSTRIAL & LABOR RELATIONS**     1994
Brighton University / Middlesex College / CUNY     New York, New York
*Concentration: Human Resources Management*

**BACHELOR OF SCIENCE IN BUSINESS ADMINISTRATION**     1991
Brighton University / Middlesex College / CUNY     New York, New York
*Conferred Magna Cum Laude • Concentration: Human Resources Management*

### Computer Competencies
MS Office • WordPerfect • Lotus 1-2-3

### CAREER TRACK

**HUMAN RESOURCES**
1996 - Present
United Medical of Staten Island, Inc.     Freeport, New York

Establish functional excellence and integrate resources into cohesive, high performing organization. Champion positive management / staff cultural change; assist with employee relations issues to ensure integrity and accountability. Contribute to cost control through reduction in absenteeism and cross-training. Review systems, processes and internal controls.

- *Help plan, organize and direct all aspects of employee benefits, compensation and labor relations training; interpret and implement collective bargaining contracts.*

- *Process compensation and disability forms; update personnel files; generate reports on HRIS system; ensure compliance with governmental and hospital regulations and policies.*

- *Promote special functions such as employee awards and United Way campaign.*

Continued

*Confidential Resume of*

**MAREN E. WHITMAN** Page 2

### ADJUNCT LECTURER
1996 - Present

Middlesex College - CUNY          New York, New York

Plan, coordinate and implement instruction in various human resources courses including Compensation Management, Employee Relations, Personnel Management and Management Theory. Create motivational learning environment. Employ positive classroom management strategies. Demonstrate holistic curriculum design and positive reinforcement skills.

- *Develop and deliver instructional content of assigned courses; evaluate and update course content; relate desired skills to each other and to appealing real-life tasks and opportunities.*

- *Encourage appreciation of individual talents, skills and potential through cooperative learning techniques; collaborate with departmental faculty and staff colleagues.*

### REGIONAL HUMAN RESOURCES RECRUITER
1994 - 1996

KBK, Inc          Queens, New York

Pioneered new territories and spearheaded high-volume recruitment of exempt and non-exempt employees. Utilized planning, organizing and leadership skills in multiple concurrent tasks. Determined realistic goals and set priorities to meet deadlines. Achieved management objectives and quality performance standards. Ensured compliance with EEO/AA policies and procedures.

- *Promoted company at job fairs, colleges and universities and community organizations; generated newspaper advertisements; trained managers in effective recruitment methods.*

- *Facilitated orientations, administered tests, checked references, processed status changes, explained benefits; spoke quarterly on "Time Management" and "Effective Presentations."*

### WORD PROCESSING LEAD OPERATOR
1990 - 1994

Rochambeau & Higgins          Albany, New York

Contributed technical expertise encompassing all aspects of document formation for busy metropolitan legal firm. Directed and supervised activities of word processing operators. Demonstrated resourcefulness and initiative. Recognized and defined issues; analyzed relevant information; considered alternative options to solve problems.

- *Utilized knowledge of computer functions to streamline operations; performed trouble-shooting and assisted supervisor with ongoing company-wide software problems.*

- *Kept current on range of computer capabilities; applied new technologies to organizational needs; trained legal assistants in creating complicated and varied documents.*

---

### ORGANIZATIONS & ASSOCIATIONS

National Honor Society in Business Administration
Society for Human Resource Management

REFERENCES AND FURTHER DATA AVAILABLE UPON REQUEST

## Accounting Manager—Traditional Chronological Format

*Confidential Resume of*

# MICHAEL D. PARKER

137 Miner Road
Silver Springs, Colorado 87703
(555) 555-7901
Email: parkerm@linear.com

## OBJECTIVE

To obtain an upper level management position with a dynamic company
in which I can utilize and strengthen my financial, personnel and sales management abilities.

## PROFESSIONAL EXPERIENCE

NEXT CENTURY TECHNOLOGIES, INC. - Denver, Colorado
**SENIOR ACCOUNT MANAGER**        February 1998 - Present

- Developed account base within a new vertical market for corporation.
- Total project management.
- Business process review and performance benchmarking.
- Return on investment analysis, capital expenditure validation.
- Solutions development, testing and implementation.
- Establish business partner services.

GOULD SERVICES / NATIONAL BANKING CORPORATION - Denver, Colorado
**EXECUTIVE ACCOUNT MANAGER**        April 1997 - February 1998

- Responsible for identifying, cultivating and securing revenue from major institutional money managers.
- Areas of concentration: Colorado and Utah.
- Assisted with network implementation of services, as well as S.E.C. compliance.
- In just four months, became number one producer amongst peers.

COLORADO SPRINGS LEASING CO., L.P. - Colorado Springs, Colorado
**DISTRICT MANAGER**        December 1994 - March 1997

- Complete financial management of four profit centers with combined annual revenues in excess of 10 million dollars.
- Oversee all employee activities, labor union relations, O.S.H.A. issues and environmental compliance programs.
- Establish and track labor efficiency systems.
- Administer continuous improvement processes.
- Develop and implement fiscal budget and progress toward structured strategic plan.

*Continued*

*Confidential Resume of*

**MICHAEL D. PARKER** Page 2

**BRANCH MANAGER** January 1993 - December 1994

- Responsible for initiating corporate operations at four new facilities in Colorado, Utah, and Idaho.
- Personally finished in top 5th percentile amongst peers for sales results in both years of eligibility, winning numerous awards.
- Doubled branch revenues in under 24 months through new account generation and national account cultivation.
- Maintain monthly customer visitation schedule.
- Establish sales assistance program with manufacturer's representatives.

**P&P LEASING CORPORATION** - Colorado Springs, Colorado
**DISTRICT BRANCH MANAGER** September 1988 - January 1993

- Oversee five profit centers consisting of over 900 vehicles, with 64 employees.
- Duties include fiscal management, break-even analysis and rate calculation, sales coordination and implementation, receivable and payable supervision, property management, inventory control, personnel hiring and disciplinary action, insurance and regulatory awareness.

**OPERATIONS MANAGER** May 1987 - September 1988

- Daily supervision of rental operation with nine employees.
- Developed sales prospectus and marketing efforts, successfully expanding customer base and revenues.
- Worked delinquent receivable accounts.
- Designed and implemented management trainee program.
- Assisted with computer system design and prototype development allowing for automation within this division.

**EDUCATION**

**BACHELOR OF ARTS AND SCIENCES**, 1985
Colorado State University - Denver, Colorado

**MAJOR AREAS OF STUDY**

*Business Management, English, Marketing, Economics, and Public Relations*

**ACTIVITIES**

Varsity Lacrosse Team Captain
Member Big Brother and Big Sister Organization
Member Varsity Club

REFERENCES AND FURTHER DATA AVAILABLE UPON REQUEST

## Treasury Manager—Concise One-Page Resume

**HENRY DUNST**

28 Henshaw Boulevard • Bethel, Pennsylvania 49714
(555) 555-1478
email: hdunst@JobGroup.com

## TREASURY OPERATIONS

**Project Management • Process Improvement • Cost Control**

*Offer excellent understanding of today's business and banking conditions, programs and alliances to customize and integrate state-of-the-art strategies and systems. Establish superior procedures for financial and operational control to manage and conserve resources and ensure data integrity.*

### POSITIONS HELD

United Kingdom Bank Plc. Philadelphia, Pennsylvania
**OPERATIONS OFFICER -** FOREIGN EXCHANGE / FUNDS TRANSFER      1994 - Present

Provide focused leadership for staff of 4. Update Corporate mandates; authorize release of electronic Interbank and Corporate payments. Reconcile daily Foreign Exchange currency positions. Design, develop and deliver detailed monthly FX statistic and activity reports.

- *Conducted quarterly systems contingency tests; prepared for federal and internal audits; created and updated procedures manual for Operations; charted staff performance.*

**SUPERVISOR -** MONEY MARKETS / DERIVATIVE PRODUCTS      1992 - 1994

Contributed expertise critical to organizational efficiency and business growth. Maintained Money Market Cash Book position for Operations. Prepared payments for SWIFT ST200 system. Reconciled Options / Futures positions for Trading Room. Led quality performance.

- *Updated daily market rates; analyzed all derivative documentation; processed Vanilla Swaps, Swaptions, OTC Options, Currency Options, Future Rate Agreements, CMOs and High Yield Bonds.*

**CLERK -** INVESTIGATIONS / RECONCILIATION      1988 - 1992

Participated in providing accurate, high quality financial reporting services. Reconciled internal and external nostro accounts and overdraft statements. Generated spreadsheets of all accounts weekly. Matched incoming and outgoing transactions; investigated and reported discrepancies.

- *Combined resourcefulness with initiative; exercised habits of persistence and attention to detail; ensured accuracy and security of account handling, reporting and management.*

### EDUCATION

| | |
|---|---|
| COURSEWORK TOWARD BACHELOR OF SCIENCE IN MARKETING<br>Pennsylvania State University | 1990 - Present<br>Philadelphia, Pennsylvania |
| CERTIFICATE IN TRADING FOR NON-TRADERS COURSE<br>CERTIFICATE IN DATA PROCESSING - Welsh Business Institute | 1998<br>1987 |
| COURSEWORK IN BUSINESS MANAGEMENT<br>❑  Hartsdale Community College | 1982 - 1986<br>Hartsdale, Pennsylvania |

### COMPETENCIES

Lotus • Excel • WordPerfect • Word • SWIFT • DEVON • BLOOMBERG • REUTERS

## Secretary—Concise, One-Page Resume

### CECILIA K. DEMARCO
2568 Commonwealth Street
Cambridge, Massachusetts 10754
(555) 555-0174

**OBJECTIVE:** A position in administrative support which will fully utilize diversified administrative experience, including employee relations, organizational and interpersonal skills, combined with a willingness to assume greater responsibilities and challenges. Seeking a position that will utilize knowledge and understanding acquired through experience in both union and brokerage environments while offering opportunities for professional advancement and growth.

**EXPERIENCE:**
**8/90 - Present**

**BOSTON DISTRICT OFFICES  217 Mass Avenue, Boston, MA**
Administrative Assistant / Secretary

- Assist President and Vice-President with small projects, mailings, type correspondence, memos, weekly and monthly activity reports.
- Assist Secretary-Treasurer with follow-ups of membership dues reports; calculate figures for per capita reports; process and post retiree dues monies.
- Heavy telephone interfacing with membership, City Officials, City Agencies and other Union Officials; answer, screen, route calls and take detailed messages.
- Conduct follow-ups of membership status to ensure that the City's Welfare Fund monies are distributed properly for each member.
- Provide membership information; answer benefit related inquires and resolve complaints; make subsequent follow-up calls to gather / relay information as needed; meet requests; greet visitors.
- Update membership database records; provide membership counts; maintain and update membership mailing list; process new enrollments, terminations, title and department changes.
- Provide general clerical support including ordering and maintaining office supplies; filing, faxing and photocopying; open, sort and distribute mail.
- Type correspondence utilizing MS Word 7.0 and WordPerfect for Windows 6.0.

**5/89 - 5/90**

**TTY BETAMAX            300 Boylston Street, Boston, MA**
Receptionist / Office Assistant
- Assisted management with daily operations.
- Answered, screened and routed calls on active 8 line phone system.
- Met and greeted clients and visitors.
- Typed correspondence, memos and labels utilizing WordPerfect for DOS 5.1.
- Opened, sorted and distributed mail and inter-company correspondence.

**10/88 - 5/89**

**BRISTOL BROTHERS & CO.  47 Liberty Street, Boston, MA**
Money Market Clerk
- Researched and reviewed money market accounts for errors; balanced money market funds; issued debits and credits to clients accounts.
- Extensive phone contact with clientele; answered account-related inquiries and resolved complaints.

**5/88 - 9/88**

**MINUTEMAN EXCHANGE      Bay Financial Building, Boston, MA**
Volume Control Clerk
- Assisted brokers on trading floor collecting and matching tickets.

**EDUCATION**
**9/87 - 3/88**

**SUFFOLK REGIONAL COLLEGE  Concord, Massachusetts**
Courses in Accounting and Psychology

**9/83 - 5/87**

**RIDGEMONT HIGH SCHOOL  Ridgemont, Massachusetts**
Completed the required studies and additional studies in Secretarial, Bookkeeping and Italian.

**SKILLS:** Typing 50 wpm • Knowledgeable of Microsoft Word 7.0 • Light knowledge of Excel 7.0 WordPerfect for Windows 6.0 • Knowledge of Internet • Fluent in Italian

REFERENCES AVAILABLE UPON REQUEST

## Network Administrator—Military Background Deemphasized

*Confidential Resume of*
### PHILIP E. FRENCH

Sotomunju Hoje 2 Dong • 366 Kunji Hymadai Apt. 701-20 Ho
Tokyo, Japan 120-090
*Phone:* 82-2-555-9919 • *Fax:* 82-2-555-2615

## NETWORK ADMINISTRATOR

**Planning • Design • Email • Hosting • Filtering • Security • Training**

*Offer proven leadership contributions to internetworking, technology planning, diffusion of new technologies and academic computing. Energetic and dependable. Multidisciplined, innovative and resourceful. Identify opportunities, 'make things happen' and consistently achieve objectives.*

### CERTIFICATION

**Microsoft Certified Professional (MCP)**
**Microsoft Certified Professional + Internet (MCP+I)**
**Microsoft Certified System Engineer (MCSE)**

Networking Essentials - 1999
Internetworking with Microsoft TCP/IP on MS Windows NT 4.0 - 1999
Implementing and Supporting MS Internet Information Server 4.0 - 1999
Implementing and Supporting NT Server 4.0 in the Enterprise - 1999
Implementing and Supporting NT Workstation 4.0 - 1999
Implementing and Supporting NT Server 4.0 - 1999

### COMPETENCIES

Operating Systems/Server Software: MS Windows NT Server 4.0 • MS Windows NT Workstation 4.0 • MS Windows 95, 98 • MS Windows 3.0, 3.1, 3.11 • MS DOS • Internet Information Server 4 • Exchange 5. Application Software: MS Office 97, 95 • Excel 97, 95 • Access 97, 95 • PowerPoint 97, 95 • MS Outlook 97 • MS Outlook Express • MS Exchange • MS Internet Explorer 3, 4x, 5 • Front Page 97, 98 • MS Schedule + • Page Maker • HTML Hardware • Dell • Hewlett Packard • Compaq. Studying MS Exchange Server 5.5 • Proxy Server • SMS • SQL 7.0 • JavaScript • MS Visual Studio Enterprise Edition • MS Visual Basic • MS Visual C++ • MS Visual Database Tools • MS Visual FoxPro • MS Visual InterDev • MS Visual J++ • Power builder 5.

### CAREER TRACK

**WEB & LAN ADMINISTRATOR / NT SYSTEM ENGINEER**
1995 - Present
Armed Services and Ground Militia - 34th Support Group, Volunteer Program - Tokyo, Japan

Optimize performance of LAN / WAN network. Support mission critical operations. Establish guidelines and priorities; identify required resources; coordinate with others. Champion change; create a shared vision of future beneficial networking activities. Monitor progress; evaluate outcomes. Improve organizational efficiency and effectiveness.

* *Perform trouble shooting for 1,000 client computers; maintain exchange mail server; WINS server, DNS server and RAS server; foster cooperation and communication.*

* *Sustain user accounts and system security and Network monitoring; develop insight and solutions.*

Continued

PHILIP E. FRENCH

### ENGLISH PROGRAM COORDINATOR
1996 - 1998
Shoki Free University - Tokyo, Japan

Selected, trained, scheduled and supervised staff of 10 Americans and 13 Japanese to deliver English language instruction. Designed and developed online English simulation program.

- *Researched new and emerging technologies with diverse applications; set up institute—intranet with 10 computers for instructors and lab with 48 computers for students.*
- *Installed English and Korean Microsoft programs such as Windows NT 4.0, Windows 98, Office 97; tested systems and ensured technical compatibility's and minimal downtime.*

### NETWORK ADMINISTRATOR / TEACHER TRAINER
1990 - 1996
Tokyo University - Tokyo, Japan

Provided leadership in areas of creativity, technical expertise, quality assurance and project management. Interviewed and evaluated students; taught extension courses. Recruited and selected 200 Sogang Language Program (SLP) teachers for 16 institutes. Conducted monthly Teacher Training Program (TTPs). Instituted LAN connecting all SLP institutes to system.

- *Maintained English / Korean Language Institute's Intranet / Internet system; performed troubleshooting and repair of hardware, software, components and programs. Maintained RAS server.*
- *Developed recruiting system; negotiated contracts with teachers and owners, resolved contract violations; directed Bank of Korea program, The Republic of Korea Presidential Security Service and six other programs.*

### ENGLISH INSTRUCTOR
1988 - 1990
Yamagoto Group - Human Resources Center - Tokyo, Japan

Taught English to all new employees of major manufacturer. Introduced material in orderly, comprehensible and increasingly holistic manner, relating skills to each other and to appealing real-life tasks and opportunities. Encouraged appreciation of individual and group abilities.

- *Interviewed and evaluated students; planned and implemented group activities related to peer support and role modeling; develop effective teaching materials.*

**Previous positions include:**
REGIONAL COORDINATOR - Central Kansas College • 1986 - 1988
US ARMY - STAFF SERGEANT • 1975 - 1986

## EDUCATION

| | |
|---|---|
| **BACHELOR OF ARTS IN BUSINESS ADMINISTRATION** | 1988 |
| Central Kansas College | Belmont, Kansas |
| **BACHELOR OF SCIENCE IN APPLIED LINGUISTICS** | 1997 |
| Hawaii State University | Honolulu, Hawaii |

**Additional courses, seminars and workshops include:**
Networking Essentials - 1999
Internetworking with TCP/IP using Microsoft Windows NT 4.0 - 1999
Creating and Managing a Web Server using IIS 4 - 1999
Supporting Microsoft Windows NT Server 4 Enterprise Technologies - 1999
Administering Microsoft NT Server 4.0 - 1999
Supporting Microsoft NT Server 4.0 Core Technologies - 1998

REFERENCES AND FURTHER DATA AVAILABLE UPON REQUEST

## Gaming Industry Executive—Profile Highlights Accomplishments

*Confidential Resume of*

# VICTOR G. MARCIL, JR.

100 Burberry Close
Lewiston, Missouri 66023
*Home:* (555) 555-4211 • *Fax:* (555) 555-3829

## Gaming and Hospitality Executive

**Casinos • Hotels • Marketing • Convention & Leisure Sales
Riverboat Casino • Construction • International Marketing**

*Forward-thinking, results-oriented, large-scale producer. Motivational leader experienced in industry-leading operations, with demonstrated track record spearheading new business development and market expansion, generating record-level sales and profits. Insightful and decisive; innovative and creative; team builder; imaginative and resourceful. Able to marshal resources, launch and coordinate initiatives, and execute multi-faceted plans.*

### PROFILE

- **Management Skills:** Skilled in directing all Casino and Hotel Operations. Strong organizational technical and conceptual abilities. Innovative strategist, practical decision-maker, artful problem solver, insightful change agent. Initiated Slot and Table Game Casino Marketing, Convention, Leisure Sales and Convention Service departments from conception to full operation.

- **Management Style:** Gain consensus; build and train flexible, cross functional teams; Challenge individuals and organizations to continually produce the competitive edge.

- **Financial Development:** Engineered $15,000,000 (180%) EBITDA turnaround in one year; grew casino win to $95,000,000 in 18 months, a 30% increase with 35% operating profit; Increased baccarat drop $100,000,000 over 3 years; involved in $250,000,000 of Casino, Hotel and Riverboat design and construction.

- **Results-Oriented:** Developed high energy, creative, efficient management teams for Casinos, Hotels and Riverboat Casino operations; maintained over 90% hotel occupancy for 12 years.

### PROFESSIONAL EXPERIENCE

**RKO OPERATIONS**                                                    1997 - 1999
Intellitalk, Inc.                                                    St. Louis, Missouri

Involved in all aspects of strategic planning, policies, procedures, operations, purchasing, marketing, sales, customer service, quality assurance, manufacturing, production, inventory, fulfillment, vending, integration of new acquisitions and $2,500,000 office renovation.

**PRESIDENT / C.O.O.**                                              1996 - 1997
Sunset Square Casino                                                Las Vegas, Nevada

- Utilized management expertise to engineer organization efficiency and business growth with 1,650 employees to effect 180% increase in EBITDA on $60,000,000 of revenue in one year

- Oversaw Vice Presidents in Casino Operations, Marketing, Finance, Security, Surveillance, Human Resources, Food and Beverage, Housekeeping and Maintenance.

- Directed complete renovation of Sunset Square Hotel & Casino: 282 rooms, restaurant, lounge, health club and 110 table games. Launched grand opening with 1,350 employees.

**VICTOR G. MARCIL, JR.** Page 2

**PRESIDENT & C.O.O.** 1993 - 1996
Jack & Joker Riverboat Casino Riverside, Mississippi

❑ Directed all day-to-day operations in Casino, Finance, Marketing, Marine, Sales, Food and Beverage, Security, Housekeeping and Maintenance. Marshaled strong planning, organizing and leadership skills to set priorities for staff of 950 at riverboat casino and pavilion with 1,000 slots, 48 table games, 400-seat buffet, gourmet room, lounge and gift shop producing $95,000,000 in revenue.

❑ Designed and built new $26,000,000 riverboat casino increasing casino capacity **30%**.

❑ Evaluated new gaming jurisdictions and laid groundwork in Iowa, Missouri, Virginia, Indiana, Colorado, Mississippi and Louisiana.

❑ Completed comprehensive revision of internal controls and employee handbook.

**PRESIDENT & C.O.O.** 1989 - 1992
**EXECUTIVE VICE PRESIDENT** 1986 - 1989
Border Hotel & Casino Reno, Nevada

❑ Managed 15 department heads in daily operations of Strip Resort with 2,000 rooms, 125,000 sq.ft. casino, 1650 slots, 48 table games, 4 showrooms, 5 restaurants, 1,950 staff and annual revenue of $175,000,000. Championed team structure; ensured effective selection, motivation and training of management. Created and drove comprehensive budgets of $22,000,000 for Operations, $24,000,000 for Marketing and $33,000,000 for Food and Beverage that increased profit margins and financial stability and enhanced customer service. Coordinated $21,000,000 budget for Entertainment and negotiated vendor contracts. Noted for establishing tight financial controls and efficient operational procedures.

❑ Collaborated on 1,000-room hotel tower, 70,000 sq.ft. convention complex, 2 restaurants, 4 showrooms and 85,000 sq.ft. casino expansion.

❑ Instituted Slot, Table Game and International Marketing programs—grew Baccarat drop $100,000,000; extended over $80,000,000 in casino credit in six years.

❑ Developed complimentary criteria for all casino programs.

❑ Extensive international and domestic travel experience in Casino, Convention and Leisure Marketing.

**Previous positions include:**

VICE PRESIDENT - HOTEL OPERATIONS, Border Hotel & Casino • 1984 - 1986
VICE PRESIDENT - SALES & MARKETING, Border Hotel & Casino • 1979 - 1984
VICE PRESIDENT - SALES & MARKETING, Outback Hotel & Casino • 1978 - 1979

**EDUCATION**

**BACHELOR OF SCIENCE IN HOTEL ADMINISTRATION** 1975
Nevada State University at Reno Reno, Nevada

**Additional training and professional development:**

Westford Hotel Corporation - National Convention Sales Manager • 1975 - 1978
Front Office Operations - Athena Hotel and Casino - Las Vegas • 1972 - 1975
Hotel Internship Program - Grand Sphinx Hotel and Casino - Las Vegas, Nevada • 1974

REFERENCES AND FURTHER DATA AVAILABLE UPON REQUEST

## Hospitality Sales—Education Highlighted

*Confidential Resume of*

# DANIELLE M. HOLMES

685 Santa Maria Avenida, #9B
Pacific Cove, California 98975

(555) 555-8359

## HOSPITALITY SALES

**Forward-Thinking, Results-Oriented, Solution-Driven Achiever**

*Energetic and dependable contributor with strong client communication skills and years of success in the hospitality industry. Innovative, resourceful and inventive. Identify opportunities, help people and consistently achieve objectives. Offer understanding of today's business conditions, programs and alliances to customize and integrate state-of-the-art strategies and systems.*

### LEARNING CREDENTIALS

**BACHELOR OF SCIENCE - Human Resources**                         1998
Walton College                                          Columbus, Ohio
    **Major: Hotel, Restaurant and Institutional Management • *GPA in Major 3.85***
    COLLEGE MERIT SCHOLAR • BECKER SOCIETY SCHOLARSHIP RECIPIENT (4 Years)

**Study Abroad**: Winter 1998
London, England - A study of the social, cultural and geographical elements of a major metropolis

**Internship**: February - December, 1997
DOLCE VITA, COLUMBUS CULINARY CENTER, Ohio
*Intensive front and back of the house training involving rotations through 17 positions including sous chef and dining room manager. Gained solid experience in Russian, French and American styles of food service.*

**Activities**:
*Officer* - National Society in Hospitality
*Officer* - Kappa Omicron Nu (Human Resources Honor Society)
*Member* - Mortar Board Senior Honor Society
*Member* - Eta Sigma Delta (Hospitality Honor Society)

***Computer Skills***:
Desktop Publishing • Micros Restaurant Software • Lotus • WordPerfect
Microsoft Word and Excel • World Wide Web • Internet • E-mail • Fidelio Software

### CAREER TRACK

**GUEST SERVICES MANAGER-IN-DEVELOPMENT**
1998 - Present
Blue Coast Bed & Breakfast - Pacific Cove, California

Utilize communications skills and interpersonal relations to clarify and meet customer needs and cultivate continued loyalty through courteous, attentive service. Champion "Standard of the Week" and staff morale; learn effective management techniques; help encourage co-workers to perform as self-directed teams. Review Guest Services staff payroll and submit to Accounting.

*Continued*

- *Recognize and define issues and concerns; develop insights; assimilate complex information; anticipate and prevent problems; suggest alternative solutions as necessary.*
- *Analyze room rate efficiency; monitor credit report; closely monitor daily house count; attend Rooms Merchandizing meetings; assist in supervision of Night Audit.*
- *Ensure monthly report deadlines are met for Central Reservations, Market Segment and Travel Agent check registers.*
- *Manage cash handling and all aspects of Front Office computer system; oversee key control, Lost & Found, guest laundry, message and mail delivery; monitor PBX console.*

### ASSISTANT TO GENERAL MANAGER
1997 - 1998
Columbus Culinary Center

Contributed training and customer service expertise to meet retail production goals, management financial objectives and quality performance standards. Established quick rapport with co-workers and patrons. Fostered communication and cooperation. Ensured highest standards for customer service and cleanliness.

- *Tasked new staff assignments quickly and efficiently; prepared all food items sold in retail portion of restaurant; maintained attention to detail in front of the house retail activity.*

### AMBASSADOR COORDINATOR
1995 - 1998
Walton College / Office of Admissions - Columbus, Ohio

Exercised planning, organizing and leadership skills to set priorities and ensure effective recruitment, motivation, training, performance appraisal and recognition of campus tour guides. Updated training on points of interest, academic buildings, libraries and laboratories; fine arts, performing arts and athletic facilities; dining and social centers; and personal stories.

- *Directed scheduling of over 65 tour guides; worked to establish consistency in factual presentations while valuing cultural, ethnic, gender and other individual differences.*

### FRONT DESK AGENT
1996 - 1997
Bexley Hill Tavern - Columbus, Ohio

Received and sent messages; made and confirmed reservations. Answered inquiries pertaining to hotel services, guest registration, shopping, dining, entertainment and travel directions. Kept current directory of emergency services. Updated records of room availability and guest accounts. Actively solicited guest input; sought to accommodate special requests.

- *Applied new technologies to organizational needs; utilized HMS front desk computer and reservation systems.*

### STAFF / Catering Service
1994 - 1996
Walton College - Hopkins Student Union - Columbus, Ohio

Effectively organized materials, equipment, supplies, service areas and rooms scheduled for special events. Provided prompt and efficient service to guests; checked plate presentation and food temperature and quality before plates left kitchen. Served effectively with co-workers in high-pressure environments for functions with up to 300 guests.

REFERENCES AND FURTHER DATA AVAILABLE UPON REQUEST

## Accounting Manager—Traditional Format

# AARON KRAKOW

189 Florence Street • Tampa, Florida 56912
(555) 555-0845
Email: akrakow@JobGroup.com

## ACCOUNTING MANAGER

### Comprehensive Financial Record Services

*Offer contributions and direction to efficient corporate financial and records management and process improvement. Recognize and define issues; consistently achieve objectives. Persistent, reliable, detail-oriented. Implement new technologies; utilize degreed training and highly developed computer software skills. Coordinate work effectively for financial and operational control to conserve resources and ensure data integrity. Clearly communicate complex accounting concepts.*

### PREVIOUS POSITIONS

**ACCOUNTING MANAGER**                                    1996 - Present
CityCorp. Health System                                  Tampa, Florida

Spearhead planning, organization and coordination of accounting and auditing activities for affiliated companies in system. Establish guidelines and priorities; identify required resources. Compile budgets for affiliated companies. Formulate and recommend improvements to financial policy and procedure critical for managing cash flow. Assist in implementing accounting systems to execute analysis, costing and forecasting and process A/R, A/P and payroll. Perform General Ledger activity. Assist CPA firm in year-end and interim audits.

- *Supervise preparation of monthly journal entries; review invoicing and payments; analyze and reconcile balance sheet accounts; prepare monthly financial reports and supporting schedules.*

- *Produce financial statements for 3 affiliate companies; reconcile all inter-company general ledger accounts; oversee reconciliation of bank statements.*

- *Assist with new technologies to meet needs; integrated accounting system for newly acquired corporation; implemented ADL system and all acquiring and secondary systems.*

- *Maintained, updated and reviewed General Ledger.*

**STAFF ACCOUNTANT**                                      1993 - 1996
Miami Central Medical                                     Miami, Florida

Provided accurate, timely, comprehensive high quality financial reporting services. Performed assessment, accounting and audit procedures on cash accounts and subsequent events. Fulfilled diverse operational assignments and advisory services—general business planning, tax planning, budgeting. Researched, traced, analyzed and summarized investment activity. Compared and investigated expense fluctuations. Conducted year-end audit.

- *Identified complex issues; analyzed relevant information; developed insights and implemented timely solutions with enhanced sensitivity to cost and efficiency.*

- *Assisted in managing corporate assets and liabilities to ensure financial stability and maximize returns.*

- *Performed General Ledger, monthly entries and discount analysis.*

### LEARNING CREDENTIALS

**BACHELOR OF SCIENCE IN ACCOUNTING**                     1996
Keyston College                                          Jacksonville, Florida

*GPA 3.4*

### COMPETENCIES

Excel • Lotus • WordPerfect • MS Word • Quattro Pro • ADL System

REFERENCES AND FURTHER DATA AVAILABLE UPON REQUEST

## Paralegal—Concise One-Page Format

# OLIVER KAPPEL

10047 West Bale Court, Denton, NC 23076
(555) 555-5700
Email: kappelo@find.com

## PARALEGAL

*Energetic and dependable contributor with proven leadership abilities, bilingual expertise, outstanding interpersonal and computer skills, and 6+ years of proven client service experience. Offer a consistent record of success. Foster cooperation, demonstrate initiative and integrity, write with clarity, and utilize resourcefulness in conjunction with a capacity for work and achievement.*

### CAREER TRACK

**LEGAL ASSISTANT**                                   1996 - Present
Law Offices of Arthur P. Blumfeld              Winston, North Carolina

Demonstrate strong organizational abilities and bilingual communication skills in expediting a broad range of legal procedures. Research and compile precedent case information for attorney reference. Assist with analyses and the formulation of conclusions. Prepare memoranda involving definition of issues and statutes. Conduct client interviews and compile demand packages. Draft correspondence, interrogatories and answers. Preserve statements and evidentiary material in preparation for trial.

- *Attend mediation and settlement conferences; establish solid rapport with co-workers, professionals and staff; gained a reputation for relational excellence.*
- *Combine resourcefulness with initiative and a drive for success; coordinate work effectively with exceptional time management skills.*
- *Continually pursue a high level of quality in proofreading, correcting vital case data, and in the overall management of information.*

**LEGAL ASSISTANT**                                   1992 - 1996
Francis Xavier, Esq.                               Wheeling, Maryland

Duties included research, conducting client interviews, drafting correspondence and pleadings, digesting deposition transcripts, scheduling depositions and motion hearings, and trial document preparation.

### TRAINING

**PARALEGAL CERTIFICATE,** 1998
Simpson University
*Honors • Paralegal of the Year*

Simpson University, Legal Studies Institute
*Alumni Association Director / Organizer*

**ASSOCIATE DEGREE,** 1999 - Present
Carson County Community College

**Seminars:**

Settlement, Demand Packages and Technology - September 1996
Legal Writing Workshop • CLA Exam - March 2000

### RELEVANT SKILLS

Fluent in Spanish • Outstanding Communication, Drafting and Organizational Skills
Proficient in WordPerfect 7.0 • Windows 95 • Lexis-Nexis

## Administrator with Military Background

*Confidential Resume of*

# REBECCA  NELSON

5 Waverly St. • Marytown, Virginia 26012
*Home*: (555) 555-6365 • *Work*: (555) 555-2221
www.JobGroup.com/resumes/rnelson.htm
*Email*: prtygrl@netscape.net  *or*  rnelson@JobGroup.com

---

*Communications Field*

## ADMINISTRATIVE MANAGEMENT

*- four years of outstanding experience -*

PROFICIENCY IN:
**Personnel Administration / Development • Supervision
Technical Expertise • Public Sector Savvy • Troubleshooting**

*Aggressive and persuasive leader, at ease in fast-paced, high stress environments requiring critical attention to detail, and independent decision-making. Dedicated team player motivated to the highest performance standards. Characterized as insightful, analytical and inventive with proven ability to 'make things happen.' Recognized for endless initiative and competitive spirit. A team builder and staff potentializer. Innovative and multidisciplined with solid business acumen, deft influencing skills, and a proven record of success. Consistently achieve goals and objectives.*

---

### CAREER TRACK

UNITED STATES NAVY
Costa del Sol / Germany / Virginia     *1995 - Present*

**COMMUNICATIONS TECHNICIAN / SUPERVISOR**                   1998 - Present
Naval Computer Telecommunications Station                   Costa del Sol

Provide strong planning and organizing skills in the direct supervision of 4 communications specialists operating sophisticated communications equipment—voice, broadcast and satellite. Continually reveal technical proficiency and its impact in assigned areas of responsibility. Orchestrate daily operations, recognize and define issues, analyze data, and encourage solutions to resolve problems. Monitor and maintain appropriate statistics in an accurate and timely manner. Effectively cope with stress; make difficult decisions as needed.

- *Expertise in fiber optic, T-1 and T-3 links, voice, high / low speed data, packet switching networks, satellite and microwave links, and telephone communications.*

- *Exercise final authority regarding the receipt, accountability and distribution of classified and unclassified messages regarding national strategic affairs.*

- *Skilled in conducting system performance tests and providing component level troubleshooting on a variety of circuits.*

**COMMUNICATIONS TECHNICIAN**                   1996 - 1998
Naval Security Group Activity                   Naples, Italy

Demonstrated superior technical and operations expertise in utilizing state-of-the-art communications systems and equipment including mainframe and IDNX based systems, terminals, patch panels, modems, multiplexers, and communications security devices. Assured digital and analog signal quality using such test equipment as analyzers, transmission distortion test sets, and signal analysis equipment. Provided overall leadership in the areas of creativity, quality assurance, technical expertise, and operational management. Responded immediately to emergency situations working with technical support personnel to diagnose and resolve problems accurately and quickly. Facilitated interactive technical assistance to other personnel.

*Continued*

*Confidential Resume of*

**REBECCA NELSON**     Page 2

- *Managed the command materials system account, the largest first-line accounting system in the United States.*
- *Administered all facets of receipt, accountability, security, distribution and destruction of highly classified materials.*
- *Designed / developed training presentations / programs / classes on communications procedures, systems, equipment and operations.*

**BASIC / TECHNICAL TRAINING**                                                    1995 - 1996
Naval Technical Training Center                                          Clearwater, Florida

## LEARNING CREDENTIALS

**CONCENTRATION IN BUSINESS ADMINISTRATION AND MARKETING**
Maryland State A&M College - Baltimore, Maryland

**TECHNICAL TRAINING**
Naval Technical Training Center - Clearwater, Florida

*Additional Courses, Workshops, Seminars, Professional Development*:
Numerous training exercises and inspections throughout entire tour of duty

## CLEARANCES

Hold Top Secret SCI Clearance through Department of Defense

## PERSONAL

Willing to perform work-related travel / Willing to relocate
Separating from the United States Navy, November 1999

REFERENCES AND FURTHER DATA AVAILABLE UPON REQUEST

## International Business Expert with Self-Employment History

*Confidential Resume of*
# LUCY NEWMAN
PO Box 2078
Newfield, Texas 80754
(555) 555-3797 • Fax: (555) 555-3798

www.JobGroup.com/resumes/lnewman.htm
Email: LN25@flash.net *or* lnewman@JobGroup.com

## INTERNATIONAL BUSINESS DEVELOPMENT EXECUTIVE

WITH NEARLY 20 YEARS OF CORPORATE / PROJECT FINANCE, DEVELOPMENT, SALES /
MARKETING,
CONTRACT NEGOTIATIONS, TAX AND LEGAL EXPERIENCE

*Seasoned, results-driven professional with established track record for negotiating and structuring complex, multi-faceted transactions, managing multi-level projects and generating multi-million dollar profits. Recognized for unbounded creativity with cutting edge strategic methods, demonstrated multidisciplined talent in solving complex problems, skilled in mobilizing initiatives, and innovative in packaging programs. Expert negotiator with sterling reputation among lawyers, accountants, legislators and multi-cultural clients. Enthusiastic and energetic with superior strategy development and leadership skills combined with a refined business sense.*

### CAREER HISTORY

**PRESIDENT**      1983 - Present
HB Monetary Advisors, Limited      Austin, Texas

Broad, diverse and varied responsibilities encompass all facets of sales and financial administration of multi-level projects for the hospitality, gas & oil and mineral industries with multi-cultural specialization. Analyze risk management, pro-forma and infrastructure of projects; ascertain viability and feasibility; and provide advisory expertise in all areas of process improvements, maintenance, asset restructuring and utilization, contract negotiations, planning, and operations. Configure organizational structures for complex projects; recruit and manage professional teams; provide superlative customer service and support.

- *Negotiated and closed more than $375,000,000 income-producing, property transactions.*

- *Played an integral consultative role in negotiating a complex insurance anomaly resulting in a $500,000,000 income stream for 20 years.*

- *Secured more than $45,000,000 in private placement loans from securities industry and obtained $100,000,000 CD for insurance product.*

- *Expert in federal, state and local regulations; testified in R.I.C.O. matters and served as expert witness in bankruptcy cases.*

- *Absent any investment, earned client $1,000,000 in 1 week.*

- *Developed Costa Rican corporation; consulted with numerous clients including Mumford Corporation and Public Outreach Commission of Texas.*

*Continued*

*Confidential Resume of*

**LUCY NEWMAN**                                                                Page 2

**SALES MANAGER**                                                      1977 - 1980
Kristal Distributing Company / Diamond Wholesale Liquor Company          Austin, Texas

Marketing and sold product lines throughout territory with accountability for developing and motivating staff, increasing market share and penetration, brand management and pricing, purchasing, importation and logistics.

- *Parlayed sales more than 300%, maximized profits and improved organizational efficiency.*

## EDUCATION AND TRAINING

**BACHELOR OF SCIENCE**                                                          1982
Quinlan College                                                            Odessa, Texas

*Coursework included Spanish, Finance, Real Estate and Investments*

**Real Estate Broker • Mortgage Broker Exempt Status
Juris Doctorate Candidate**

COMPUTER PROFICIENCIES
Windows 95 • Microsoft Office • Internet

**Lab Technician,** 1980 - 1983 • Hummel & UT Medical Schools
Conducted research and experiments to patent cell fusion process; published results.

## INTERESTS & ACTIVITIES

Active Volunteer for
UNITED WAY • PALAMINO MUSEUM • RIVIERA ZOO • NATURE CONSERVANCY

## PERSONAL

FLUENT IN SPANISH & LATIN AMERICAN CULTURE • NATIVE AMERICAN CULTURE
WILLING TO RELOCATE

REFERENCES AND FURTHER DATA AVAILABLE UPON REQUEST

## Operations Manager with Single-Job Background

*Confidential Resume of*

# GEOFFREY MILSON

93 Powderhouse Lane, Weymouth, New Hampshire 14742
*Home*: (555) 555-2256   *Work*: (555) 555-2307
*Email*: ggm879@look.com *or* gmilson@WorkGroup.com

## OPERATIONS MANAGEMENT

**Production   Packaging   Marketing   Distribution**

*Energetic, results-oriented dedicated team player with years of proven management success. Strong conceptual and organizational abilities. Proactive decision-maker. Innovative strategist; resourceful and inventive. Able to identify opportunities, make things happen, and consistently achieve objectives. Aggressive trouble shooter; artful problem solver; insightful change agent.*

### CAREER TRACK

**PLANT MANAGER / MARKETING MANAGER**                    1995 - Present
New Hampshire Ice House - Yankee Frozen Foods            Concord, New Hampshire

Exercise strong leadership skills for 50-ton plant with 300+ customers in 25 counties. Direct and coordinate production, packaging, distribution and marketing to obtain optimum efficiency and economy of operations and maximize profits. Establish policies, guidelines and priorities. Identify required resources. Review production and sales reports. Plan with others to promote product and increase market share. Monitor progress; evaluate outcomes. Direct investigation of customer issues regarding quality, tolerances and delivered condition of products.

> *Ensure effective recruitment, selection, motivation, training, performance appraisal and recognition of staff; build flexible, cross-functional high-performing teams.*

> *As Marketing Manager, conduct market research; organize systems and procedures to increase visibility and maximize outreach, customer satisfaction and profitability.*

> *Orchestrate marketing efforts for 600+ customers served by multiple production facilities; achieved 50% sales increase in 4 years; instituted audits and cut losses 10%.*

> *Propel new products and new business; utilize persuasion, negotiation and authority to formulate beneficial agreements; plan, coordinate, time and position effective advertising.*

> *Restructured routing; reduced mileage and delivery time; increased overall efficiency.*

**Previous positions include:**

ROUTE SALESMAN   PLANT WORKER   TRUCK HELPER

### LEARNING CREDENTIALS

**CANDIDATE FOR BACHELOR OF SCIENCE IN MARKETING**        1998 - Present
Exeter Business Institute                                 Exeter, New Hampshire

**ASSOCIATE OF SCIENCE IN BUSINESS**                      1995
Piermont College                                          Atkinson, New Hampshire

REFERENCES AND FURTHER DATA AVAILABLE UPON REQUEST

## Entertainer—An Eye-Catching Design for a Creative Professional

*Confidential Resume of*
**KIP WOODLAW**
37 Manning Drive
Freeport, Delaware 35521
Residence: 555-555-0621 · Fax: 555-555-3543

**WRITING / PRODUCTION / PROGRAM DEVELOPMENT**
*Talented comedian, actor, writer and producer of variety shows, comedy nights and concerts. Experienced in all facets of program development and promotion, treatments for TV / film comedy programming, and radio campaigns. Manage creative talent, cast music videos, write and record music parodies, develop poetic satires and commercial spoofs.*

**PROFILE**

**Production & Promotion Expertise**
*Skilled Organizer, Decision-Maker, Problem-Solver*
- Managed all phases of production and promotion of variety shows, comedy concerts, a 2-year comedy night and numerous others at over 20 locations. Booked radio talent, selected appropriate advertising mediums and marketing tools, designed and produced results-getting advertisements, wrote and recorded radio spots. Booked hotel accommodations, air and ground transportation.

**MULTITALENTED PROGRAM DEVELOPER**
*Perceptive Innovator - Enjoy Experiment with New Ideas*
- Co-developed an urban radio campaign and pitched Shayna Mitchell, the featured speaker, for SIP FRESH BEVERAGES. Performed voice over work on developed spots. Develop treatments for TV and film comedy programming. Worked creatively with several comics at all levels: from premises to finish bits and formatting within repertoire. Experienced agent and manager; troubleshoot problems with quick, positive solutions.

**ENGAGING COMMUNICATION**
*Stand-up Comedian for Over 10 Years*
- Persuasive motivator, deft at directing creative talent. Lead by example, inspire with enthusiasm. Cultivate excellent relations with a host of up and coming and well-known personalities such as Jerome Wilson, Howie King and Wesley Johnson. Presented warm-up routines for sitcom and game shows including 'Annihilation'. Wrote 'Henry and Harry' on a collaborative basis with Pete Somers of 'After Hours Live'.

**ACTED IN EIGHT FEATURE FILMS**

| Title | Starring | Studio | Director |
|---|---|---|---|
| *Roundaway Girl* | Joey Libby | Apex Productions | Theo Rubin |
| *Stepdaddy* | Shawn Jett | Breakstone Pictures | Alexander King |
| *Rainbows at Sunset* | Jeffrey Boxer | Millennium Films | Bill Deluca |
| *The Spy* | Edgar Milton | This Century Films | Daniel Abrams |
| *Mystery Woman* | Kellie Fox | Square Peg Cinema | Fred Dubois |
| *Singin' Pixie* | Koby Simpson | Apogee Studios | Jermal Jones |
| *Badd Boyz* | D'Wayne Shiff | Posey Pictures | Steve Balkman |
| *Crybaby* | Sidney Fremmer | Harvey Movies | William Franz |

## Customer Service Manager—Concise One-Page Format

# KELLY BROWN

32 Oceanview Place #7A
San Diego, California 90561
(555) 555-8588

## ACCOMPLISHED MANAGER

### Business Development & Customer Service

*Talented, energetic professional with demonstrated communications talents, staff training and development acumen and direct sales skills. Resourceful, imaginative and assertive with proven persuasive presentation skills and unusual ability to maximize employee performance utilizing interpersonal dynamics. Insightful; listener; team builder and staff motivator. Seek a challenging position where training, strong organizational / sales abilities, interpersonal skills and 14 years of experience will be fully utilized and lead to career growth and advancement opportunities.*

## CAREER TRACK

**STATION MANAGER** 1989 - Present
Affordable Auto San Diego, California

Direct all aspects of daily operations for highly competitive rental operation. Marshall strong planning, organizing and leadership skills to set priorities for staff of 45 and consistently meet sales goals and quality performance standards. Merchandise vehicles utilizing effective sales techniques. Interact with customers to ensure satisfaction. Produce weekly payroll. Apply new technologies to station needs; utilize and train corporate acquisitions in system software.

♦ *Provide constant initiative and insight regarding products and services; manage up to 1,200 daily rentals (average 800); achieve sales exceeding $2,000,000 per month.*

♦ *Ensure effective staff selection, motivation, training, counseling, performance evaluation and recognition; lead regulatory awareness and compliance with company policies.*

♦ *Troubleshoot delivery and quality issues; analyze relevant information; suggest options, encourage alternative solutions; resolve matters in customer-friendly, cost-effective way.*

♦ *Monitor staff to ensure optimal efficiency of customer interviews including price quotes, options, identification, explanation of procedures, credit verification and incremental sales.*

♦ *Achieve outstanding customer satisfaction and repeat business through high operating efficiencies, reliability and quality performance.*

**DESK CLERK** 1985 - 1989
Bayside Grill and Motel Long Beach, California

♦ Rented hotel rooms, made reservations, resolved customer service issues, trained new employees.

## ADDITIONAL TRAINING

**Received - Customer Service Certificate for occupation in the travel industry**
Co-Opted Schools, Inc. - San Diego, California

*Additional courses, seminars and workshops include:*
Diversity Training Course to increase experience in varied work force demographics
Two day seminar to allow for accelerated training of new employees
Received sales training and provided training in proper modes of increasing sales revenue

REFERENCES AND FURTHER DATA AVAILABLE UPON REQUEST

## Construction Manager—Concise One-Page Resume

*Confidential Resume of*
# ROBERT Mc CLOUD

24 Borley Lane
Savon, Louisiana 30752
*Phone:* (555) 555-9164  *Fax:* (555) 555-7915

## GENERAL MANAGER

**Strategist - Motivator - Coordinator - Trouble Shooter - Project Manager**

*Innovative, resourceful and inventive. Able to identify opportunities, make things happen, and consistently achieve objectives. Offer multifaceted perspective from manufacturing, operations, inventory control and general contracting. Establish superior procedures to enhance resources. Demonstrate achievement developing highly focused teams motivated to achieve ambitious goals.*

### CAREER HISTORY

**CONSTRUCTION MANAGEMENT**                                              1993 - Present
Jolie Industries                                                          Lafayette, Louisiana

Contribute vision and management expertise critical to organizational efficiency and business growth for general contractor with principal client the U.S. Department of Interior. Establish business policy, guidelines and priorities, financial and operational strategies. Identify required resources. Formulate, submit and follow through with proposals; negotiate and sign contracts. Target, interview and hire appropriate subcontractors. Monitor progress; evaluate outcomes.

❑ *Oversee personnel, purchasing, material management and cost control for simultaneous jobs ranging from road or pipeline construction to commercial and residential construction.*

**PURCHASING & INVENTORY CONTROL ADMINISTRATOR**                          1991 - 1993
Sunbelt Camera Works                                                      New Orleans, Louisiana

❑ Responsible for strengthening the company's position during buyout process.

❑ Redesigned inventory control procedures, updated purchasing techniques, reduced antiquated inventory, evaluated and negotiated vendor services and supply contracts.

❑ Established profit margins, developed profitable re-order points, and co-designed computer generated management reports.

**PLANT PRODUCTION MANAGER**                                              1988 - 1991
Partex                                                                    New Orleans, Louisiana

❑ Directed plant operations during night production process which included supervision of a staff of 50 employees in 8 departments.

❑ Responsible for introducing latest manufacturing techniques which increased operator productivity by 40%, improved overall production output by 450%, and reduced turnaround time by 75%.

❑ Implemented TQM, JIT and Konbon Pull Method manufacturing techniques.

### EDUCATION

**BACHELOR OF BUSINESS ADMINISTRATION IN BUSINESS MANAGEMENT,** 1987
Tulane University - New Orleans, Louisiana

REFERENCES AND FURTHER DATA AVAILABLE UPON REQUEST

## Investment Manager—Functional Format

# SUSAN B. ROUSSA

Post Office Box 964
Cargill, MI 76912
(555) 555-2413 / (555) 555-5958
Email: SMILER@tracker.net

### FINANCIAL SERVICES

WITH 15+ YEARS OF FINANCIAL PLANNING / MANAGEMENT, INVESTMENT,
ACCOUNTING, TRUST AND TAX EXPERIENCE

### SKILLS / ABILITIES / ACHIEVEMENTS & VALUE OFFERED

▲ **Knowledgeable / Experienced:** Offer a BS in Business and Accounting and 15+ years of extensive experience in banking, financial and accounting environments. Expertise includes corporate and individual tax accounting, securities, trust accounts and audit operations. Completing **CFP** program, Fall 1999.

▲ **Strong Interpersonal / Communications Skills:** Possess people and service sensitivity. Articulate speaker with excellent writing abilities. Consistently develop good rapport with staff, professionals, government officials and clients. Skilled troubleshooter.

▲ **Demonstrated Management Flair:** Self-starter with strong planning and leadership skills. Increased the number of trust and individual accounts from 150 to 270 within 2 years at LINCOLN & TUNY. Formulated policy and procedure for DANBURY SCHUSTER LLP; increased accounts from 170 to 220.

▲ **Well Organized:** Improved time use, productivity and quality performance at LINCOLN & TUNY by restructuring trust and individual account files and introducing a tickler file system. Managed tax preparation, including Direct Fast Tax activities, and administered 220 trust accounts for DANBURY SCHUSTER LLP.

▲ **Analytical / Detail Oriented:** Utilize exceptional research skills in tracking figures, persons, information, and in verifying data. Ability to identify and make use of trends for financial advantage and / or marketing purposes.

▲ **Computer Skills:** Utilize both mainframes and PCs with Windows and DOS. Proficient with Excel, Fast Tax, Pro FX, LOTUS 1-2-3, 1040 Solution, Shepard's Gift Tax, BNA Tax Planning, and Microsoft Word applications.

### CAREER HISTORY

**INVESTMENT MANAGEMENT**                                             1998 - Present
J/T Company                                                                    Detroit, Michigan

Perform accurate, timely, comprehensive high quality financial reporting services. Research, analyze and compile materials in preparation for purchase and sales of Initial Public Offerings; make appropriate recommendations. Review company prospectuses. Stay informed on laws, policies, administrative priorities, trends and special interests. Trade securities. Monitor daily market indicators to sell stock holdings in timely fashion. Correspond with brokers and underwriters. Transmit correspondent letters to Savings & Loan banks to open accounts.

❑ *prepare reports; maintain balance sheet and G/L; produce annual balance sheets.*

❑ *Establish Coordinate daily IPO sheets; update weekly syndication schedule from brokers; review monthly statements; guidelines and priorities; apply new technologies to organizational needs; develop and maintain various schedules on Microsoft Excel.*

❑ *Prepare and distribute payroll; identify and assemble required financial information; prepare and file quarterly and annual federal and state tax returns.*

**SUZETTE B. ROUSSA**                                                        Page 2

**MANAGER, TRUST ADMINISTRATION**                                        1996 - 1998
Danbury Schuster LLP

Promoted to provide professional leadership, technical expertise and oversight to the firm's 3 trust administrators with accountability for quality assurance and customer service satisfaction. Planned, organized and assigned work and supervised the execution of all trust agreements. Determined client goals, developed plan and income projections, accruals, market value comparisons. Prepared Fiduciary Income Tax returns; estimated quarterly tax payments, foundation and employer payroll tax reports; maintained efficient tax system operations.

- *Assured accuracy in client deposits, transfer of funds and distributions; analyzed and reconciled trust accounts and inventories.*
- *Cultivated and maintained excellent professional relations with attorneys, administrators, co-trustees, beneficiaries, investment brokers, custodial bank officials, tax accountants and other professionals.*
- *Trained, motivated and evaluated employee performance; administered personnel functions.*
- *Carried out special projects involving trust policy / procedures, stock market fluctuations and accounting systems; recommended quality improvements to senior level staff.*

**TRUST ADMINISTRATOR**                                                    1994 - 1996
Danbury Schuster LLP

Contributed administrative, managerial and technical expertise critical to the organizational efficiency and financial health of this prestigious firm. Directed Fast Tax System operations and tax preparation throughout the year, working effectively with administrators. Administered 170 trust accounts executing openings / closings, discerning client goals, projecting income, accruals and market value comparisons. Analyzed trust accountings and inventories.

**TAX ACCOUNTANT: FIDUCIARY AND INDIVIDUAL**                              1988 - 1994
Lincoln & Tuny

Planned, coordinated and executed tax planning. Prepared federal and state income tax returns for all types of trust accounts, private foundation returns, individual and gift tax returns. Researched securities activities for client accounts, prepared quarterly estimated tax payments; verified current account figures on mainframe computer system. Corresponded with firm partners, legal counsel and government representatives to troubleshoot problems and correct discrepancies. Generated statements and account activity reports; maintained confidential files.

**TAX ACCOUNTANT: CORPORATE**                                            1987 - 1988
Masconomet Bank

**STAFF AUDITOR: OPERATIONAL AND FINANCIAL**                                  1987
SilverStock FSB

**TAX STAFF ACCOUNTANT: CORPORATE AND INDIVIDUAL**                            1986
Glen Kinnear & Company

**TAX STAFF ACCOUNTANT: CORPORATE**                                      1984 - 1986
Treasury of States, FSB

### EDUCATIONAL CREDENTIALS

**BACHELOR OF SCIENCE IN BUSINESS & ACCOUNTING**, 1987
Forrest College - Bloomfield, Michigan
AMERICAN INSTITUTE OF BANKING COURSES  1040 SOLUTIONS SEMINAR  PRO FX SYSTEM  FAST TAX SYSTEM
REFERENCES & FURTHER DATA AVAILABLE UPON REQUEST

## Seasoned Manager/Journalist—Age Camouflaged

*Confidential Resume of*

# FRED HARRIS

529 Greys Street
Cold River, Florida 33315
(555) 555-1758

2414 Tupello Road
Santa Bell, Florida 33309
(555) 555-9552

Email: fharris@Jobnet.net

## SENIOR EXECUTIVE MANAGEMENT
*- with 15+ years of outstanding experience -*

Expertise in:
**Strategic Planning / Market Analysis / New Product Design
Advertising Concepts / P&L Responsibilities / Negotiating / Public Relations
Networking & Partnering / Troubleshooting / Creative Production**

*Seek out and assume high visibility roles. Skilled in assessing marketplace and devising plans to improve competitiveness and penetrate saturated markets. Find great challenge in the realms of ideas and theory-defining, testing, proving. Personally motivated by opportunities to create innovative approaches to business service delivery, the planning of events, or public relations activities. 'Own' each project from inception to completion including all negotiating, deal making, advertising, and promoting.*

*Demonstrated experience in growing business revenues, conceptualizing strategies, and providing hands-on management to achieve goals. A gifted communicator adept at networking, alliance building, team-building, persuading, and motivating. Write and speak with strength, clarity and style. Nationally recognized at the highest levels for instructional excellence. A problem-solver, change agent, competitor and over-achiever. Streamline processes, infuse innovation. Considered gregarious, high energy, and diplomatic.*

### CAREER TRACK

**EXECUTIVE MANAGEMENT**
SMART SERVICES

1992 - Present
Dallas, Texas

A full service organization offering targeted member services, basic training and instruction, certifications, and specialized benefits to clients and members. Directed, from *start-up*, all aspects of daily operation. Negotiated equipment purchases and leases. Hired, developed and motivated staff. Devised and implemented all advertising and promotion. Communicated with licensing agencies and other governmental entities. Framed the business plan. Resolve customer service issues, administer banking and other financial issues including insurance, benefits, and all P&L factors. Expedite alliance / partnering arrangements enhancing organization's perception as a national entity. Configure pricing.

❑ *Achieve consistent **25% net profit** each year, the highest level of its kind within the nation, in this industry group.*

❑ *Provide critical leadership in all short- and long-range business and organizational planning leading to outstanding financial and operational results.*

❑ *Troubleshoot and resolve complex and / or sensitive issues; appropriate time and tasks to consistently meet deadlines and objectives.*

❑ *Dynamically promote organization through creative presentations, motivation of staff, and the development of targeted marketing approaches.*

Continued

**FRED HARRIS**  Page 2

**REGIONAL MANAGER / AREA PUBLISHER**  1987 - 1992
NEWSCO INC. - TRAVEL PUBLISHING DIVISION  New York, New York

Managed key accounts for Calvin Thompkins-owned operation involving major national and international companies and airlines, car rental services, hotels / resorts, and tourism organizations at state and national level. Identified unique market niches; formulated strategic marketing plans; established goals; hired and trained high performing staff. Designed systems and procedures to maximize efficiency, productivity, customer satisfaction and profitability. Identified opportunities, promoted concepts, effectuated action, made things happen. Consistently overachieved objectives.

❑ *Doubled annual advertising revenues in 3 years to $5,000,000 per year.*

❑ *Proposed and developed a South West Regional Office.*

❑ *Fueled the aggressive development and expansion of special product offerings and innovative supplements that stimulated circulation and increased revenue.*

**ASSOCIATE PUBLISHER**  1982 - 1987
HATCHER WORLDWIDE  New York, New York

Spearheaded publication of 7 international magazines produced in English, French, Japanese and Arabic. Targeted split-run editions to focus on the distinct business environments of each circulation area worldwide. Contributed management expertise, creative leadership, sales and marketing savvy critical to organizational efficiency, financial health and business growth. Orchestrated multiple operations to ensure timely completion within budgets. Consistently met deadlines. Motivated others by establishing quick rapport with professionals and staff at all levels. Continually generated new ideas and responded quickly to new opportunities.

❑ *Personally created concepts, marketing approaches, and ongoing strategies for each publication.*

❑ *Devised promotional programs which included presentations on international business topics to universities and foreign trade organizations*

❑ *Fostered excellent professional and community relationships.*

**Positions prior to 1982 include:**

**SALES MANAGER,** RUTHERS PRESS - New York, New York

**NEWSPAPER REPORTER / FREELANCE WRITER**
SNOW MOUNTAIN PRESS / DEXTER CAULFELD NEWS / FREEDOM WATCHER
CONCORD CRIER / SURREY POST, England

**EDUCATIONAL BACKGROUND**

**BACHELOR OF ARTS - Economics**
Surrey University, England

*Additional Certifications:*
United States Coast Guard Master's License
Certified Sailing Instructor    Professional Soccer Coach

**PERSONAL / INTERESTS**

Willing to perform work related travel  /  Willing to relocate

Skippered 10,000 Trans-Pacific Ocean miles
Coached two youth soccer teams to state championships

REFERENCES AND FURTHER DATA AVAILABLE UPON REQUEST

## Manufacuting Engineer—High Profile in "Selling"

*Confidential Resume of*
### VASANTH NABAVI

21 Prudential Street, Apartment 140
Somerville, New York 01459
(555) 555-7431
www.JobGroup.com/resumes/vnabavi.htm
Email: vnabavi@JobGroup.com

*Quality Control*

## MANUFACTURING PROCESS ENGINEER

**Turning Demand into Growth, Technology into Value,
Competition into Opportunity**

*Energetic and dependable contributor with highly developed communications abilities, manufacturing expertise, interpersonal and computer skills. Innovative, resourceful and inventive. Identify opportunities and consistently achieve objectives. Offer multifaceted perspective with excellent understanding of today's high tech environment, business conditions, programs and alliances to customize and integrate state-of-the-art strategies and systems. Proactive decision-maker, motivated team player, artful problem solver. Persuasive and pragmatic. Possibility thinker with persistent initiative, deft influencing skills and technical acumen. Excel in commitment.*

### CAREER TRACK

Chem Pro Labs
Albany, New York
**MICROELECTRONICS QUALITY ASSURANCE ENGINEER**
1999 - Present

Demonstrate strong planning, organizing and leadership skills to set priorities for multiple, simultaneous staff activities and consistently meet service goals and management objectives. Collect and review inspection data for conformance with customer expectations and company and industry quality performance standards. Schedule outside testing and analysis as required.

❑ *Keep up to date on market conditions, government regulations and industry competition; apply knowledge to quality assurance, product reliability and manufacturing techniques.*

❑ *Prepare, issue and update process control charts; spearhead and structure qualification testing of new manufacturing processes; energize activities of Material Review Board.*

**MICROELECTRONICS MANUFACTURING PROCESS ENGINEER**
1996 - 1999

Contributed vision and management expertise critical to organizational efficiency. Established guidelines and priorities; identified required resources; planned and coordinated with others. Processed engineering experiments and specification writing. Provided technical support to manufacturing; upgraded equipment. Monitored progress; evaluated outcomes.

❑ *Programmed and maintained Cerdip and Cerpac plating and marking machines; performed hermeticity testing; supported cap welding, seam sealing and glass frit; utilized SPC tools.*

❑ *Recognized and defined issues; enlisted cooperation of labor force; analyzed relevant information and rejects; developed insights; provided alternative solutions.*

Continued

*Confidential Resume of*

**VASANTH NABAVI**

New Amsterdam Automated Systems
**SYSTEM ENGINEER**

New York, New York
1995 - 1996

Provided leadership in areas of technical expertise, quality assurance and project management. Developed and implemented methods, systems and procedures to assure cost-efficient technical direction. Configured computers; provided engineering and design support.

❑ *Performed programming, installation and service for all point-of-sale products; tested systems to ensure technical compatibility and minimal downtime.*

❑ *Applied new technologies to organizational needs; ensured staff and management were capable, trained in system use and comfortable with results.*

**Additional positions include:**

INSTRUCTOR - Electronic Technology Institute - San Francisco, California , 1997
*Electronic Fundamentals, Theory and Lab*
PEER TUTOR - Preston School of Technology - San Francisco, California, 1994 - 1995
*Calculus, Circuit Theory, Electronic Measurement, Financial Accounting*

---

**LEARNING CREDENTIALS**

**BACHELOR OF SCIENCE IN ELECTRONIC ENGINEERING TECHNOLOGY**
Preston School of Technology

1995
San Francisco, California

*GPA 3.3, Dean's List*

**Co-op assignments include:**

BELL - SST - Hanover, Oregon, 1994
*Built, tested and specified prototype electronic boards; repaired production boards; designed new products; built test equipment; supervised testing; diagnosed electronic boards*

HANCOCK & BUMBLE - Lovi, Kuwait , 1992
*Tested and repaired heavy-duty motors; assembled new instruments and electronic circuits; interfaced with customers; wrote technical instruction speculation sheets*

---

**COMPETENCIES**

Microsoft Word , MS Excel, Bilingual in Arabic and English

---

**PERSONAL**

Willing to perform work-related travel / Willing to relocate

REFERENCES AND FURTHER DATA AVAILABLE UPON REQUEST

## Clerk with Military Background

*Confidential Resume of*

# CLAUDIA ST. JOHN

368 Madden Street, Clive, Iowa 54410

(555) 555-2591

### CAREER SUMMARY

*Results oriented assistant with proven initiative, integrity, resourcefulness and analytical / decision making ability. Capable of communicating effectively with management personnel, clients, associates and visitors in various disciplines and at all levels of responsibility. Expertise in organizing and coordinating efforts toward the achievement of desired objectives. Characterized by others as goal oriented, high energy, and disciplined with strong comprehension, ability to identify and resolve problems, and creative in finding and implementing timely / appropriate solutions. Relied upon for a consistent record of achievement fostering cooperation and communication among superiors, subordinates and peers. Coordinate work with superior time management skills.*

### CAREER HISTORY

UNITED STATES ARMY
*Fort Thom, Florida, Fort Worth, Texas, Madchent, Austria, 1994 - 1999*

**ADMINISTRATIVE CLERK / RECEPTIONIST**
125th Base Support Battalion

1996 - 1999
Madchen, Austria

Demonstrated strong planning and organizational skills in executing daily administrative responsibilities for the Command Sergeant Major and the Battalion Executive Officer. Implemented effective operating and management control systems. Set priorities to fulfill multiple and simultaneous staff activities. Organized meetings, set calendars, interacted with soldiers, civilians, and high level personnel. Performed duties of the Commander's secretary in her absence. Established and maintained excellent relationships with all staff personnel.

❑ *Maintained time and attendance data for approximately 35 civilian employees and assisted in resolving pay problems.*

❑ *Gathered information, analyzed circumstances and made numerous referrals to proper agencies and authorities for many soldiers, family members and civilians.*

❑ *For three months, served as the Installation Pass Officer for various commercial enterprises.*

**ADMINISTRATIVE CLERK / RECEPTIONIST**
Training & Operation Planning Offices

1995 - 1996
Fort Worth, Texas

Assisted many personnel in the Training & Operation offices. Answered, screened and routed calls to the appropriate staff members. Typed or word-processed documents and correspondence. Expedited / maintained specialized records including fingerprinting. Prepared slides for quarterly training briefs reviewed by both the Commanding and Deputy Commanding Officers. Planned, organized and implemented effective operating, accounting and management systems. Interacted effectively with staff and enlisted personnel and visitors.

❑ *Coordinated professional development school enrollment, involving application submissions and other related information, for nearly 900 enlisted soldiers and officers.*

*Continued*

*Confidential Resume of*

**CLAUDIA ST. JOHN**                                                  Page 2

**ASSISTANT ORDERLY ROOM CLERK**                                      1994 - 1995
B Company, 75th Adjutant General Battalion                         Fort Thom, Florida

Performed a broad range of administrative support functions involving extensive filing of information, typing of correspondence, and compiling / processing daily status reports for the unit. Monitored supplies and reported low levels or shortages to appropriate staff members.

❑  *Screened newly arrived personnel to ensure proper credentials and duty instructions.*

❑  *Promoted in less than 6 months to Administrative Clerk in Training & Operation Planning Offices.*

**Previous Positions**

**REGISTRAR**                                          January 1993 - September 1994
Madison College                                                       Linden, Iowa

**MEDICAL ASSISTANT**                                   (Concurrent) April - June 1994
Stephen Chester, MD                                                   Linden, Iowa

**MEDICAL ASSISTANT**                        (Concurrent) September 1993 - April 1994
Anthony Hopper, MD                                                    Linden, Iowa

---

## TRAINING CREDENTIALS

**CERTIFIED MEDICAL ASSISTANT**                                             1993
Youth Enrichment Program                                             Cokely, Iowa

**DIPLOMA**                                                                 1990
San Sebastian Charter High School                             San Sebastian, Tobago

*Additional courses, seminars and workshops include*:
45 credit toward Bachelor's degree
University of Iowa, Anselm College, European Division
Beverly College, European Division , Wheaton College, Clive, Iowa
Understanding Human Behavior - Department of Defense

Basic First Aid - American Red Cross
Instructor Candidate Course - American Red Cross
Paris, France

**Computer Skills:**
Microsoft Word   Access   PowerPoint   Excel
Microsoft Outlook (e-mail)   Calendar Creator Plus

---

### PERSONAL

Willing to perform work related travel / Willing to relocate
Enjoy fitness activities, crocheting, reading, travel, photography

REFERENCES AND FURTHER DATA AVAILABLE UPON REQUEST

## Educator—Clear, Attractive Presentation

# LANCE W. SCOTT

17 West Road, Post Office Box 1877
Sterling, Wisconsin 67633-1877
*Home:* (555) 555-4487 *Work:* (555) 555-9861 *Fax:* (555) 555-9721
www.JobGroup.com/resumes/lwscott.htm
Email: lwscott@JobGroup.com

### CAREER OBJECTIVE

A challenging EDUCATION RELATED or HUMAN SERVICES position where Master's degrees in Education and Administration, highly developed organizational abilities and interpersonal skills, and 18+ years of teaching and administrative experience will be utilized and offer professional growth opportunities.

### CAREER TRACK

MADISON SCHOOL DEPARTMENT - Madison, Wisconsin   1983 - Present

**PROGRAM DIRECTOR :** SPECIAL EDUCATION DEPARTMENT                     1998 - Present

Plan, coordinate and implement lesson regimen that addresses various learning styles and abilities. Create an active motivational learning environment. Utilize positive classroom management strategies that promote learning excitement and self-expression within a controlled behavioral framework. Demonstrate creative and flexible approaches, varied initiatives and positive reinforcement skills. Collaborate with other departments and service providers to ensure appropriate inclusion of Special Education students in all subject classes and school programs and activities.

❑ *Assist Headmaster in fulfilling all Chapter 766 responsibilities; participate in development and implementation of Annual School Plan; train, supervise and evaluate all professional staff.*
❑ *Oversee development and coordination of curriculum goals and objectives and distribution of instructional materials; ensure timely maintenance of accurate student records.*
❑ *Achieve demonstrated success with parental involvement; maintain responsive communication with parents, students and staff involved in Special Education programs.*

**EVALUATION TEAM LEADER:** DAWSON MIDDLE SCHOOL                     1995 - 1998

Established excellent professional relations with teachers, parents and pupils as a basis for critical evaluations. Scheduled, planned and coordinated assessment conferences in accordance with state regulations and local procedures. Chaired all evaluation meetings and follow-up reviews and re-evaluations. Coordinated and advised on writing and submission of Individual Education Plans. Communicated with parents and any involved agencies on their children's progress; provided clear explanations and assistance; initiated process for outside counseling or therapy if required.

**SPECIAL NEEDS TEACHER:** PROCTOR MIDDLE SCHOOL                     1990 - 1995

Developed relevant lesson plans and curriculum for adolescents with poor learning skills. Presented clear explanations and demonstrations of basic subjects. Provided an environment conducive to learning through active exploration and creative activities. Managed time to allow students to develop productivity and exploration skills. Maintained good rapport with the class.

*Continued*

**LANCE W. SCOTT**    Page 2

**PROGRAM ASSISTANT:** FAIRVIEW ELEMENTARY SCHOOL    1984 - 1990

Provided support and discipline services for teachers and administrators. Worked directly with guidance counselors in handling problem students and served as liaison to Headmaster; helped in assessing individual student needs; initiated contact with parents and other involved parties.

**SCIENCE TEACHER:** HOOVER JUNIOR HIGH SCHOOL    1983 - 1984

Taught children at middle school level a variety of science topics including Biology, Life Sciences, Earth Science and Physical Science, as well as history and social studies. Compiled course materials and aids for demonstrations; devised experiments in which students took part. Instructed in scientific method involving students making predictions, conducting procedures, observing and recording data and drawing conclusions.

### LEARNING CREDENTIALS

**MASTER OF SCHOOL ADMINISTRATION,** 1997
*(GPA - 3.5)*
**MASTER OF EDUCATION IN MODERATE SPECIAL NEEDS,** 1992
Howard Pierce College - Keene, New Hampshire
*(GPA - 3.6)*

**BACHELOR OF ARTS IN SOCIOLOGY / EDUCATION,** 1983
University of Vermont - Burlington, Vermont
*(GPA - 3.5) Dean's List   President's List*

**ASSOCIATE OF SCIENCE IN LAW ENFORCEMENT,** 1981
Massapequa Community College - Lynn, Massachusetts
*Dean's List*

**Additional Courses:**
*Assessment in Reading, Language and Learning Disabilities*
*Beginning Reading Materials*
Syracuse Graduate School of Education - Syracuse, New York

*9 courses in School Law; Business; Personnel; Curriculum; Analysis of Teaching;*
*Social, Legal, Ethical Issues; School / Community Relations and Administration*

### CERTIFICATES & LICENSES

Wisconsin Teaching Certificates:
*Moderate Special Needs, History, Social Studies, Behavioral Sciences*
*Intensive Special Needs, Principal / Assistant Principal (All grades)*
*Supervisor / Director (All), Administrator of Special Education (All)*

Certificate in Computer Basics,   Advance Computer Training

### MILITARY SERVICE

Military Police, United States Army

### ORGANIZATIONS & ASSOCIATIONS

Wisconsin Teachers Association
Disabled American Veterans Auxiliary

REFERENCES AND FURTHER DATA AVAILABLE UPON REQUEST

## Aviation Safety Expert—Selective Highlighting of Relevant Details

*Confidential Resume of*

## PETER S. MAGGIO

876 Clear Brook Road
Seattle, Washington 80735
(555) 555-6648

www.WorkGroup.com/resumes/psmaggio.htm
*Email:* slugger@resource.net *or* psmaggio@WorkGroup.com

## SAFETY / AVIATION

### Forward-Thinking, Results-Oriented Professional

*A self-starter with proven ability and leadership in fields of Aviation and Safety. Deliver high quality projects from inception to completion, with safety, on schedule and within budget. Innovative, resourceful and inventive, with ability to identify opportunities, make things happen, and consistently achieve objectives. Establish superior procedures for analysis and operational control. Serve as motivational team leader, aggressive troubleshooter and artful problem solver.*

### CAREER TRACK

**SAFETY ADVISOR**                                                                        1997 - Present
Rock Creek Excavating Company                                               Seattle, Washington

Plan, implement and coordinate program to reduce or eliminate occupational injuries, illness, deaths and financial losses. Identify and appraise conditions that could produce accidents. Identify hazards and loss-producing potential of operations and processes. Develop and deliver accident-prevention, HazMat awareness and loss-control programs.

❑ *Maintain liaison with outside organizations such as fire and rescue units to assure information exchange and mutual assistance.*

❑ *Establish guidelines ensuring safe environmental conditions and equipment maintenance to OSHA standards; issue personal safety clothing and equipment.*

❑ *Conduct drug screenings and present safety training for multiple crews of over 50 personnel in safe operations, health and environmental issues.*

❑ *Institute and monitor Hazard Register; record daily and near-miss reports on health and safety aspects of crew operations.*

**OWNER / OPERATOR**                                                                      1995 - 1997
Hanger 15                                                                                            Bend, Oregon

**SAFETY OFFICER**                                                                           1983 - 1988
3rd Military Intelligence Battalion                                                   Berlin, Germany

Managed, conducted and recorded Standardization and Training for the three companies, including but not limited to the personnel, aircraft and assets assigned to the 3rd Military Intelligence Battalion.

❑ *Responsible for maintaining the avionics, ejection seats and survival gear employed in the OVID Mohawk. The shop received four superior ratings.*

❑ *Second in Command in the OVID Mohawk Aerial Sensory Aircraft.*

Continued

*Confidential Resume of*

**PETER S. MAGGIO** Page 2

**HEAD TROUBLESHOOTER / ASSISTANT HEAD LINESMAN** 1977 - 1981
Morris Oil Supply Bend, Oregon

> Initiated the program and received training to perform basic maintenance of the Opsies Telemetry System in the field, saving thousands of dollars in down time and lost production.

❏ *Rocky Mountain Exploration Helicopter Crew #330.*

## LEARNING CREDENTIALS

**BACHELOR OF SCIENCE,** 1995
Rensselear Polytechnic University - Rensselear, New York
*Major: Aeronautical Science   Minor: Safety*

*Certified Commercial Pilot with single engine land and sea,
multi engine land and instrument airplane privileges and ratings.*

U.S. Army Intelligence Center and School  - Fort Steven,Texas, 1983
*Second in the graduating class.*

Camden High School - Camden,Oregon, 1975

## LICENSES & CERTIFICATIONS

Certified to train personnel in CPR, First Aid, and Advanced Rescue to Red Cross Standards. Certified to train Personnel in ATV operations to the ATV Safety Institute Standards. Certified Ground School Instructor with the Federal Aviation Administration. Certified Commercial Pilot with approximately 1,000 hours civilian time and 586 hours right seat military time.

## MILITARY SERVICE

**Safety Officer 3rd Military Intelligence Battalion, 5th corps, U.S. Army Europe**

Flew right seat in the OVID Mohawk, conducting surveillance radar mapping missions on the Russian, German and Yugoslavian borders. I was responsible for operation of the radio's navigation and the Side Looking Airborne Radar (SLAR) systems.

Created, developed and headed an ALSE training program which exceeded all requirements and greatly enhanced the safety and cohesion of the Fixed Wing Army Aviation Community in Europe.
*I received two Army Achievement Medals.*

Initiated and co-authored the ALSE Training Handbook, which was integrated into the U.S. Army Training Command.
*I received an Army Commendation Medal and the Meritorious Service Medals.*

Developed a preventative maintenance program for the Digital Data Link System, critical for the Airborne Radar System, improving mission readiness by 10%.
*I received a Certificate of Appreciation*

REFERENCES AND FURTHER DATA AVAILABLE UPON REQUEST

## Internatinal Operations Manager—Detailed, Three-Page Resume

*Confidential Resume of*

# BRIAN DUMONT

98 Spruce Place
Bar Harbor, Maine 08861-0965
*Home*: (555) 555-4001  *Fax*: (555) 555-3120

*Email*: brian3@discover.net

*Consultant / Senior Executive*

## INTERNATIONAL OPERATIONS
- more than 20 years of outstanding experience -

TALENTED, BILINGUAL PROFESSIONAL WITH PROGRESSIVE ACCOMPLISHMENTS AND
EXPERTISE IN THE AREAS OF BUSINESS DEVELOPMENT, FINANCIAL PACKAGING,
GOVERNMENT RELATIONS, SALES AND MARKETING, PRODUCT DEVELOPMENT,
OPERATIONS MANAGEMENT, CUSTOMER SERVICE.

*Combine extraordinary market cognizance with a practiced business sense. Offer proven leadership contributions to new business development, acquisitions and divestitures, corporate turnarounds, private / public interactions. Energetic and dependable with highly developed communication and interpersonal abilities, technical savvy, and international expertise. Innovative, resourceful and inventive with unusual ability to identify opportunities, effectuate action, and consistently achieve goals and objectives. Offer multifaceted perspective with excellent understanding of today's business conditions, programs and alliances to customize and integrate state-of-the-art strategies or systems. A possibility thinker with indefatigable initiative, deft influencing skills and marketing acumen. Articulate and persuasive speaker; excel in defining complex problems, write with clarity.*

### ACHIEVEMENTS & VALUE OFFERED

❑ **Obtained** several mandates to perform strategic investment analyses for pulp and paper companies as well as paper chemical companies and to represent these companies in investing in North America and Europe.

❑ **Co-managed** and later sold a diversified multi-plant manufacturing company with 5 divisions and 1100 employees.

❑ **Created** a new sales strategy leading to increased sales and generating substantial profits for a Fortune 100 manufacturing company.

### CAREER TRACK

**DIRECTOR OF SALES AND CORPORATE AFFAIRS**          October 1998 - Present
Winterbottom Sales Association.                                    London, England

At invitation and request of company president assumed full-time position of Director of Sales and Corporate Affairs in place of a previous consultant role. Fuel the continued expansion of product offerings and sales growth for this brand new production facility for recycled pulp. Formulate strategic marketing plans, establish goals, recruit / manage / motivate high performing personnel. Continue a highly visible role in government relations, especially through lobbying.

❑ *Drive growth of the commercial foundation by identifying and cultivating specific market niches.*

❑ *Consolidate shareholders' investment and increase the visibility of this new industry within the pulp market.*

❑ *Negotiate with municipalities and collectivities waste management contracts. Lobby at all levels of government in order to obtain favorable new legislation.*

Continued

**BRIAN DUMONT**     Page 2

**SENIOR PARTNER**                                                                   1993 - Present
NUPAPER INDUSTRIES                                                    Augusta, Maine, USA

Key member of a 5-person start-up team directing a $195,000,000 off-balance sheet non recourse project financing, www.nu/paper.com, with primary responsibilities in the financial and public sector arenas. Serve in such capacities as political representative, lobbyist, and problem solver. Selected the legal advisor and the local investment banker.

❑ *Actively negotiate with private debt lenders and equity, government agencies, and suppliers for grants and subordinated debt.*

❑ *Concluded take-or-pay offtake contracts, supply contracts for raw material, energy and water. Obtain permits to construct and operate.*

❑ *Interact with independent engineers to clearly demonstrate product demand and other critical issues.*

**INDEPENDENT CONSULTANT**                                                       1988 - Present

Perform a range of highly selective external consultations for major companies focusing on such areas as strategic planning, market analysis, feasibility studies, evaluations and due diligence reviews.

❑ *Advise international firms on mergers / acquisitions, divestitures and joint ventures, in conjunction with an associate.*

❑ *As financial consultant, successfully restructured financing of two companies.*

❑ *Designed and facilitated an extensive marketing-feasibility study for expansions of North American operations in the fields of chemicals and consumer products.*

**PRODUCT MANAGER**                                                               1981 - 1988
Grant Chemical / Beta Science Corp                                             Paris, France

Provided vision and management expertise crucial to product development, quality assurance, operations evaluations and improvements, sales and marketing. Negotiated contracts and secured projects with major clients. Utilized far ranging expertise to develop customer base, design, test and evaluate production processes and equipment, and to consistently grow both sales and profit.

❑ *Introduced an American company to the European market and rapidly achieved a 60% market share of the fine papers industry.*

❑ *Developed / utilized extensive knowledge of mill operations to facilitate machine trials, new product development, and modifications in process parameters.*

**COO AND CEO**                                                                   1975 - 1981
Pierre Montagna S.A. (Subsidiary of Louis Picard and Guy Devereaux)          Galette - Vancouver, Canada

Administered all aspects of business / financial operations for two manufacturers of consumer products distributed worldwide. Utilized expertise in planning, communication, and leadership to devise and implement overall business plans, operational budgeting and forecasting, strategic planning, sales / marketing approaches, labor relations, acquisitions / divestitures, purchasing and distribution techniques. Established results-driven policies and procedures. Identified actual and potential problem areas and implemented well-reasoned solutions to ensure maximum effectiveness.

❑ *Initiated distributor and franchise operations for the sale of company's products throughout Canada and the United States.*

❑ *Resolved an intense personnel-management relationship that involved 850 unionized members in a politically sensitive and intense climate.*

Continued

**BRIAN DUMONT**      Page 3

## LEARNING CREDENTIALS

**MBA - Finance**                                              1985
Boston University                                  Boston, Massachusetts

**BACHELOR OF SCIENCE - Industrial Engineering and Management**      1975
University of California                            Santa Cruz, California

**MATH-SUP - Equivalent to a Master in Mathematics**      1973
McGill University                                     Toronto, Canada

*Additional courses, seminars, workshops, professional development:*

Baccalaureate C (Sciences, Mathematics, Physics, Chemistry), Montreal 1972
❑   Diploma, (certificate in Management), Boston University, 1982

CPPA and TAPPI courses on all aspects of Papermaking and Chemistry
Self-taught Information Technology
Trilingual (English - French - German)

### CERTIFICATES & LICENSES

Private Pilot License

REFERENCES AND FURTHER DATA AVAILABLE UPON REQUEST

## Customer Service Specialist—Minimal Education Credentials

*Confidential Resume of*

# JOSEPH STANTON

90 Clancy Street
Roswell, Arizona 77591
(555) 555-2479

www.JobGroup.com/resumes/jstanton.htm
Email: jstanton@JobGroup.com

### CUSTOMER SERVICE

Telephone and Data Entry Skills

### CAREER HISTORY

**CLAIM REPORTING SPECIALIST**                          1998 - 1999
Fast Response Systems                                 578 Bridge Avenue
Manager: Linda Eppel                                     Tucson, Arizona

Work duties:
- Taking insurance claims over the phone
- Personal, Commercial, Auto, Liability and Property Insurance
- Data Entry
- Customer Service
- Setting up rental and auto body work

**CUSTOMER SERVICE**                                      1997 - 1998
Mercury Shoes                                     Roswell Shopping Center
Manager: Donna Comstock                                 Roswell, Arizona

Work duties:
- Sales / Managing store; Opening and closing store
- Customer Service
- Paperwork; Cash Handling
- Security of merchandise,
- Stock and Inventory Control

**ASSISTANT MANAGER / SALES ASSOCIATE**                   1994 - 1997
Lowe's Shoe Store                         Desert Vally Mall / Felices Court
Manager: Pat Yarmark              Desert Valley, Arizona / Felices, New Mexico

Work duties:
- Sales of Merchandise - Footwear and Athletic Wear
- Stock

**FRONT DESK CLERK**                                            1994
Garfield Hotel                                     Desert Valley, Arizona
Manager: Meetal Nima

Work duties:
- Checking in and out of guests
- Cash Handling
- Setting reservations
- Phone

REFERENCES AND FURTHER DATA AVAILABLE UPON REQUEST

## Software Producer—Focus on Projects

*Confidential Resume of*
**COLIN FRAKES**
11 Hollow Street · Sutton Mill, Washington 65095
Tel: 555-555-4531 · Fax: 555-555-6921 · Email: cfrakes@mavis.com

**MULTIMEDIA SOFTWARE PRODUCTION - MANAGEMENT**
Creative professional with expertise in multimedia entertainment design, development, management and promotion; asian/american communications; and consulting.

**PROFILE**
- **Game Production and Promotion.** Conceptualize, design, program and manage all facets of 3D / 2D image production, animation and sound. Made significant contributions to "Super Ova" for BIONATUREX HOLOGRAMS, "Yamaguchi Sito" (Kobiniki) and "Mr. Trick" (Dunui) for SLAYER COMPUTER PROGRAMS.
- **Management Skills:** Self starter with strong planning and leadership skills. Experienced in recruiting and managing independent professionals for the development of sound / music and artwork. Well organized; effectively reduce projects to manageable tasks, determine relativistic goals and schedules, delegate assignments.
- **Knowledge of Asian Culture:** Served as corporate liaison, translating communications between SLAYER and 7&UTI COMPANY in the U.S. Interpreted 7&UTI software documentation for Asian co-workers. Developed an extensive resource network that included an Asian partner to facilitate business dealings.
- **Productivity Minded:** Analyzed SLAYER operations and formulated conclusions on hardware / software necessary to create maximum productivity. Utilized ability to converse in Mandarin Chinese, the only language spoken in the company, to make recommendations to senior management.
- **Technical Expertise:** Proficient with Macintosh (System 7.5); also utilize IBM PCs (Windows and DOS), Masscomp Mainframe (UNIX) and DEC VAX (VMS). Applications include Adobe PhotoShop, StrataStudio Pro, MS Word, QuarkXPress, Adobe Premiere, Macromedia Director and numerous others. Program in 'C'. Adept at broadcast video and audio editing and production, including desktop video and on-line editing equipment.

**PROFESSIONAL EXPERIENCE**

**BIONATUREX HOLOGRAMS** - Tacoma, Washington
1995 - Present
> Worked on all facets of production and promotion of the CD-ROM game "Super Ova"; managed freelance sound / music and artwork professionals.

**SLAYER COMPUTER PROGRAMS** - Beijing, China
1993 - 1994
> Member of the design / programming team for "Mr. Trick" and "Yamaguchi Sito."

**JING GRAPHICS** - Beijing, China
1991 - 1992
> Contributed to conceptualization, design and development of the CD-ROM game, "Shining Man Maze".

**WMIW AM RADIO** - Mercer Island, Washington
1990 - 1991
> Engineered and broadcast live shows; produced and edited news programs and advertising.

**FREELANCE CONTRACTS - CHINA**

**COMMERCE POWER COMPANY, PUBLIC RELATIONS DIVISION**
1990

 Produced television title graphics for "L'Auberge" resort hotel.

**ROUNDHILL TERRAIN CONTROL**
1990

 Developed a multimedia presentation of "Goofy Gopher" excavation machine.

**COLONIAL CRYSTALWORK**
1990

 Developed computer graphics to portray glass production on kiosk video in welcome
 lobby.

**BEIJING DEPARTMENT OF WATER**
1990

 Created a faucet maintenance instructional video.

**HAN JO CORPORATION**
1990

 Produced a new product multimedia presentation that was used to secure development
 funding.

**EDUCATION**

**MASTER OF SCIENCE- Computer Engineering,** 1991
Beijing Polytechnic University - Beijing, China

**BACHELOR OF SCIENCE- Computer Graphics,** 1990 - 1991
Spires College - Tacoma, Washington

**CERTIFICATE OF DISTINCTION- Computer Graphics,** 1989 - 1990
Tacoma Technical Center - Tacoma, Washington

**HIGH SCHOOL DIPLOMA,** 1989
Kenneth Dover High School - Mount St. Helen, Washington
*Valedictorian*

**PERSONAL**
International Drivers' License
Willing to relocate and perform work related travel

REFERENCES & FURTHER DATA AVAILABLE UPON REQUEST

## Rabbi—Creative Use of Language for a Spiritual Leader

*Confidential Resume of*
**REVEREND SAMUEL UPTON**
190 Ferris Street
Monte Vista, Arizona 67713
*Phone :* (555) 555-4582 · *Fax:* (555)555-8137

**ELOQUENT SPIRITUAL LEADER**
**Mentor with Dynamics Communication and Leadership Talents**
*Energetic and insightful reverend with proven leadership, highly developed communications abilities, impersonal and outreach skills and years of educational experience. Empowers, motivates and guides others through the strenuous issues of divine demand and human attainment. Innovative, resourceful and inventive consultant with unusual ability to identify possibilities and opportunities, effectuate action, 'make things happen' and improve the lives of countless individuals, couples and families. Offers proof that traditional religious practice is not simply a matter of formulas rigidly observed, but of profound unities underlying everyday life, of time and eternity interesting.*

**PROFESSIONAL EXPERIENCE**

**SPIRITUAL LEADER**
1996 - 1999
Mountain View Congregational Church
Monte Vista, Arizona

Demonstrate a natural ability to lead and work with others in the study of the Bible. Establish quick rapport with workers, professionals and staff at all levels. Inspire congregation to believe and participate as their duty and necessity, because it is right. Develop strong lay leadership team. Exercise tact. Enhance human and community relations. Assist in Congregation's overall good works, such that they may say, "We shall go down to our house justified."

- *Recognize and define complex issues; identify relevant information; encourage alternate solutions and plans to solve problems in a judicious and timely fashion.*
- *Move worship and spiritual observance from any perceived association with the dull, insipid or irritating to the reality of the exciting, deeply moving and comforting.*

**PRINCIPAL**
1992 - 1996
Fellowship Academy
Mesa, Arizona

Apply extensive experience to encourage teachers to address various learning styles and abilities and the safety, comfort and happiness of every young person. Create and active motivational learning environment. Utilize positive classroom management strategies that promote learning excitement and self-expression within a controlled behavioral framework. Demonstrate creative and flexible approaches, positive reinforcement skills, sincerity, enthusiasm and years of absolute success with parental involvement.

- *Supervise training for special observances, including baptismal rites, as times set aside, when friendships and relationships become strengthened or renewed, when peace seems to return and energies flow in surprising ways.*
- *Direct and assist staff to express the normal and vital ways in which the living God is active and at work in the lives of his people and the wider world.*

**SPIRITUAL EDUCATOR**
1991 - 1994
WCMA-AM / WTRI AM
Phoenix, Arizona

Share relevant, penetrating Scriptural insights into the human condition and practical applications. Provide deeply felt, spontaneous meditations which encompass Biblical texts, scholarship, news items and personal asides, with imaginative leaps meant to inspire dedication and action. Cultivate a rich resource network. Conceptualize fresh approaches. Utilize unique storytelling skills to hold young and old spellbound; excel in explaining complex concepts. Respond with insight, care and concern to the needs, feelings, capabilities and interests of others.

- *Introduce text and theme; seek to provide listeners with clarity and relevance through a marriage of rhetorical skill, textual and theological substance and personal challenge.*
- *Use persuasion and authority to achieve consistent, audience-pleasing results; have been renewed for over 13 years, disseminating Scripture on daily and weekly programs.*
- *Appeared in special series on WGBH-TV (Channel 3) and NTI-TV (Channel 9) and on several Cable TV programs.*

**ORGANIZATIONS & ASSOCIATIONS**

Advisory Board - Big Brother / Big Sister
Heed Prevention Program for Young Adults
Christian Task Force · Holy Family Services
Amnesty International

**CHIEF PUBLICATIONS**

*Whispers of the Persecuted*
Santa Fe: Rising Son Press, 1997

*Various cassette tapes and videos of lectures and presentations*
Phoenix: Trinity Recording

**HONORS & AWARDS**

Society of American Communal Service Award
Outstanding Educator's Award - American Christian Institutions
Alumnus of the Year - Holy Spirit Day School
Distinguished Spiritual Leadership Award - Christian Reclamation Project
Humanitarian Award - International Organization of Congregational Churches

**INTERESTS & ACTIVITIES / PERSONAL**

Extensive travel throughout the U.S., Israel, Europe
Willing to perform work-related travel / Willing to relocate

REFERENCES AND FURTHER DATA AVAILABLE UPON REQUEST

## Golf Pro—Resume Highlights Both Athletic and Business Skills

*Confidential Resume of*
# WILLIAM T. BREWSTER

390 Spring Drive
Adams, New Jersey 25409
Home: (555) 555-1849  Work: (555) 555-3795

www.JobGroup.com/resumes/wtbrewster.htm
Email: wtb3@genius.net *or* wtbrewster@JobGroup.com

## PGA CLASS A PROFESSIONAL

*Highly successful golf professional with proven leadership and communication / training abilities, excellent interpersonal skills, superior organizational talents, and an outstanding track record. Innovative, resourceful and inventive with unusual ability to identify opportunities, make things happen, and consistently achieve goals and objectives. Strong orientation to students of the game, other professionals and staff, and a range of corporate supporters, vendors, and clientele. Demonstrate strong ability to integrate marketing, sales and service strategies, alliance building techniques, and personal commitment to the game to meet and exceed existing goals and objectives. Author of books, designer of web page, Golf business consultant and Certified Ski Instructor.*

### SKILLS, ABILITIES AND ACHIEVEMENTS / VALUE OFFERED

❑ **Special Aptitude:** Experienced in P & L, planning, implementation and established teaching programs for junior, beginners and video/computer lessons. Abilities in Clinic/Seminar presentations, event promotion and negotiation. Have taught over 20,000 lessons and am Colbert/Ballard certified. Organized food service, provided supervision and coordinated events.

❑ **Management:** Coordinated, scheduled and supervised as many as twenty-five employees. Trained three teaching assistants in how to teach simplicity in basics. Designed and supervised construction of a 20,000 sq. ft. short game area.

❑ **Customer Services:** Worked as manager outside of golf industry for a tire company which stressed good customer relations and phone etiquette. Was chief liaison between membership and management of 700 member Haverford Country Club.

❑ **Public Relations:** Reached 7th position of top ten money winners in Mid-Atlantic section. Assisted many renowned touring professionals with demonstrations and clinics. Redesigned and supervised construction of 6,000 square foot small business.

❑ **Tournament Skills:** Ten years experience organizing and implementing club tournaments. Initiated and implemented Mid-Atlantic Assistant Pro/Pro Championship 1988 / 1989. Initiated and implemented Junior Club championships.

### CAREER TRACK

| | |
|---|---|
| **INTERMEDIATE / BEGINNER GOLF CLASS INSTRUCTOR** | 1999 |
| Burgess College | Garyville, New Jersey |
| **HEAD GOLF PROFESSIONAL** | 1997 - 1998 |
| Elizabeth Family Golf Center , | Elizabeth, New Jersey |
| **STORE MANAGER** | 1993 - 1994 |
| Wheel Inspection by Tire Treaders | Trenton, New Jersey |
| | *Continued* |

**WILLIAM T. BREWSTER**                                                                          Page 2

**PGA PROFESSIONAL TEACHER / PLAYER / CONSULTANT / AUTHOR**                       1990 - 1997
New Jersey & New York

**ASSISTANT GOLF PROFESSIONAL**                                                              1983 - 1990
Haverford Country Club                                                           Haverford, New Jersey

**ASSISTANT GOLF PROFESSIONAL**                                                              1978 - 1983
Bright River Country Club / Rose Hill Country Club                        Garyville, New Jersey

### LEARNING CREDENTIALS

**PGA Class A**  Appointment, 1983

Business College, Applied Sciences School, Wesley College, 1988
Wesley, New York

New York University, Business School, 1971 - 1972
New York, New York

U.S. Army NCO School, 1970
Fort Bruce, Florida

Central California University, School of Education, 1965
Laradino, California

### AWARDS & RECOGNITIONS

Designed and wrote web page, 1999
Colbert / Ballard Certified, 1997
Authored - *Golf 101: The Novice's Golfing Guide, 1993*
Sidwell Stewart Golf Club Repair School, 1993
Won Assistant Pro-Pro Championship CenCal, 1989
Top Ten Money List CenCal, 1989
Napa, CA brothers received college golf scholarships, 1988, 1990, 1983 - 1990 students
1994 California Junior Golfer of the year, 1976 - 1983 student
Senior student qualifies for the Senior US Open, 1999, 1997 - 1999 - student
Golf club consultant to Kamazu, p.r.o.Golf, San Jose, California - 1993
Certified Ski Instructor - Park City, Utah 1974

REFERENCES AND FURTHER DATA AVAILABLE UPON REQUEST

# Web Sites for the Job Hunter

Internet sites with listings of useful features that will aid you in your search. Many are great sources for job postings and career resource centers. The following listings represent only a handful of sites geared toward the job seeker. To find more, search the Internet using these keywords: *jobs, careers, classifieds, jobsearch, careers, headhunters, resume posting, job fair.*

## GENERAL SITES

**www.monster.com**

Research companies

Store/send resume

Search jobs by industry and location

Online career resource centers

Chat rooms to share or find information

**www.nytoday.com**

Operated by the *New York Times*

Extensive listings for the New York City metro area

Search for a job and apartment simultaneously

Search by industry, keyword, and date

Resume posting and job fair listings

Company profiles

**www.hotjobs.com**

Research companies

Post resume and apply for jobs online

Job search by location, company, and industry

U.S. and international job listings

Free e-mail

**www.headhunter.net**
Search 200,000+ jobs by industry, location, or salary

All listings less than two months old

Resume posting and apply for jobs online

Career resource center

**www.careersite.com**
Resume posting

Career resource center

Job listings from major companies

Search by personal profile, industry, and location

**www.jobcue.com**
Resume posting

Search by personal profile

Online interviews and job applications

Special sites for computer and medical jobs

**www.jobsonline.com**
Electronic headhunter

Job aptitude test

Resume posting

200,000+ listings by industry and location

Average salary guide for several industries

**www.fedjobs.com**
Lists federal and government job listings

Job Hunter's Tool Box—job info, application tools

Resource centers, job search by agency and location

Listings for overseas, United Nations, and private sector

Create a personal profile

**www.ecampusRecruiter.com**
A good site for people new to the workforce or changing careers

Lists entry-level jobs and internships targeted at college students

Thousands of listings by industry and location

**www.headhunt.com**
>Operated by the Council Network
>Lawyer recruitment
>Listings by specialty and location

**www.experience.com**
>Resume resource center
>Financial advice for the job hunter
>Lists industry contacts and salary guides

**www.careers.wsj.com**
>Job search by keyword or industry
>Job hunting advice
>Lists salary guides and company profiles

**www.ajb.dni.us**
>"America's Job Bank"
>Operated by the U.S. Department of Labor
>Linked to state employment offices
>1,000,000+ job listings
>Links to online career resource centers

**www.careermosaic.com**
>Job service for college students and professionals
>Employer and job profiles for several industries
>Information center for new graduates

# INDUSTRY-SPECIFIC SITES

**www.foodheadhunters.com**
>(food preparation and service)

**www.helpwantedexpo.com**
>(professional and executive online career fair)

**www.higheredjobs.com**
>(college and university job listings)

**www.doleta.gov**
>(industry listings from the U.S. Department of Labor)

**www.peacecorps.gov**
(volunteer work)

**www.journalismjobs.com**
(for aspiring and experienced journalists)

# OTHER SITES

**www.gotajob.com**
(search for a job nationwide)

**www.careerpath.com**
(all the information to get you a new career)

**www.bestjobsusa.com**
(national listings for all levels of experience)

# Trade Journals, Industry Guidebooks, and Directories

V aluable sources of information to help you find job opportunities and learn more about your industry or any industry in which you're interested.

## ADVERTISING

*Advertising Age*
*Ad Week*
*Brandweek*
*Direct Marketing Magazine*
*Journal of Advertising Research*
*Marketing News*
*Potentials in Marketing*
*Standard Directory of Advertising Agencies* ("The Red Book")

## AEROSPACE

*Aerospace Daily*
*Aerospace Engineering*
*Air Jobs Digest*
*Aviation Week & Space Technology*
*Business and Commercial Aviation*
*Space Commerce Week*

# APPAREL AND TEXTILES

*Apparel Industry Sourcebook*
*Apparel Industry Magazine*
*Apparel News*
*Apparel Trades Book*
*Dawson's Textile Blue Book*
*Fairchild's Textile & Apparel Financial Directory*
*Fashion Newsletter*
*Garment Manufacturer's Index*
*Membership Directory, Americal Apparel Association*
*Textile Hi-Lights*
*Textile Research Journal*
*Textile World*
*Women's Wear Daily*

# ARCHITECTURE

*AIA Membership Directory*
*AIA Journal*
*Architectural Record*
*Architectural Review*
*Architect's Directory*
*Building Design & Construction*
*International Directory of Architects and Architecture*
*National Membership Directory, Society of American Registered Architects*
*Progressive Architecture*

# AUTOMOBILE

*ASIA Membership Directory*
*Automotive Age*
*Automotive Executive*
*Automotive Industries Insider*
*Automotive News*
*Jobber Topics*
*Ward's Automotive Reports*
*Ward's Automotive Yearbook*

# BANKING

*ABA Banking Journal*
*American Bank Directory*
*American Banker*
*Bank Letter*
*Bank Management*
*Banker's Magazine*
*Banker's Monthly*
*D & B Reports*
*Financial Yellow Book*
*Moody's Bank and Finance Manual*
*Savings and Loan Association Directory*

# BOOK PUBLISHING

*American Booksellers Association Newsletter*
*Editor and Publisher*
*Innovative Publisher*
*Library Journal*
*Publishers Weekly*
*Publishing Trends and Trendsetters*
*Small Press*
*Writer's Market*

# BROADCASTING, RADIO, AND TELEVISION

*Billboard*
*Broadcast Communication*
*Broadcasting and Cable*
*Broadcasting Magazine*
*Cable World*
*Communication News*
*Radio World*
*Ross Reports*
*Television Broadcast*
*TV Radio Age*
*Variety*

## CHEMICALS

*Chemclopedia*
*Chemical and Engineering News*
*Chemical Business*
*Chemical Industry Update*
*Chemical Week*
*Chem Sources*

## COMPUTERS: SOFTWARE, HARDWARE, AND CONSULTING/INFORMATION MANAGEMENT

*BYTE*
*CIO*
*Computer Communications Review*
*Computer Industry Report*
*Computer World*
*Data Communications*
*Datamation*
*EDI News*
*The Industry Standard*
*InformationWEEK*
*Infoworld*
*Internet Business Report*
*Link-Up*
*Network World*
*Networking Management*
*Online*
*PC Computing*
*PC Letter*
*PC Magazine*
*PC Week*
*Red Herring*
*Software Magazine*
*Wired*

## CONSTRUCTION

*Builder*
*Builder and Contractor*
*Building Design and Construction*
*Construction Review*
*Constructor*
*Membership Directory, Associated Builders and Contractors of America*

## COSMETICS, TOILETRIES, FRAGRANCE

*Beauty Fashion*
*CTFA Newsletter*
*The Cosmetic, Toiletry, and Fragrance Association Membership Directory*
*Cosmetic World News*
*Cosmetic and Toiletries*
*Fragrance Foundation Reference Guide*
*The Rose Sheet*

## DRUGS AND PHARMACEUTICALS/BIOTECHNOLOGY

*American Druggist*
*Biotechnology Advances*
*Biotechnology Directory*
*Drug Topics*
*Health News Daily*
*Marketletter*
*Pharmaceuticals Manufacturing of the U.S.*

## EDUCATION

*ACADEME*
*Chronicle of Higher Education*
*Education Week*
*Executive Educator*
*Instructor*
*School Administrator*
*Teacher*
*Teaching Pre-K-8*
*Technology & Learning*
*Today's Catholic Teacher*

# ELECTRONICS/TELECOMMUNICATIONS

*Communications Daily*
*Communications News*
*Electrical World*
*Electronic Business*
*Electronic News*
*Electronics*
*Sourcebook, North American Telecommunications*
*Technology News of America*
*Telecommunications Week*
*Telephony*

# ENGINEERING

*Building Design and Construction*
*Chemical Engineering Progress*
*Civil Engineering Magazine*
*Electronic Engineering Times*
*Engineering News Record*
*IEEE Membership Directory, Institute of Electrical and Electronics Engineers*

# ENTERTAINMENT

*American Theatre*
*Backstage*
*Billboard*
*Blue Book Hollywood Reporter*
*Broadcasting and Cable Magazine*
*On Location Magazine*
*Show Business News*
*Stage Managers Directory*
*Theatre Times*
*Variety*

## ENVIRONMENT

*E: The Environment Magazine*
*Environmental Business Magazine*
*Environmental Science and Technology*
*Environmental Times*
*Environment Report*
*EPA Journal*
*Pollution Engineering*

## FINANCE AND INVESTMENT BANKING

*Barron's Financial Weekly*
*BusinessWeek*
*CFO*
*Corporate Finance Letter*
*Corporate Financing Week*
*Financial Executive*
*Financial World*
*Journal of Finance*
*Securities Trader Association Traders Annual*
*Stock Market Magazine*
*Traders Magazine*
*Wall Street Letter*

## FOOD/BEVERAGE

*Beverage World*
*Brewing Industry News*
*Fancy Food*
*Food and Beverage Marketing*
*Food and Wine*
*Food Industry News*
*Food Management*
*Foodservice Product News*
*Frozen Food Age*
*Gourmet*
*Journal of Food Products Marketing*
*Lempert Report*
*Progressive Grocer*
*Thomas Food Industry Register*
*Tri-State Food News*
*Wines and Vines*

## GOVERNMENT

*AFSCME Leader*
*Federal Employee News Digest*
*Federal Jobs Digest*
*Federal Staffing Digest*
*Federal Times*
*Government Executive*
*The Government Manager*
*The Public Employee Magazine*
*Public Employee Press*
*Federal Yellow Book*

## HEALTH CARE

*American Journal of Nursing*
*American Journal of Public Health*
*Business and Health*
*The Dental Assistant*
*Healthcare Executive*
*Healthcare Marketing Report*
*HMO Magazine*
*Hospitals*
*Journal of American Medicine*
*Modern Healthcare*

## HOSPITALITY

*Club Management*
*Food and Wine*
*Food Management*
*Hotel and Motel Management*
*Hotel and Resort Industry*
*Meetings & Conventions*
*Nation's Restaurant News*
*Restaurant Business*
*Restaurant Hospitality*

## HUMAN RESOURCES

*HR Executive*
*HR Magazine*

## INSURANCE

*American Insurance Association*
*Best's Insurance Reports*
*Best's Review*
*Financial Times World Insurance*
*Independent Agent*
*Insurance Advocate*
*Insurance Journal*
*Insurance Week*
*National Underwriter*

## LAW

*American Bar Association Journal*
*American Lawyer*
*Harvard Law Review*
*Lawyer's Weekly*
*The National Law Journal*
*Of Counsel 500*
*The Paralegal*
*The Practical Lawyer*

## MAGAZINE PUBLISHING

*Folio*

## MANAGEMENT/CONSULTING

*Academy of Management Journal*
*Academy of Management Review*
*ACME Newsletter*
*Business Quarterly*
*Consultants and Consulting Organizations*
*Consultants News*
*Executive*
*Harvard Business Review*
*Management Review*

# PUBLIC RELATIONS

*Bacon's Publicity Checker*
*Communication World*
*O'Dwyer's Newsletter*
*PR News*
*PR Reporter*
*Publicist*
*Public Relations Journal*
*O'Dwyer's Directory of Public Relations Firms*

# REAL ESTATE

*American Real Estate Guide*
*Journal of Property Management*
*National Real Estate Investor*
*Real Estate Issues*
*Real Estate News*
*Real Estate Review*
*Realty and Building*

# RETAILING AND WHOLESALING

*Apparel News*
*Chain Store Age*
*Fairchild's Financial Manual of Retail Stores*
*Inside Retailing*
*Journal of Retailing*
*Merchandising*
*Women's Wear Daily*

# SPORTS AND RECREATION

*American Fitness*
*Athletic Business*
*Athletic Management*
*Business Fitness*
*Fitness Management*
*Parks and Recreation*
*Sports Industry News*
*Sports Market Place*

## TRAVEL/SHIPPING/TRANSPORTATION

*Air Travel Journal*
*ASTA Travel News*
*Aviation Week and Space Technology*
*Business and Commercial Aviation*
*Daily Traffic World*
*Mass Transit*
*Tours and Resorts*
*Travel Agent*
*Travel Trade*
*Travel Weekly*
*Urban Transport News*

## UTILITIES

*Electric Light and Power*
*Public Power*
*Public Utilities*
*Telephone Engineering and Management*
*Telephony*

# NOTES

# NOTES

# NOTES

# NOTES

# NOTES

# NOTES

# NOTES

# NOTES